Robert Schumann

ROBERT SCHUMANN

The Life and Work of a Romantic Composer

MARTIN GECK

Translated by Stewart Spencer

The University of Chicago Press · Chicago and London

MARTIN GECK is professor of musicology at the
Technical University of Dortmund. He is the author
of more than two dozen books, including *Johann
Sebastian Bach: Life and Work*.
STEWART SPENCER is an independent scholar
and the translator of more than three dozen books.

The University of Chicago Press, Chicago 60637
The University of Chicago Press, Ltd., London
© 2013 by The University of Chicago
All rights reserved. Published 2013.
Printed in the United States of America

22 21 20 19 18 17 16 15 14 13   1 2 3 4 5

ISBN-13: 978-0-226-28469-9 (cloth)
ISBN-13: 978-0-226-28471-2 (e-book)
ISBN-10: 0-226-28469-7 (cloth)
ISBN-10: 0-226-28471-9 (e-book)

Originally published as *Robert Schumann. Mensch
und Musiker der Romantik.* © 2010 by Siedler
Verlag, a division of Verlagsgruppe Random House
GmbH, Munich, Germany.

Geisteswissenschaften International — Translation
Funding for Humanities and Social Sciences from
Germany. A joint initiative of the Fritz Thyssen
Foundation, the German Federal Foreign Office,
the collecting society VG WORT, and the German
Publishers and Booksellers Association.

FRONTISPIECE: Lithograph of Schumann by
Gustav Heinrich Gottlob Feckert (1820–99) after
a painting by Adolf von Menzel (1815–1905).
Menzel worked not from life but from one of the
daguerreotypes taken in Hamburg in March 1850 by
Johann Anton Völlner. (Photograph courtesy of the
Heinrich Heine Institute of the Regional Capital of
Düsseldorf.)

Library of Congress Cataloging-in-Publication Data
Geck, Martin.
[Robert Schumann. English]
Robert Schumann: the life and work of a romantic
composer / Martin Geck; translated by Stewart
Spencer.
    pages cm
Originally published as Robert Schumann: Mensch
und Musiker der Romantik, 2010 by Siedler Verlag.
Includes bibliographical references and index.
ISBN-13: 978-0-226-28469-9 (cloth: alkaline paper)
ISBN-10 0-226-28469-7 (cloth: alkaline paper)
ISBN-13: 978-0-226-28471-2 (e-book)
ISBN-10: 0-226-28471-9 (e-book)
1. Schumann, Robert, 1810–1856. 2. Composers—
Germany—Biography. I. Title.
ML410.S4G29613 2012
780.92—dc23
[B]   2012007981

♾ This paper meets the requirements of ANSI/NISO
Z39.48–1992 (Permanence of Paper).

Contents

Prologue

The organs associated with *precaution* are admirably well developed, —
anxiety that is even said to stand in the way of my happiness, — *music*, —
the *power of poetry* — noble *striving* — great artistic but noble *ambition* —
great *love of the truth* — great *honesty* — great *benevolence* — "*emotional
through and through*" — *sense of form* — *modesty* — *strength of purpose* —
(Noël's phrenological studies on my head — Maxen, June 1)[1]

These lines are taken from Schumann's diary entry of June 1, 1846, when the
composer and his wife were visiting Maxen Castle near Dresden. The castle
and its estate were owned by a retired army major, Friedrich Serre, whose love
of art was matched only by his wealth. The Schumanns had been invited to
lunch, after which Schumann played whist and was introduced to a "Captain
Noël," who that same evening undertook a "remarkable phrenological examination" of him, an examination also recorded in an entry of the same date in
Schumann's housekeeping book.[2]

The captain in question was the English phrenologist Robert R. Noel, who
was visiting Dresden to discuss his ideas with the local physician, painter, and
natural scientist Carl Gustav Carus and to prepare the second edition of his
*Phrenology, or A Guide to the Study of This Science, with Reference to More
Recent Research in the Field of Physiology and Psychology*, which was to be
published soon afterward by Christoph Arnold in Dresden and Leipzig.

Phrenology — the attempt to deduce a person's characteristics from the
shape of his or her skull — was currently enjoying a boom. And to the extent
that the measurements that were taken on these occasions were of particular interest to criminologists, Schumann no doubt would have felt a certain
squeamishness on presenting his head for the well-known phrenologist's inspection, a squeamishness inevitably mixed with the strange and yet by no
means unusual desire to learn something new from a third party. And he was
rewarded for his pains: the anxiety that had caused him so many problems in
his daily life could now be put down to a "fateful predisposition," whereas all
the other tendencies noted by Noel were admirable in their different ways:

noble aspirations, noble artistic ambition, a love of the truth, a sense of form, and strength of purpose.

Of course, the phrenologist knew who he was dealing with that evening in June 1846, and there is no doubt that he was sufficiently familiar with the ways of the world and the mores of his profession not only to inspect Schumann's skull but also to draw on other evidence to ensure that his prominent client, if a little agitated, was able to return to his fellow guests with his head held high. A century and a half later, the present author is moved by Noel's portrait of Schumann, for, however vague it may be, there is no doubt that if his description were used in a quiz, anyone tolerably familiar with the history of music would guess that the subject of the inquiry was Schumann rather than Beethoven, Wagner, or Meyerbeer, for we are dealing here with an ambivalence entirely characteristic of the composer. On the one hand, we have the diagnosis of cautionary foresight and anxiety, feelings that tormented Schumann and repeatedly made him seem to suffer from "weak nerves" and at times to become misanthropic. These are characteristics that, creatively speaking, encouraged him to work on his own personality rather than confront others with his envy, criticism, or condescension. Rarely in his *Neue Zeitschrift für Musik* did Schumann rake any of his colleagues over the coals. Nor did he insult his contemporaries in private conversation. The fact of the matter is that he did not like arguments or sneering criticism but had the greatness to hail the young Johannes Brahms as his successor and to acclaim Berlioz as a genius of French romantic realism even though he could not in fact abide the *Symphonie Fantastique*.

On the other hand, Schumann evinced an admirable courage in repeatedly facing up to the world and fighting for what he believed in, beginning with his protracted struggle to win the hand of Clara Wieck. It was a struggle that ended only when the courts decided in the lovers' favor. Then there was Schumann's concern for the welfare of his increasingly large family, which was held together for the most part by Clara, though Schumann too was responsible in no small way for helping to maintain it. More than anything, his anxieties did not prevent him from accompanying Clara on her concert tours or from attending parties and conducting choirs and orchestras. The fact that at the outward high point of his career he assumed the duties associated with the post of director of music in Düsseldorf and that this may have exceeded his powers and ultimately led to his final breakdown was perhaps only to have been expected.

Prior to his collapse, however, Schumann was not lacking in professional competence. He revealed great skill in negotiating with publishers; and, as we shall see in chapter 3, his feat in setting up the *Neue Zeitschrift für Musik* without any outside help amounted to a stroke of genius both as a business enterprise and in terms of the cultural politics involved. Nor can we forget his courage in artistic matters. Largely self-taught as a composer, the young Schumann was sufficiently astute to stick in the first instance to piano music, initially regarding "composing at the piano" as his essential métier, quite apart from the fact that piano music was easy to publish. From the age of thirty, however, he sought to advance ever further into the field of music First, it was whole sets of songs for voice and piano that reflected his growing self-confidence, before these in turn gave way to instrumental works for more elaborate resources, chamber music, and finally, oratorios and an opera. Toward the end of his career, he managed with his *Rhenish* Symphony to write a piece whose zest for life and mood of relaxation would have redounded to the credit even of a composer more carefree than Schumann.

In short, it was more than mere ambivalence that Schumann's immediate circle of friends, as well as large sections of the public, had to deal with and which they largely tolerated; there were also extreme tensions. In this regard we should not underestimate cultured society in the nineteenth century. After all, who would nowadays offer someone like Schumann the post of music director in Düsseldorf with the knowledge that he was perhaps not the right person for the job in terms of the town's public image? Half a century ago, the Hungarian writer Béla Hamvas summed up the nineteenth century in lines that bespeak his astute understanding of the situation: "This was a century of madmen — Hölderlin, Schumann, Gogol, Baudelaire, Maupassant, Van Gogh, and Nietzsche. Today we are no longer able to go mad."[3] And, we could go on, no more are we able to tolerate madmen who do not conform to our own brand of madness.

This is not the place to pursue the thesis of a link between genius and madness, for all that that theory was popular in the nineteenth century. Instead, it is sufficient to draw attention to a world in which an artist could be left to go his own way relatively unscathed and without losing face in the process, even if that artist did not fit into the grand scheme of things. Nonconformity had not yet been subsumed within the subculture of society but tended rather to embody the bad conscience of the well-to-do burgher who still suspected that all would be lost if maximizing profits were to become the predominant maxim.

From that point of view, the present study of Schumann was written not just out of a sense of admiration for a difficult man who prior to his breakdown never abandoned his struggle; it is also motivated by respect for a society that may not have glorified him as an artist and musical intellectual but which judged him by standards other than those of his marketability.

We ourselves would not be able to enjoy Schumann's music or be moved by it if his own contemporaries had not laid the foundations for the tradition which, like a calmly meandering river, continues to bear us along today. That Schoenberg's music is less popular than Schumann's is above all due to the fact that it is more difficult to understand, but part of the reason is also to be found in the barrier that the composer and his audience erected between themselves. Schoenberg's own elitist calculations meant that the general public was left to eat at a table of its own, while audiences in turn regarded the composer as an oddity.

It is fortunate that in Schumann's case everything worked out for the best. His music contains enough popular elements to ensure that it reached a wide audience, and it has enough elitist qualities to turn its composer into the progenitor of a kind of music that, reflective and refracted in character, might be described as modern in the sense that, unlike the music of the "heroic" middle-period Beethoven, it cannot be reduced to a single structural and narrative common denominator but shimmers in many contexts. Schumann very much demanded that we as listeners should play a part in the re-creative process — in other words, we should create our own "meaning" from the notes that enter our consciousness within the framework of contexts that may either lie open for all to see — in a work's headings, for example — or which may be written in invisible ink, as it were, leaving us listeners to make it visible.[4]

Schumann's Humoresque op. 20 for piano solo includes twenty-four bars marked *Hastig* (rapid), to which the composer has added a third stave between the other two. It is clear that what Schumann called this "inner voice" is not meant to be played — to attempt to do so would be neither technically possible nor musically meaningful, for the notes that make up this "inner voice" already appear an octave higher in the right hand. Why, then, did Schumann notate this "inner voice"? And what is it supposed to signify?

At this point we need to examine Schumann's own aesthetic views and, more especially, his admiration for the romantic writer Jean Paul.[5] In doing so, we shall also draw a little closer to Schumann as a human being, for he is known, after all, to have heard inner voices at many points in his life. Is the biographer guilty of a fall from grace if he fails to draw a neat dividing line between life and works but presents them as if they are inextricably interwoven?

Bars 251–56 ("Hastig") of Schumann's Humoresque, op. 20, for piano,
with the "inner voice" that is not meant to be played.

If we take this view to its logical conclusion, we shall see that the question is one of style, rather than one of principle.

In writings on music there is what we might call a "lofty style" in which analysis pure and simple reigns supreme. Here all nonmusical and biographical questions are regarded as distasteful or, at best, as pointers to the true essence of the music. Whatever one thinks of so rigorous an approach, it strikes me as unduly limiting in the present case, because Schumann himself had no time for this "lofty" style. Of course, analysis was one of the tools of his trade just as it is for any writer on music, but whenever he used it, he also allowed his imagination to wander freely and indulge in images, metaphors, and general aesthetic and historical digressions. He was familiar with both sides of the coin: music was only itself and at the same time it could be experienced only in the many contexts within which our lives unfold. That is why he could write to his colleague Carl Koßmaly on May 5, 1843: "With me, the man and the musician have always sought to express themselves simultaneously."[6]

The present study follows Schumann in adopting a "middle style" that no more shies away from examining the composer's music than it avoids the wider context. (As an example of the "lower" style — and the term is not meant in a pejorative sense — we might cite Peter Härtling's novel *Schumanns Schatten* [Schumann's shadow].) Although the phrase "middle style" might seem to imply a compromise, it in fact amounts to no more than any other discourse about art: whether we attempt a more subtle structural analysis or examine the wider context, none of these approaches can replace the actual experience of art.

The more we know about a composer, the less we can discount his life, even if it is above all on the strength of his works that we love and admire him. Even though the "life" does not explain the "works," there is — as Roland Barthes has put it — a "Surplus-Value" to examining the one against the background of the other. Barthes explains this approach with reference to Proust's *In Search of Lost Time,* arguing that although it would be foolish to think that by investigating a writer's background, we might find ourselves in possession of the key to understanding his or her works, "the projection of the reader in the work" becomes clearer, as also do both the "desire for the keys" and our "*imaginary* link with the Work."[7]

It is no accident that Barthes used a modern novel, rather than Cervantes's *Don Quixote*, for example, to develop his ideas: the closer the relationship between an artist's life and works and the present day, the more we may be able to empathize with that artist — or at least we imagine that this is the case. And the converse is also true: the more an artist is part of the modern world, the more firmly that artist is as a rule convinced that it is neither possible nor permissible to keep his or her private life out of his or her art. In my own view, Schumann is the first *composer* whose life and works were fused together in a symbiotic relationship. It was not least because of this that I decided to write the present biography not only in a "middle" style but also in a "mixed style." In my biographies of Bach and Mozart, I discussed their lives and works in separate chapters, whereas in the present case there is a much greater degree of dovetailing.

With Schumann in particular, it seemed to me sensible to adopt the line of reasoning proposed by Barthes. Of course, the phrenological study of Schumann's character mentioned at the start of this prologue says nothing uniquely compelling about him as a human being, however much it may have fascinated the composer himself. Still less does it say anything about his works. But it elicits interest and, together with many other remarks, it encourages the "desire for the keys," as discussed by Barthes. As Barthes indicates in his typically subtle way, this desire is the erotic longing of the author who repeatedly tries to approach the object of his love — the music — through the person of the composer, without ever quite achieving that objective. If the empirical facts, of which there is no shortage in Schumann's case, are not twisted or obscured but are used as a spur to further reflections, then the "mixed style" is every bit as serious as a tool of purely formal analysis, which for its part is based on many preconceptions that generally remain unchallenged.

Hans-Georg Gadamer was entirely serious when he asked whether the only scientific aspect of the humanities was the necessary "psychological tact" that reveals itself as a "function of both aesthetic and historical Bildung [culture]."[8] Although this may disappoint those readers who expect art to be explicable, it also places great demands on anyone who writes about art and artists inasmuch as it commits him or her to upholding the claim that Schumann himself prefaced to the first issue of his *Neue Zeitschrift für Musik* in 1835: "Every genius must be studied on the basis of what he himself wants to achieve." At the same time, however, it leaves the writer with no other choice but to examine the numerous contexts that make it clear why Schumann may rightly be described as a "universal genius of romanticism."[9]

I'll complete the Intermezzos after all, to appease my critics.

(Schumann's diary entry, June 1, 1832)

Scattered among the twelve main chapters of this study of Schumann are nine "intermezzos," a term that may remind readers not only of the composer's op. 4 but also of the eighteenth-century opera intermezzos involving two characters and a comic plot that had nothing to do with the principal action and that was performed on the forestage during the entr'actes. The present intermezzos are not intended to be comic in character, nor are they independent of the main narrative, but they nonetheless focus on single elements in Schumann's output or even on a single movement. Readers may omit them if they wish, but in doing so they will be like those eighteenth-century operagoers who slipped out of the auditorium and in that way risked missing the best part of the evening's entertainment.

Robert Schumann at the age of fifteen or sixteen. This colored miniature on card is the only surviving portrait of him as a young man. The anonymous artist depicted him wearing a fashionable blue jacket and sporting a ring and a watch chain — he appears here as the attractive scion of an upper-middle-class family, making it easy for us to believe in his artistic ambitions and also his success with women. The portrait was once owned by Schumann's daughter Marie and is now a part of the holdings of the Robert Schumann Museum in Zwickau. (Photograph courtesy of the Robert Schumann Museum, Zwickau.)

CHAPTER 1

Early Years (1810–28)

*It isn't yet clear to me what I really am: I don't think that I'm lacking
in imagination, at least no one claims that I am: but I'm not a deep
thinker: I can never follow the thread of an argument to its logical
conclusion, however well I may have started out. Only posterity can
decide if I am a poet — for this is something that no one can become,
unless they already are one.*

The seventeen-year-old Schumann's diary entry in *Days of Youth*[1]

I f Beethoven's international reputation may be said to have reached its first
high plateau between 1809 and 1813, then this was also the period when he
produced three important heirs, albeit unbeknownst to him: Mendelssohn
was born in 1809, Schumann in 1810, and Wagner in 1813. It was a powerful
triumvirate, with Schumann in the middle. Unlike Wagner, Schumann did
not see himself as the reincarnation of Beethoven, but unlike Mendelssohn,
he wanted to do more than merely honor Beethoven's legacy. Schumann saw
in Beethoven's music a harbinger of that "new poetic age" that he himself
wanted to shape through his own active contribution.[2]

If this has a ring of optimism to it, then that is how it was meant. And yet it
is not the optimism of a man like Beethoven, who saw himself as Napoleon's
equal and was convinced that Napoleon had ushered in a whole new era in
world history. Like Hegel, Hölderlin, and Goethe, the "heroic" Beethoven
saw the French emperor as the Prometheus of his age — conveniently over-
looking Napoleon's acts of usurpation. And the hopes that were placed in
Napoleon as a ruler were not unlike those that Beethoven held as an artist: "In
the world of art, as in the whole of our great creation, freedom and progress
are the main aims."[3]

Of course, this remark suggests nothing so much as an act of defiance on the part of a composer fighting a rearguard action, for it dates from July 1819, by which time the real-life Napoleon had been living the life of an exile on Saint Helena for four years; few of Beethoven's contemporaries still thought of the erstwhile emperor as a Promethean figure. Political reality was very different, for a new era had begun that later historians have tried to sum up with terms such as "the Restoration," "the persecution of demagogues," and *juste milieu*, the last of these an expression of contempt used to dismiss the rule of Louis-Philippe established in the wake of the July revolution of 1830 and geared to the concept of compromise and muddling through. In Germany, the period between 1815 and the March revolution of 1848 is usually referred to as the *Vormärz*. This was a period that Schumann later looked back on with rather more positive feelings: "This whole time had the most stimulating effect on me. I was never more active, never happier in my art."[4]

This political and social background needs to be borne in mind by any writer who sets out to present an unblinkered view of Schumann's early years—exactly the same is true of contemporary writers such as E. T. A. Hoffmann and Heinrich Heine. Schumann's phrase about "a new poetic age" is, of course, ambiguous, directed, as it is, in part against the unbending and arid representatives of the *juste milieu*, whom he described in a clearly political context as "philistines." At the same time, however, Schumann himself did not wage this war with the aim of bringing about political, revolutionary upheaval. Rather, it was as an artist that he wanted to assert himself in the face of the oppression perpetrated by the spirit of the age.

However contradictory it may sound, the young Schumann was a man who, unlike Mendelssohn but like Wagner, bore within him the potential for political resistance but who, initially at least, exercised that potential only within the framework of his own artistic beliefs. What this meant in practical terms emerges from a passage in a composite review that he published under the title "Shorter and Rhapsodic Works for the Pianoforte" in his own *Neue Zeitschrift für Musik*:

> Musical upheavals, like their political counterpart, affect our lives in every
> last detail. In music one notices the new influence even in that area where it
> is wedded to life in the coarsest and most physical way: in dance. With the
> gradual disappearance of the hegemony of counterpoint, miniatures such
> as the saraband, gavotte, and so on vanished from the scene, hoop skirts
> and beauty spots went out of fashion, and wigs became much shorter. The
> minuets of Mozart and Haydn rustled past with long trains on their dresses

as listeners stood by, silent and well-behaved in a middle-class kind of way, bowing a good deal and finally withdrawing; one still saw the occasional solemn wig, but bodies that had previously been stiffly corseted now moved far more freely and gracefully. Soon the young Beethoven arrived, breathless, embarrassed, and distraught, his hair long and unkempt, his brow and breast as open as Hamlet's, an eccentric who caused much bewilderment; he found the ballroom too confining and too tedious, preferring to rush outside into the dark, snorting at fashion and ceremonial, yet at the same time avoiding the flowers in his path in order not to trample them underfoot.[5]

When Schumann wrote this, he was twenty-five, but he was able to express himself in this way because the education he had received in his childhood and adolescence had been not only grounded in the traditional humanities but also politically abreast of the times. Indeed, the driving force throughout this period in general was the acquisition of such an education. The fact that Haydn, Mozart, Beethoven, and Schubert could never have written such a text is due in part to their lack of Schumann's literary talent. But above all they had not enjoyed even a tenth of the education Schumann had. Born within fifteen months of each other, Mendelssohn and Schumann were the first musicians to receive a proper formal education, which no doubt helps to explain why they understood each other as well as they did during the time they both spent in Leipzig. No less striking, however, is the differing use to which they both put that education. But let us start at the beginning: with Schumann and his parental home.

Schumann was born in Zwickau in Saxony, some fifty miles to the south of Leipzig. His parents' house stood on the town's neat and tidy main square on the corner of Münzstraße. By 1955–56, the building was no longer considered safe and was torn down and replaced by what is now the Robert Schumann Museum, its façade reconstructed on the basis of the original structure. It now houses the world's largest collection of Schumann manuscripts and also contains a museum, a recital room, and a research center. Schumann was only fourteen or fifteen when he drafted his first curriculum vitae, an account of his life that is already astonishingly mature:

My biography, or the main events of my life. I was born in Zwikau [*sic*] on 8 June 1810. I have only the vaguest recollection of my childhood years; until my third year, I was a child like any other: but my mother then went down with a nervous fever and because it was feared that I too would be infected, I was sent to stay with Frau Ruppius, the wife of the present mayor, initially for a period of six weeks. — These weeks slipped by very quickly, for it must be said to her credit that she was good at raising children: I loved her and she became a second mother to me. In short, I remained under her truly maternal supervision for two & a half years: each day, however, I would call on my parents, but otherwise I did not trouble myself with them any further. [. . .] I was a God-fearing child, innocent and physically attractive, I worked hard & at the age of 6 ½ I enrolled at the private school run by Herr Döhner, who is now the official preacher in Freiberg but who was then the archdeacon, a highly cultured and well-respected man: I was seven when I started to learn Latin, eight when I began French and Greek, and 9 ½ when I joined the fourth class at our Lyceum.[6]

Schumann then goes on to note:

I was eight when — would you believe it? — I learned all about Cupid's arts: my love for Superintendent Lorenz's daughter Emilie was truly innocent, & I shall never forget the occasion when, just as we were leaving a French lesson, I handed her a desperate, but still unfinished love letter in which I had wrapped a penny (presumably so that she could buy a dress for herself). O, such sweet simplicity![7]

Even as an eight-year-old, Schumann claims to have been fond of going for long walks "completely on my own" and of pouring out his heart to nature.

Also, I & my brother & a number of our school friends had a very attractive theater where we were well known and even notorious in Zwikau [*sic*] because we sometimes took in 2–3 thalers, performing everything completely extempore, making terrible jokes & taking nothing seriously. It was at around this time that I fell in love with Ida Stölzel, & although I was only 9 ½ I wrote several poems to her. [. . .] We loved each other dearly for two years, a childlike love that we never abused in any way: we were always kissing: I bought her sweets with the four groschen that I was given every Sunday — in short, I was hap[py].[8]

The next two pages of the manuscript are missing, but the seventh includes a poem with which the then twelve-year-old youth bade farewell to his childhood sweetheart, claiming that he was now "weary" of her "moods":

Einst war die Zeit der süßen Gegenliebe,
Die sie mir, lang' u. lang' geschenkt,
Doch Nattern nähr'n jetzt andre Triebe,
Und anders hat's ein Geist gelenkt:
Sie war, die Zeit: dahin ist sie geflohen,

In Trauerflor ist sie gehüllt:
Doch nun mein Geist, dank ihm, dort oben,
Daß er den Wunsch dir nie erfüllt.[9]

[Those were the days of sweetest love's delights, / A love she granted me so long ago, / But now a serpent's venom blasts and blights / That love, which ghosts have dealt a fatal blow. / That time is past, all mem'ry of our love / Is swathed in widow's weeds. But now, O fires / Of this my spirit, thank the Lord above / For never having granted your desires.]

Before the manuscript breaks off after ten pages, Schumann also refers to his mother, the daughter of a surgeon from Zeitz:

I almost forgot to describe the few brief trips that I made. In 1818 — in other words, more than seven years ago now — I visited Carlsbad with my mother, where she wanted to take the waters, while I myself was there to cheer her up and entertain her: we remained there for five weeks, but it seemed more like a week, for me especially. I got up at half past seven, sometimes even between 4 and 5, in order to walk along the promenade. I then went out for a walk with my mother until half past ten & wrote or read until noon, we then ate, I went for a stroll on my own until around 3, either in the town or out into the countryside — in short, it was a wonderful life that we led & without doubt the best time of my life. I did not have a care in the world, there was nothing to cause my brow to furrow — ah! with what sweet and wistful sadness I sometimes recall the hours I spent there and especially my favorite place — this was a rock on which a crucifix stands, not far from Marianensruh. [. . .] I saw very many famous people there, including Napoleon's brother, Jérôme, the former king of Westphalia, and his sister Elise, who was married to a Prince Bachchochi [*recte* Bacciocchi] & who was very similar to Napoleon, also Prince Blücher, with whom my mother spoke: he was an extremely kind man who spoke to everyone.[10]

In the course of his life, Schumann constituted and constructed his own image of himself through a whole range of autobiographical accounts, including notes, diary entries, housekeeping books, and correspondence books, to say nothing of his numerous letters. For an artist who tended to be reserved in his personal dealings with others, the written word was an indispensable form of self-reassurance. The German proverb "Wer schreibt, der bleibt" (he who writes leaves a lasting impression) is mostly used in an ironic sense, but for Schumann it acquired a positively existential dimension that applied not only to his literary activities but also to everyday events in general. In his diaries Schumann kept a close record of all that happened to him, often going into minutely meticulous detail. The result is of inestimable value not only from a biographical point of view but also as a source of contemporary cultural history.

Between 1840 and 1844, these diaries were largely replaced by the "marriage diaries," in which Schumann and his wife wrote alternate entries, often reacting directly to each other's contributions. As a result this dialogue between husband and wife can be used — at least tentatively — to reconstruct a kind of *Scenes from Married Life*. Here the differing temperaments of the two diarists often clash with striking force. And however much the two writers may have attempted to gloss things over and invest their lives with a certain stylistic elegance, there is no doubt that these three marriage diaries are rather more honest than the diaries Cosima Wagner wrote as a conscious legacy for her children in an attempt to present her husband to posterity, if not as an idealized figure then at least in a transfiguring light.

Starting in 1837, the Schumanns' housekeeping books provide us with a continuous and impressively detailed account of his income and expenditure. Or at least this is the impression that they give, for it is impossible, of course, to know if certain transactions have been omitted on purpose or simply overlooked. But the housekeeping books, which were kept, in part, in parallel with the Schumanns' diaries, also include other notes, turning them, too, into miniature diaries that further document the composer's constant attempt to impose a sense of permanence on the transience of life and in that way to create a prop with which to support himself. From April 1846, Schumann also included intimate details of his marital life: a kind of F-sign, first found on April 13, 1846, seems to indicate sexual intercourse and appears four more times between then and the end of the month.

Let us return, however, to Schumann's earlier period and to the text that he wrote in 1824. It is one that deserves to be taken seriously from an autobiographical point of view, for even if later writers may have been able to correct a handful of details, they cannot establish a more authentic picture than the one that Schumann paints of himself here. Above all, however, this early account of his life affords important evidence of the way he saw himself: he was an attractive child (this is confirmed by early portraits) who felt drawn to the opposite sex from an early age and to whom women were attracted in turn. He was happy to be educated in the humanities, an education on which he set out from an early age in keeping with contemporary practice among members of the educated middle class. And he saw himself as an aspiring artist who wrote poetry, a youth who precociously and with wisdom beyond his years reflected on his own life and who enjoyed acting, which he saw as more than just a source of harmless fun. In keeping with his age and background he lived in an emotionally charged world in which a certain eccentricity was interpreted as an early sign of genius — who knows what current titles on this subject he took down from the groaning shelves of his father's library and read from cover to cover.

Schumann's father, August, sold and published books, in which capacity he was highly successful. His own father had been a pastor in Thuringia, but he and his brother Friedrich had opened a publishing house in Zwickau that brought out German translations of works by Byron and Walter Scott, some of them translated by August himself. The firm also published the *Vollständiges Staats- Post- und Zeitungs-Lexikon von Sachsen* (Complete state, post, and newspaper lexicon for Saxony), a standard reference work in eighteen volumes. Moreover, August Schumann was one of the first German publishers to issue cheap editions of the classics, making him the inventor of the modern paperback. He wrote numerous literary and scientific texts and in 1813, in his *Erinnerungsblätter für gebildete Leser aus allen Ständen* (Memoranda for educated readers from all social classes), he wrote: "What binds the Germans together as a nation is their literature. As long as this remains for them, they need not fear the tempests that threaten the fate of all other nations."[11]

August Schumann was fifty-three when he died in 1826, leaving his wife to bring up their fifth and last child, Robert, on her own. Like most mothers, she wanted only the best for him and did what she could to foster his talent, while insisting that he should study law on leaving school, a course of action that he adopted only reluctantly. Although mother and son remained close until her death in 1836, their relationship was not free from tension. Johanne Christiane tended to dwell on the darker aspects of life, while her son reacted with feelings of guilt and occasional defiance:

Dear Robert,
Your last letter left me so deeply shaken that ever since I received it I have sunk back into my old state of depression. [...] I am not reproaching you for this, because this would not get us anywhere — but I cannot approve of these views of yours, still less can I approve of your actions. If you examine your life since your dear father's death, you will have to admit that you have lived only for yourself. How will it all end?[12]

Schumann's mother was reacting to a letter in which her son had asked for her permission to be allowed to put an end, once and for all, to his "*twenty-*

year struggle between poetry and prose or, to put it another way, between music and jurisprudence."[13] The tone of Schumann's reply was not exactly considerate:

> If I were to stick to law, I'd shoot myself from boredom as an unpaid assistant. Heaven forfend, but I could one day go blind, and then music would be the finest form of deliverance for me. [. . .] I have to send a number of franked letters to Heidelberg but I don't have a penny to pay for the postage. What will the world think of me? My piano is horribly out of tune, but I can't afford a tuner etc. etc. I even lack the money to buy a pistol with which to shoot myself.[14]

"But to be serious for a moment," Schumann goes on in the same letter, a sentiment that sounds plausible when we recall that five years earlier, in 1825, his elder sister, Emilie, had indeed taken her own life. The fact that Schumann failed to attend his mother's funeral in 1836 after she had repeatedly appeared to him in his dreams "warning" him or "angry" with him[15] should not necessarily be seen as an attempt on his part to distance himself from her or as a sign that he could not handle the situation, still less as an act of ultimate self-emancipation, for he had arranged to meet Clara Wieck in Dresden at that very time. Following the meeting, he wrote to Clara on February 13, 1836: "This was an emotional day for me for many reasons — the public reading of my mother's will and the accounts of her death. But behind it all is your radiant likeness."[16]

Schumann was hoping to find in the then sixteen-year-old Clara the sense of home that his parents' house could no longer offer him, for all that it had previously afforded him excellent opportunities to develop. While living with his parents, he had never had any financial worries, his mother was an amateur singer, and his father had done all he could to encourage his son's aptitude for music — an aptitude that, like his love of poetry, had made itself felt at an early age. Eugenie Schumann recalled how as a child her brother had delighted their mother by singing the song "Schöne Minka, ich muß scheiden" "with tender, splendid emphasis and a fine sense of rhythm."[17] Then, when he was about seven, he began piano lessons with the local organist, Johann Gottfried Kuntsch. For a time he also had cello and flute lessons with one of the municipal musicians, Carl Gottlieb Meißner.

Although Schumann also needed to practice, he still had plenty of opportunities to indulge his favorite musical pastime and to improvise on the piano. His famous review of Berlioz's *Symphonie Fantastique*, which he published in 1835, opens with a reminiscence of a scene from his "earliest childhood," when "late at night, while everyone in the house was asleep, he crept into the music room as if in a dream and, with his eyes shut, went over to his old piano, now ruined, and played chords and wept."[18]

Truth or fiction? Whatever the answer, Schumann did not have to content himself with communing with the piano in the intimacy of his own drawing room; he had ample opportunity to take part in the musical life of Zwickau, which included Lutheran church music, regimental band music, and a theater where opera performances were given at irregular intervals. In 1823, for example, the young Schumann attended a performance of Weber's *Der Freischütz* that inaugurated the new theater in the Clothiers' Hall. No doubt he also took an interest in the subscription concerts held in the function rooms at Däumler's Tavern, as well as in the open-air concerts in the grounds of the town's beer cellars. These performances were presumably notable for their limited resources and imperfect technical standards, but they would have been good enough to provide the young boy with a more than adequate degree of musical stimulus.

Schumann was eleven when, standing at the piano, he accompanied a public performance of Friedrich Schneider's popular oratorio *Das Weltgericht* (The last judgment) at the town's St. Mary's Church. That same year — 1821 — he also began to appear in public at the Literary and Musical Entertainments that were held at the city's grammar school, or Lyceum. At his first appearance there he played a set of Pleyel's piano variations for four hands with one of his fellow pupils at the school, and by 1828 he was sufficiently adept to perform an arrangement of Friedrich Kalkbrenner's Piano Concerto op. 61.

In 1822 — inspired by his participation in the performance of Schneider's *Das Weltgericht* — Schumann produced a setting of Psalm 150 for soprano and contralto soloists, piano, and orchestra. It was his first completed composition. In a diary entry of 1846, he wrote, "I am almost ashamed to look at it now; I lacked all knowledge and wrote it just as a child would have done; but also without any outside stimulus."[19] It was not least in order to equip himself with such knowledge that he formed a school orchestra in 1823. It met at his parents' house, using the parts that Schumann was able to order from his father's bookshop. In a series of texts to which he gave the collective title *Blätter und Blümchen aus der goldenen Aue* (Leaves and florets from the golden meadow) and in which he accounted for his life as a young artist, he made the following entry under the heading "Musical Notes": "On 7 December [1823] the first musical evening's entertainment was held at my place under the directors Robert Schumann and Carl Praetorius." The performance began with a sinfonia for strings, horns, and flutes by Ernst Eichner. Schumann made a conscientious note of the names of all the performers, adding, "This piece, although a little old-fashioned, passed off very well and with no mistakes." The seventh item on the program was a set of variations for piano and flute by Johann Wilhelm Wilms, described by Schumann as "a splendid composition; invariably playful with no sense of stiffness; admirably performed by Hoffmann on the flute; his tone is bright, refined, and clear; his sense of rhythm firm and gratifyingly good; his cadenzas flawless. I'd almost say that it is a shame that this man doesn't have another teacher."[20]

There is no doubt that the thirteen-year-old Schumann was not only a musician but also a critic and, above all, a writer and poet. As a result, the *Blätter und Blümchen* volume contains not only notes on musical events in the town but also a whole range of literary texts of one kind and another: poems, an attempt at a drama headed *Der Geist* (The ghost), two descriptions of nature and a travelogue in the form of fictional letters, "the sayings of classical Greek and Latin authors," the sort of lines more usually associated with autograph albums, dedications and aphorisms, excerpts from newspaper articles and from Christian Friedrich Daniel Schubart's *Ideen zu einer Ästhetik der Tonkunst* (Ideas on a new aesthetic of music), a survey of poetic meters, and a list of the "Lives of Famous Musicians." Of course, Schumann too hoped to become famous very quickly, with the result that we find him copying out a newspaper article on Mendelssohn, who, only a year older than himself, was already a national celebrity.

It is hard to resist a smile when we read the heading that Schumann gave to his play *Der Geist*: "Otto the Murderer's Departure from This World. Sentence Handed Down by the Schwarzenberg Criminal Court on the Day of His Execution, 27 November 1823." This was the date not of some quasihistorical event but the day on which Schumann wrote down the scene or declaimed it to some listener or other. No less amusing is the echo of many a literary model that occurs in the following poem:

Einst wenn die Abendröthe
des schönen Lebens ist.
O euch ihr Menschen wünsch ich
des Lebens lange Frist
Dieweyl ihr seyd zum Segen
Der Menschen auserkoren.

Doch wenn ihr auch vergehet
So lebt ihr immer fort.
Im blauen Himmelsraume
Dort wo die Frommen sind.[21]

[One day the dusk of fairest life / Will shroud this sullen vale of tears. / A long and healthy life till then / I wish all men and women here / On earth as long as it's your fate / To be a blessing to mankind. / But even when you pass away, / You'll still live on forever more / Within the empyrean vault / Where God's own congregation dwells.]

What matters here is not the literary quality of this or that product of the young Schumann's imagination and whether or not it lies above a notional average, for there have always been thirteen-year-olds capable of remarkable achievements in this regard. What is fascinating is something else, namely, the resolve with which the young boy worked away at a game plan that he had already sketched out in his head: he was determined to become an artist of genius. This view of himself already bears within it a number of traces of decadence, something that Schumann's school friend Emil Flechsig may have been exaggerating only a little when he recalled from a distance of half a century that

> even in his early youth Schumann had felt an insane preference for men of genius who were destroyed by their work. The eccentric Lord Byron had earlier been his ideal, his wild and self-destructive life striking him as having an infinite grandeur to it, while the fantastical life and suicide in Jena of Franz Anton Sonnenberg—famous as the poet of *Donatoa*—left a tremendous impression on him. As early as the 1820s he already knew about the period of almost forty years that Hölderlin had spent in a benighted state of mental imbalance, a state to which he referred with feelings of awe. Beethoven's shock of unruly hair over his somber countenance seemed to him to be a true artist's face that he was almost fond of imitating.[22]

Schumann's image of himself—and it is this that concerns us here—was marked by the awareness that however productive they may be, the fantasies associated with megalomania are no guarantee of an artist's successful career. Rather, such an artist has to work hard and strive tirelessly to educate himself. If Schumann was able in adulthood to resist the destructive forces within him for such a long time, this was due in no small part to the fact that as a child he had already worked out a picture of himself, which, undoubtedly modeled on that of his father, ensured that well-planned and systematic activities would serve as a bulwark against the fears that threatened to overwhelm him. This helps to explain why the young Schumann not only wrote poems but prepared a detailed list of them — it was effectively the first catalog of his works. And not only was he inspired by the very idea of men of genius, he was only fourteen when he was allowed to assist his father on a projected "Portrait Gallery of the Most Famous Men and Women of All Nations and Ages."

From this point onward, Schumann's literary ambitions increased and even appear to have eclipsed his musical interests. At the same time, the focus of his attention shifted from more or less naïve poeticizing and theatrical improvisation to an interest in current literary discourse. In December 1825 he joined forces with ten of his fellow pupils at the Lyceum to form a Literary Society aimed at "initiating" its members into "German literature." The minutes of this society, which in the main were kept by Schumann himself, list a total of thirty discussion evenings between 1825 and 1828, the year in which its members all left school. Among the subjects discussed were Schiller's plays, Friedrich Schlegel's treatise on early German literature, and Fichte's *Addresses to the German Nation*.

In 1826, Schumann began an initial volume of "German Essays" that ran to fifteen separate entries, starting with an "Observation, Written from a Beautiful Region near Zwickau." The fourth essay was entitled "On the Randomness and Futility of Posthumous Fame," the sixth "The Resignation of Ariadne on Naxos," the seventh "Address on the Close Relationship between Poetry and Music," and the fifteenth "Why did Tragedy not Flourish among the Romans?" These fifteen essays represent a selection of those that he wrote as part of his regular assignments at school, making it clear that even as a schoolboy Schumann drew no distinction between duty and inclination.

Although the Literary Society's program occasionally featured romantic writers, it was above all in his private reading that Schumann departed most markedly from the Lyceum's canonical syllabus. His personal preferences were for E. T. A. Hoffmann, Ludwig Tieck, and Jean Paul, whose *Flegeljahre* (The awkward age) became his self-styled "bible" after 1827. A year later he noted in his "Hottentottiana," as he called his student diary, "I often wonder where I would be if I had never got to know Jean Paul."[23]

This represented a considerable advance on the classics that were the prescribed texts at the Lyceum and that Schumann undoubtedly took very seriously. Just as the young people of the *Sturm und Drang* (Storm and Stress) generation had identified with Goethe's *Werther*, so the avant-garde of Schumann's age was passionate about Jean Paul's two vexing figures of

Vult and Walt, to say nothing of Hoffmann's wild-eyed genius Kapellmeister Kreisler and the romantic fairytale characters from Tieck's *Phantasus*. Here we already have a premonition of the "new poetic age" that we shall shortly examine in much greater detail.

First, however, we need to get Schumann through his school-leaving examination on March 15, 1828. This must have been a comparatively painless experience, not least because it was not until 1830 that Saxon schools introduced a proper test for final-year students. Relatively poor results in math meant that he failed to achieve the highest grade of 1a, but he nevertheless left the school with a personal recommendation from his headmaster, Friedrich Gottfried Wilhelm Hertel, on whose revised edition of Forcellini's great *Lexicon totius latinitatis* he was invited to work, an invitation he evidently felt unable to refuse. In a letter, he explained that this meant "a fair amount of corrections, copying out excerpts, looking things up, and reading through Grüter's inscriptions." It was hard work, but it also meant that "a few extra pennies" found their way into his purse.[24] At the public graduation ceremony he recited a poem, "Tasso," that he had written in the meter of a Horatian ode. It was his final work in German and begins: "The twilit day lay resting, and off into the silver / Evening's clouds the cerulean swan flew, smiling." According to a later reminiscence, Schumann was supposed to deliver the poem from memory but stumbled, though without being in the least disconcerted by his lapse.

In spite of his fondness for purple prose and poetry, Schumann was also capable of parody. Three months after he left school—and perhaps encouraged by the new freedoms associated with student life—we find him parodying Goethe's "Erlkönig":

Was raspelt es dort in den Spänen[,]
Vater, mir ist so schwül.
Das Kind weinte bittere Thränen[,]
Weinte der Thränen zu viel.

Sey ruhig, mein Kind, in den Spänen
Naget wohl eine Maus.
Der Vater weint selber Thränen[.]
Es ward ihm selber so graus.[25]

[What's rustling in the shavings there? / Father, I feel so hot. / The child was weeping bitter tears, / Of which there were a lot. / Calm down, my child, it's just a mouse / That's gnawing through the wood. / His father, too, was all in tears, / Scared witless where he stood.]

This may be no masterpiece, but it is a useful indication of the fact that at this date Schumann was a contented individual with a positive attitude toward life, a point underscored by a letter he wrote to his friend Emil Flechsig on December 1, 1827, in which he referred to an outing to Schneeberg, where a group of his friends entertained their fellow drinkers at a local hostelry. They sang student songs and recited Schiller's poem "The Glove" at the request of a portly peasant — Schumann was later to set this poem to music. He himself took his place at the piano: "I played a free fantasy on Fridolin [by Schiller]; the peasants opened their mouth in surprise as my fingers moved so tipsily over the keys. At the end, there was drunken dancing: we spun the peasant girls round to the music." Inevitably the occasion was invested with a literary note and described as "worthy of a Van Dy[c]k."[26]

Schumann must have felt particularly at his ease in the home of the Zwickau businessman Carl Erdmann Carus, where he was a welcome guest not least because of his contribution to his host's musical soirées, when Schumann was introduced to the string quartets of Viennese classicism. It was here, in 1827, that he got to know Agnes Carus, the wife of a local physician, and soon fell hopelessly in love with her, sending her lengthy poetic effusions. Earlier objects of his undying affection had been Nanny Petsch and Liddy Hempel: "Three goddesses stood on the Olympus of my dreams," he wrote in his *Pilgrimages of Youth*: "Agnes at the front, Nanni in the middle distance and Liddy in the background, which sounds almost ambiguous."[27]

We would be doing the young Schumann an injustice if we saw him only as a bookworm or as a loner obsessed with his own artistic interests, for it is clear that he was also interested in politics. In a detailed and carefully minuted interrogation, his headmaster wanted to know if he was aware of the activities of a secret student society. Since the events in question dated back to 1821, the now fourteen-year-old Schumann was able to deny any knowledge of the matter, a denial that under the circumstances sounds plausible. But the whole incident brought home to him from an early age the concrete implications of denunciation and persecution.[28] It was presumably from his father that Schumann inherited his lifelong political ambitions, however vague these ambitions sometimes may have been. As the frontispiece of the 1819 volume of his *Memoranda for Educated Readers*, August Schumann chose a portrait of the student Karl Ludwig Sand, who shortly beforehand had caused a furor with his politically motivated murder of the reactionary writer August von Kotzebue. The young Schumann could also see Sand's likeness hanging in his parents' drawing room.

Following in his father's footsteps, Schumann noted in 1827, "Political freedom is perhaps the true midwife of poetry: it is this that is most needed for poetry to flourish: in a country where there is serfdom and bondage and so on, true poetry can never thrive: I mean the poetry that permeates public life as an inflammatory & inspirational force."[29] That this was no passing phase in Schumann's development is clear from a letter that he wrote in 1828 to his school friend Eduard Moritz Rascher, who by then was president of the Literary Society that Schumann had founded at the Zwickau Lyceum. As for "the young fruit tree that I have planted," Schumann wrote, he urged his correspondent to show "the greatest possible caution, for otherwise the authorities may easily track it down not least because the Leipzig student organization is currently threatened with a serious inquiry, which would spell the end of all our fun." Schumann then came to the heart of the matter and explained why "under the present circumstances" he had "no intention of joining the actual student organization": although the movement was "undeniably based on a splendid idea and an ideal principle," it was pointless "sitting in a bar & discussing wild & nebulous ideas" in an attempt to put all these laudable aims into practice: "This is not the way to reform the world or Europe or Germany or Saxony or Leipzig or any human being or student." Fifteen hundred students were not enough "to re-educate millions." People must realize that "the world can never be cut to the size they want but only to the way that time, molding it by degrees, dictates." At the present point in time "no sense of nationality can be created" because "those who want it are not elected by the nation."

"And so it follows," Schumann concludes, "that concepts such as nationhood etc. are mere figments of the imagination that fly in the face of the spirit of the age and are incompatible with it." This belief was confirmed by Schumann's feeling that the students he met in Leipzig were often no more than "weak, sickly, biased, & recalcitrant creatures." They must first become "human beings" and find a "more moderate, more humane, and more beautiful middle ground" between opposing extremes. Only then was it possible to forget "all political goals & demagogic figments of the imagination."[30] For a youth who had only just turned eighteen, this was an astonishingly mature reflection that requires no further comment here but which readers are invited to bear in mind in due course when we come to consider Schumann's attitude during the revolutions of 1848 and 1849.

An Awkward Age

S ome of the books that we read can save our lives — literally or meta-phorically — and it is no accident that the young Schumann described Jean Paul's *Flegeljahre* (The awkward age) as his "bible." When, at the age of seventeen, he wondered how he would view the world if he had not encountered Jean Paul's writings, Jean Paul himself had been dead for only three years and from a literary point of view was still very much alive. Schumann may well have looked on him as a kind of elder brother — as some-one who knew what was what.

Writers on Schumann have long since acknowledged that the heroes of Jean Paul's novel, Vult and Walt, are the models for his own aesthetic con-structs, Florestan and Eusebius: Vult is the musician, Walt the poet. Moreover, the two characters, for all their differences, represent a unity that Schumann himself, as an aspiring artist, undoubtedly found immensely fascinating. It is one to which we shall often have occasion to refer in the course of the follow-ing pages.

But there is something else that deserves to be mentioned here, and it is scarcely less significant — namely, the background against which the novel is set, for this was the only conceivable biotope in which Schumann could breathe freely. Even more importantly, the whole of the novel pulsates with music: "Richter [i.e., Jean Paul] poeticizes musical fantasies," Novalis wrote enthusiastically.[1] Vult's flute may be heard from every point of the compass, and there are concerts in every better kind of garden. How fortunate it was, moreover, for Schumann as a would-be professional musician that he found in his model not only a writer whose heart had "ears," allowing him to rhap-sodize in verse about the divine impact of music,[2] but also one who was an expert on music conversant with terms such as *"reiner Satz"* ("pure composi-tion"), "enharmonic change," and "consecutive (or parallel) fifths." Jean Paul was also a writer who wanted listeners to be guided by their feelings of the moment and also to be able to follow the structure of a piece — after a concert that Walt had praised to the skies and that had moved him to tears, Vult asks:

> But *how* did you hear it? Did you listen ahead and retrospectively, or did the piece just pass by in front of you? The common people are like cattle hearing only the present, not the two polar times, only musical syllables, not the syntax. A good listener remembers the antecedent of a musical period in order to be able to form a clear grasp of the consequent phrase.[3]

Schumann would have shouted with joy on reading such sentences, which are almost without precedent in the literature of the age: not only did they provide him with sustenance for his soul, they also prepared him for his coming vocation.

Within the artistic biotope of Jean Paul's novel, music permeates not only weekends and holidays but also the quotidian round. And the same is true of poetry: Walt writes flowery verse, and the twins work on a novel with the title *Hoppelpoppel, or The Heart*. Even the title reveals the clash between the finite and the infinite and between profound emotion and the droll. But the brothers become even more caught up in reality when they send their opening chapters to the Leipzig publisher Magister Dyck and receive a reply to the effect that he "may publish pleasantries by Rabener and Wezel, but never ones like these."[4]

Jean Paul — depicted in the drawing overleaf in an ironically exaggerated pose — is referring here to two of his rivals, Gottlieb Wilhelm Rabener and Johann Karl Wezel, both of whom wrote satirical novels. As such, the reference finds Jean Paul engaging fully with real life, and in this respect too he could reckon on the interest of the young Schumann, who was, after all, the son of a publisher and bookseller. As such, he was enough of a scholar and a bookworm to enjoy the literary allusions with which Jean Paul peppered the footnotes of his "pleasantries" in a way that was half serious and half ironic. Most memorably of all, the music dealer Johann Carl Friedrich Rellstab appears in *Flegeljahre* in apparent anticipation of Schumann's own life — Rellstab was the father of Ludwig Rellstab, who, as we shall see, was to make life difficult for the composer of the *Kinderscenen*.

All in all, then, there was a constant interplay and overlap between reality and fiction, between actual experience and a riotous imagination, between daily concerns and far-fetched plans, and between fears and feelings of happiness. The young Schumann would not have been affected by all this if *Flegel-*

Jean Paul. (Courtesy of agk-images, Berlin.)

jahre had not demonstrated that one could live one's life as if a character in a novel by Jean Paul. When we recall that he began to study law in keeping with his mother's wishes even though he was powerfully drawn to music and poetry, then it will be clear that in this respect, too, the novel struck him as profoundly consoling. Of the two protagonists, Vult, as a professional musician, was the more down-to-earth, while the more sensitive poet Walt muddles through as best he can as a notary. Could jurisprudence and the arts be reconciled after all?

As a musician, Schumann admired Beethoven, describing him as "the Jean Paul of music."[5] But his thinking was not yet sufficiently advanced for him to be able to follow his model in matters of compositional rigor. Here he preferred to stick to the rampant imagination of a writer like Jean Paul, who was less "demanding" than Beethoven and who "invited" visitors to enter his biotope. And Schumann must have welcomed the fact that *Flegeljahre* keeps breaking off at random points in its narrative instead of moving toward a glorious finale like one of Beethoven's symphonies. At this date Schumann would probably have foundered on such high-flown concepts, whereas Jean Paul was able to show him the way forward. Although his earliest works are on a far smaller scale than *Flegeljahre*, they reveal a similar head-in-the-clouds mentality. Jean Paul encouraged Schumann to listen to the "inner voice" to which he would later pay homage on a separate stave in his Humoresque op. 20.

"I'm now having myself painted in miniature; if it's a good likeness, I'll send it to you; the beautiful new crimson coat costing eighty-five florins is also featured in it," Schumann informed his mother in a letter written from Heidelberg on February 24, 1830 (*Jugendbriefe von Robert Schumann* 22). It is in fact a bluish-black coat that he can be seen wearing in the miniature above, which was painted on ivory by an unknown artist. On the back is a golden S with a red band representing the student society of Saxoborussia. Schumann gave the miniature to his fiancée, Ernestine von Fricken, and it is now owned by the Heinrich Heine Institute in Düsseldorf. (Photograph courtesy of the Heinrich Heine Institut, Düsseldorf.)

CHAPTER 2

Student Years (1828–34)

*Music gives me everything that people are unable to give, and the piano
tells me all about the lofty feelings that I myself cannot express.*

Schumann to his mother, August 31, 1828[1]

Mulus was the term applied to students between the time they left
school and the start of their university course. As such, it described a person who, like a mule, did not know exactly where he
belonged. In much the same way, the seventeen-year-old Schumann, about to
study law in Leipzig at his mother's behest and against his own better judgment, still did not know where he was really heading. And yet he had a clear
idea of the first thing he would do after matriculating at the university: he
would undertake a pilgrimage to Bayreuth. It would not, of course, be to visit
Wagner, who had yet to found the Bayreuth Festival (although he could have
watched the fourteen-year-old Wagner writing his schoolboy drama *Leubald*
in Leipzig). Rather, it was to see the places associated with Jean Paul, including the writer's grave. "I am just returning from the famous Rollwenzel," he
told his brother Julius on April 25, 1828, "Jean Paul was a regular visitor here
for twenty-six years of his life."[2]

Schumann was accompanied on his visit by one of his friends from school,
Gisbert Rosen. Together they then traveled to Munich via Augsburg, for
Schumann was anxious to meet Heinrich Heine, whose *Reisebilder* (Travel
pictures) and *Buch der Lieder* (Book of songs) meant almost as much to him
as Jean Paul's novels and the short stories of E. T. A. Hoffmann. Heine accorded the two students an affable welcome at his house in the city and afterward took them on a guided tour of the art gallery in the Leuchtenberg Palace.

Schumann's diary contains the laconic note: "Witty conversation — ironic little man."[3]

Schumann's first term at university brought him back to earth with a bump: "I can take no pleasure in cold jurisprudence, the frigid definitions of which crush you from the outset," he told his mother. "I won't study medicine, and I can't study theology."[4] Her reply made him feel "so sad that I can draw only sad conclusions about your mental and physical state."[5] In spite of his feelings of guilt and no matter what he may have told the outside world, he had already made up his mind to do something different. But was it music? It is impossible to say for certain.

By this time, ideas such as "universal poetry" and "the total artwork" were already in the air. The first of them had been put into circulation by the early romantic poet Friedrich Schlegel, while the second is first explicitly mentioned by Karl Friedrich Eusebius Trahndorff in his *Aesthetics, or Teaching of Philosophy and Art* (1827). Although he was an avid reader, Schumann tended to avoid writings on philosophy, but he followed current discussions on an art that admitted to no particular interests and that could certainly not be reduced to the tools of an individual trade. Rather, such an art should contribute to society as a whole and at the same time usher in the social changes that politicians had failed to achieve but which continued to haunt the minds of contemporaries in the form of a vision of a utopian future.

Although Schumann later kept his distance from his two close contemporaries Liszt and Wagner, there was one point on which they shared a number of common beliefs in the 1830s, namely, the search for ways of ensuring that the grand idea of a universal art might acquire a physical, tangible form.

However much Schumann may have been exercised by this question, there was nothing unworldly about his brooding. He retained a sense of pragmatism after leaving school, refusing to put all his eggs in one basket but seeking to keep open his options as a pianist, journalist, and composer. We shall shortly discover the extent to which he succeeded in this aim. For the present, here are the opening shorthand entries in his project book in which he documented his life between 1828 and 1834:

University life 1828.
Emil Flechsig as roommate — enthusiasm for Jean Paul, Franz
    Schubert — compositions: polonaises for four hands, songs etc. —
Student activities —
Götte from Braunschweig — Renz, dissolute, but good-natured fellow
Moritz Semmel

Piano lessons with Wieck—
Often with Dr. Carus—Marschner—
Quartet evening in winter: Glock, Täglichsbeck, Sörgel.
Quartet for piano & strings—
1829
To Heidelberg at Easter—travel there with Wi[l]libald Alexis—
Living with Rosen and Semmel
In August & September visit Switzerland and Italy.
Winter 1829–30, dissolute life spent drinking and playing the piano a lot—
Fritz Weber from Trieste, now a doctor in London—
Henriette Hofmeister—
1830 June or July decision in favor of music
(Papillons—Abegg Variations) Röller.
Visit to Baden-Baden. Violinist Ernst.
Previously (Easter 1830) visit Frankfurt with Töpken to hear Paganini.
July Revolution 1830.
Visit Strasbourg with Röller & Auerswald.
In fall 1830 return to Leipzig over the Rhine & Detmold—
Bad period.
Board with Wieck. Chopin's appearance.
Mechanical studies taken to excessive lengths. A few lessons with
    Music Director Kupsch.[6]

These entries date from 1843 and until recently have been published in only fragmentary form. Schumann was concerned with imposing some sense of order on his diaries and closing any gaps that he found there, with the result that these jottings lack the spontaneity of others drawn up at an earlier date. On the other hand, they focus on what the then thirty-three-year-old Schumann felt was memorable after an interval of a dozen or so years. First and foremost the present-day reader is struck by the names of many of Schumann's fellow students, all of whom were the same age as he was: Georg Auerswald, Emil Flechsig, Wilhelm Götte, Johann Friedrich Renz, Eduard Röller, Gisbert Rosen, Moritz Semmel, Theodor Töpken, and Friedrich Weber. Presumably Schumann not only enjoyed their student company but also shared with them the urge to nudge society along the road of intellectual advancement. Semmel, who was related to Schumann by marriage, proved such an exceptional law student that he later became a local magistrate in Gera. But during his student days, he adopted the nom de plume "Justiziar Abrecher" (literally, a legal adviser who settles old scores) as a member of Schumann's League of David, about which we shall have more to say in due course.

It is also symptomatic of Schumann's whole thinking at this time that in the course of his travels he was moved to visit the writer Willibald Alexis, his senior by twelve years, who was then editing the *Konversationsblatt* in Berlin, a periodical which in 1830 merged with the liberal *Der Freimüthige*. In 1835, Alexis resigned in protest at increasing censorship, a move that demonstrates the extent to which the *juste milieu* was then bearing down on many contemporaries with all its oppressive weight. It is no accident, therefore, that in spite of the brevity of his jottings, Schumann found time to mention the July revolution that broke out in Paris in 1830. And the words "Bad period" presumably relate to the unrest in Leipzig in the September of that same year. His diary 5, which contains notes on his visit to Strasbourg, includes a whole series of entries on this subject, one of which reads: "Copied out French Lord's Prayer from original in Strasbourg." The prayer begins: "Our Late King, which art a scoundrel; thy name be accursed; thy kingdom never come; thy will be done neither in France nor elsewhere; give us this day our 46 million florins that thou owest us & forgive us our trespasses for not having sent you packing long ago."[7] Schumann also copied out a report from the *Journal des Débats* announcing that in the course of the uprising in Leipzig, burghers and students had made common cause in their hostility toward the authorities.

These facts cannot and should not be overlooked by anyone wanting to understand the young Schumann, nor should their importance be exaggerated, for most of the entries in the aforementioned travel diary are of a nonpolitical nature. In describing his own experiences Schumann adopts a tone that is either objective or — in the manner of Jean Paul — half effusive and half ironic, making it clear that music is permanently in his thoughts. And it is music, together with the cultivation of his circle of friends, that dominates the summary of his student years quoted above.

Law is not mentioned once in this summary, an omission confirmed by Schumann's friend Emil Flechsig: "He enrolled as a law student, I bought a briefcase for him, and he added his name to the list of students who would be attending the lectures by Krug and Otto, but that was the full extent of his involvement in the course at the Academy. Otherwise he never set foot in a lecture hall."[8] This may well be a wild exaggeration, for Schumann himself assured his mother that he regularly attended classes and wrote out what he heard there "with mechanical efficiency" as there was nothing else he could do.[9] But Flechsig's account must contain at least a grain of truth.

Flechsig seems to have been Schumann's roommate, lending his well-heeled friend a helping hand and perhaps earning the right to free accommodation in return. According to the composer Johann Friedrich Täglichsbeck, who during this period played quartets with Schumann:

> Schumann was living on the Brühl with his roommate Flechsig, a lively enough lad, though he rarely put in an appearance at our musical soirées. It was an exceptionally elegant student apartment consisting of two pleasant rooms situated next to each other and looking out over the front of the building. One of the rooms could even be described as large and was admirably suited to music-making. The whole arrangement revealed a certain affluence, as did a very good grand piano that belonged to Schumann and that graced the larger of the two rooms.[10]

As Täglichsbeck also recalled, Schumann was fond of sitting at this instrument and playing waltzes and duets by Schubert, a composer he particularly admired. Together with the cellist Christian Gottlob Glock, a perpetual student who later became the mayor of Ostheim, they also performed Schubert's Piano Trio in B-flat Major op. 99:

> Once we had reached the point where our ensemble playing seemed to us to be adequate, Schumann organized a musical soirée to which we invited not only several music students but also, as our principal guest, the piano teacher Friedrich Wieck. The unforgettable evening ended with a brilliant supper at which the champagne flowed rather too freely, prostrating each and everyone who was present — except, perhaps, our host.[11]

Schumann clearly knew how to live. But he also had regular lessons with Wieck, who was a well-known teacher. He practiced assiduously and composed not only a number of songs that were well received by the Braunschweig director of music, Gottlob Wiedebein, but also a piano quartet. When filling out his passport, he toyed with the idea of listing his profession as a "music scholar." And in his "Hottentottiana" he kept a detailed account of excerpts from his reading matter as well as aphorisms, reflections, and observations about himself. On the horizon lay the idea of a novel to be called *Selene*. In short, he had still not decided to become a professional musician. Time and again music became literature, and literature music: "When I listen to Beethoven's music," he wrote, "it is as if someone were reading Jean Paul to me: Schubert is more like Novalis, Spohr is the Ernst Schulze or the Carlo Dolci of music."[12] (Schulze was an epic poet who died prematurely in 1817, Dolci a Florentine painter of the seventeenth century. Both were morbidly religious.)

Of course, the young Schumann was fascinated not only by the connection between literature and music but also by the link between champagne and music: in one of his earliest writings, which appeared in the Leipzig *Allgemeine musikalische Zeitung* in December 1831, he has his League of David troupe of music enthusiasts saying of Chopin's Variations on "Là ci darem la mano" from Mozart's *Don Giovanni* that "The whole thing is in champagne," rather than the expected "The whole thing is in B-flat major."[13] It is a metaphor well suited to the situation, making it all the more regrettable that Schumann omitted this witticism from his collected writings. What he find there instead is another comment about Chopin that is symptomatic of his sympathy for the Polish liberation movement of the 1830s: if the Russian tsar "knew to what extent a dangerous foe threatened him in Chopin's works, in the simple tunes of his mazurkas, he would ban this music. Chopin's works are cannons buried among flowers."[14]

There was no shortage of "student excesses," as Schumann called them.[15] For a while he took up fencing, and as for his experiments with narcotics, we find him noting in his diary:

> Strong cigars make me feel high & poetic; the more my body is relaxed, the more my mind is excitable. Whenever I am drunk or have been physically sick, my imagination floats higher & more freely the next day. While drunk I can do nothing, only afterwards. Black coffee also makes me drunk, if not black-humored.[16]

However exciting this may sound, Leipzig had already lost its charm for Schumann after only two terms. He felt drawn instead to Heidelberg, where he was less visible to his worried mother and his circle of family and friends in Zwickau. But Heidelberg was also the home of Justus Thibaut, who taught Roman law at the local university, providing Schumann with an excellent excuse to move to the town. In fact, it was Thibaut the amateur music lover who drew the young Schumann there. Not only had Thibaut written a slender volume, *Über Reinheit der Tonkunst* (Purity in music), but he also conducted a choir dedicated to the performance of early music.

Before Schumann moved to Heidelberg for the winter term of 1829–30 and could enthuse about the "wonderful, godlike" Thibaut,[17] he traveled extensively, taking boat rides up and down the Rhine and not hesitating to send his mother a typical "Rhineland menu," even though she could not have been entirely happy with her son's conspicuous consumerism:

Delicious soup
Beef or cutlets with three kinds of vegetable
Asparagus with ox tongue
Meat pies
Fricassee of veal or steamed liver
Eel or salmon
Fresh salmon
Stuffed pigeon pie
Three kinds of roast and the finest dessert[18]

This may also be a suitable place to reproduce the postscript to a letter that Schumann wrote to his future landlady in Leipzig, Johanne Christiane Devrient, on September 15, 1837, explaining what she could serve him when he came to board with her:

Menu of a Thrifty Individual

Nothing fatty or sweet. Favorite foods:
Beef with rice, dumplings, pearl barley & the like.
Veal, mutton, pork, more rarely, if it's not too fatty. All kinds of roast meat as
    long as they're not fatty —
Desserts, none, none at all.
Egg dishes, fine.
Soup, consommé, yes please.
Fruit, bottled fruit, no.
Salads, pickled, all.
Fish, all except for eel.
Vegetables, yes please, except for sweet ones such as carrots etc.[19]

Between late August and late October 1829 Schumann visited Switzerland and Italy — it was almost a grand tour of the kind undertaken by Mendelssohn at almost the same time — they missed each other in Venice by only a year.

Back in Heidelberg, Schumann began to practice the piano in earnest, and on January 24, 1830, he played Moscheles's Alexander Variations in the concert hall attached to the town's museum:

Stumbled at the beginning — final variation perfectly played — endless
applause, congratulations etc. ——— to Borngasser's — Smollis and
Krug from Leipzig — with Arnold & Beelitz from Berlin, with Jung
from Rheinbayern, with Labes from Danzig [modern Gdańsk] — the
drunken Counts Schulenburg & Hohenthal — people delighted — kind

Director Hofmann—Lemke—praised to the skies—Faulhaber—H[err]
Lind—Jung delighted—staggered home delighted—at 2 o'clock.[20]

Schumann's diary entry for Sunday, January 24 sounds like the beginning of a promising career as a virtuoso. But within two days we find three words hidden away among a number of other entries: "My numb finger."[21] From that point on, there were numerous such signals, most of them coinciding with Schumann's decision to become a professional musician. He was presumably unfamiliar with the word "stress," but it may well apply to a situation that he undoubtedly felt to be rife with conflict: for him, it was the tone-poet or, more prosaically, the composer who embodied the profession of musician, but as an unknown young man it was impossible for him to earn his living as a composer, which left only a career as a pianist.

But is this what Schumann really dreamed of becoming? After all, it was only a few years later that he set up the *Neue Zeitschrift für Musik* with the avowed aim of combating what he felt were the lapses in taste on the part of composers such as Henri Herz and Franz Hünten,[22] two popular salon pianists who, thanks to Schumann's invective, became synonymous with mindless virtuosity. Chopin and Liszt would have been preferable as models and they were certainly admired by Schumann from a very early age, but as his contemporaries, they too were at the start of their careers. As a result, Schumann had to find his own way and, understandably for a youth who had not yet turned twenty, this journey was to prove a bumpy one.

On the one hand, Schumann practiced, made music, read, and wrote poetry, while on the other he attended one party after another, all of them involving dancing, alcohol, and flirtatious liaisons. His diary entry for February 8, 1830, reads simply:

This is the most dissolute week of my life,
This is the most dissolute week of my life,
This is the most dissolute week of my life
--my life.[23]

In April 1830 he and Theodor Töpken traveled to Frankfurt to hear Paganini. He was deeply impressed by the violinist's playing, which was virtuosic, but not in a superficial way. Rather, there was an element of shamanism or sorcery to it that consorted well with the "black" romanticism that Schumann liked. Finally, on July 30, 1830, Schumann had reached the point where he felt able to write to his mother and inform her of his decision to become a musician. She responded by asking Friedrich Wieck about her son's abilities. Wieck advised her to summon Schumann back "to our cold dull Leipzig" from Heidelberg, the "warmth" of which was "causing his imagination to become even more overheated." On this condition he offered to turn Schumann into "one of the greatest living pianists," which "in view of *his talent* and *imagination*" he claimed to be able to do

> within three years. He will play with greater intelligence and warmth than Moscheles and more magnificently than Hummel. As proof I offer you my own eleven-year-old daughter, whom I am just beginning to present to the world. As for composition, our Cantor Weinlich [the cantor of St. Thomas's Church, Theodor Weinlig] would certainly be adequate for now.[24]

Schumann's mother was not convinced, however, and suspected — not without good reason — that the well-known piano teacher was thinking above all of his own reputation. Moreover, Schumann himself was by no means certain of what he wanted to do. He continued to practice like a man possessed, but on September 25, 1830, he was obliged to admit to a friendly physician, Ernst August Carus (the husband of Agnes Carus, whom we have already met) that in the course of the previous winter there were times when he was no longer able to think about "finger exercises and scales." Rather, he had "reached the point when, whenever I had to double under my fourth finger, my whole body would twist convulsively and after six minutes of finger exercises I felt the most interminable pain in my arm — in a word, it felt as if it were broken."[25]

Although he turned up for his first lesson with Wieck in October 1830, Schumann was not really enamored of either his teacher or of Leipzig, but preferred the idea of studying in Weimar with Hummel, who had been a pupil of Mozart. He was also thinking of writing an opera, *Hamlet*, on which the worthy Weinlig would almost certainly have been unable to help him. And yet he remained in Leipzig — not least because he was in serious financial difficulty. Indeed, he was less and less able to survive on the bills of exchange that his mother sent him on a regular basis. As a result, he sank further and further into debt. At least for the present, then, travel was out of the question.

On January 21, 1831, Schumann wrote to his mother, begging her to send him one hundred thalers:

> God knows, I'm not lying when I say that during the last two weeks I don't think I've eaten a roast or meat more than twice, but simply potatoes. [...] Poverty may well be the worst thing that could happen to a person because it cuts you off completely from human society. I'm now beginning to understand this, and there's much that I regret.[26]

He pawned a number of his books and a watch that his mother had given him and waited for June 8, the day on which he came of age and would receive the money his father had left him. He used it to settle his debts and was even able to buy a grand piano on which he practiced zealously under the watchful eye of Friedrich Wieck, in whose house he lived for a time. In September 1831, father and daughter then set off on a seven-month concert tour, leaving Schumann to his own devices.

Soon afterward, Schumann reported in his project book on the "paralysis" of his "right hand."[27] In spite of this, he continued his attempts to strengthen his third finger, this time using a "cigar mechanism"[28] (presumably a kind of device intended to immobilize the finger). But this helped only for a time, and by August 9, 1832, he was obliged to admit that "my whole house has become an apothecary's."[29] He was now taking "animal baths," bathing his hand in alcohol, and applying a herbal bandage at night.

Lessons with Wieck continued, and after a course of some kind of electrical treatment had proved, if anything, counterproductive, Schumann reported to his mother on June 28, 1833: "I'm now having my hand treated homeopathically."[30] He still appears to have taken an optimistic view of the situation, but another passage in the same letter must give us pause for thought:

> A group of young and well-educated people, mostly music students, has sprung up around me, a circle that I in turn am drawing closer to Wieck's house. Most of all, we are taken by the idea of new, major musical journal.[31]

By now Schumann had largely abandoned the idea of a career as a virtuoso, and he seems to have done so without any great regret now that other opportunities had opened up to him in this field.

Schumann's hand injury raises two further points. First, there is evidence that in later years, whenever he was playing piano duets with Clara or other colleagues, he would avoid using the index finger of his right hand. This contradicts the traditional view that the problem affected his ring finger and his little finger. Second, excessive or inappropriate exercises may have made his problems worse, but according to current thinking, an alternative explanation may be found in the phenomenon of focal dystonia: certain parts of the brain are hyperactive, preventing the muscles from working and in that way destroying the coordination between brain and hand.[32] The neurologist Oliver Sacks has described this phenomenon with reference to the American pianist Leon Fleisher who, as a result of similar problems, was able to play only works for the left hand for a period of three decades. Fleisher was then shown ways of dealing with a disorder that may have been physiological or even hereditary in origin.

Schumann was unable, of course, to wait for such medical advances, but in 1833 he was able to see himself in the role of an up-and-coming composer — to say nothing of his literary and journalistic ambitions. After all, his earliest piano pieces had already appeared in print by this date, and on November 18, 1832, the opening movement of his unfinished *Zwickau* Symphony in G Minor had received its successful first performance in his hometown.

If we believe Schumann's diaries, the period that he spent in Leipzig in 1832 and 1833 was marked — in spite of these few minor successes — by increasing self-doubts. "You are too insignificant to be sought out & too proud to go looking," reads a typical entry from October 7, 1833. "In a society in which I cannot be the first, I would prefer to be nothing, rather than second or third."[33]

The death of his sister-in-law Rosalie, to whom he had felt very close, plunged him into a state of immediate depression, and when his brother Julius died only a short time afterward, he wrote to his mother on November 18, 1833:

> I expect you think that I don't have the courage to travel to Zw[ickau] on my
> own because I am afraid of what might happen to me there. Breathlessness
> keeps alternating with momentary blackouts, albeit less frequently than
> in recent days. If you had any idea of what it is like to be affected by this
> melancholic, sunken-eyed sleep of the soul, you would forgive me for not
> having written.[34]

He had taken rooms on the fifth floor of a property at 21 Burgstraße, but within a few weeks he had moved down to the second floor as he could not overcome his fear of heights. In the same context, we find him writing in his diary, "Torments of the most terrible melancholia from October to December — I had been seized by the idée fixe that I was going mad." But the very next entry reads: "Sobriety. Work as a writer. Idea for the League of David further elaborated."[35]

As early as 1831, Schumann's diary mentions his relationship with a young woman known only as Christel, to whom he gave the League of David name of "Charitas." The following entry has been interpreted by a number of writers as evidence of Schumann's admission that he had syphilis:

> The wound was bad in the morning & Glock [the eternal student
> mentioned earlier] made a face — the pain was keen & corrosive — it's

like half a—give me a whole lion that tears me apart but not a little one that just gnaws! […] In the afternoon Chr[istel] pale—exchange of information—only guilt gives birth to Nemesis.[36]

"Charitas is coming today."[37] This is the last meaningful entry on the subject of Christel in Schumann's diary. It is dated July 13, 1832. Immediately above it are the words "Clara is kind-hearted." At this date, Clara was twelve, and on his regular visits to the Wieck household, Schumann would tell her fairy stories. By the following year there are the first vague signs that he was starting to fall in love with her. On July 13, 1833, for example, Schumann, who had fallen ill with the "ague," wrote to his "dear kind Clara":

> I want to know if you're alive and what you're up to—there is nothing about this in your letter. I almost wish you didn't still remember me as I'm becoming visibly thinner with each passing day and am shooting up like a beanpole without the leaves. The doctor has even forbidden me to pine so much—namely, for you—because it affects me so badly.[38]

This is the fourth of the 442 letters that Schumann and Clara Wieck exchanged before they were married in 1840. In her reply (no. 5), Clara gently chided him, "You can surely imagine the sort of life I'm leading! But how can I be all right when you no longer come and visit us?"[39] By this date Clara had already appeared in public in Paris and at the Leipzig Gewandhaus and had written a number of works, including the *Caprices en forme de valse* op. 2. In August 1833 she dedicated her *Romance variée* op. 3 to Schumann. In a long letter that he addressed to her on July 10, 1834, he acknowledged her as a member of the League of David and, as such, as someone worth taking seriously in the group's discussions on the subject of poetry.

At the same time, this letter is impressive evidence of the sort of romantic approach to epistolary effusions that flourished in the wake of Jean Paul: individuals and events from real life would merge with artistic figures and other fantasies. Schumann was in fact reacting to a letter from Clara that she had signed: "Your friend Clara Wieck. Clara Wieck. Doppelgänger." "Your letter," he wrote, "was *you*. You stood before me, talking, laughing, and, as always, leaping from matters of great seriousness to others that were mere fun, playing with veils as diplomats do—in short, the letter was Clara—the doppelgänger."[40]

To be precise, the first part of the above quotation actually appears in the holograph as "Your letter   *you*." The space between the second and third words is filled with a further word that Schumann has written in pencil with a deliberate lack of clarity. The letter contains a further twenty such words that Schumann then explained in a postscript:

> In great haste and in spite of my being very busy, I am preparing a kind of lexicon of the unclearly written words that I've placed in brackets. As a result the letter may be very colorful and piquant. The idea is by no means inglorious. Addio, clarissima Cara, cara Clarissima!
> really — sufficed — chords of a ninth — tender — a — year — Rosenthal — chocolate — was simpler — galley — grieved — was — Eusebius — neatly — makes — bright — July evenings — window — right — preacher — Robert Schumann — [41]

This tendency to confuse different categories and to invest them with a sense of mystery was dear to the hearts of the romantics — the reader may be reminded here of E. T. A. Hoffmann's novel *The Life and Opinions of the Tomcat Murr Together With a Fragmentary Biography of Kapellmeister Johannes Kreisler on Random Sheets of Waste Paper*, which is based on the notion that while writing out his views on life, the tomcat occasionally used for his draft pages from a biography of Kreisler, which the composer erroneously set as part of the text. The romantics' demand that poetry should be a part of our lives and that life should be poured into poetry was applied by Hoffmann to an elaborate work of literature, whereas Schumann privileges the elements of fun and jest. But the claim to be taken seriously as art also shines through here inasmuch as lines of music are included within the text of these letters, such music serving not just as a banal illustration but as a symbol of something that must otherwise remain unsaid.

In the summer of 1834 Schumann became engaged to Ernestine von Fricken, which suggests that at this date his feelings for Clara amounted to no more than a friendship between two artists in the spirit of romantic art. Of course, Schumann acknowledged Clara as a physical human being, but in his eyes she was also Zilia or Chiara, to give her the names by which she was known to the League of David. And it is the League of David that will engage our more detailed interest in Intermezzo II.

Figments of the Imagination

The satirical tale about the clockmaker BOGS who after his death applies to be "received into bourgeois society" was written jointly by two German romantics, Joseph Görres and Clemens Brentano. First published in 1807, it was intended as a critique of the philistinism of the ordinary burgher whose life ran like clockwork. In particular it questioned the belief that skull measurements might say something about a person's normality or abnormality.

From the outset, BOGS, who is depicted opposite in a line drawing from the 1807 edition of the satire, senses that his attempts to gain acceptance will meet with resistance: after all, he is not "normal" because he is soon thrown off balance by music. And in fact, he receives a provisional notification informing him that his "mad ideas about music" are incompatible with "land, state, and rifle club," which is why he is required to behave "normally" while attending a concert: "If you attend this concert and can prove that you were not unduly affected by it, your application for membership may proceed."[1]

BOGS does as he is told but has to admit that on listening to a Haydn symphony he has again been beside himself with emotion:

> A thousand flames poured from the violins, and a thousand salamanders bathed in them, and from the violas and violoncellos a thousand philistines emerged, but Samson sprang from the timpani and struck them dead with his jawbone, and as they sank, the evening sky turned red, before the light faded and moonlight poured from the trumpets.

Such rhapsodizing was hardly to the liking of the "land, state, and rifle club," which duly invited a team of doctors to examine "the clockmaker's state of health." Three physicians, Schnauznas, Gamaliel, and Sphex, began a detailed examination and took various measurements. In the process they ob-

The clockmaker BOGS as depicted in the first edition of *The Strange Story of the Clockmaker BOGS* (1807), by Johann Joseph von Görres and Clemens Brentano. (Photograph by the author.)

served that BOGS had two different faces, one with dark eyes and a bulging brow, the other with hazel eyes and a receding forehead. Worse, they even noticed that his two skulls were differently shaped:

> A bump on one was invariably canceled out by an indentation on the other: high spirits, low spirits, arrogance, humility, stolidity, fickleness, murderous intent, dove-like docility, thievishness, and the desire to catch thieves all negated each other in turn, so that no one could work out the subject's actual nature and qualities.[2]

The doctors became curious and used an endoscope to get inside BOGS's brain, the walls of which were found to be hung with thousands of microscopic clocks that were no longer striking in time with each other as a result of the concert that BOGS had been instructed to attend: BOGS was no longer "ticking" properly. And when his body was suspended from a thread and left to swing freely, the head no longer pointed to the North Pole and the feet to the South Pole, as they should have done. Instead, the positions were reversed. The symphony had disoriented him.

Readers will recall the phrenological studies on Schumann's head that were mentioned earlier. According to Noel's diagnosis, there was "nothing really abnormal" about the composer. Was Schumann really relieved to hear this, as I assumed was the case? At least as an artist, he was striving to escape from the bonds of normality, for he was far closer to the romantics Görres and Brentano than to the "normalist" Noel. He was also closer to his idol E. T. A. Hoffmann, who in his fairytale *Master Flea* allows a certain Peregrinus to look inside the brain of the sleeping Dörtje Elverdink with the help of a tiny microscope. Winding their way through the network of veins and arteries were

> brightly flashing silver threads, probably a hundred times finer than those of the finest spider's web, and these threads, which appeared to be endless since they coiled out of the brain and lost their way in a certain something that could not be made out even with a microscopic eye, were confusing in the extreme.[3]

This talk of confusing imagination and imaginative confusion inevitably recalls two of Schumann's other idols, Jean Paul and Heinrich Heine. Jean Paul's *Titan* contains the sentences: "Suddenly individual notes on a flute flew up from the leaves up there on the mountains — more and more flew out and joined them, fluttering around in a state of beautiful confusion."[4] And in *Das Buch le Grand*, Heine notes enthusiastically that "the world is so delightfully confused."[5]

Schumann himself has provided us with an example of this "delightful confusion" in the form of the letter puzzle that he sent to Clara. But whereas that particular document was intended as no more than a joke, the subject will acquire a much greater seriousness in the course of the following chapters, which deal with the way in which he transfers this idea to his art. What concerns us here is not simply a few entertaining letters but the whole concept of an important music periodical; and not just individual compositions such as "Traumes Wirren" (Dream's Confusions) but a basic theme of his whole creative output.

The worst thing that could happen to an artist like Schumann would be to subject him to the sort of examination that the clockmaker BOGS had to endure and to seek to draw a distinction between "normal" and "abnormal" characteristics — and this is true even if we take a charitable view of the "abnormal" features and see them as somehow attractive. The shock that BOGS felt on hearing the Haydn symphony is already built into Schumann's works from the outset — and not only into his own. "Cantor, beware of the storms!

The lightning will not send out any liveried servants to warn you before it strikes. At best there will be a storm followed by a bolt of thunder!"[6] This comment on the part of Schumann/Florestan will be examined in greater detail in the course of the following pages. It refers to the shock of the opening bars of the final movement of Beethoven's Ninth Symphony and to a cantor who thinks he can explain such things in theoretical terms and tick them off as having been dealt with.

There is only one thing that would be worse, and that would be to attempt to reduce Schumann's individuality as a composer to questions of biography and character, for we could then start looking for personal defects in the case of Görres and Brentano, E. T. A. Hoffmann and Jean Paul, Heine and Eichendorff. If post-Renaissance art has a task to perform, then it is to call into question our understanding of normality. And in Schumann's case it is admirably successful in meeting this aim.

"By the way, don't be alarmed! I'm growing a mustache," Schumann added in a postscript to his letter to his mother of April 9, 1834 (*Jugendbriefe von Robert Schumann* 238). The present silhouette presumably dates from the same period. A note in Clara Schumann's hand attests to its authenticity. One wonders if she received it as a gift at this time. When Wagner had a silhouette of himself prepared the following year, he gave it to his fiancée, Minna Planer. (Photograph courtesy of the Robert Schumann Museum, Zwickau.)

CHAPTER 3

The *Neue Zeitschrift für Musik*

*In the short time that we have been operating we have learnt a good
deal. Our thinking was clear from the outset. It is straightforward,
and it is this: to acknowledge the past and its products, and to draw
attention to our belief that in art the new and the beautiful can derive
their strength only from a source as pure as this — and then to combat
the recent past as inartistic, the only substitute for that past being an
increase in the merely mechanical. Finally we shall then help to prepare
and usher in a new poetic age.*

Neue Zeitschrift für Musik, January 2, 1835[1]

I t was while reading his favorite novel, Jean Paul's *Flegeljahre*, that
Schumann was introduced to Vult and Walt, whom he soon came to
regard as close friends. The former was a wily flute player, the latter a
dreamy poet. Together the twins built castles in the air. And it was Vult and
Walt who were the immediate inspiration behind Schumann's own set of
twins, whom he mentions for the first time in July 1831: "Some entirely new
people have entered my diary today — two of my best friends, even though
I've never set eyes on them before. They are called Florestan and Eusebius."[2]
Schumann regarded them as poetic reflections of his own "dual nature,"
which he was "keen to fuse together as a single person."[3] At the risk of oversimplification, we could describe Florestan as the extrovert, sanguine idealist,
Eusebius as the more introverted, or at least a more thoughtful dreamer. They
were quickly joined by Master Raro and Zilia, the worldly-wise Raro being a
cover identity for the idealized figure of Friedrich Wieck, while Clara Wieck
lay behind Zilia, Chiara, and Chiarina, a composite figure notable for her understanding and appreciation of art.

Florestan, Eusebius, Master Raro, and Zilia were all founding members of the League of David that Schumann summoned into existence at this time. Just as real life and fiction, sentiment and a sober attitude to life were inextricably linked in Jean Paul's *Flegeljahre* and just as the political and social present was concealed behind the poetic world of his *Unsichtbare Loge* (Invisible opera box), so Schumann's League of David led a volatile existence, switching between fiction and reality and between the quotidian and mystification. This is the poeticization and romanticization of a life that has to be lived in the real world but which is bearable only as an alternative construct in the individual's imagination — only with our own fantasy can we play with this life, rather than allowing it to play with us.

Anyone wanting to help in preparing for a "new poetic age" cannot do so, of course, as a loner or as an eccentric familiar with nothing beyond the confines of his or her own diary. Rather, they and their "community" need to engage with the world. And so we find Schumann at the end of 1833 publishing a kind of unfinished novel with the heading: "The Member of the League of David. Communicated by S*. Leipzig's world of music. First article." It appeared in *Der Komet*, a Leipzig-based periodical highly regarded by the Young German movement of the time. The following excerpt allows us the best possible insight into Schumann as a young writer:

Above me, a window was quickly thrown open, and behind it I recognized in the half-shadow an angular, wry-nosed roundhead. Just as I was looking up, something like finely scented leaves fluttered down and played around my temples: they were scraps of paper that had been thrown down from the window. Back at home I felt as if I were rooted to the spot when I read the following on a sheet wrapped up in some heavier paper:

Our Italian nights are continuing. Florestan the idealist has gone quieter than ever in recent days and seems to have something on his mind. But Eusebius let slip a few words that roused the Old Adam in him. After reading a copy of Iris, the latter said: "But he's gone too far." — "What? How's that? Eusebius," Florestan started up at this point, "Rellstab [Ludwig Rellstab (1799–1860), an influential Berlin music critic hostile to the romantic movement and the editor of the music magazine Iris] has gone too far? Is this infernal German politeness to last for centuries? While the literary factions oppose each other and engage in open feuding, art critics simply shrug their shoulders, evincing a degree of reserve that cannot be understood or sufficiently condemned. Why not simply dismiss those who have no talent? Why not throw the insipid and moribund out of court, together*

*with the presumptuous? Why not stick warning notices on works that end
where criticism begins? Why do writers not have a newspaper of their own
in which they can inveigh against critics and challenge them to be even ruder
about their works?* [. . .] *It is time to stand up to the defensive and offensive
alliance forged between meanness and defiance before it overwhelms us and
there is no longer any prospect of putting an end to the whole of this wretched
situation. But what do you think, Master Raro?"*

You know Raro's *affecting way of speaking, which is made even stranger by
his Italian accent, how he strings sentences together, before taking them apart,
fitting them together again, entwining them even more tightly, then summing
up everything again at the end and seeming to say: "That's what I meant."*

*"Florestan," retorted the Master, "what you say is true, even though I
cannot approve of the way you express it. Remove the mask when the highest
gifts and abilities of the mind are concerned.* [. . .] *Does not secretiveness give
the appearance of —"*

Here the sheet of paper was torn, but on the back were the words:

*"Inventor! You have been chosen for greatness and for the good! You are to
become a member of the League of David and translate the League's mysteries
for the world — that is, the League that is to strike dead the philistines,
musical and otherwise! Now you know everything — now you must act! Yet
those actions must not be provincially narrow-minded but confused and
insane. Master Raro, Florestan, Eusebius, Friedrich, Bg., St., Hf., Knif,
Balkentreter to St. George."*[4]

In keeping with its heading, "Leipzig's Musical Scene," the article also discussed current events in the city, not contenting itself with a mere reference
to a savage attack on Chopin's Mozart Variations in Rellstab's *Iris* but allowing its readers to see a concert review that the first-person narrator effectively
copies out before their very eyes. The writer, who signed himself simply as
"E." (presumably Eusebius), also mentioned the name of Clara Wieck, a local
heroine in the musical life of the city, and advised her to perform keyboard
concertos by Bach and Handel.[5]

Inevitably the review itself was interrupted, adding to the sense of tension:
"I had reached this point in copying out the piece when a handsome, black-
haired youth entered the room and silently handed me a letter. — "Who are
you?" But he was already on his way out. What was in the letter? "I want to
say it in your ear ——————— Did you hear?""[6]

The motif of the scraps of paper found by the narrator clearly recalls the
word games in E. T. A. Hoffmann's *Tomcat Murr* and Jean Paul's *Leben Fibels*

(Life of Fibel). And the same is true of Schumann's trick of having the narrator interrupt his task of copying out the review and whispering the contents of a letter in his reader's imaginary ear. And we do not have to waste time wondering whether the aforementioned writers made things easier for themselves with their romantic humor than their imitators, for with Schumann we find something new and, indeed, unique inasmuch as he integrates into his poetic text elements of professional music criticism which, far from being abstract, are related to concerts currently taking place in Leipzig.

It is hard to imagine a more exciting trial run for a new periodical, as Schumann turned his plans into a game drawing on elements from both real life and the world of poetry. But it was a game also designed to inspire him with the courage to tackle such a major project. At the same time, we may observe a twenty-three-year-old who, in spite of all the emotional crises he had been through, was able to reconcile ideality and reality in an astonishingly professional manner. Notwithstanding his lofty aim of giving a voice to musical romanticism, he never for a moment lost touch with reality: the new journal needed a publisher, subscribers, distributors, advertisers, and reliable contributors.

The first issue of the twice-weekly *Neue Zeitschrift für Musik* appeared on April 3, 1834. It ran to 4 pages and had a print run of 400 copies — no mean figure when we recall that Schiller's *Horen* had an average print run of 1,000 and that Cotta sold 2,500 copies of his daily *Morgenblatt für gebildete Stände*. In any event, Schumann's publishers, Johann Ambrosius Barth and August Robert Friese, were pleased, although Friese later expressed his unease when Schumann's own contributions began to appear less frequently and the circulation figures dropped in consequence. By 1843, the paper had only 340 subscribers, but the income Schumann derived from his publishing activities was still enough to provide him with a solid financial basis.

According to the masthead of the first year's issues, the paper was "Published by an Association of Artists and Friends of Art," but by the second year this had changed to "Published in Association with Several Artists and Friends of Art under the Overall Responsibility of R. Schumann." This revised wording was a more accurate reflection of the situation: until he sold the paper in 1846, Schumann edited it, and it was effectively a one-man business. And he ran it well. Although unworldly in many respects, he was down-to-earth in other ways, and from 1834 he kept a detailed list of all the letters he sent or received, all of them carefully numbered, with a brief summary of their contents in a separate column. He continued to keep this list up to date until

1854, and even though it soon included Schumann's other correspondence, it was based initially on a desire to ensure that the paper was from the outset run along orderly lines.

According to this list, Schumann sent out some 2,500 letters, the originals of which are now scattered all over the world and in many cases lost altogether. But what remains is still a respectable body of evidence. Schumann's handwriting was never easy to decipher, and even his contemporary, Eduard Hanslick, noted by way of a joke: "Everyone to whom I showed the page in question looked at the final words of the first letter he sent me in Prague and insisted that they read 'In this fetid hole,' whereas what they actually said was 'In this fervent hope.'"[7]

By contrast, the 5,500 or so letters that Schumann received have survived almost in their entirety and are gathered together in several thick volumes in the Biblioteka Jagiellońska in Kraków. Although they are invaluable for the light that they throw on contemporary events, they have yet to be properly examined and to yield all their riches. It is interesting, perhaps, that Schumann singled out a selection of these letters, including the ones he received from Mendelssohn, and kept them in a "family chest" specially reserved for such "relics." This particular group of letters is now in the University of Dresden Library.

In Schumann's day, letters were delivered with often astonishing speed, making it easier for him as editor of the *Neue Zeitschrift für Musik* to maintain a network of contacts between publishers, supporters, writers, local correspondents, and subscribers. And in terms of contemporary discourse on musical aesthetics, we are fortunate that when it came to collecting information, he did not sit back and wait for news to break — nor did he run the risk that many a newspaper editor in the twenty-first century has to face and drown in a floodtide of news items. Rather, he went about his business with very real pleasure and affection, eager, as he was, to know what was going on in the world of music and to provide a focus of interest in the pages of his newspaper. It was not long before his readers were being invited to submit reports from their own hometowns and cities, for which they would be paid a fee of fifteen thalers per printed page. Such reports, Schumann insisted, should not be "arid notices typical of foreign correspondents but living pictures of the musical conditions that obtain in all of these places."[8]

Inevitably there were problems, but in general Schumann succeeded in filling his columns with reports from cities as far afield as Paris and St. Petersburg. And yet he was also keen to keep his readers informed about new publications in the world of music. And to the extent that this introduced a political element to his activities, it is time to examine the position of the *Neue Zeitschrift für Musik* within the context of three rival periodicals and against the background that Schumann himself sketched out:

> The present age is characterized by its factions. Just as the world of politics can be divided up, so the world of music can be broken down into liberals, middlemen, and legitimists or into romantics, modernists, and classicists. On the right sit the members of the old school, the contrapuntalists, antiquarians, folklorists, and anti-chromatists, and on the left hand are the youths, the Phrygian caps, the despisers of form, and the brazen geniuses, among whom the Beethovenians are a class apart. In the *juste milieu*, young and old commingle and vacillate. Here the majority of the products of the day are to be found, here are the creatures of the moment, fathered by it and destroyed by it.[9]

According to this taxonomy, *Caecilia* belonged in the reactionary, "classical" camp of the old "contrapuntalists." It was a conservative periodical that was chiefly interested in the theory of music, arguing that, historically speaking, music had culminated in the figure of Mozart. According to *Caecilia*, the music of late-period Beethoven was an aberration. *Iris im Gebiete der Tonkunst* (Iris in the field of music) was Rellstab's publication. Although less rigorous in its approach, it adopted a highly skeptical view of all avant-garde developments. In 1833, for example, Rellstab felt called upon to make a symbolic gesture and dismiss Chopin's Mazurkas op. 7 on account of their "earsplitting dissonances, tortured transitions, piercing modulations, and repugnant distortions of the melodic line and rhythm."[10] Shortly afterward, Rellstab adopted an equally hostile tone in his review of Schumann's Intermezzos op. 4 and *Kinderscenen* op. 15, while the *Neue Zeitschrift für Musik*, in its "Letters from Paris," responded by taking exception to Rellstab's harsh critique of Chopin's Mazurkas.[11]

The "middlemen" of the *juste milieu* were represented by the *Allgemeine musikalische Zeitung*, which had been published in Leipzig since 1798 and, as such, was the maiden aunt among music journals and the main rival to Schumann's new enterprise. In fact, Schumann himself contributed on occasion to the *Allgemeine musikalische Zeitung*, but he hated it on account of its lack of passion and indifference and preferred to number himself—not without a dash of irony—among the romantics to the left of center, the "despisers of form," and "brazen geniuses." And perhaps it was specifically with himself in mind that he devised the subcategory of the "Beethovenians."

This subcategory also included Adolph Bernhard Marx, who edited the liberal *Berliner Allgemeine musikalische Zeitung* from 1824 until it folded in 1830. Schumann could with some justification regard his own *Neue Zeitschrift* as Marx's belated successor, even though the focus of his interest lay elsewhere. Far more than Marx, Schumann was keen to promote an exchange of ideas and engage with the contemporary musical scene in what he hoped would be a productive way. As for the extensive reviews section of his paper, he pursued his own agenda, one that was both pragmatic and based on sound principles. His fixation on piano music was pragmatic but also a little self-interested, for in his eyes it remained the clearest possible mirror of the musical zeitgeist. And in terms of his subscribers' practical interests, there is no doubt that piano music played a predominant role, second only to songs, which were initially treated rather shabbily by the *Neue Zeitschrift*. But works scored for larger forces were also discussed in its pages — even the first year's issues contained reviews of such recent works as Auber's opera *Gustave III, ou Le bal masqué* (Gustavus III, or the masked ball) and Carl Loewe's oratorio *Die eherne Schlange* (The iron snake), although neither piece was written by Schumann, whose famous reviews of Berlioz's *Symphonie Fantastique* and Schubert's Symphony in C Major (*Great*) appeared a little later.

Three columns were intended to reflect the topicality of Schumann's periodical: "Reviews," "From Our Own Correspondents," and "Chronicle." There were also "Essays on Theory" and "Belles Lettres," which allowed the editor to live hand-to-mouth and put off dealing with submissions he disliked. Even so, he was obliged to compromise in this regard: the short stories by Johann Peter Lyser about Handel, Bach, Beethoven, and Mozart may not have been to his liking, for they were markedly inferior to a multilayered romantic masterpiece like E. T. A. Hoffmann's "Chevalier Gluck" and lacked characters as complex as Kapellmeister Kreisler, who threatens to stab himself with an augmented fifth while wearing a coat in C-sharp minor with a collar in D major.

But Lyser — better known as a draftsman and portrait painter who included Beethoven among his sitters — was a member of the League of David, and Schumann was generally tolerant of their works whenever it was a question of reviewing them. He may also have been fascinated by Lyser's dissolute life as an artist: the latter had tried his hand at the most varied professions and on one occasion had had to be rescued from a debtor's prison by Mendelssohn. He was also friendly with Heine. Prematurely deaf, he ended his days in a poorhouse in Altona. In a review devoted to new dance compositions,

Schumann wrote a tribute to Lyser under his League of David name, Fritz Friedrich: "On the other hand a whole carnival dances in the German Dances [by Schubert]. 'And it would be great,' Florestan shouted in Fritz Friedrich's ear, 'if you got out your magic lantern and used shadows to recreate the masked ball on the wall.' He rushed away, jubilant, and was soon back."[12]

The writer and folksong collector Anton Wilhelm Florentin von Zuccalmaglio led a similarly peripatetic, albeit less restless, existence. His 130 or so articles appeared in the *Neue Zeitschrift* between 1835 and 1850, some of them signed "Village Sexton Wedel." Although "Gottschalk Wedel" was capable of satire, he was generally content to enthuse in such a naïvely generous way about the manifold miracles of music that Schumann was able to announce on December 17, 1835: "Wedel has been appointed to the League of David."[13] Present-day readers will be familiar with Zuccalmaglio's name, if at all, as the author of the quietistic poem "Kein schöner Land in dieser Zeit" (No fairer land in the present age), but a more belligerent side emerges from the poem "Die Liedertafeln" (The glee clubs), the last verse of which reads:

> Was jetzt in Liedersprudeln gährt,
> Der Freiheit Preis und Wonne,
> Und was den Tag uns festlich klärt,
> Der Strahl der neuen Sonne,
> Es kann in Männerthaten glühn,
> Wie nur die Feinde drohen.
> Das Lied wird dann vom Schwerte sprühn,
> Gesang zu Schlachten lohen.[14]

> [The fountainhead of song now seethes / With freedom's joy and full-toned praise, / The day, transfigured, now bequeaths / A new sun's incandescent rays: / Men's deeds can glow with lambent fire, / Our foes can threaten as they may. / Our songs will flash with swordplay's ire, / Our battle songs shall light the day.]

Schumann showed a good deal of courage when he quoted this poem on the title page of the issue of January 27, 1837, for at a time when every publication had to meet with the censor's approval, such consciously vague threats were as likely as not to cause political offense. And although Schumann could not have foreseen at this stage the revolutions of 1848 and 1849, such threats would have been welcome to him precisely because of their ambiguity: in no circumstances was his newspaper to be a magazine for philistines; and playing with fire is always fun.

Schumann's use of the word "philistines" derives from the language of students, but his concern for the most part was the clash between artists and the willfully inartistic, a meaning already explored by Goethe in one of his "Parables":

Gedichte sind gemalte Fensterscheiben!
Sieht man vom Markt in die Kirche hinein
Da ist alles dunkel und düster;
Und so sieht's auch der Herr Philister:
Der mag denn wohl verdrießlich sein
Und lebenslang verdrießlich bleiben.[15]

[Songs are like painted windowpanes! / In darkness wrapp'd the church remains, / If from the market-place we view it; / Thus sees the ignoramus through it. / No wonder that he deems it tame, — / And all his life 'twill be the same.]

Schumann was determined that artists rather than pedants should write for his *Neue Zeitschrift*, and he applied this precept not only to the articles that were "literary" in the narrower sense of the term but also to the reviews section. His aim of having new works reviewed above all by composers is one that he achieved mainly by writing the reviews himself, although he was also willing to give space to divergent opinions. When he reviewed Spohr's symphony *Die Weihe der Töne* (The consecration of tones), for example, he appended a second review by the respected Viennese composer and music theorist Ignaz von Seyfried; and when he discussed Berlioz's *Symphonie Fantastique*, he prefaced his review with a piece that had appeared in the *Revue musicale* condemning the work in no uncertain terms — it was this piece that had alerted him to the existence of Berlioz's composition. And so we find him writing on June 19, 1835:

We have had the piano score in our hands for some weeks now. It was with horror that we saw and played it. Gradually, however, our opinion took shape and was so clearly at odds with that of Monsieur Fétis that we decided to offer our readers a brief and free translation of his review. Our own assessment will follow as soon as possible. Until then we would encourage those who are interested in the exceptional to familiarize themselves with this symphony.[16]

The *Neue Zeitschrift* then published a piece signed by "Florestan" that was largely poetic in character, but Schumann followed this up with a longer article, which he signed himself and which offered a more detailed account of the compositional aspects of the work. It was thanks to Schumann that within a year a work by Berlioz had received its first performance in Germany and, moreover, in Leipzig. True, it was not Mendelssohn who introduced the work to his Gewandhaus audience but — probably — the city's Euterpe Society that gave the successful local premiere of the overture to Berlioz's unfinished opera *Les francs-juges*.

Berlioz published a letter of thanks to Schumann in the *Revue et Gazette musicale*, and the *Neue Zeitschrift* covered the ensuing controversy raised by the merits and demerits of a work that struck many contemporaries as newfangled in the extreme. The yea-sayers were represented by the Weimar composer and music theorist Johann Christian Lobe, their opponents by the honorary member of the League of David, Florentin von Zuccalmaglio. With hindsight we can only congratulate Schumann for opening the columns of his newspaper to the debate about Berlioz and for instigating the lively discussion that was conducted thereafter in much of Germany and Austria.

It would be little short of a miracle, of course, if everything had gone according to plan in the case of a newly established newspaper that appeared with such striking frequency. But although Schumann knew that he would often have to compromise, he stuck to his principle of maintaining the paper's distinctive style, no matter how varied and random the individual details may have been. Their subject matter may have been different, but all the contributions were to be imbued with the same spirit of poetry that was to help pave the way for the "new poetic age" of which he dreamed.

In order to signal that every issue was held together, as it were, by an invisible poetic bond, Schumann adopted the model of Cotta's *Morgenblatt für gebildete Stände* and prefaced it with a motto of its own. The very first issue, for example, began with a Shakespearean quotation rich in allusive symbolism:

> Only they
> That come to hear a merry bawdy play,
> A noise of targets, or to see a fellow
> In a long motley coat guarded with yellow,
> Will be deceived.[17]

Schumann took over many quotations from the *Morgenblatt*, in some cases even within a day or so of their initial appearance there. On June 19, 1834, for example, he reproduced a couplet from Byron's *Childe Harold's Pilgrimage* that the *Morgenblatt* had used only two days earlier:

And yet how lovely in thine age of woe,
Land of lost Gods and godlike men, art thou![18]

As the motto for the next issue, Schumann chose a distich from one of Goethe's *Roman Elegies*:

Thou art indeed a world, oh Rome; and yet, were Love absent,
Then would the world be no world, then would e'en Rome be no Rome.[19]

In each case the choice was apt, for the main article was devoted, respectively, to the world of Italian music and to the specific situation in Rome.

Schumann had already written his *Papillons* op. 2 when for the July 28, 1835 issue of *Neue Zeitschrift* he chose lines from the *Elements of Natural History* by the German naturalist and philosopher Lorenz Oken:

The butterfly is in every respect the highest insect. Its consummate life consists of a mere fluttering. A butterfly lives simply in the air and in the light. Its body is made up almost entirely of wings, its ability to set foot on the ground has, as it were, been forgotten. The most beautiful colors have settled upon it; its life is one of pleasure and love.[20]

Perhaps the composer saw a parallel here with his own life as an artist.

Schumann was clearly eager to use these mottos as a way of helping his readers to understand that the world of music was immeasurably enriched if *belles lettres* played its part — regardless of whether it was Shakespeare, Byron, Herder, Goethe, Schiller, Jean Paul, Lenau, or Herwegh. At the same time these mottos allowed him to throw open a window on those distant landscapes of the mind in which he wanted his periodical to be located.

But Schumann managed to achieve even more than this, weaving what can only be termed a spiritual bond around his paper's daily news items: it is a bond that bears the name of the League of David. When setting up the paper, he had in fact refrained from announcing that the "artists and friends of art" who supported him were members of the League, preferring instead to play a clever game of hide-and-seek and telling Zuccalmaglio that "for many people the mysterious nature of the whole affair has something appealing about it and, like all that is concealed from view, it exerts a particular power."[21]

Not until the nineteenth issue did an article appear under the heading "The League of David." In it, Eusebius, Florestan, and Raro took it in turns to express their views on Johann Nepomuk Hummel's pianoforte *Études* op. 125. A footnote explained that "Unfortunately we are still unable to offer a full explanation of the heading 'League of David,' but the valued reader may expect one soon as the unknown hand that has already signed itself 'Euseb.,' 'F–n,' and 'Florestan' in previous issues has given us ample reason for hoping as much. Ed."²²

The "explanation" at the end of the thirty-eighth issue likewise has a cryptic ring to it as the *Neue Zeitschrift* was still appearing at this date without any explicit mention of Schumann:

> Many rumors are circulating concerning the identity of the members of the League who have signed this article. Since we are unfortunately still obliged to withhold the reasons for drawing a veil over our identity, we are asking Herr Schumann (assuming that he is familiar to an honorable editorial office) to represent us with his name. The Members of the League of David. — I shall be pleased to do so, R. Schumann.²³

The game that Schumann as editor was playing with his public was nothing if not bold: when would his readers, on whom he depended for the journal's continuing existence, start to feel disoriented? For Schumann as an artist, conversely, this remained not just a game but also a process of positively existential significance — he would never have felt comfortable as the stolid editor of a serious paper. Rather, readers should be able to regard his newspaper as a part of that poetic total artwork that he wanted to help to create. And such a work was inconceivable without cryptic puzzles and masquerades and without the role-playing and changes of identity typical of E. T. A. Hoffmann and Jean Paul. The last-named in particular could be described as the *Neue Zeitschrift*'s spiritus rector, or inspiration.

Even the opening sentences of the "Shrovetide Address" that Schumann placed in the mouth of his alter ego, Florestan, in April 1835 had, of course, contained clear pointers to what readers should understand by the term "League of David": "Assembled members of the League of David, that is, youths and men dedicated to the destruction of the philistines, musical and otherwise, the bigger the better" — thus Florestan addressed his comrades from his seat at his grand piano,²⁴ before going on to discuss an actual musical event in the form of a performance of Beethoven's Ninth Symphony in the Gewandhaus in Leipzig under the retiring music director August Pohlenz.

It was not only Pohlenz's complacency that annoyed Schumann/Florestan but also, and above all, the philistines in the audience. "David against the Philistines" was his motto. And in the course of his article Schumann/Florestan not only drew a comparison between himself and Jean Paul's balloonist Giannozzo, who looks down implacably on human dealings from his lofty vantage point, he also struck a severely practical note, arguing that to perform a work like Beethoven's Ninth for a subscription audience, no matter how charitably disposed it may have been, was tantamount to casting pearls before swine. In the face of such a timeless work, rhapsodic enthusiasm was the only possible response. But this did not preclude constructive criticism:

> You gave me a beautiful moment there, director of music! You caught the tempo of the theme in the basses [the well-known melody accompanying the words "Freude, schöner Götterfunken" in the final movement] so wonderfully that I forgot much that had angered me in the first movement where, despite the modestly veiled performance marking "Un poco maestoso," one hears the whole slowly striding majesty of a god.[25]

This was a dig at Pohlenz, but it avoided the sneering condescension and aesthetic hair-splitting about tempo decisions found in so much music criticism. Rather, Schumann was typically concerned to reconcile his own personal experience of the work—an experience that always drew on poetry and imagery—with the fixed form of the piece as it appeared in the published score and performance markings. A century later Hans-Georg Gadamer would declare the fusing of the horizons of work and observer to be the necessary precondition for any process of understanding: the mere "reproduction of an original production" of content and form can never be successful or even remotely adequate.[26] For Schumann, this was self-evident, and the place where these different horizons met was the metaphor.

When Schumann writes that the "whole slowly striding majesty of a god" speaks to him from the opening of the Ninth Symphony, then he does not mean that this was the impression that Beethoven necessarily wanted to create, for Schumann offers other possible interpretations here:

> Others listeners were more graphic. For them, the symphony represented the story of the origins of humankind—first chaos—then the divine "Let there be light!" And the sun rose upon the first human, who was delighted with such magnificence—in short the whole first chapter of the Pentateuch![27]

This, then, was the symphony as a whole. But Schumann did not want to suggest indiscriminate associations. Rather, he took the term "progressive" seriously in the sense understood by Friedrich Schlegel when he wrote about "progressive universal poetry,"[28] rightly interpreting it as an invitation to use the work of art as the starting point for further thought. This, then, was the task of that particular kind of romantic criticism of the arts to which Walter Benjamin devoted his attention in his doctoral dissertation, "The Concept of Art Criticism in German Romanticism," in 1919, a study that continues to prove enlightening even today.

But let us return to David's struggle with the philistines, a battle that finds expression above all in the reviews section of the *Neue Zeitschrift für Musik*: inferior pieces concerned only with empty effects and lacking in imagination were either ignored altogether or dismissed out of hand. In the second issue of the paper, the *Grande Fantaisie et Variations* op. 10 by the young Sigismond Thalberg — soon to be acclaimed by audiences in the same breath as Liszt — came within the critic's line of fire:

> A piece like this, the supreme and, indeed, the only aim of which is its desire
> to please, is not one that we can condone in spite of its individual beauties,
> its pianistic style, and its evident attempt to avoid the merely ordinary. If a
> young composer has not only natural talent, as Herr Thalberg does, but
> also understanding, he has no need to fear that he will sound ordinary if
> he simply passes on what he feels and perceives within him. But if he fails
> to appreciate this principle and if he is not even aware of its existence but
> worships the fashion of the day as his god, and if he subordinates his talent
> to the applause of the crowd, then everything that he may do to preserve his
> deeper qualities will be a waste of effort. And so it is with Herr Thalberg.
> His composition is nothing more than a new and more elegant version of
> works by Herz and Czerny with an extra dash of erudition.[29]

Although this review was probably not written by Schumann, it nonetheless sums up the beliefs of the members of the League of David: they had declared war on the opportunism that necessarily leads to superficiality, and they praised the powers of the imagination that the artist conjures up within himself. The *Neue Zeitschrift* never tired of drawing attention to composers who lived up to this ideal and who included not only members of a much earlier generation but also some of the major figures on the contemporary musical scene, such as Chopin, Liszt, Mendelssohn, and Henselt, as well as lesser-known artists. And who will hold it against the editor for mentioning his own piano works?

The fact that his Sonata in F-sharp Minor op. 11 was twice discussed in detail demonstrates the way in which the members of the League of David conceived of music criticism — not as a review in the traditional sense but as a form of poetic discourse. Much the same spirit had already informed the famous piece that August Wilhelm Schlegel had published in the *Athenäum* a generation earlier, when he had divided his discussion of a series of paintings among several different voices. In the case of Schumann's Sonata, the views of the two critics were divided between separate articles, but the same spirit of poetry pervades them both. The tone was set by the Königsberg musician Eduard Sobolewski with his essay "Observations and Dreams after the F-sharp Minor Sonata by Florestan and Eusebius." Instead of describing the work, he indulged in a series of historical reflections and poetic images, before ending with the words:

> Just play the sonata again and again. — Of course, it does not contain things
> that you can hold up for display, no finery, no gewgaws, no thin piping
> sounds in the very highest register, no somersaults, but *only music*; and yet,
> if your heart is free from constraint, then you may calm your emotions in its
> sounds. It is an antidote to poison. It too grieves with time over time.[30]

Carl Ferdinand Becker's assessment of the piece appeared three weeks later with the programmatical sentence: "This work is an authentic sign of the romanticism that has been woken up in the present day and that is now gaining ground all around us." Becker — an authority on the Leipzig musical scene at this time — then spoke of a "new school," which he defined as follows: "Those who place themselves at the head of this school, with its poetic painting through sounds, are Berlioz, Liszt, Hiller, Chopin, Florestan, and Eusebius."[31] By naming Florestan and Eusebius, but not Schumann himself, Becker was adhering to the composer's own guidelines: after all, he had published the sonata under the names of his two "best friends."

If Mendelssohn, who was currently carving a niche for himself as the undisputed star of Leipzig's musical scene, was missing from Becker's list, it was because "even before this new example of our aspirations he has already demonstrated such great independence that, even without wanting it and without working toward that goal, he stands there as of his own accord as the principal voice of this poetry in music, without, however, having sidestepped beautiful prose in art."[32] In other words, however much Becker was alive to Mendelssohn's neoclassical romanticism, he — Becker — was championing the young fantasts at this particular moment and in their own particular forum.

The four "Effusive Letters" Schumann published in the third volume of his *Neue Zeitschrift* are "reviews" in an altogether more distinctive sense.

They appeared under the headings "Eusebius to Chiara," "[Chiara] to Euse-bius," "[Florestan] to Chiara," and "[Serpentin] to Chiara" (Serpentin being Schumann's fellow contributor and initial friend, Carl Banck). They wrote effusively not only about one another but also about the pleasures that were afforded by the current state of music in Leipzig and that provided an excuse for an exchange of views on musical poetry.

Among these pleasures was "early music." When Clara Schumann, Men-delssohn, and Louis Rakemann played Johann Sebastian Bach's Triple Con-certo for three keyboards, Serpentin felt impelled to write to Chiara:

> I found Eusebius resting his head on this sheet yesterday evening and
> sleeping soundly; he looked fit to be painted and kissed, as if he were still
> dreaming of Zilia's concert, about which he was wanting to write to you. We
> are sending you the whole piece of paper. But don't laugh at old Sebastian's
> concerto for three keyboards, which Zilia played with Meritis and gentle
> Walt from the League of David, but be like Florestan, who said that it will be
> perfectly clear to one what kind of a wretch one is.[33]

("You must change your life"—thus Rainer Maria Rilke was to end his sonnet "Apollo's Archaic Torso" two generations later.)

It is fascinating to watch Schumann build up a small empire with his *Neue Zeitschrift für Musik* and how he fused reality and vision, poetry and politics, public and private concerns, and artistic ideals and self-promotion to create a miniature total artwork.[34] No one else was able to do this—neither E. T. A. Hoffmann nor Jean Paul nor Heinrich Heine. The fact that he needed this performance art—and it is one that would have done credit to a member of the Fluxus movement—in order to lend a sense of stability to his own per-sonality and that, as a stranger in the world, he could evidently communicate with it only in this way does not make it any less compelling. But it is hardly surprising that he was unable to maintain this level in the longer term and that the *Neue Zeitschrift für Musik* gradually acquired a greater normality and that Schumann himself wrote for it less and less frequently.

In this sense, Schumann's opening remarks in the 1839 volume seem al-ready to be a little more detached, their note of resolve notwithstanding. As such, they provide a suitable conclusion to the present chapter:

> It may be possible to use German art to raise the level of our appreciation
> of all things German by drawing attention to older models or by preferring
> those younger and more talented artists whose most outstanding

representatives one hears described as romantics — and this elevation may even now be seen as the goal of our aspirations. At all events, the recurrent theme that holds this thought together may be found in the history of the League of David, a league which, even if its appearances are restricted to the realm of fantasy, boasts members who are identifiable less by their outward insignia than by an inner similarity. In the future, too, they will seek to raise a bulwark against mediocrity in word as well as in deed.[34]

Schumann in 1839, lithograph by Joseph Kriehuber, a portraitist in great demand in Vienna at this time. It was commissioned by the publishing house of
Mechetti, which between 1839 and 1841 published five of Schumann's works:
the *Arabesque*, op. 18; the *Blumenstück* (Flower Piece), op. 19; the Humoresque,
op. 20; the four *Nachtstücke* (Night Pieces), op. 23; and the Heine *Liederkreis*
(Song Cycle), op. 24. Schumann himself later said that "none of my portraits
is of much value, with the possible exception of Kriehuber's" (*Briefe. Neue
Folge* 317). (Photograph courtesy of the Robert Schumann Museum, Zwickau.)

CHAPTER 4

The Early Piano Pieces

*I am affected by everything that happens in the world: politics,
literature, people — I think about everything in my own way, and
this then seeks to vent itself and find an outlet through music.
That is why many of my compositions are so difficult to understand
because they relate to remote interests, including even significant
ones, and because everything remarkable that happens in this age
moves me and I then have to express it in my music.*

Letter to Clara Wieck, April [15,] 1838[1]

C omposing is not the same as composing. In the case of the young
Schumann it makes sense to distinguish between two fundamentally
different attitudes, the first naïve and practical, the second reflective
in the highest degree.

Children sing and, when they have a chance to do so, they pick out little
tunes on an instrument. Here we see an aptitude for a naïve type of composing
that is lost if it is not encouraged or gradually channeled into more practical
forms of composition. Until Beethoven's day composition was primarily a
craft that required an adherence to traditional rules. The simple pleasure that
the innocent listener may derive from Mozart's music rests not least on the
fact that this music clearly follows certain rules while transcending them in an
altogether inspired way: the composer does not strike at the very foundations
of music as defined at that time but seeks, rather, to build his musical visions
upon those foundations. When seen from Mozart's standpoint, composers
learned to write music much as they learned any other trade, while gradually
adding new elements of their own.

Much the same appears to have been the case with the young Schumann, at least as far as his intentions were concerned. True, he had little in the way of regular composition lessons but took his cue, as if of his own accord, from the models that he found all around him — and he was by no means unsuccessful in this regard. As we have already noted, he was eighteen when he sent some of his songs to Gottlob Wiedebein, asking the latter to cast an eye over them. The response was so positive that he felt encouraged to turn his hand to "proper" symphonies, overtures, piano concertos, and string quartets, and did indeed make a start on a number of such projects. The best-known product of these early attempts at composition is the opening movement of the unfinished *Zwickau* Symphony, a movement that was performed on no fewer than three occasions in 1832–33.

Although a writer as knowledgeable about Schumann as Peter Gülke has plausible reasons for hailing this early attempt at a symphony as a "stroke of genius,"[2] there is no denying Schumann's debt to Mozart and Beethoven. No less obvious is the way in which for whole sections he does little more than juxtapose compositional set-pieces. He himself expressed the view at this time that many years of study would have been necessary if he were to have had any lasting success in this genre, but this — he believed — would also have meant that he would not have found his own voice as quickly as he did. And it was this that took priority, as is clear from the note of irritation in the lines that he addressed to Clara Wieck in January 1839: "Don't on any account call me Jean Paul the second or Beethoven the second again; if you do, I really could hate you, even if only for a moment; I want to be ten times less than others but be *something in my own right*; please don't call me etc. etc. any more."[3]

Schumann wanted to be an original genius, a category introduced into artistic discourse by the *Sturm und Drang* movement of the previous century and one which in the context of the history of music first proved to be decisive in discussions on Beethoven, whose works reveal the qualitative leap from a form of composition that had largely conformed to social expectations and been regarded as a craft to a type of creativity according to which every work by a composer had at least to equal what had gone before it in terms of its originality, even if it could not surpass it. Whereas Haydn wrote over one hundred symphonies, Mozart completed only a little over forty, while Beethoven gave each of his symphonies such a distinctive profile that nine had been the limit for him. This was no longer the age of absolutism, when two dozen sandstone putti, standing outside in the park, had become so weather-beaten that after two generations they had had to be replaced as a matter of course. Now nine masterly bronze busts were displayed inside a museum, where a tenth could no longer be added. At least that is how Brahms viewed the situation regarding the symphony when he exclaimed at the age of almost forty: "I shall never write a symphony! You have no idea how someone like me feels when he can always hear a giant marching along behind him."[4]

The young Schumann had neither the staying power of a Brahms nor Brahms's specific goals. Although he wanted to honor tradition, he had no intention of serving it. Rather, his aim was to engage in active warfare against the philistines. David had only one weapon with which to defeat Goliath — his sling. This presupposed reduced forces, initially the piano, and small-scale forms such as dance movements and sets of variations. Of course, a writer of symphonies could also play the part of David, and Schumann would undoubtedly have conceded that his colleague Hector Berlioz had marched into battle against the French philistines with his *Symphonie Fantastique* emblazoned on his banner. For the present, however, this was not Schumann's way. Only when improvising at the piano did he feel that his life had achieved a genuine authenticity — it was as if he had switched to the instrument after reading the works of E. T. A. Hoffmann and Jean Paul and had translated into music the states of mind that he found in those writings. In making these states his own and restoring them to their rightful place in an uncomprehending and soulless world, he set an appropriate example.

"It would be a petty art that had only sounds but no language or signs for states of mind," Schumann wrote in his "Book of Thoughts and Poems," in which he made sporadic entries between 1831 and 1833.[5] And in spite of the respect that he felt for Chopin and Mendelssohn, he was bound to admit that on this point his musical heroes from the past had made greater advances than many musicians of the present day, with their tendency toward shallowness:

> When I think of the supreme kind of music, as bequeathed to us by Bach
> and Beethoven in a number of their works, and when I speak of the rare
> states of mind that the artist is to reveal to me, and if I were to demand that
> with every one of his works he takes me a step further into the spirit world
> of art and if I were to demand poetic depth and novelty everywhere, in
> individual detail and in more general terms, I should have to search for a
> long time.[6]

The "artistic roots" of counterpoint were so well hidden in the fugues in Bach's *The Well-Tempered Clavier*[7] that we can appreciate them as "character-pieces of the highest kind and in part as truly poetic creations."[8] As a result,

Schumann was delighted to note, "an observer with no mean knowledge of music could think that a fugue by Bach was a study by Chopin—an assessment that is a credit to both composers."[9] If Schumann held Beethoven in such high regard, it was not least because of his late quartets, which seemed to reveal to him "rare states of mind" in a particularly undisguised form. Nor should we forget his admiration for Schubert, whose A Minor Piano Sonata D. 845 inspired him to write about it as follows a decade after its composition:

> The first section is so calm, so dreamy that it may move us to tears; and yet it is so simply constructed out of only two pieces that one has to admire the sorcerer who was able to dovetail and contrast them in so strange a way. [...] If we wanted to say anything about the inner nature of Schubert's works in general, it would be this: he has musical sounds for the subtlest emotions and ideas and even for events and for the conditions in which we live. Myriad as the forms human thought and desire can take, Schubert's music reflects them all. What he sees with his eyes and touches with his hand is transformed into music; he casts down stones, and from them living human forms rise up just as was the case with Deucalion and Pyrrha. He was the most distinguished composer after Beethoven who, as the mortal enemy of all philistinism, created music in the highest sense of the word without regard for strict mathematical forms and without the use of contrapuntal aids.[10]

But how could a beginner who even at the piano did not write like Bach, Beethoven, and Schubert, for example, find a suitable language for his own "states of mind"? For Schumann, this was not so much a technical question involving the rules of composition as one that raised wider aesthetic issues. He had to mature as a romantic and find his own tone of voice. Bach, Beethoven, and Schubert wrote in a "romantic" style without being aware that they were doing so. The age of the "neoromantics" had now dawned, to quote the title of a novel by one of Schumann's artistic friends, Julius Becker. And whereas Beethoven had been around thirty years old when he had decided to strike out in what he himself described as a "new direction," Schumann was only twenty when he started to look for the key that would turn him into a romantic composer.

His "Leipzig Book of Life" contains diary entries for the months between May and August 1831 and includes an invitation to the members of the League of David that was summoned into existence at this time: "Step closer & behave in a real romantic way!"[11] But the diary was also concerned with the question of actual composition. According to Florestan/Schumann, the composer's new (and unfinished) piano concerto was his first work to be written in a style "that tends toward the romantic."[12]

Looking back on his life from the vantage point of 1846, Schumann was inclined to date his "birth" as a romantic composer to an even earlier period: "I still have a very clear memory of a passage in one of my compositions (1828) that I told myself was romantic, a passage in which a spirit at variance with the older character of music first revealed itself to me, and a new life of poetry seemed to open itself up to me."[13] As Schumann explained, the work in question was the Trio from the Scherzo in his early Piano Quartet in C Minor, allowing us to examine the passage to which he was referring, even if it ultimately fails to embody the sort of "aha" experience that Schumann himself ascribed to it. More enlightening in this regard is a glance at his earliest published works, for these are surely unequivocal examples of the poetic and romantic music that Schumann wanted to bequeath to the world.

He could hardly have made a more impressive or auspicious start than with his Abegg Variations op. 1, an undervalued work that appeared in print at the end of 1831. And while it is true that the work was the result of a series of experimental dry runs on Schumann's part, it magnificently illustrates his future "program" and with astonishing light-handedness combines what he *wanted* to achieve with what he *could* achieve at this particular point in time.

What he wanted to achieve is summed up in a motto included in his "Book of Thoughts and Poems": "I don't like those people whose lives are at variance with their works."[14] His aim, then, was to write a piece that grew out of his own experience but which brought a poetic element to the quotidian in the spirit of his idol Jean Paul and placed it in a romantic light. Among these everyday experiences was his work on Moscheles's Alexander Variations op. 32 during his months in Heidelberg in the winter of 1829–30. It was an effortful exercise that took him to the very limits of his abilities as a pianist and left him wondering if it would not be more satisfying to write a set of piano variations of his own rather than playing those by another composer. The sequence of two notes, A–B-flat, that occurs in the Alexander Variations returns, therefore, in the Abegg Variations as something uniquely his own.

During his time in Heidelberg, Schumann also became friendly with fellow student August Lemke, who was an admirer of Meta Abegg, a pianist highly regarded in court circles. Although Schumann appears to have had little contact with this daughter of a town councilor from Mannheim, he was evidently fascinated by her family name, which he translated directly into music. As such, he seems to have been the first nineteenth-century composer to play with the letters of the musical alphabet in this way, a game almost certainly inspired by Jean Paul's *Flegeljahre*, in which a comic piano tuner draws Walt's attention to the fact that his surname, Harnisch, is "musical."

Schumann was aware, of course, that he had a famous predecessor in this field, Johann Sebastian Bach having used the letters of his name — in German nomenclature B–A–C–H = B-flat–A–C–B — in the unfinished Contrapunctus XIV of his *Art of Fugue*. Imitators soon followed. For his part, Schumann was fortunate that the name "Abegg" generated a sequence of notes that produced a highly original waltz theme rather than the awkward fugue subject generated by Bach's name. The fact that the theme also sounded attractive in retrograde — that is, the notes are played in their reverse order — merely added to the motif's appeal. It was neither a "simple" waltz nor "simple" salon music that was coaxed from this material but music with a multiple perspective.

> Schläft ein Lied in allen Dingen,
> Die da träumen fort und fort,
> Und die Welt hebt an zu singen,
> Triffst du nur das Zauberwort.

> [A song's asleep in everything / That dreams inside our heads unheard. /
> And so the world will start to sing / If you can find the magic word.]

Joseph von Eichendorff published these lines under the eloquent title "Wünschelrute" — a magic wand that will make the wisher's dreams come true. And all of us who can relate to the young Schumann's zest for life will find that this metaphor is by no means exaggerated: although he was able at this period to compose with an elegance whose effortlessness he later lost, there was always a depth to what he wrote. It was with a secret delight that he sought to invest his work with a certain mystique by dedicating it to the nonexistent figure of the "Comtesse Pauline d'Abegg." But even when Schumann's mother expressed her bemusement at his fictitious dedication, Schumann struck a fantastical, cryptic note, claiming that "the countess is an old bag of twenty-six, very intelligent and musical but haggard and ugly."[15] Only as part of such a puzzle does the work of art come into its own.

It is not only the dedication to a fictitious person that causes confusion, for the music, too, opens up a whole range of new and bewildering perspectives. As we have already observed, Schumann's thoughts were full of Moscheles's Alexander Variations during the final stages of the work's composition, and there are also echoes of Chopin's variations on Mozart's duet "Là ci darem la mano." Even though he could not compete with the much younger Clara

Wieck when it came to performing the piece, he was still determined to demonstrate what he was capable of achieving as a composer, just as he would have wanted to prove to his contemporary Chopin that he was in no way his inferior when it came to lightness of tone and musical poetry.

In short, Schumann wanted to ensure that a common- or garden-variety name should become a "magic word" that now took on a life of its own in his music; his "companions" on the piano — Moscheles and Chopin — were to accompany him in his music, too; this particular work was to be poetic *and* brilliant; and it was to hold up a mirror to rare states of mind *and* be acceptable in the salon. The best possible proof that this is the case may be found in the fact that the listener is only vaguely aware of the amount of thought that went into the work but never smells the midnight oil. Listeners do not need to decode the five-note motif A–B-flat–E–G–G, nor do they have to know the variations by Moscheles and Chopin to be impressed by Schumann's piece, which lasts between seven and eight minutes in performance. Even the way in which Schumann varies his theme is original, for whereas Moscheles and Chopin operate along entirely traditional lines, taking a complete theme as their starting point and for the most part retaining its harmonic, melodic, and metrical patterns, Schumann adopts a far freer approach in keeping with the heading of his final movement, "alla Fantasia."

Following in the footsteps of his revered Bach, Schumann can introduce his five-note theme wherever and however he likes. And when he does so as furtively as is the case in the first variation, where the theme appears in the inner parts, then the result has an undeniable "romantic" charm to it. And much the same is true of the gradual disappearance of the A–B-flat–E–G–G theme toward the end of the final movement, where Schumann sets the pianist the task of playing a chord made up of all five notes and of then successively releasing each note in turn. Deleted from later editions, this playful device may pass the listener by, but it warns the performer against treating the piece as no more than harmless fun.

Although the Abegg Variations op. 1 may be less multilayered than many of the later piano pieces, they are nonetheless entirely typical of Schumann, and if the writing does not yet contain as many of the luxuriant arabesques that are to be found in *Kreisleriana*, for example, the formal design tends to recall a succession of independent fantasies rather than a set of variations rigidly constructed around a single theme. One element that is completely new and that even the young Chopin had yet to match is the way in which the ever-present virtuosity is introduced into piano writing of mercurial and almost nervous sensitivity, with a constant crossing and interlocking of left and right hands — not just spatially but metrically and rhythmically, too. What is at stake here is not parity between the two hands, for Bach had already achieved this in his keyboard works, nor even the tendency for the two hands to drift apart such as we find in Beethoven's late piano music but the tiny shifts and little games of hunting and harrying that turn the actions of playing and listening into a high-wire act without a safety net and force the performer to keep on striving to maintain his or her balance.

This is not intended to suggest that these acrobatics dominate the work to the exclusion of all else. As is only appropriate with musical poetry of this order, the narrative elements are fully able to hold their own, encouraging a sensitive writer on Schumann like Hans Joachim Köhler to describe the second variation, with its "basso parlando," as an "undisguised love scene without witnesses" and to hail it as "both the most poetic and at the same time the most stylistically advanced section of the work."[16]

It may have been the Abegg Variations that Moscheles had in mind when he wrote in his diary in 1836:

> The finger acrobatics have a place in Thalberg's new works, which I am currently playing through; but for wit, I turn to Schumann. With him, romanticism strikes me in such a novel light and his genius is so great that I am bound to keep immersing myself in his works in order to weigh up the qualities and weaknesses of this new school in an accurate set of scales. He has also sent me his recently published sonata "Florestan and Eusebius" with the flattering remark that I alone can properly review it and would I mind doing so for his new music journal in Leipzig?[17]

In referring to "weaknesses," Moscheles may have been thinking of an aspect of Schumann's piano pieces that is more prominent in his twelve-part *Papillons* op. 2, which appeared in print in 1832, than in his op. 1: his willful tendency to indulge in terse and aphoristic formulations which, compositionally speaking, may be traced to Beethoven's late quartets, while their poetologic influence is clearly Jean Paul. There is nothing here to appeal to listeners addicted to harmony and enamored of easily accessible narrativity, still less for lovers of beautiful, fully rounded forms, hence a diary entry dated May 28, 1832, following a musical soirée in the Wieck household: "*Papillons* seems not to have put the company in the picture — they looked at each other in a strange way & were unable to grasp the rapid shifts in it. Also, Clara played it less well than she did on Saturday & must have been mentally & physically tired."[18] Schumann knew his audience's taste, but when he wrote to his mother in the context of *Papillons* and announced, "Now I'm starting to understand my existence,"[19] he may also have meant that he felt most himself in music that was more difficult to grasp. But he was also building a bridge between his music and the listener: "There are secret states of mind in which a word from the composer can lead more speedily to a better understanding and for which the listener is bound to be grateful."[20]

It was in this spirit that he replied to the critic Ludwig Rellstab, offering to help him to understand *Papillons* after Rellstab had dismissed the Abegg Variations in a fit of ironical contempt:

> If I am taking the liberty of adding a few words about the origins of *Papillons*, then this is less for the edification of the editor of *Iris* than for the poet and kindred spirit, Jean Paul, for the thread that is intended to bind them together is barely visible to the naked eye. Your Excellency will recall the final scene in *Flegeljahre* with its masquerade — Walt — Vult — masks — Wina — Vult dancing — exchange of masks — confessions — anger — revelations — hurrying away — final scene, and then the brother leaving. I have often turned over the final page, for the ending seemed to me merely a new beginning — I was barely aware of being at the piano, and in this way one butterfly after another came into being.[21]

This is the wording of Schumann's letter as preserved in the draft that he copied out in a book specially designed for that purpose, and it fully reflects the work's genesis. In his own private copy of Jean Paul's novel he singled out eleven typical sentences and marked them with corresponding references to the first eleven movements of *Papillons*. The note "Pap. 3," for example, appears next to a sentence about Walt looking around on the dance floor:

> But it was mostly a giant boot sliding around the dance floor that caught his attention, for the boot was wearing *itself*, which it continued to do until such time as a patriarchal schoolmaster looked at it so earnestly and reprovingly with his ferule that it became confused, looking at itself and examining its carter's shirt in the belief that it had committed some indiscretion.[22]

This scene is particularly appropriate in the context of the third of the *Papillons*, for the movement begins with a dance tune that, earthy in character, is initially played by both hands in unison before being accompanied in a strikingly ungainly manner and finally appearing in canon, *fortissimo*. This canon is a splendid image for the giant boot that is placed inside itself, and at the same time it throws an important light on Schumann's claim that he learned more about counterpoint from Jean Paul than from anyone else. There is something contrapuntal about a poetic and romantic style that evokes associations of mysteriously intricate, wildly luxuriant or simply bizarre phenomena that the philistine finds disconcerting.

In much the same way, the final movement of *Papillons* may be interpreted in a figurative sense. Here the elegant theme is overwhelmed by the stolid Grandfathers' Dance that traditionally ended weddings and similar festivities; and the final diminuendo includes the sound of a clock striking six in the morning — the ghosts have fled. Then, right at the end, we hear an effect familiar from the Abegg Variations as the pianist plays a seven-note chord before gradually releasing each note in turn to leave only a solitary A. Even during a much earlier period, there had been pieces of music that had died away in a meaningful manner, but most composers had adopted a more naïve approach to this device than the young Schumann: the note A that remains at the end is all that remains of the *Papillons* theme, which in the course of this final movement is quite literally deconstructed — that, at least, is how a postmodernist writer would express it, albeit without being able to express the fact that this act of deconstruction is so carefully constructed that construction and deconstruction, even if they do not cancel each other out, are at any rate held in a state of precarious balance.

We may, of course, choose to see a connection between this quest for balance in the young Schumann's works in general and his own psychological makeup, and yet this would be of little consequence if he had not succeeded in reworking this quintessential Schumannesque theme in such a way that listeners can identify with a personal characteristic that has become a musical theme. True, this ability to identify with Schumann and his music will initially apply only to those listeners who have a schizophrenic attitude to their own age and who suffer as a result. Here the idea of the freely acting ego gains momentum in the wake of the *Sturm und Drang* movement and German idealism, while this same ego simultaneously sees itself hoppled and gagged by the *juste milieu*. The fact that there is invariably a political dimension to all of this is clear from works such as the *Faschingsschwank aus Wien* (literally, "Carnival Prank from Vienna," but more usually translated as "Carnival Scenes from Vienna") op. 26.

Schumann concealed two quotations in this last-named work: the Grandfathers' Dance familiar from *Papillons* and the *Marseillaise*. And yet both quotations are almost unrecognizable, again allowing us to speak of deconstruction. And there is no doubt that this deconstruction is intentional. The

Grandfathers' Dance represents a tradition that had outlived its own usefulness, while the *Marseillaise* implies a new beginning, albeit one that the inhabitants of Vienna were unable to acknowledge openly, for in the Habsburg monarchy the *Marseillaise* was regarded as a token of rebellion — visitors were advised not even to whistle it if they wanted to avoid a run-in with the police. Schumann, who had spent much of the spring of 1839 working on his op. 26 in Vienna, was undoubtedly aware of this background — there were good reasons he was repeatedly warned by well-meaning insiders to be on his guard against censorship.

It would be wrong to place too much emphasis on the fact that he still insisted on playing with fire, even if only a little, but nor should we ignore it completely, for if nothing else it indicates the extent to which Schumann was able to hold up his "states of mind" for public inspection. Even within himself, he seems to be saying, both the outdated old and the yet-to-be-experienced new cohabited in a precarious relationship. He was not interested in mocking the one and idealizing the other but in examining an entirely realistic element in our engagement with the world: we have already quoted from his letter to Clara Wieck in which he had explained that "because everything remarkable that happens in this age moves me, I then have to express it in my music." And a work like *Faschingsschwank aus Wien* makes it clear that this must be understood in an entirely concrete way.

Schumann's *Carnaval* op. 9 was published in 1837 and amounts to a public declaration of the extent to which the theme of masks that had always fascinated him was currently the focus of his interest, not least in the headings that he gave to several of its movements: "Pierrot," "Harlequin," and "Pantaloon and Columbine." Between nos. 8 and 9, the notes E-flat–C–B–A, A-flat–C–B, and A–E-flat–C–B are notated beneath the heading "Sphinxes." These notes are not intended to be played and certainly do not constitute a piece of music in their own right but provide a code that can be deciphered as soon as they are linked to the work's subtitle: *Scènes mignonnes sur quatre notes* (Charming scenes on four notes). These are the four notes that are spelled out under "Sphinxes" and provide the music with its basic motific material, like a poetic ribbon that winds itself round the colorful sequence of scenes featuring not only commedia dell'arte characters but also two of Schumann's colleagues, "Chopin" and "Paganini," as well as figures from the world of the League of David, "Florestan," "Eusebius," "Chiarina," and so on.

This gave Schumann a chance to show off his "dual nature": an expressive Adagio characterizes the meek and dreamy Eusebius, although it is clear from the complex quintuplets and septuplets that accompany him that there is nothing phlegmatic about him, while a wild outburst headed "Passionato" and beginning with the notes A–E-flat–C–B sums up the sanguine Florestan, who is bursting with the urge to act. Elsewhere Schumann explains how we should imagine such an idealist: "What is the point of dressing a roving youth in a grandfather's fur dressing gown and sticking a long pipe in his mouth in the hope that he will become more settled and better behaved? Leave him his long hair and loose-fitting clothes! — Florestan."[23]

Performers and listeners still do not know what A–E-flat–C–B means. (In German notation these notes are A–Es–C–H.) Are we supposed to guess that there was not only a B–A–C–H (in English notation, B-flat–A–C–B) but also a S(= Es)–C–H–[UM]–A–[NN] (in English notation, E-flat–C–B–[UM]–A–[NN])? But even then we would still not know that we are also dealing with A–S(= Es)–C–H and hence with the Bohemian home of Ernestine von Fricken, to whom Schumann was briefly engaged to be married. Schumann himself belatedly offered a vague and somewhat cryptic explanation of the letters when he reviewed *Carnaval* in his *Neue Zeitschrift* in 1840, glossing them as "the name of a little town where a musical acquaintance of mine lived," and as "mere letters of the scale that also happened to be a part of my own name." It was, he concluded, "one of those games that since Bach's time are no longer new."[24]

Nothing more is needed. At the risk of leaving much that is unexplained and not even properly examined, the air of mystery surrounding the work may not be destroyed. If the "states of mind" that the piece reflect are dragged out into daylight, then the spell will be lost, and musical poetry will be turned into nothing more than banal and petty craftsmanship. Encodings of this kind serve not least to protect the artist, a goal that they achieve in what is almost a psychopathological context:

> It is a good thing that mankind feels a certain timidity in the face of the workplace of genius: we do not want to know about the causes, tools, and mysteries of the creative process, just as nature herself proclaims a certain delicacy by covering her roots in the ground. [. . .] We would discover terrible things if we could get to the bottom of the origins of every work.[25]

These sentences are taken from Schumann's review of Berlioz's *Symphonie Fantastique*. Here he was at pains to point out that in his eyes not even the most impassioned work is an autobiographical document. While making no secret of the work's private context, such an approach leads us away from that context in order to deal with "states of mind" that any member of the League of David can grasp without further ado. If the ninth of the *Davidsbündlertänze* op. 6 begins in the first printed edition not with music but with the note, "At this point Florestan finished what he was saying, and his lips twitched painfully," this reflects the state of mind of Florestan as a member of the League of David, not that of Schumann himself. Is it possible, however, to separate the two? Which of them wrote to Clara, asking her to "Play them [the *Davidsbündlertänze*] occasionally at nine in the evening!"?[26]

It is no accident that the masquerades associated with the Shrovetide carnival provided the young Schumann with themes that he found particularly appealing, leading not only to the composition of *Papillons*, *Carnaval*, and *Faschingsschwank aus Wien* but also inspiring him to write "Florestan's Shrovetide Oration" following a performance of Beethoven's Ninth Symphony, an article that we have already examined, just as we have already noted the "whole carnival" which, according to Schumann, found expression in Schubert's German Dances.

Carnaval was never intended to surpass these German Dances. Nor, indeed, could it do so. Its aim, rather, was to continue their tradition in a neoromantic vein. In the final line of his poem "To a Lamp," Schubert's contemporary Eduard Mörike had written of the "genuine artistic creation" that "what is beautiful seems blissful within itself." It was a sentiment shared by Schubert. But the emphasis is on the word "seems": not only to our own ears but presumably to Schumann's as well, Schubert's German Dances can be no more than a dim reflection of the naïve beauty of old. Whereas Schubert completes the step from the naïve to the sentimental, the young Schumann takes the process a stage further by graduating from the sentimental to the reflective; and in the extreme case, criticism transcends beauty.

Even in the case of *Papillons*, Schumann wrote, "This self-destruction of *Papillons* may have something critical about it, certainly there is nothing artistic here. A glass of champagne may be inserted between the individual movements." Otherwise, "the changes are too rapid, the colors too garish."[27] In a letter that he addressed to Clara Wieck from Vienna, Schumann indicated that this was arguably even more true of *Carnaval*:

> You often perform *Carnaval* for people who as yet know nothing else by me — wouldn't the *Phantasiestücke* be better from this point of view? In *Carnaval* each piece cancels out the next, something that not all listeners can tolerate, whereas they are bound to feel more comfortable with the *Phantasiestücke*.[28]

Certainly, the "thread" that is provided by the notes A–E-flat–C–B and that is intended to hold the piece together is rarely clear to the listener, with the result that the procession of masked figures, which is further obscured by such intermediary stages as "Réplique," "Reconnaissance," "Valse allemande," "Aveu," "Promenade," and "Pause," creates a far more bizarre impression than a succession of Schubert dances, dances which are far more likely to "seem blissful within themselves." Whereas the last-named pieces refer to nothing but the dance type that they depict, Schumann's music evokes far-reaching associations not least through the confusing variety of the titles given to the individual movements. There are also allusions of a compositional kind inasmuch as Schumann quotes musical gestures familiar from Chopin and Paganini, while also harking back explicitly to *Papillons* with the mischievous comment: "(Papillon?)." The music also refers expressly to the Grandfathers' Dance: "Thème du XVIIème siècle" (Theme from the seventeenth century). And in the final movement, which is headed "Marche des 'Davidsbündler' contre les Philistins," there is a brief echo of the main subject of the final movement of Beethoven's "heroic" Fifth Piano Concerto (bars eleven and twelve in the right hand of the piano part): here Beethoven is invoked as a confederate.

This "march" makes it clear to performers and listeners alike that Schumann's headings are no substitute for their own reflections on the work. Where else can we find a march in waltz time? And how is it possible to distinguish between the musical gestures that are intended to place an ironic gloss on the philistines' muscle-bound antics and those that represent a good-humored satire on the power fantasies of the members of the League of David? Schumann writes as if his adversaries are pulling together on the same rope, allowing him to clarify his own aesthetic position: music is not intended to paint a picture, and headings do not represent a program in the strict sense of the term. When Ludwig Rellstab wrote dismissively about the programmatic element in the *Kinderscenen* op. 15, Schumann retorted angrily, "I expect he thinks that I place a screaming child in front of me and pick out the notes to go with it. The opposite is the case. And yet I do not deny that I had a few children in mind when I wrote these pieces; on the other hand, the headings came later, of course, and are really no more than relatively subtle pointers to the execution and interpretation of these works."[29]

This brings us to the multisectional cycle in which the young Schumann was particularly concerned with obvious meaning and was able to justify this with aesthetic arguments: childhood is innocent — at least against the background of the miniature scenes which according to Schumann himself "depict reflections of an older person and for older people."[30] A tone that he himself described as "blissful"[31] and that he had occasionally struck in the *Fantasiestücke* op. 12 is perpetuated here. In a letter to Clara, Schumann wrote of the "old and eternal conditions and moods that rule us"; he would demonstrate to her "at the piano by means of some of the *Kinderscenen*" that "the intimate, the simply lovely, and the unaffected" could also be "romantic."[32]

It did not have to be the "infatuated howling"[33] that Schumann found so unbearable in the music of Carl Banck, who was one of Clara's admirers. But these "funny little things" had to be played "lightly & delicately & as joyful as our future."[34] And perhaps in German? In any event, Clara wrote to Schumann from Paris in March 1839, referring to the title "By the Hearth": "The hearth is German, [. . .] this coziness cannot be found by any French hearth."[35]

This is not simply a spur-of-the-moment remark, nor even an attempt on the part of the young pianist to define her position in the hurly-burly of an international metropolis, which she was visiting without her father to watch over her. Rather, the background is the musico-aesthetic discourse that was central to Schumann's thinking and familiar, of course, to Clara. In 1837, for example, he had written a favorable review of Stephen Heller's Impromptus op. 7 that had included the following profession of faith:

> I am heartily sick of the word "romantic," even though I have not spoken
> it ten times in my entire life; and yet — if I wanted to give our young seer a
> title — that is what I would call him, and how! Thank God our composer
> knows nothing of that vague, nihilistic sense of disorder behind which many
> people seek romanticism, nor does he know about the crude, materialist
> daubings so beloved of the French neoromantics; on the contrary, he
> generally feels things naturally and expresses himself astutely and clearly.[36]

Schumann presumably took over the terms "nihilism" and "materialism" from Jean Paul's *Preliminary School of Aesthetics* — he felt that at least in part Liszt's piano music was nihilistic, Meyerbeer's operas materialistic. In *Papillons* and *Carnaval* he may have come within an inch of the frontier with nihilism, but there is no doubt that he exorcised this danger with his *Kinderscenen*, which he regarded, rather, as "German." In doing so, Schumann gave the lie to all who would like to pin him down to a particular compositional creed that saw itself above all as a form of criticism — criticism of the shallowness and intellectual laziness of the *juste milieu* and of the hankering after empty effects of its favorite performers. Such features may help to characterize the piano works of the young Schumann, but they certainly do not dominate these pieces to the exclusion of all else.

It is tempting to believe that Schumann had a number of children in mind when he wrote his *Kinderscenen*, especially when we recall how thoughtful he could be toward children. In April 1838, in a letter that he addressed to Clara, who was at that date in Vienna, basking in her newfound glory as chamber virtuosa to the imperial and royal court, he writes:

> A little boy who lives in one of the other apartments in this building was here a moment ago — he and his friends sometimes call on me — and he said that he too could write; he then drew some big things and asked me if I could tell him what he'd written. Isn't that sweet? The boy thinks that the letters were there before the thoughts. I had to laugh.[37]

But it is equally tempting to believe Schumann when he writes that it was only after the event that he thought up titles such as "Of Foreign Lands and Peoples," "A Curious Story," "Blind Man's Bluff," "Pleading Child," "Happy Enough," "An Important Event," "Dreaming," "At the Fireside," "Knight of the Hobbyhorse," and so on. More generally, he had the following to say on this subject:

> Now and again people have criticized these headings for works of music and claimed that good music does not need such pointers. Of course, it doesn't: but nor does it lose any of its value as a result, and it is the safest way that the composer has of pre-empting any obvious misconception of the work's character. If poets try to encapsulate the meaning of a whole poem in a heading, why should musicians not do the same?[38]

Schumann's titles tell us what he himself had in mind when he was playing or listening to the piece in question and in that way they provide us with an example of imaginative listening. This idea is particularly important in the case of the *Kinderscenen*, because without the narrative concept stated in the title we would undoubtedly regard these pieces as a less coherent collection and derive less enjoyment from them. It makes no difference whether the individual headings reflect the contents of the movements as precisely as they do in numbers such as "Blind Man's Bluff" and "Child before Falling Asleep" or whether they offer only a vague indication as in the case of "Dreaming" and "Of Foreign Lands and Peoples," the opening movement whose title is justified only to the extent that it deals with matters of interest. The exact nature of these matters of interest remains open.

The fact that "Dreaming" was to become arguably Schumann's most popular piece is due not only to its title, of course, even though that heading is the first point of contact between the composer on the one hand and performers and listeners on the other. "What is it called?" a person asks on his first encounter with a child. "It's called 'Dreaming,'" Schumann replies. "Hello, 'Dreaming,'" players and listeners respond.

In general, there are good reasons Mendelssohn decided not to include explanatory headings with his *Songs Without Words* for these works bear no trace of Schumann's unbridled desire to lend each of his pieces a unique and unrepeatable set of characteristics, even at the risk of leaving them difficult to categorize. For the most part, the *Songs Without Words* can be ascribed to a particular kind of "affect" or emotion: "wild," "lively," "elegiac," "chorale-like," and so on. To duplicate these emotions by means of titles would risk reducing these pieces to the level of salon music. Although the buyer may suspect what to expect from them, he or she would feel no real desire to explore them any further. The opposite is the case with the *Kinderscenen*, in which the headings stir childhood memories and make us curious to see how these memories may be reflected in "art music." And inasmuch as these miniatures may last only a matter of a few seconds and can scarcely be reduced to traditional models, listeners may be able to make good use of such hints.

This also applies to "Dreaming," which is less conventional than it seems at first sight. Admittedly, it is the most self-contained and compact of the pieces that make up the *Kinderscenen* and to that extent is comparable to one of Mendelssohn's *Songs Without Words*, with the result that it does not necessarily require an explanatory heading. And yet, however clear its form may appear to be, its inner life is so rampantly luxuriant that nonspecialist listeners will be able to respond to it chiefly on an emotional level — at least to the extent that they are willing to engage with the "rare state of mind" implied by the title.

The specialist reader may be reminded of a diary entry in which the young Schumann discusses "dreams" and "fantasy" at length: "Notes in themselves cannot really paint what the emotions have not already painted."[39] And we may imagine Schumann improvising and dreaming at the piano, just as he saw himself when beginning a review of Mendelssohn's *Songs Without Words*: "Who has not sat at an upright piano in the fading light (a grand piano often seems to strike too courtly a note) and unwittingly sung a quiet tune while improvising?"[40]

But what do our feelings "paint" in the case of "Dreaming"? And what does the music say about this particular waking dream? At stake here is the contradiction between our experience of natural beauty and the futile longing of the romantic artist who yearns to merge with that beauty as a single entity. Natural beauty is found in any song that is written in a well-balanced ternary form, with a melody that strives gently upward like the one at the start of "Dreaming." Hans Pfitzner saw only this natural beauty when he observed: "What a miracle of inspiration! What can one say about it that would increase the understanding of a person who is not completely overcome by this melody, which constitutes the whole piece and in which inspiration and form practically coincide? Nothing." And he goes on: "The person who cannot appreciate this will not be convinced by rational arguments, and there is nothing that can be said to counter their attacks except to play the tune and say: 'How beautiful!' What it expresses is as profound and clear, as mystical and as self-evident as the truth."

Writing in 1920, Pfitzner was defending artistic inspiration against the intellectualism of the Second Viennese School that he sought to pillory, but in doing so he overshot his target, not least when claiming: "Great works of art spring from the unconscious, not from the conscious."[41] What matters here is that in composing "Dreaming," Schumann was deliberately flying in the face of the ideal of natural beauty; and even though it may initially have been "feeling" that "painted" this scene, as he himself expressed it, it is "understanding" that is subsequently needed here. Only by means of careful compositional calculation was Schumann able to achieve the metrical shifts that allow him to transform a phrase of four bars in 4/4 time—harmless enough on paper—into a sequence of bars in 5/4, 3/4, 2/4, 2/4, and 4/4 time. Even the initially failed attempts of the "Dream" melody to climax in the central section of the piece owe their cunctative impact to a compositional approach of considerable subtlety.

It is this that the German writer on music Peter Gülke had in mind when he wrote, "Not least of the miracles of this piece is the fact that it brings together within the narrowest possible confines symmetries, repetitions, and linear procedures and yet can still appear to be dreamily aimless and purposeless."[42] Nothing like it is found in Mendelssohn's *Songs Without Words*, where there is no sense of contradiction between natural flow and constant congestion. I recall some of my own dreams in which I have tried in vain to resolve such contradictions, and although Schumann does not succeed in doing so, he does manage to integrate them in his music, initially through improvising and experimenting at the piano, but then in purposeful composition that does not shy away from several false starts before a successful and definitive version is found.

At first sight, the series of four etchings *Times of Day* by the romantic painter Philipp Otto Runge create a wholly agreeable impression and from that point of view are comparable to the surface aspect of "Dreaming," but Goethe's commentary is worth quoting here, for these images "are a veritable labyrinth of obscure relationships, causing the observer to feel dizzy from the almost unfathomable nature of their meaning." Exactly the same is true of Schumann's "Dreaming"; we shall do justice to its title only by interpreting it in the context of the heading "Dream's Confusions" from the *Fantasiestücke* op. 12.[43]

This brings us back once again to the more general problem of the works' headings. If performers and listeners take the title "Dreaming" seriously rather than treating it as a popular, romantic label, they will find it easier to fathom the piece's deep structure, which tells us something about the *heaviness* of the dream. That this is no hair-splitting may be clear from a comment by the linguistic philosopher Ludwig Wittgenstein: the feeling that "It was a long, long time ago" is not typical of *all* instances of the concept of self-recollection, yet this feeling undoubtedly exists, and its most consummate expression, in Wittgenstein's view, may be found in a piece from Schumann's *Davidsbündlertänze*.[44] Would Wittgenstein—an amateur music lover—have been able to tell this if he had encountered the piece in question without its heading, "As From a Distance"?

Whereas this question must remain unanswered, there is no doubt about another, related phenomenon: Wittgenstein's association of ideas certainly makes sense, but he could have made the connection only because the piece is short, in which respect it resembles the other miniatures from Schumann's early cycles. Or, to put it another way, no composer would be able to sustain the feeling of "It was a long, long time ago" over an entire sonata movement or a whole symphonic movement without turning his initial idea into a wearisome program or simply remaining misunderstood. Only a fleeting idea can trigger the shock that Umberto Eco has defined as a decisive hallmark of the creative metaphor. It is, he says in this context, drawing on a language of peculiar vividness, a "perception catastrophe" triggered by the use of the metaphor.[45]

It was in this spirit that Schumann broke a lance for "shorter" works in a review that he published in 1835 under the title "Shorter and Rhapsodic Works for the Pianoforte," claiming that such music creates an impression "through the lightning flash of the mind, which must develop, control itself, and ignite all within the space of a moment." Only rarely, he went on, did composers succeed in doing this: "All beauty is difficult, brevity the most difficult of all."[46]

Of course, the young Schumann was concerned not just with brevity but also with aphorisms, fragmentation, and rapid change, concerns he had already demonstrated in *Papillons* and *Carnaval*. But in the case of *Papillons*, the meters and periodic structures of dance forms had for the most part provided the listener with semantic clues, while a similar function had additionally been served in *Carnaval* by the programmatic titles. He adopted an even more radical approach in the Six Intermezzos op. 4: in spite of their title, these intermezzos were not inserted between other movements but are treated as compositions in which dependence achieves a state of independence — the first time in the history of music that this had been done.

Schumann originally intended to call these works "Pièces phantastiques." In an essay titled "Loving Schumann," Roland Barthes writes in a positively rhapsodic vein about their definitive title and the idea that is associated with it. He believes that Schumann's music — not least as a result of the titles that he gave to his works — invariably points to reality:

> For Schumann the world is not unreal, reality is not null and void. [...] But this reality is threatened with disarticulation, dissociation, with movements not violent (nothing harsh) but brief and, one might say, ceaselessly "mutant": nothing lasts long, each movement interrupts the next: this is the realm of the *intermezzo*, a rather dizzying notion when it extends to all of music, and when the matrix is experienced only as an exhausting (if graceful) sequence of interstices.

In this context Barthes recalls the French writer on the aesthetics of music, Marcel Beaufils, who believed that the literary motif of the carnival was basic to Schumann's early piano works: "The Carnival is truly the theater of this decentering of the subject (a very modern temptation) which Schumann expresses in his fashion by the carousel of his brief forms."[47]

Another Schumann expert, Hans Joachim Köhler, has described the Intermezzos as an "auto-psychologically oriented work."[48] His phraseology may be more cautious, but it amounts to much the same thing, for the "rare states of mind" reflected in Schumann's music imply the experience of "decentering." Anyone playing or listening to the Intermezzos is not only fascinated by the subtle riches of the music and by what, at the time, was the unique boldness of their language, they will also risk being shocked at the disjointed way in which the ideas are strung together.

The situation is made additionally difficult by the speed at which most of these pieces are to be played and by the obsession with motific and thematic detail. Life, according to a comment that applies not only to the op. 4 Intermezzos, continues to evolve in intermezzos, which for their part are in a constant state of flux: the artist may try to capture every moment but he can never reach the famous heart of the matter or the core of his own being, for no such thing exists. In Schumann's eyes, such a quest would be more profitably directed at Bach and Beethoven.

The deconstructionist elements in Barthes's view of Schumann are regarded by experts and music lovers alike as evidence of arrogant philosophizing. And yet it makes sense to treat Schumann as a composer who in spite of his profound desire for beauty and coherence in art was never satisfied with the mere semblance of meaning. It is also worth noting in this context that of his early piano works Schumann later gave his unqualified approval only to the Intermezzos op. 4 and the Toccata op. 7.

Notwithstanding all the hard work that went into it, the Toccata is indeed a masterpiece of gestural concision within the narrowest confines. In Schumann's day, the term "toccata" was used for a technically demanding concert study, but in his hands it acquired a sense of the fantastical and restless while retaining its element of extreme technical difficulty. Even so, the motoric unrest of the writing repeatedly reveals a charmingly songlike motif that bears a marked affinity not only to the motif associated with love's bliss in the duet between Lohengrin and Elsa in act 3 of Wagner's opera but also to Clara Schumann's later song, "Er ist gekommen in Sturm und Regen," more especially at the words "Wie konnt' ich ahnen." In the second section it is briefly supplanted by a two-bar *krakowiak* motif already heard in the lively opening bars but which for a time appears to go off the rails or at least to mutate into a *galop* or quick polka. The repeated notes in this passage have an almost uninhibited physicality to them, a feature rarely found in Schumann's music. Toward the end of the piece, everything is brought back to an even keel, of course, and the piece's toccata character is preserved.

We may regard the Toccata op. 7 as a well-spiced piano study not worth making a fuss about, but we may also interpret it as a detailed record of Schumann's "rare states of mind" at the piano: practicing double octaves like a man possessed, he could also see before his mind's eye the figure of Clara who, ideally, was practicing the piano elsewhere in Wieck's house at exactly the same time. Then more earthy elements clamor for attention: the memory of wild student pub crawls and dancing. There are even contemporary references; the *krakowiak* can be seen as a symbol of the Polish nation whose failed struggle to achieve independence exercised Europeans at the very time that the Toccata was being written. It also inspired the young Wagner to write his Polonaises in the winter of 1831–32.[49]

At some point or other almost every composer feels the urge to tackle large-scale forms: even the miniaturist Anton Webern was mildly shocked to discover when rehearsing a new work that it had turned out shorter than he had imagined when writing it. Schumann, too, was still in his mid-twenties when he admitted his high opinion of the sonata as a genre, reckoning it to be a "higher form of art" and associating hard work and "lofty aspirations" with it.[50] On the other hand, he had absolutely no wish to be thought of as a classical composer, which is why he staked everything on originality in his First Piano Sonata in F-sharp Minor op. 11, a piece first performed in 1835 and notable above all for its daring harmonies: which other contemporary work, for example, modulates with such exceptional rapidity?

And yet both the tonal excesses and the interpolated passages of recitative illustrate a tendency on Schumann's part to explore the world of the piano fantasy, a genre to which he was to turn explicitly only some years later in his op. 17 Fantasy in C Major, a three-movement work full of allusions of a private and professional kind. In a letter to Clara, Schumann described its opening movement as "arguably the most passionate thing I've ever written: a profound lament for you."[51] Apart from this pointer to the "unhappy summer of 1836,"[52] the work also contains a contemporary artistic point of reference in that Schumann planned to donate the fee for it to a Beethoven Monument that Liszt was planning. Both motifs — Schumann's love of Clara and his love of Beethoven — are encapsulated in four lines by Friedrich Schlegel that he prefaced to the work in the form of a motto:

> Durch alle Töne tönet
> Im bunten Erdentraum
> Ein leiser Ton gezogen
> Für den der heimlich lauschet.

> [Through every sound there sounds / In earth's most motley dream-world / A sound so soft and drawn / For him who lists in secret.]

Of course, we need to listen carefully and also know our Beethoven to be able to identify this "soft sound" that permeates the C Major Fantasy, for it is a phrase from the beginning of "Nimm sie hin denn, diese Lieder" (Take these songs then) from Beethoven's song cycle *An die ferne Geliebte* op. 98.[53] The element of "secrecy" consists in the fact that Beethoven's theme is initially so well concealed that we can only suspect its identify. In its original form, the melody becomes audible only in the Adagio at the end of the movement. In other words, Schumann "unveiled" Beethoven musically before the actual Beethoven Monument was unveiled in Bonn in 1845. But the idea behind the work extends beyond Schumann's reason for writing it. Although the movement is nominally in C major, it tends for the most part to avoid this key rather than seeking it out, and it is not until the end that it achieves the unambiguity of the sort of C major that allows us to regard Beethoven as a figure of light. In other words, Beethoven's music helped Schumann to survive the dark times in the world of contemporary culture, while Clara functions as an anchor in the face of existential problems.[54]

The Fantasy op. 17 was composed immediately *before* Schumann wrote his *Kreisleriana: Fantasien für Piano-Forte* op. 16, in which he created a large-scale work of undeniable greatness, *not* by appealing to an icon in the history of music but by discovering that greatness within himself and by drawing on a genuinely romantic spirit that was uniquely his own.

"No, What I Hear Are Blows"

In Schumann's *Kreisleriana* (Opus 16; 1838), I actually hear no note, no theme, no contour, no grammar, no meaning, nothing which would permit me to reconstruct an intelligible structure of the work. No, what I hear are blows: I hear what beats in the body, what beats the body, or better: I hear this body that beats.[1]

It is with these words that Roland Barthes begins his essay "Rasch," echoing others that E. T. A. Hoffmann had once placed in the mouth of his Kapell-meister Johannes Kreisler:

> There often flares up inside me an insane and dissolute longing for something that I am seeking outside myself by means of restless activity because, hidden away inside me, there is a dark secret, a confused and mysterious dream about a Paradise of supreme contentment that even my dream cannot name but only suspect.[2]

Of course, Barthes's aim was not to imply that Schumann's *Kreisleriana* has a program derived from E. T. A. Hoffmann. Rather, he "reads" the work in an intensely "corporeal" way and in doing so eschews all other attempts to fathom its meaning. Certainly, Schumann's op. 16 stands apart from his other early piano works in that — apart from its title — it contains no obvious allu-sions to the figure of the fantastically insane Kapellmeister to whom Hoff-mann had first raised a memorial in his collection of essays *Kreisleriana* and, later, in the aforementioned *Tomcat Murr*.

Unlike *Papillons*, *Carnaval*, and the *Davidsbündlertänze*, *Kreisleriana* could get by without its title or at least survive as a "Fantasy," "Humoresque," or "Arabesque" — in every case in a typically Schumannesque sense. What is so magnificent about this thirty-minute work, which is made up of eight pieces, is that although it is concerned with the "rare states of mind" to which Schumann returned again and again, that concern is remote from any obvious, tangible program.

In spite of this, there is no doubt that each of the pieces that make up *Kreisleriana* (a Latin plural, implying that each individual number is a *Kreislerianum*) represents an attempt on Schumann's part to write a musical sequel to Hoffmann's essays. And this is significant in more ways than one. None of his predecessors or contemporaries had written a piece of music that took over the title of a literary work unless it was a mere setting of its text. Schumann, however, had no intention of providing a musical setting of Hoffmann's collection of essays but aimed, rather, to compose a work in their spirit and if possible outdo his model. Hoffmann chose the title *Kreisleriana* in order to be able to republish a series of essays, most of which had previously appeared in the *Allgemeine musikalische Zeitung*. They were reissued in a self-contained form in his *Fantasiestücke in Callots Manier* (Fantasy pieces in the manner of Callot). Not all of them are concerned with the figure of Kreisler, and they are all so varied in terms of their density, length, and basic character that they could never have served as the point of departure for a set of piano pieces that writers have often compared with Bach's Goldberg Variations and Beethoven's Diabelli Variations.

Fortunately, Schumann was precisely what he always demanded his followers should be: a productively "re-creative" artist. As a result, he was able to take the fragmentary aspects of the character offered to him by Hoffmann and generate a Kapellmeister Kreisler who is very much his own brother: a profoundly romantic artist who seeks the essential and the absolute amid common, everyday concerns, finding consolation for the insipidity of the current musical scene by turning to Bach, rhapsodizing about the "high value of music" in his "musical and poetic club," and suffering untold agonies on account of his inability to give adequate expression to his musical fantasies. In art as in life Kreisler repeatedly came up against his own limitations until he finally went mad. But what is that when compared to the daily madness of society?

Schumann does not describe this in his *Kreisleriana* in the same way as he depicts the struggle between the members of the League of David and the philistines in *Carnaval*. But he writes with Kreisler looking over his shoulder, and it is Kreisler who gives him the courage to indulge a fantastical imagination unsupported by any program and to create a cycle that explores what Franz von Schober had called "life's untamed circle" with a tremendous wealth of ideas but without the sort of safety harness that Bach and Beethoven had had at their disposal in the form of an initial theme on which their respective sets of variations are based. It is now Kreisler/Schumann who provides the theme.

But back to Barthes. When he writes about *Kreisleriana* that he hears only "what beats in the body, what beats the body, or better: I hear this body that beats," his words are deliberately provocative and intentionally unsupported by any explanation. One of Barthes's distinguished colleagues in Paris, the linguistician Julia Kristeva, sought to give this phenomenon names that at first sight do not go together: chora and — borrowing an expression from the cultural semiologist Mikhail Mikhailovich Bakhtin — carnival.[3] "Chora" is a vague term dating back to Plato and applied to a phenomenon that more recent writers have tried to approach from a psychoanalytic standpoint. For Kristeva, it is the "semiotic bed" of early childhood expressions, especially those dating from the prelinguistic period. These expressions are dictated by physical needs and are only apparently uncoordinated and meaningless. In fact they have their own rhythms, which are determined by the situation of the moment and are innocent of any *a priori* reasoning. Kristeva includes all of this under the heading of the "genotext," which she defines as "the sum of unconscious, subjective, and social relations in gestures of confrontation and appropriation, destruction and construction — productive violence."[4]

Processes that, in the case of the "chora," occur unconsciously in the interaction between mother and child are raised to the level of a conscious principle by the carnival and the culture of laughter, both of which undermine the social order, locating themselves outside the realm of our prevailing morality, and in many respects operating according to the laws of dreams. Art historian Florens Christian Rang, who is remembered chiefly for his powerfully expressionist exchange of views with Walter Benjamin, once declared in this context that "the modern freedom of the life of the mind and of the psyche has leapt into this age of ours in the guise of a Shrovetide caper."[5]

Composers and musicologists have singled out a number of striking aspects of *Kreisleriana* and spoken of them with admiration. All can be related to current discourse about chora and the carnivalesque. Of particular interest here are the elements of the improvisatory, aphoristic, volatile, fragmentary,

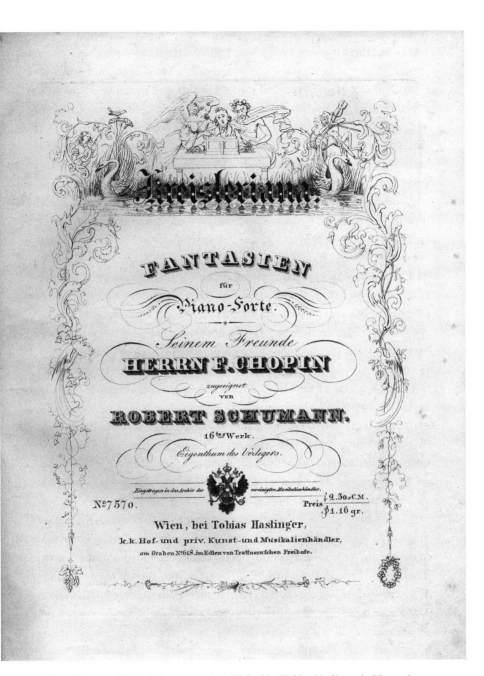

The title page of *Kreisleriana*, op. 16, published by Tobias Haslinger in Vienna in 1838. (Photograph courtesy of the Robert Schumann Museum, Zwickau.)

incomplete, ambiguous, wildly rampant, confusing, veiled, and sensorily il-
lusory . . . the list could easily be extended. All of these elements may be
identified by means of analysis as melodically, metrically, harmonically, and
formally specific to this work.[6] If I were writing for an audience of specialists,
I would be happy to provide any number of relevant examples, beginning
with the very first bars, where the movements of the right and left hands are
so displaced that not only does the very stability of the metrical structure
seem to be threatened, but harsh dissonances are produced. In general, the
bass appears to limp behind the rest by as much as an eighth note, but if one
tries to bring it into line, then the music becomes meaningless in a different
way. In other words, we cannot even rely on the assumption that the shift
bears any relation to a previous sense of order that would enable us to make
sense of it.[7]

This brings us on to a sore point of purely formal analysis, and it is at these
attempts to rationalize the situation that Barthes quite rightly expressed his
misgivings. It is impossible to do justice to the distinctive features of this — or
any other — music by describing them against the background of a deviation
from the norm, for far too often such an approach leads to statements of what
the work is *not* about. But this is not true of chora and the carnivalesque as
interpretive tools, for these both involve experiences that are not judged by
any secondary "normality" but which obey primary structures. Of course,
even these tools have their limits, for Schumann's approach to composition
was not naïvely anarchic. He made entirely conscious use of the tension between the rational and calculable on the one hand and a living, sideways attack
on the other, even if the instinctual drives of the unconscious may lie behind
such a conscious approach.

This highlights a fundamental difference between Hoffmann's Kreisler and
Schumann's. In his essays, short stories, and novels Hoffmann was unable
to resolve the tension between the ideal of a heavenly art and the "infinite
incoherence" of human activity discussed by Jean Paul in his *Preliminary
School of Aesthetics*.[8] Indeed, it is possible that it was never his wish to do so.
As a result, he vacillates in *Tomcat Murr* between the world of the pedantic
pussycat and that of the chaotic Kreisler: the stylistic device of alienation is
intentional, and it is left to the reader to integrate these disparate elements on
a higher level.

Not so for Schumann the musician: however disjointed and fractured his
Kreisleriana may seem, the work, when seen as a whole, is fully integrated,

even if the superficial listener may not appreciate this fact, which tends to be played down by the proponents of deconstruction. Of course, there are "blows" and the semantic openness that Barthes regards as the work's essential attributes. But Schumann himself stressed that it nonetheless has a higher sense: "There is a really wild love in some of these movements, as well as your life and mine and many of your glances," he told Clara in a letter of August 3, 1838.[9] Four months earlier he had already written that "my music now strikes me as so strangely intricate, in spite of all its simplicity, it seems so eloquent and heartfelt, and that's how it affects everyone when I play it for them."[10]

This does not sound like disintegration, and there is no doubt that there are many elements of cohesion in *Kreisleriana*, elements that specialists have not overlooked, even if they may have been guilty of underestimating their importance. For example: six of the eight pieces are in ternary form, A–B–A, although the straightforwardness of this form may be more apparent from the notes on the printed page than from any impression that a listener may form at an initial hearing. A seventh piece is essentially cast in rondo form. Above all, however, Schumann's comment on the work's "intricacy" proves to be accurate, an intricacy evidenced not only by the complexity of the part-writing, which has few counterparts at this period, but also by the motific links between the individual pieces, older material often being taken up again within a new context.

There is also a wealth of allusions that invest the work with a special significance. A recurrent scalar motif recalls the "Andantino de Clara Wieck" on which the set of variations in the Piano Sonata op. 14 is based:

Sehr innig und nicht zu rasch.

The recurrent scalar motif first heard at the start of the second *Kreisleriana*, op. 16 ("Very inward and not too fast") and reminiscent of the "Andantino de Clara Wieck," on which the second movement of the Piano Sonata op. 14 is based.

One wonders if Schumann was referring to this when he wrote, "You and an idea of you [play] the main part."[11] In the fifth piece, he explicitly quotes from his own Intermezzo op. 4, no. 1. And finally we have "old Bach." The contrapuntal writing in the second piece and also in the central section of the seventh is so clearly inspired by *The Well-Tempered Clavier* that Schumann's friend Julius Becker could refer specifically to the "link between modern music for the pianoforte and Bach's classicism" in his book *Der Neuromantiker*.

Even more revealing is the comparison that Becker draws between Hoffmann's Kreisler and Schumann's: whereas the former "veers forever between the two extremes, the ideal and the real, and whereas the ideal draws him upward, while the real drags him downward, life becomes a torment for him. Schumann, by contrast, is not ruled by these two elements, for it is he who rules over them. He is able to unite them in a tremendous show of strength."[12]

And it is undoubtedly true that Schumann does not introduce his quotations in a flag-waving way, nor does he use irony to refract the work's many facets. Still less does he construct a series of contrasts. The Clara theme — if we may call it that — emerges from the contrapuntal interiority of the second piece in a way that may be "intricate" but which also suggests an example of "simple" nature. And at the very end of the movement a second "Clara" motif steals in and demands to be heard. It is the same motif as the one that occurs in the opening movement of the Piano Fantasy op. 17: "Take these songs then."

With that, Schumann's identification with Hoffmann's Kreisler is over. As the composer and creator of *Kreisleriana*, he is not as inwardly torn as the Kapellmeister who has given the work its name. Rather, he composes in manifold guises. The gestural language is both strict and formless; the delicate poetry of musical sounds appears alongside expressions of wild frenzy; the music affects us physically while also being thoroughly spiritualized. Sometimes it creates the impression of composure and meditation, while at other times it seems distracted. For a moment we feel that everything is bright and clear, only for our sense of time to vanish as we feel ourselves sinking into the morass. The notes are carefully written out right down to the very last nuance, and yet there are passages whose rapid tempo means that we can hear them only as an oscillating layer of sound. Although Schumann does not shut himself off entirely from the idea of objectivity, he does operate with a polyvalent structure whose meaning listeners must establish for themselves.

Discussing the music of the second third of the nineteenth century, Hugo

Riemann — one of the forefathers of modern musicology — observed a movement away from "architectural" forms to their "psychological" equivalent.[13] From this point of view, Schumann was able to learn a thing or two from individual piano sonatas by Beethoven and Schubert, notably Beethoven's *Tempest* Sonata op. 31, no. 2. At the same time, however, he went substantially further. Although the second of the *Kreisleriana* pieces may be described as a rondo from an "architectural" point of view, it basically describes an emotional, psychological process that can be expressed in the image of a rondo. The "Clara" theme that we mentioned a moment ago (see music example on page 85) is like a star that shines with a welcoming light before being briefly obscured, only to reappear again from behind the clouds. Sometimes it is present only as a yearning anticipation. According to Adorno, it was in the second of the *Kreisleriana* pieces that Schumann "first discovered [. . .] the gesture in which music recalls something long forgotten rather than simply unfolding it directly."[14] The result reveals psychological credibility rather than formal rigor. And yet, like all tonal music, *Kreisleriana* is lit by the sun of traditional harmony, a sun in whose light even what is most remote appears to be connected and to belong together. The principle of *concordia discors* — concord within discord — is integral to Schumann's music and cannot be ignored, a circumstance that should give food for thought to those who define romantic aesthetics and the romantics' view of the world only from the standpoint of philosophy and poetry.

In his writings on the theory of discourse, Jürgen Link has observed that literary romanticism "consciously" produced "incoherencies and contradictions," which it did, in part, as an "option in support of civil society and against the bureaucratic central state."[15] But Schumann's music deserves to have a say here, for what triumphs in this music is not Hoffmannesque or Jean-Pauline incoherence but an admittedly idiosyncratic variety of the "real idealism" that we shall examine in greater detail in chapter 11 and that was to be explicitly introduced into musico-aesthetic discourse a decade after *Kreisleriana*.[16] Although literary scholars refer constantly to music as the principal medium of romantic art, they have devoted too little time and attention to looking for works of music that can be compared with *Tomcat Murr* and *Flegeljahre* as concrete, equally valid products of art. In his *Kreisleriana*, however, Schumann created a work that could contribute materially to discourse on the criteria appropriate to romantic art if only we were prepared to examine it in the sense sketched out above.

A generation before Schumann, Friedrich Schlegel demanded that the romantics should produce a "progressive universal poetry" that would not be limited to literature but would also include "the sigh, and the kiss that the child, writing poetry, breathes into its artless singing."[17] This demand finds a belated but convincing echo in Schumann's *Kreisleriana* that is no less compelling than many of the literary works of the time. By refusing to take over the subject matter of Hoffmann's *Kreisleriana* and by eschewing every other kind of imitation, Schumann succeeds in continuing the tradition in the form of "absolute" music, as understood by the romantics, and in so doing he exemplifies the sort of romantic critique of art whose creative and productive element was singled out for particular attention by Walter Benjamin.[18]

More than any other work from this period, *Kreisleriana* is clearly located at a point of intersection. On the one hand, Schumann was still committed to the cosmological thinking according to which music is the expression and reflection of the sense of order immanent in the whole of nature, and to that extent he has no time for the "nihilistic disorder behind which many people seek romanticism." At the same time, however, he is a true contemporary, ever watchful and ever capable of absorbing into his music the contradictions in his own life and in the lives of others. As such, he may be said to have stolen a march on E. T. A. Hoffmann, who explored these contradictions in his literary works but who remained extremely tame as a composer.

And so both approaches may be justified. On the one hand, we may hear *Kreisleriana* as uncontested musical poetry, which is how Schumann advised his fiancée to listen to it, while on the other we may regard it as a bold precursor of modern art beyond any idealistic horizon. Writing under the heading "The Middle Ages of James Joyce," Umberto Eco examines our "experience of a new and changing image of the world, one which throws imagination and intelligence, sense and reason, fancy and logic into discord."[19] Eco, in fact, was not writing about *Kreisleriana* but Joyce's *Finnegans Wake*. And yet everything must start somewhere. And as far as music is concerned, Schumann's bold opus is by no means a bad place to begin. Nor am I alone in holding this view, which is shared by the contemporary philosopher and music lover Slavoj Žižek: "It is my assertion that the formal structure of Schumann's music reflects the paradox of modern subjectivity: it provides a theatrical staging of the barrier or hurdle — the impossibility of 'becoming oneself' and of realizing one's own identity."[20]

The present intermezzo should not be allowed to end with such a negative definition but with some lines from Jean Genet's prose-poem *The Tightrope Walker*. If we regard the rope as the music with which the composer feels at one with the dance, then it is by no means absolutely necessary for "him himself" to dance:

> If your love, your skill, and your cunning are great enough to discover the secret possibilities of the wire, if the precision of your gestures is perfect, it will rush to meet your foot (clad in leather): it will not be you that dances but the wire.[21]

Schumann in 1839. This distinctly uninspired oil painting is by an unknown artist who signed himself simply as "Fr. Klima." It is believed to depict Schumann and is now in the Schumann Museum in Endenich. The sitter is seen wearing a ring in his left ear — at that time a relatively common token of middle-class respectability rather than one of student revolt. One wonders if it represented an attempt on Schumann's part to impress his prospective father-in-law, Friedrich Wieck, who was stubbornly opposed to the relationship between his daughter and her admirer.
(Photograph courtesy of the Municipal Museum, Bonn.)

Probationary Years in Leipzig (1835–40)

What will the new year bring? I often feel a sense of apprehension.
To remain abreast of the age and to be equal to all its manifestations,
to help the world to progress, to fight, and to remain independent —
regardless of all inner and more private turmoil, I often feel quite dizzy.

Schumann to his sister-in-law Therese Schumann, New Year's Eve 1836[1]

The present chapter is concerned in the main with Schumann's relations with Clara Wieck — the phrase "probationary years" refers
above all to the time when he was engaged to be married to a woman
whom we have already met as his "muse." First, however, we need to say
something about her predecessor, Ernestine von Fricken, who first appeared
in Leipzig in the spring of 1834. "My friend Ernestine von Fricken arrived
on April 21 in order to study the piano with my father," Clara noted in her
diary.[2] Three years older than Clara, Ernestine was the adopted daughter of a
landowner from Asch in Bohemia. She boarded with the Wiecks, and when
Wieck sent his daughter to Dresden for a longer period of study, Ernestine
and Schumann found themselves drawn into each other's company. In the
end, they became secretly engaged.

The fourteen-year-old Clara, who had just been confirmed, observed
these developments both from close quarters and from afar and felt a growing
sense of jealousy. Wieck, we know, would have welcomed any union between
Robert and Ernestine, as his daughter would then be out of danger. He wrote
to Baron von Fricken, describing Schumann as "somewhat whimsical and
obstinate, but a generous, splendid, effusive, highly gifted, and intellectually
profoundly well educated individual — in short, a musician and a writer of

genius."[3] Ernestine returned to her native Asch in September 1834 without having learned very much from Wieck, prompting Clara to dip her pen in venom:

> She was like a plant which as long as it is watered and remains where it is can be maintained with a great deal of effort and trouble, but as soon as it is moved, it withers and gradually dies as it no longer has the accustomed care and rest. The sun shone down too strongly on it — the sun in this case being Herr Schumann.[4]

In his biography of Clara Schumann, Berthold Litzmann claimed that it was her father who entered these sentences in her diary, but it is clear from the original, now in the Robert Schumann Museum in Zwickau, that they are in Clara's own handwriting. Even so, Litzmann is not entirely wrong, for Wieck initially kept the diary for his daughter and for a long time afterward continued to supervise all that she wrote in it, so that it is entirely possible that he more or less dictated this particular entry.

Four years later, Schumann himself explained the situation to Clara, who by now had replaced Ernestine as his fiancée:

> At that time I was forever running to my doctor in a terrible state of agitation and telling him everything — I kept fainting, I was so afraid that I simply did not know which way to turn, nay, I could not even vouch for the fact that I would not take my own life, so utterly helpless was the state in which I found myself. Don't be alarmed, my angel from Heaven, but simply listen to what I have to say. The doctor was kind enough to console me & finally said with a smile: "Medicine won't help; find a woman, she'll cure you at once." Things became easier for me; I thought it was working; you were not really very worried about me & were yourself at a crossroads, no longer a child but not yet a young woman. And then Ernestine came along — a young woman as good as any that the world has ever produced — it's her, I thought: she'll save you. I wanted to cling to a feminine being with every ounce of my strength.[5]

But Schumann's matrimonial interest in Ernestine seems to have been very short-lived. His diary for 1835 contains a breathless entry: "Drifting away from Ernestine in the summer & autumn — ah! — With Klara [sic] every day — received a watch ribbon from her on June 8." A second note, "Broken off with Ernestine,"[6] must date from the end of 1835. Both entries were belatedly added in 1838, but they are presumably an accurate reflection of the earlier situation. The news that Ernestine was adopted and therefore not entitled to inherit may have contributed to the break-up, but this is all idle speculation as Ernestine will have had no real chance from the outset: even at that early date the bonds between Clara Wieck and Schumann — or perhaps we should say "between Chiara and Florestan/Eusebius" — were already too close, for what is decisive about this relationship is the element of a friendship between two artists, a friendship that sustained both parties in a way that was almost literally necessary for their survival. "I loved you only as a friend — then as an artist," we read in the letter from which we have just quoted.[7] It may be added that Ernestine married in 1838 but that within a year she was already a widow. She was only twenty-eight when she herself died of typhus in 1844.

And Clara? Schumann was without doubt a physically attractive young man and, his youth notwithstanding, already successful. At the same time, she knew his weaknesses and problems at firsthand, and some of the things that he admitted to her about the threat to his inner life could certainly have struck her as a warning. Initially, however, she enthused about Schumann as an artist, an enthusiasm that makes sense only if we see her not as an adolescent fantastically gifted as a pianist but as an artist sufficiently respected by Schumann to be accepted as a member of his League of David. Here was the spiritual home that she felt that her father had failed to provide.

For his part Friedrich Wieck was a musically cultured man whom Schumann, in his initial euphoria, was likewise willing to enroll in his League of David under the name of Master Raro. Wieck never wanted his daughter to be a piano-playing machine but was eager to give her a "general education."[8] Her visit to Dresden was intended not least to allow her to further her studies in composition and singing. In short, Wieck was keen for his daughter to become a successful composer. And yet the care that he lavished on her does not preclude the possibility that the relationship between father and daughter was not only worryingly close but also artistically repressive, allowing the young Clara few opportunities to develop and almost literally driving her into the arms of Florestan and Eusebius, where she was enticed by hopes of the kind of artistic happiness that she could not find in her acclaimed concert appearances and in salon conversations. In early 1835, Wieck accompanied his daughter on a hugely successful tour of northern Germany, functioning as both her escort and her impresario, but his complaint clearly hints at the situation that we have just outlined: "Clara plays reluctantly and really does not want to go on. What is a virtuoso without vanity?"[9]

Clara felt an urge to aspire to greater heights in art, the same urge that Wieck — with some disquiet — observed in Schumann, for all that he did not regard him as a suitable son-in-law. By cleaving to Schumann in artistic matters, Clara was not being disloyal to her father's precepts, but was expressing a side of herself that had remained resolutely unexplored with Wieck, who demanded outward success and an ability to cope with life.

But how could Wieck have had any deeper understanding of an artistic union between two lovers that is unique in the history of music? And this brings us to an important point: the lovers' drifting apart and finding each other again, with all the concomitant emotional struggles, feelings of confusion and happiness, and the outbursts of despair that accompanied them on their journey through life from their very first kiss in November 1835 to their engagement on August 14, 1837 and, finally, to their wedding on September 12, 1840, would barely claim our attention unless they were inextricably linked to the lovers' lives as artists. No one, apart from novelists and their readers, would be interested in the fact that after asking Wieck in vain for Clara's hand in marriage in September 1837, Schumann despaired of ever being able to marry her, with the result that he may have resumed his liaison with "Christel." And what would it matter that Clara was by no means averse to being courted by other young gentlemen, including the composer Carl Banck, whom Schumann ridiculed in the pages of his *Neue Zeitschrift* as Herr de Knapp (Master Short), much to Clara's annoyance?

If Schumann and Clara made such heavy weather of their developing relationship, it is because of their differing artistic ambitions. And Wieck was not solely to blame for the fact that for long periods the lovers lived apart. Rather, it was their professional lives that drove a wedge between them: Clara was away on tour while Schumann was taking soundings elsewhere, notably during his visit to Vienna, where he wanted to explore the possibility of establishing his *Neue Zeitschrift* in the city. It was very much while they were away from home that they were most dependent on mutual support. From that point of view their correspondence served at the very least to confirm their own sense of artistic identity—the letters that passed between them in a single year, 1839, run to almost five hundred pages.

But there was more to it than that, for it was in art that they felt closest—in a literally physical way. Of course, there were plenty of areas of sensitivity—when Clara reported on her successes in the concert hall in January 1838, she went on to strike a note that was not a little piqued: "You won't be able to understand this enthusiasm [on the part of the audience] as you simply don't know what I'm capable and incapable of achieving—you know me far too little as an artist."[10] The letter was posted in Vienna, where she had just been appointed chamber virtuosa to the imperial and royal court and — in spite of all the upheaval — completed her opp. 9 and 10. For all that Schumann lavished great praise on these two works, there is no doubt that he was incapable of always adequately appreciating Clara's achievements, although he continued to write letters filled with sighs of longing that provided Clara with a different kind of support. On Easter Saturday that same year, while he was hard at work on his *Kreisleriana*, he wrote to her in Vienna:

> When will you stand beside me while I am sitting at the piano — ah! we shall both weep like children! I know, it will overwhelm me. So be cheerful, my heart! Your beautiful slender figure is always standing beside me, and soon you'll be mine. — But I want to tell you about the other night. I woke up and couldn't get back to sleep — and since I was thinking about you so much and sinking ever more deeply into the life of your soul and your dreams, I suddenly said with tremendous inner strength, "Clara, I'm calling you" — and then I heard right next to me: "Robert, I'm here with you." I was overcome by a kind of horror at the way in which spirits can communicate with one another over great tracts of land. But I shan't do it again, this calling out to you; it really affected me.[11]

Sentences like these may encourage readers with an interest in depth psychology or even in psychopathology to indulge in all manner of speculations about Schumann's state of mind, but we should not forget that there were other romantics, too, who regarded music as a real, material force that had the power to enter not only minds but bodies, too. Clara's own compositions, which provided Schumann with material for his *Kreisleriana*, may well have ensured that in particular situations he could also feel her physical presence.

That the experiences described by Schumann were also artistic experiences or at least the harbingers of these is clear from *Dichterliebe*, his setting of poems by Heinrich Heine that dates from two years later. Here, for example, we read:

> Allnächtlich im Traume seh' ich dich
> Und sehe dich freundlich grüßen,
> Und laut aufweinend stürz' ich mich
> Zu deinen süßen Füßen.

> [All night in vision behold I thee, / And see thee greeting me kindly; / And loudly weeping then throw I me / Before thy sweet feet blindly.[12]]

Would Schumann have made these lines his own if he had not been familiar with the experience that they describe? Or, to put it another way, would he have told Clara about his own private experiences in such a concisely telling way if he had not already admired Heine's *Book of Songs?* Just as the League of David reflects the indissoluble knot between reality and fiction, so the lives of Schumann and Clara Wieck appear to reflect a similar bond between the two. Once again it is hard not to recall Friedrich Schlegel's idea of a "universal poetry," for it is very much this idea that is realized here — not just in terms of the interplay between the different arts but also with regard to the oneness of life and art.

Even the ruses that the lovers were forced to adopt in their dealings with Wieck are not without a poetic dimension. Since he had prohibited his daughter from writing to Schumann and did everything in his power to enforce that ban, the couple had to communicate by using assumed names or else they had to find friends willing to write and receive letters in their name. Writing to Clara in Vienna, Schumann ended one of his interminable missives: "Madame de Dimitrjeff (de Varsovie). Poste restante. You'll receive my next letter at this address."[13]

"Another letter from me should arrive at 'Haußner's' in Dresden on Wednesday morning," Schumann wrote on another occasion. "If you're afraid that your frequent visits to the post office may attract attention, let me know before Tuesday."[14] Clara was certainly afraid that her movements would arouse suspicion, and so we find her replying to Schumann: "*I can't collect any more letters from the post office — they know me there!* It was in mortal fear that I left the building today as the man looked at me so ironically and asked: 'What's the young lady's first name?'" She ended with an urgent entreaty: "Couldn't Dr. Reuter go and see N[anny] when her parents are out for an early morning walk, or meet her and give her a letter to enclose?"[15]

But neither Clara herself nor her chambermaid, Nanny, nor Moritz Reuter, who was friendly with the couple, could help out on every occasion, so Clara was reduced to writing to Schumann in Vienna in October 1838 in a state of some agitation:

> I'm expecting a letter from you tomorrow, assuming I can see Reuter — even this source is now cut off from me since Father is threatening to make inquiries to see if Reuter is bringing me news. — Give me an address that I'll use when I write to you while I'm on tour, I don't dare write to you at your own address as Father had said that he'll be able to take his usual steps in every town and city.[16]

Even when they were together, the problems did not go away. In the fall of

1838, for example, Schumann was staying with his sister-in-law, Therese, in Zwickau, but even then the lovers could meet secretly in Leipzig only when Wieck was away. Clara wrote to Schumann on September 22 in a state of some desperation: "Father still hasn't settled on a date." But a postscript headed "Sunday 5 o'clock" reports the glad tidings: "Father's leaving at 6, we're just about to take him to the coach station, so come soon—best wishes."[17] Schumann replied at once:

> The coaches are so unreliable at present. So listen: I'm almost sure that I'll be able to come past your house tomorrow evening (Tuesday) at 8. So do whatever is necessary to ensure that we may be able to speak. [...] You're quite right that I can't keep my return to L[eipzig] a secret, but no one will see me until Thursday, so we'll have Tuesday & Wednesday to ourselves.[18]

We can sense the difficulties that the lovers had to endure, but one suspects that there was also an element of pleasure in their secret arrangements and that they enjoyed this game of hide-and-seek; simply devising the many false names under which letters were left at the post office for general delivery must have added to their sense of fun. Schumann's piano music is full of such masquerades, and the activities of the League of David, as reported in the columns of the *Neue Zeitschrift für Musik*, derive much of their appeal from their cryptic qualities and disguises. Here, too, then, there is the same oneness of life and art.

So abundant is the surviving material that the chronicler would soon be obliged to abandon his narrative in a fit of resignation if he wanted to report on all the vicissitudes of the lovers' period of engagement in the order in which those events unfolded. A preferable approach would be to see them as a single event with a multiplicity of different facets. In this way we may also come closer to an essential aspect of Schumann's early piano music, for the individual pieces that make up *Carnaval*, the *Davidsbündlertänze*, and *Kreisleriana* do not form a coherent sequence but must be perceived as a single tableau.

This view of these works reflects a comment that Schumann once made about a set of Schubert waltzes:

> The way in which the rest of them circle around it [the *Sehnsuchtswalzer* op. 9, no. 2], more or less spinning a cocoon with their gossamer threads, while a rapt thoughtlessness permeates each and every one of them so that listeners in turn are robbed of the ability to think and believe they are still playing the first one when they have already reached the last—this way is very good.[19]

This swirling together of life and work is unique in the history of music and would be inconceivable in the case not only of Mendelssohn but of Wagner, too. True, Wagner "needed" his relationship with Mathilde Wesendonck to summon up the emotional intensity that he required for *Tristan und Isolde*, but conceptually speaking the two are unconnected. This was not true of the young Schumann, whose musical works were created from the spirit in which he lived, just as his life was grounded in the spirit in which he created his music. Of course, each of these two forms of discourse can be considered on its own, but it is more useful if, as "re-creative listeners" we take them both together.

It remains for us to consider the legal proceedings between the parties, an affair that, like many a private prosecution, is not without its carnivalesque qualities, even if it lacks any sense of romantic poetry. The Germans have a proverb, "Trennungen verbinden" ("separations bind us together"), that Wieck chose from the outset to ignore, and this was arguably his biggest mistake. On the other hand, it is easy to understand why he underestimated the obstinacy of the two lovers, for which other underage daughter would have dared at that time to oppose her father's wishes? The case was also particularly difficult: Clara had grown up more or less without a mother, leaving Wieck to believe that he was playing the part of both parents. He took every care to educate her and accompanied her on many of her concert tours. For her part, Clara remained inwardly and outwardly loyal to him, at least up to the time of their legal altercation, as she still hoped that the matter would be settled amicably.

Wieck snapped only when he held in his hands a copy of the petition with which Clara, represented by her lawyer and urged on by Schumann, officially complained about Wieck's refusal to give his consent to the marriage. This was in the fall of 1839. Wieck was evidently incapable of grasping that he had now been cast in the role of the accused. His attitude before this point is understandable even if it fails to gain our approval. In brief, he was worried that Schumann would be unable to provide for his daughter, that she would have to abandon her career, and that she would be obliged to relinquish her inheritance to her husband. It soon became clear that he was right on all three points, even if only in part. From a twenty-first-century standpoint we may also see him as a champion of women's rights, for he was keen to ensure that his daughter was able to continue her artistic career at a time when it was usual for even well-known singers and instrumental virtuosos to retire from public life once they were married—whether they married out of love or because of the need to secure their financial future is beside the point.

On the other hand, Wieck's motivation was by no means as noble as one writer has claimed in a recent study.[20] While he was undoubtedly concerned for his daughter's welfare and well-being, she was ultimately his most prized possession and he had no wish to see it reduced in value. Nor was he willing to share her with a husband who, however much of a genius he may have been, was nonetheless lacking in stolidity. Schumann fought back with all the means at his disposal, seeking to refute the charge that he was incapable of providing for a wife and, as a sign of his decadence, that he was immoderately fond of his tipple.

In any event Schumann was able to convince the court that his finances were sound and draw a veil over the fact that he had already drawn on much of the capital acquired from the various legacies that he had received from his father, mother, and brother Eduard. He was able to adduce character references and even to present himself to the court as the holder of a newly awarded doctorate, the faculty of music at the University of Jena having bestowed this title on him on February 24, 1840, in recognition of his services to music — as was not unusual at this time, the award was made in writing and without any further formalities, including even an examination of his abilities.

The court reached its decision on August 1, 1840, granting the couple permission to marry in church "following the usual publication of the banns."[21] Despite a promise made to Clara, Schumann persisted with his libel action, and in April 1841 Wieck was sentenced to eighteen days' imprisonment. Although he did not serve the sentence, he was no longer a serious risk.

The wedding ceremony took place in Schönefeld, a village to the north of Leipzig, on September 12. The pastor was a school friend of the composer, Carl August Wildenhahn. Schumann had taken steps to ensure that his gift to the bride — a deluxe copy of his *Myrthen* op. 25 bound in red velvet — was ready in time for his stag night. An even more valuable present was a grand piano with English action worth five hundred thalers that he had smuggled into Clara's apartment in July, since Wieck had made it clear that he was not allowed to play the beautiful instrument that the celebrated Viennese piano maker Conrad Graf had given her during her acclaimed visit to the city in 1838. When the Schumanns later acquired the piano, it was above all Schumann himself who played on it. After his death, it passed into the possession of Brahms.

The couple had asked that the wedding should be a quiet affair, and the guests who assembled that evening at the home of Emilie and Julius Carl danced "very little,"[22] an abstinence in no way contradicted by an entry in

Schumann's housekeeping book, "1000 Fl. Rheinisch,"[23] which refers not to the purchase of one thousand bottles of wine from the Rhineland, as a number of writers have speculated, but to the acquisition of stocks and shares worth a total of one thousand florins in Rhineland currency.

Clara finally had the means to keep house for herself and her husband. The previous December he had given her "a new and simple cookery book" written for housewives "without any previous knowledge of cookery." He had it expensively bound, with a gilt inscription: "To My Wife, R. S." A glance at the volume, which the Robert Schumann Museum in Zwickau has reprinted as a facsimile, indicates that Clara used it; underlined entries reflect the fact that she took account of the likes and dislikes that her husband had already itemized in the list that he drew up for his landlady Johanne Christiane Devrient.

The final entry in the diary that Clara kept as an unmarried woman is dated September 12:

> My whole inner world was filled with gratitude for Him who has finally brought us together through so many reefs and rocks; it was my ardent prayer that it might please Him to keep my Robert for me for many, many years — ah, whenever I am assailed by the thought that I might one day lose him, my senses grow confused. [...] Now a new life is starting, a beautiful life, living for him whom one loves above all else, including oneself, but heavy duties lie upon me, too, and may Heaven grant me the strength to meet them faithfully like any good wife.[24]

The fact that the wedding ceremony took place on the day before Clara's twenty-first birthday, while she was still a minor, can hardly have been an accident but must have been due to far-sightedness on the part of Schumann or his legal adviser. Although the date of Clara's coming of age had played no material part in the preceding legal arguments, it was in Schumann's interest to marry her while she was a minor, because he would then be able to dispose of her fortune in whatever way he liked. It was a point that had in fact already exercised him with peculiar urgency — he was sufficiently astute to plan for the future.

However much the subject of Clara may have dominated the years between 1835 and 1840, no chapter on the couple's "probationary years" in Leipzig can ignore other important issues at this time. Schumann was no Beethoven, having to fight for custody of his nephew, and although his struggle for Clara was no less passionate, it did not inhibit his creativity in the way that Beethoven's was affected over a period of many years. In Schumann's case, crisis and creativity were by no means mutually exclusive, for loss led to a redoubling of effort. It was with justified indignation that he wrote to Clara in May 1838 to complain about her father's jibes:

> Your father calls me phlegmatic? *Carnaval* & phlegmatic — F-sharp Minor Sonata phlegmatic — loving such a young woman phlegmatic?! And you calmly accept that? He says that for six weeks I've written nothing for the paper — 1) it's not true 2) even if it were true, he knows what else I've been working on — where, ultimately, is all the material supposed to come from? I've so far supplied the paper with some eighty printed sheets of my own thoughts, not including all my other editorial work, I've also completed ten major compositions in two years — I poured my heart's blood into them — I've also spent several hours a day studying Bach and Beethoven & much of my own music — I've dealt promptly with an extensive correspondence that was often very difficult and detailed — I'm a young man of twenty-eight, a quick-blooded artist who in spite of this has not set foot outside Saxony for the last eight years but has sat here quietly — I've been careful with my money and spent nothing on drink or horses but have quietly gone my own way.[25]

Schumann refers here to ten major piano pieces. By the date of his marriage to Clara, twenty-three separate opus numbers had appeared in print — all his early piano works, together with the *Faschingsschwank aus Wien* op. 26, which was not published until the beginning of 1841. In many cases, fewer than fifty copies of each of these works were eventually sold — his piano works were rarely performed even in the Leipzig music salon of Henriette Voigt, for all that she was well disposed to Schumann as a musician. It is clear from her unpublished diaries that between 1830 and 1837, Beethoven featured a hundred and ten times in her programs, and Mendelssohn sixty times. Schumann, by contrast, was represented only five times, with single performances of *Papillons* op. 2, the *Fantasiestücke* op. 12, *Kinderscenen* op. 15, the Toccata op. 7, and the Piano Sonata op. 22, the last of which was dedicated to Henriette Voigt. In spite of all this, there were numerous positive reviews, not only in the *Neue Zeitschrift* but elsewhere, too. Mendelssohn, Liszt, and Berlioz, to name only the three most famous of Schumann's colleagues, all expressed their admiration.

In 1840, the short-lived *Blätter für Musik und Literatur* published a review full of praise for a group of five composers said to have attracted attention "with their strains of romantic magic" in what "has become known as Young Germany":

If I am to say anything brief but specific that I would ask my readers not to misconstrue, then Chopin is fond of the pithy and the emotionally charged, and also of the seamless legato; Henselt loves elfin playfulness, Thalberg a solemnity that is brilliant and wistfully solemn by turns, Schumann loves humorous depth, Liszt greatness, seriousness, and sublimity of style; but all of them love fullness and abundance.[26]

Similar comments may be found in six blue-bound volumes of press cuttings that Schumann collected between 1832 and 1851.

There were also, of course, critical voices. Carl Koßmaly, whom one tends to think of as a supporter of Schumann, had the following to say about the Fantasy in C Major op. 17:

Its eccentricity, arbitrariness, vagueness, and the nonclarity of its contours can hardly be surpassed. [. . .] To have recourse to a simile, the composer reminds us of a wealthy, distinguished man who, in the aristocratic conceit of making himself unapproachable, egotistically and stubbornly shuts himself off from the world, digs deep moats around his entire property, causes great hedges of thorn to be planted, warning shots to be fired, and traps to be laid, and so fences in and barricades himself that in the end people cannot help but be discouraged from making his acquaintance.[27]

These lines were written in 1844, at a time when — in advance of the bourgeois revolutions of 1848 and 1849 — a fundamental change was taking place in musical aesthetics, as the romantic approach, now dismissed as unduly high-flown, was replaced by a modest classicism that Schumann, too, had come to accept. As a result, he reacted with remarkable mildness to Koßmaly's review, which also contained a number of positive points: "Much about your essay delighted me beyond words; and I think you would react differently to various other points if we were to spend some time together."[28] In any event, it was Schumann himself who sent Koßmaly a "box of older compositions" as the basis for his review, adding:

You'll easily discover what is immature and imperfect about them. Most of them are a reflection of my wildly agitated earlier life; man and artist always tried to express themselves at the same time with me; and I expect that this is still true of me, even now that I have learned to take greater control of myself, including my art. Your sympathetic heart will discover just how many joys and sorrows lie buried in this little pile of music.[29]

There is no doubt that Schumann's early years in Leipzig witnessed many highs and lows. Clara's frequent absences from the city meant that he led a typical bachelor's life in which male friendships were of particular importance. Mendelssohn's appointment as director of the Gewandhaus concerts in August 1835 struck him as a great boon—a stroke of luck not only for Leipzig but for Schumann, too.

Only a year older than Schumann, Mendelssohn took up his new post with tremendous enthusiasm, encouraging Schumann to believe that the new poetic age of which he had dreamed was finally dawning. Florestan's report to Chiara on Mendelssohn's Leipzig debut was couched in correspondingly poetic, not to say rhapsodic terms:

> He sat down innocently at the piano, like a child, and captivated one heart after another, drawing them after him en masse, and when he finally set his listeners free again, they knew that they had flown past a number of islands inhabited by the Greek gods and had been set down again, safe and happy, in the Firlenz Hall.[30]

For Schumann, Mendelssohn was a prime example of the way in which a composer could write works in a poetic and romantic vein while at the same time upholding the German classical tradition. Mendelssohn championed contemporary composers and introduced his audiences to works by Chopin, Liszt, and Berlioz. But he also invested Beethoven's symphonies with a new significance and helped with the rediscovery of Bach. After reading a text on astronomy, Schumann explained to Mendelssohn the theory that when seen through a telescope men and women on earth must "look like mites on a piece of cheese" to the "higher inhabitants of the sun," prompting Mendelssohn to reply, "Yes, but I expect that *The Well-Tempered Clavier* would instill a certain respect in them."[31] And together with Louis Rakemann and Clara Wieck, whose services he was in any case fond of engaging, Mendelssohn performed Bach's Triple Concerto BWV 1063 on November 9, 1835. It was Mendelssohn, too, who helped Schumann to enter the world of chamber music—it is unlikely that the "quartet morning" that he arranged in his rooms in 1836 in order for him to gain a deeper understanding of the works that had been submitted to the *Neue Zeitschrift* for review would have taken place at all without Mendelssohn's help. In his *Reminiscences of Mendelssohn*, Schumann wrote that "his praise always meant the most to me—he was the ultimate authority."[32]

It is perhaps fortunate that the Schumann of the 1830s was too much of the impetuous member of the League of David for him to take his cue from Mendelssohn as a composer. Even so, he observed what Mendelssohn was doing and thought about what he would compose at a later date — namely, his future symphonies and chamber music. Mendelssohn was also an amiable conversationalist to whom Schumann fondly refers in his diary. An entry like this one, dated January 29, 1838, is typical:

> Cudgeled my brains over the ecossaise thing [a lost work]; in the afternoon snowballs at the window, & Mendelssohn came up — kind as ever — then went out for the first time in weeks to Connewitz — beautiful winter's day — in the evening, rather bad concert by Stegmayer in the theater — Hope to wean myself away from Poppe [the landlord of the Coffe Baum, an old Leipzig coffee house much frequented by Schumann] — really not worthy of me. Expect to receive a letter from Vienna in a week's time — I always think of her [Clara] with great affection.[33]

On another occasion, over lunch, Mendelssohn even took Schumann into his confidence, informing him that he was "engaged to be married" and was very much "bewitched" by the young woman in question.[34]

Even the briefest glance at Schumann's diary for this period reveals that he was in contact with an astonishing number of people. To take a single example:

> 26th. Monday. Beautiful day. Meeting at my house, Lipinski, Mendelssohn, David, Mosewius, Ortlepp, Nowakowski, Reuter. Nothing comes of the quartet; but then Mendelssohn, David, & Grenser casually sight-read Schubert's B-flat Major Trio — extraordinary. 27th, Tuesday morning. Stamaty back from Dresden, good-natured young man. Spend the whole week at dinner parties at the hotel with Lipinski, David, Nowakowski, Stamati [i.e., Stamaty], Mendelssohn & his sister, a lively, fiery Jewess. Dr. Frank, whose brother has arrived in town, is a small man of whom much may be expected. At the hotel in the evening told Mendelssohn about Rahel. His sister watched us in silence.[35]

Rahel is the title of the book that Karl August Varnhagen von Ense published in 1834 in memory of his late wife, the prominent literary hostess Rahel Varnhagen, who had died the previous year. Schumann had recently reprinted excerpts from it in his *Neue Zeitschrift*. Mendelssohn and his sister had both frequented Rahel Varnhagen's salon in Berlin and undoubtedly would have taken a lively interest in Schumann's remarks. In short, he was taken entirely seriously as a conversationalist.

A further entry in his diary, this time dated May 1838, commands our attention:

Sunday the 13th. Spoke at length with Prince Emil at the Museum — then Mozart concert, also attended by Walther von Goethe & Frau von Pogwisch — to the hotel with them, Frau von Goethe & the Caruses — then home — went for a walk in the evening — melancholia — I must have had the D — in me because, finding no one to talk to all evening I drank more than a bottle of wine & did the stupidest thing a day before C[lara]'s arrival. Bad hangover on Monday.[36]

Schumann's successor as editor of the *Neue Zeitschrift* was Franz Brendel, who recalled often seeing his predecessor at the Coffe Baum:

He used to sit sideways at the table so that he could rest his head on his arm, brushing away his hair, which kept falling down over his brow, his eyes half closed and dreamily inward-looking. But then he would suddenly come to life again, becoming talkative and animated, whenever there was an interesting exchange of ideas.[37]

From 1836, Schumann lived at the "Red College," a complex of buildings belonging to the university. It was here that he was looked after by the aforementioned Johanne Christiane Devrient. In one of the two rooms was the grand piano on which he composed, improvised, and played the works of other composers, including, most notably, *The Well-Tempered Clavier*. On the wall above it hung portraits of Bach, Beethoven, Clara Wieck, and Ludwig Schunke, a friend who had died in 1834 at the age of only twenty-three. On his desk were statuettes of Paganini, Liszt, and Thalberg in virtuosic poses that were more or less ironically exaggerated. When the young pianist Amalie Rieffel visited him, she was struck not only by these "terrible caricatures,"[38] but also by an engraving of a Raphael Madonna. Schumann's fondness for this work may be surmised from an excerpt from Wolfgang Robert Griepenkerl's poem, "The Sistine Madonna," that he entered in a collection of mottos for the period 1836–38:

Genius! Wohl gibt es dunkele Stunde
Wo du den Künstler verläßt, dann schneidet das irdische Leben
Kalt wie die Luft des Körpers u. ganz erliegen die Kräfte:
Aber erlösest du ihn, dann steiget er mit riesigen Schritten
Ueber die irdische Welt.[39]

[Genius! There is doubtless a dark hour when you leave the artist; then earthly life cuts cold like the air of the body & strength fails completely: but if you redeem him, he will rise with giant steps above the earthly world.]

One wonders if Schumann raised his eyes to look at this Madonna when he thought up or wrote down the section "In the Tone of a Legend" in the opening movement of his Fantasy op. 17. One does not need to be a writer of kitsch to ask this question, for anyone performing this piece is bound to welcome a more detailed explanation of the muted, hymnlike gesture that temporarily dampens the sense of agitation that the work exudes until then. It is by no means far-fetched to think of a Marian aura at this point, for in the early 1840s Schumann, in spite of his Lutheran upbringing, is known to have regarded the subject of the Virgin Mary as an "excellent text" for an oratorio.[40] And his Düsseldorf Mass op. 147 includes a particularly beautiful offertory based on the words "Tota pulchra es, Maria" (You are all beautiful, Mary).

Schumann's aforementioned visit to Vienna lasted from November 1838 to April 1839 and kept him away from his familiar surroundings. He was there to take soundings and see if he and Clara could make a living for themselves in a city that was also an important center of music. After all, Wieck had declared categorically that he would allow his daughter to marry Schumann only on condition that the couple moved away from Saxony. Vienna, where Clara had just been appointed chamber virtuosa to the imperial and royal court, seemed an obvious choice. Having no wish to be a kept man, Schumann wanted to find out if his *Neue Zeitschrift* could be successfully transferred to Vienna.

On the other hand, he had by now already begun to drift away from what had once been his favorite project: sales were falling, and the daily grind was oppressive. While Vienna could have given the paper a new momentum, various discussions with local publishers failed to produce any tangible results. Schumann was also warned that the Austrian censor was particularly vigilant, and to make matters worse, Wieck was plotting against him in faraway Leipzig. In April 1839, Schumann returned to Germany without any sign of outward success, but with a whole series of new ideas and a particular jewel in the form of Schubert's Symphony in C Major (*Great*), a copy of which Schubert's brother, Ferdinand, had presented to him. Mendelssohn gave the first performance of the hitherto unknown work at a Gewandhaus concert on March 21, 1839, even before Schumann himself had returned to the city and well before Viennese audiences had a chance to hear the symphony. Three further performances followed in December 1839 and March and April 1840, giving Schumann ample opportunity to wax lyrical about the "heavenly length" of the work in the columns of his *Neue Zeitschrift*. It was, he went on, "flooded with a romanticism" found elsewhere in the composer's output.[41] By now, Schumann was sufficiently well known as a critic in Leipzig for the publisher Heinrich Brockhaus to seek to engage his services for the *Leipziger Allgemeine Zeitung*. A messenger even turned up at Schumann's house on December 1, 1840 to ask for a review of the recent concert appearance of the violinist Ole Bull at the Gewandhaus. The messenger, Brockhaus explained, would wait until the review was ready.

Soon Schumann himself was writing "great music" for the Gewandhaus. But first there was — in his own words — a "rich blessing of songs."[42]

This plaster relief of Robert and Clara Schumann was made by the Dresden sculptor Ernst Rietschel in January 1846 at the request of the Leipzig publisher Hermann Härtel. The couple sat for the artist several times and were very pleased with the result, although there had apparently been some "arguments" in the run-up to the sittings (*Tagebücher* 3/1:412). Schumann's grandson Ferdinand added a note to the relevant entry in the couple's housekeeping book: "Hiller wanted Clara to be at the front in Rietschel's double medallion. Schumann refused, insisting that the creative artist should take precedence over the re-creative, performing artist" (*Tagebücher* 3/1:756). Copies of this relief can still be found on the secondhand market today. (Photograph courtesy of the private archive of Gerd Nauhaus.)

CHAPTER 6

The "Year of Song" (1840)

"In Foreign Lands"
I hear the brooklets rushing
This way and that in the wood.
In the wood and in the rushing
I know not where I am.

Joseph von Eichendorff, set by Schumann in his *Liederkreis* op. 39, no. 8

W e would be doing Schumann no favors by describing as "perfect" the piano pieces that he wrote before 1840. Even calling Mendelssohn's contemporaneous *Songs Without Words* perfect is tantamount to an act of canonization that is dubious in the extreme — people who want to be perfect are wary of taking risks, and was there ever a man more willing to take risks than the young Schumann? When looking back over his early piano works, he himself gave serious thought to the question of whether they demanded too much intellectual volatility from their audiences. But without the courage to essay the fragmentary and the aphoristic, he would never have written *Carnaval* or *Kreisleriana*, and there would have been none of the romantic art as understood by writers such as Friedrich Schlegel, E. T. A. Hoffmann, Jean Paul, Heinrich Heine, and, of course, Schumann himself.

But then came the "year of song," with its major cycles of lieder to poems by Justinus Kerner, Joseph von Eichendorff, Heine, Adelbert Chamisso, and Friedrich Rückert. And here one is tempted to speak, if not of perfection, then of a degree of success that is altogether breathtaking. Poetry and music embrace each other, and a romantic dream comes true, the two notions of "universal poetry" and of a "synthesis of the arts" achieving a hitherto unsuspected sense of fulfillment in the unassuming form of the piano-accompanied song.

Even as early as the summer of 1839, Schumann had written to his colleague Hermann Hirschbach: "Or are you perhaps like me—someone who all his life has placed vocal compositions below instrumental music and never regarded them as great art? But don't tell anyone I've said this!"[1] Until then, Schumann had been proud of his ability to write music with no regard for a given text or for a far-reaching set of formal rules. The listener was to "re-create" the pianist's state of mind as the latter sat composing at the piano. In the longer term, this required a certain amount of effort and was bound to give rise to self-doubts, for who, on observing the many characters and masks that scurried past them as the composer had seen them spring up, could identify the Schumann their composer wanted them to see?

It was time for something new, albeit not wholly unexpected. After all, Schumann had already written a handful of youthful songs, and there was also a diary entry from 1833 that mentions an unrealized project: "Musical poems, with underlaid songs by Heinrich Heine, written & dedicated to Heine."[2] And at a time when he was ostensibly not interested in writing songs of his own, Schumann was busily reviewing lieder by fellow composers and as if in passing formulating his own aesthetic views on song-writing. Finally, on the evening of June 25, 1838, "after a few days feeling inwardly depressed to the point of collapse," he attended a concert given by the then sixteen-year-old Pauline García and, although he was "as dead as a doornail," he found "tears flooding" down his cheeks "within the first few minutes of her starting to sing."[3]

A similar sense of liberation made itself felt as soon as he started to write songs of his own: "Dreaming & music-making now leaves me practically dead; I could die of it," he told Clara while working on *Myrthen*, his wedding gift for his bride-to-be. "Ah, Klara [*sic*], what a joy it is to write for the voice. It's a pleasure I've forgone for far too long."[4]

Looking back on this period from the vantage point of 1854, Schumann is said to have described the antepenultimate song, "Du bist wie eine Blume," as the first of his "year of song"—this version of events came to the attention of Brahms who in turn passed it on to Clara, adding that she herself struck him "wie eine Blume" (like a flower). A recently discovered source indicates that this song dates from January 23, 1840. Thereafter Schumann composed his lieder at a speed that is barely conceivable, as is clear from the dates of only the best-known cycles: most of the songs that make up *Myrthen* op. 25 were composed between early February and the middle of March; the Eichendorff *Liederkreis* op. 39 was completed in two bursts between May 1 and 9 and between May 16 and 22; *Dichterliebe* op. 48 between May 24 and June 1; and eight of the ten songs that make up Chamisso's *Frauenliebe und -leben* op. 42 were sketched on the afternoons of July 11 and 12, 1840.

Evidently Schumann found it easier to write for the voice than for the piano. Whereas a number of his previous piano pieces had needed several versions and years of polishing to produce a coherent work on the basis of ideas that emerged almost by themselves from his improvisations at the piano, his songs, though still requiring the odd correction, demanded no lengthy reflections on their formal design. Often Schumann would write down only the vocal line, while allowing himself more time to work on the accompaniment. In a letter that he wrote to Clara on February 24, 1840, he explained: "Generally I write [the songs] standing or walking, not at the piano. After all, it is a very different kind of music that is not initially carried through the fingers but is much more immediate & melodious."[5]

Is it Clara to whom we owe this spring-like outpouring of lieder? No doubt she was an important catalyst — it must in part have been the prospect of marriage that finally allowed Schumann to summon up those communicative abilities needed to write songs that draw their strength from the tension between "I" and "you." But if the floodgates opened, it was to express more than just feelings of happiness, for at least during the early part of 1840, darker moods predominated, moods triggered by years of struggle and anguish that culminated in a death wish. Heine's line "Ich hab' im Traum geweinet" (I wept while dreaming) speaks a language that is unequivocally clear while at the same time serving as merely one example among many of a whole number of songs that deal with pain and sorrow. But the medium of the song also smoothed Schumann's path from the subjectivity of the individual "I" to the subjectivity of the couple, the couple in this case being not only Schumann and Clara but also Schumann and his poet of the moment.

It is also worth stressing that Clara was not only a catalyst but also a coworker and in the case of *Liebesfrühling* op. 37, even a cocomposer. Toward the end of the 1830s, Schumann began to compile a collection of verse under the title "Copies of Various Poems for Composition." In the end, it included 169 handwritten entries, 94 of which were set to music by Schumann, 7 by Clara. Of the 169 poems, 15 were by Eichendorff and were copied out by Clara. Since these poems were almost all set to music as part of the *Liederkreis* op. 39, one would dearly like to know whether Clara was acting on

Schumann's instructions or whether it was she herself who chose these poems. Whatever the answer, it remains a fact that Schumann, as well motivated as he was well versed in literature, pursued his own independent studies: his collection of aphorisms includes thirteen texts by Eichendorff, all of which appeared in the *Neue Zeitschrift für Musik* from the spring of 1840 onward.

I am not, of course, trying to suggest that Schumann's inner drive to write lieder or Clara's inspirational proximity were all that it required to produce the impressive fruits of his "year of song," for there are also plausible pragmatic considerations to be taken into account here. As a husband, Schumann had to earn money and escape from the state of anonymity within which he had to a certain extent been able to languish as the editor of, and contributor to, his own *Neue Zeitschrift*. The paper had never been intended as a lifetime's project and was now in crisis. And piano pieces could provide a livelihood only for virtuosos capable of performing them in person in well-filled concert halls. As we know, Schumann was unable to do this, and a few favorable reviews cannot blind us to the fact that his own piano pieces, of which only a handful of copies were sold, were known above all to insiders — even Clara was wary about including them in her programs.

By writing lieder, Schumann hoped to achieve more than this. In this regard, his practicality is clear from the fact that "Lotosblume" from *Myrthen* exists not only in a version for solo voice and piano but also in a parallel version for male-voice choir, while we know that he was also thinking of writing an entire volume of four-part songs. No less deliberate was his decision to tackle complete cycles of songs in the tradition of the late Schubert and to follow up the motley bridal bouquet of *Myrthen* with other collections devoted to a single poet. Such "monothematic" song cycles were taken seriously as settings of works of literature and provided a guarantee that the composer had links with the literary scene — Eichendorff, Heine, Chamisso, and Rückert were all reckoned among the leading poets of their age.

Even more emphatically than Schubert, whom we may loosely describe as his "predecessor" in this respect, Schumann sought out poets and poems that reflected his own view of life, enabling him to identify with the subject matter and at the same time giving him room to breathe — he did not have to set aside his own emotions, nor did he have to reinvent them for each new song. Rather, he was able to read them on the lips of the poet and conjure them up through the medium of his music. Here his ability to concentrate on a single poet in the course of each cycle is of major significance. On the one hand, Schumann was able to cling to the procedures that were typical of his piano pieces and juxtapose "idiosyncratically formed miniatures"[6] that often rush past us with surprising speed — at around thirty-five seconds, "Die Rose, die Lilie, die Taube, die Sonne" holds the record in this regard. On the other hand, however, Schumann avoids the danger that one title could "destroy" the next one, a danger that he had feared in the case of *Papillons*. Now it is the poetry that functions as a link holding the songs together, or, to put it another way, it is the magnet that keeps the individual songs in alignment like iron filings, no matter how different those songs may be.

The fact that Schumann's songs for voice and piano are generally better known than his piano compositions, even though they are no less progressive than the piano pieces, is due not only to the greater acceptance of the song as a medium but also to our empirical perception that in songs the idea of the cycle is more apparent to our senses. In the piano piece the countless nuances that it contains can easily be lost in the flood of sounds, whereas listeners may more readily interpret these nuances as facets of the whole when they are combined with poetry. Even if this whole is not laid down as something incontrovertible, it can nonetheless be sensed in the symbiosis of text and music.

I use the word "symbiosis" metaphorically in an attempt to come closer to defining the underlying tendency in Schumann's musical poetry. Pointless though it may be to play off Schumann's song cycles against those of Schubert, it is still clear that they contain so many novel elements that we can legitimately speak of an aesthetic paradigm shift. Particularly innovative is Schumann's decision not to home in on the poem's formal structure but to take as his starting point what he himself termed the "new spirit of poetry." This was a spirit that he found first and foremost in the verse of Rückert, Eichendorff, Uhland, and Heine, whose poetry, he explained, was better suited to a "more artistic and more profound type of song," making it possible for the composer to "reproduce the poem in its actual depth."[7]

In many of Schubert's songs, whether strophic or through-composed, the structure of the poem provides the riverbed over which the music flows, and the piano writing, however original, serves merely an ancillary function, accompanying the voice in the truest sense of the term and further supporting the position that the voice already has within the structure of the poem. From this point of view, Schubert was still rooted in the tradition of the folksong, in which the distribution of the roles was self-evident, and although he occasionally broke out of this mold, he never seriously called it into question.

But this is precisely what Schumann did in *his* songs. He believed that as a genre, the song could pave the way for a deeper relationship between the poetic word and the poetry of the music only if the composer could break free from convention. This was not least a question of intellect; the composer should not simply enter the world of the poem but look down on it from a greater height. He could then decide impartially how a strophic poem can be wedded to music that does not have to worry about such preconceived structures. In an extreme case he could even bring to a well-ordered poem a chaos all of his own without causing everything to collapse. Although he also wrote songs in a folk tone or with the hint of a folk-like element, this was always a stylistic device to be used only when needed.

There were two reasons, above all, for Schumann's ability to think and work on the highest level when it came to lieder. First, he could count himself, if not a poet, then at least a member of the confraternity of poets. And, second, his piano pieces had provided him with plentiful experience of writing music that as far as possible avoided confining formal rules. In 1843, in the course of a review of Robert Franz's lieder, Schumann looked back on this period and described exactly what it was that had made his "year of song" possible:

> We know that between 1830 and 1834 there was a reaction against the prevailing taste. In essence, the battle was not a hard one to win, for it was designed to combat the formulas and empty phrases that revealed themselves principally in piano music. And it was in piano music that the first attack was launched, passage-work being replaced by rather more thoughtful structures.

In writing these lines, Schumann was praising the League of David, including himself. And yet he clearly saw his own role as a piano composer in a distinctly negative light when he went on: "And in reality it is perhaps the song that is the only genre in which there has been any real progress since Beethoven."[8]

In lieder composition the equivalents of "passage-work" and "empty phrases" were an unimaginative insistence on schematic patterns and insensitivity to the relationship between the words and the music. Reviewing a group of songs by Norbert Burgmüller, Schumann complained that "in Schubert's case, the idea of retaining a particular figure throughout an entire song was something new; younger song composers should be warned against this mannerism." Even Schubert often "laid it on with a trowel" when it came to his accompaniments.[9]

Not only should the piano writing be more elastic and better adapted to the specific situation, but, more generally, the composer should adopt a more finely nuanced approach to the task in hand. It was against this background that Schumann expressed his dissatisfaction with the way in which one of his colleagues had set two of Ludwig Uhland's lines, "Da wärm ich mir die Hände, / Bleibt auch das Herze kalt" (Though I may warm my hands, my heart withal is cold). In order to reflect "the contrast that is articulated here and that touches on the humorous," the composer should have devised "a more specific expression, mostly achievable through a lower register in the melodic line."[10]

The category of humor that Schumann brings into play here clearly provides a key not only to his early piano music but also to his whole aesthetic outlook on the world of song. This view is based on the conviction that subjective experience is possible only at a particular moment and even then only in the way in which the finite founders on the infinite. Eichendorff's poem "Mondnacht" (Moonlit night) contains the lines:

Und meine Seele spannte
Weit ihre Flügel aus,
Flog durch die stillen Lande,
Als flöge sie nach Haus.

[And then my soul a-sighing / Spread out her wings to roam / Through silent landscapes flying / As she were flying home.[11]]

Here the idea of returning home may be interpreted as something that has the potential to happen, whereas with Schumann it acquires an air of unreality as the vocal line ends on a chord similar to the one described by musicologists as an interrupted cadence. (In German, the term *Trugschluss* literally means "deceptive ending.") The vocal line gives the impression that the soul has made an emergency landing in the finite, and it requires the piano postlude to open up a vision of the longed-for infinite. This is romantic humor of a kind that Schumann not only encouraged other composers to adopt but which he himself was able to demonstrate in particularly striking ways.

It was with a certain sadness that the Greek-born German musicologist Thrasybulos Georgiades, for whom the unspoiled world of art music came to an end with Schubert, noted how artists of Schumann's generation set out "to free the world from the fetters of the 'public and conventional' by means of the private and subjective."[12] However justified or otherwise the critical undertone that informs this statement, there is no doubt that in his song cycles Schumann succeeded in giving voice in both words and music to a new subjectivity. Having lost its way, the confused subject — "I know not where I am" — finds hitherto unprecedented sounds for the situation in which it finds itself. Above and beyond the specific example of Schumann himself, this represents an advance in the world of art: the new is not necessarily better, but in an act of emancipation it expresses something that may already have existed but which could previously not be spoken aloud.

It may now be spoken aloud because the "embrace" or "symbiosis" of poetry and music is achieved not by any direct means but often enough in a cryptic, irrational, and fantastical way. Lawrence Kramer has noted that at many points in Schumann's song cycles,

> the text is trying, naïvely or defensively, to suppress something, to inhibit the possibility of a reading that the song insists on pursuing. A latent discontinuity in the poetry is thus made explicit in the projected form of an open tension between the poetry and the music.[13]

Schumann demonstrates a magnificent ability to play with this tension. His handling of the text cannot be determined in advance but demonstrates a degree of freedom in formal matters such that his lieder may be seen as examples of "absolute" music as defined by the early romantics in their typically generous way. These songs are "absolute" to the extent that the relationship between vocal line and piano writing can be summed up in the image of a symbiosis: the listener does not necessarily have to pay attention to the individual words because everything is "said" by the way that voice and piano chime together in total accord.

In this sense many of Schumann's songs are miniature character-pieces that can be meaningfully performed without the human voice. It is no accident that Clara Schumann published thirty of them for unaccompanied piano. Take the third song from *Dichterliebe*:

Die Rose, die Lilie, die Taube, die Sonne,
Die liebt' ich einst alle in Liebeswonne.
Ich lieb' sie nicht mehr, ich liebe alleine
Die Kleine, die Feine, die Reine, die Eine;
Sie selber, aller Liebe Bronne,
Ist Rose und Lilie und Taube und Sonne.

[The rose and the lily, the sun and the dove, / I loved them all once with the bliss of love. / I love them no more, I love but her only, / The holy, the lowly, the lovely, the lonely; / Herself the fount of every love — / The rose and the lily, the sun and the dove.[14]]

This is the original wording of Heine's poem. Schumann turned the word *Bronne* (fount) into *Wonne* (joy) and at the very end repeated the lines "I love but her only,/The holy, the lowly, the lovely, the lonely." Such a change would hardly represent an improvement to the poem if it had not been set to music, but within the context of the music it does not detract from Heine's intention. Heine's original is an emphatic love poem with a sense of elation that has become altogether breathless in Schumann's setting. Heine's poem comes close to creating the impression of a series of childish rhymes but triggers a veritable whirlwind from the composer, a naïve children's game becoming a virtuosic form of expressive dance. Schumann understood Heine — although he could easily have misunderstood the poem — and yet he still went on to create something new and different.

Is it possible, however, that he failed to hear the note of irony in Heine's poem? After all, the lovesickness from which the poet suffers incurably is thrust aside for a moment in order to allow him simply to enjoy himself as a child might do.

This brings us to the heart of a fundamental debate about Schumann's lieder. Debussy, for example, argued that his predecessor had not understood the subtle irony of poems that Heine himself characterized as "pain plunged in honey,"[15] but the real roots of this suspicion lie in German nationalist (and, later, National Socialist) anti-Semitism: commentators refused to accept that Schumann, as a sentimental German, could ever derive any pleasure from the "games played by the deracinated" Heine,[16] which is from two points of view a hazardous assumption.

In the first place, it is difficult for us today to imagine the extent to which Heine's love poetry struck a nerve with enlightened contemporaries, who did not need Schumann's literary appreciation to sense the element of irony even at those points where it is not obvious — not that this precludes the possibility of their ignoring it in specific cases. The breathlessness that informs Schumann's setting of "Die Rose, die Lilie" can be seen from the standpoint of the man who is in love and who takes himself and his enthusiasm entirely seriously. But it can also be seen from the vantage point of the observer who greets such effusiveness with the hint of a smile.

By dint of the fact that Schumann has complete control of the poem (rather than merely keeping it under control), he is able to write music that does not simply fit it like a glove but enters into a true symbiosis with it. Modern semiotics provides us with an appropriate mode of perception when it speaks of different voices, voices found not only in the novel but also in music. For a composer who had already completed *Papillons*, *Kreisleriana*, the C Major Fantasy and the Humoresque, it was self-evident that a piece would not speak with a single voice but that — to quote from Eichendorff's poem "Twilight" — "voices" would "wander to and fro."

The listener's pleasure and task consists in acknowledging each of these voices in turn. The voices do not need to be those of the poet and the composer. Vocal line and accompaniment can also function as a pair of voices. This may be a nonconflictual process, as is the case with "Die Rose, die Lilie," but it may also be profoundly effortful, as it is in another song from the same cycle, "Ich hab' im Traum geweinet," in which the listener must keep switching between close and sympathetic attention to the vocal line and an equally close interest in the piano part.

> Ich hab' im Traum geweinet,
> Mir träumte, du lägest im Grab.
> Ich wachte auf, und die Träne
> Floss noch von der Wange herab.
>
> Ich hab' im Traum geweinet,
> Mir träumt', du verließest mich.
> Ich wachte auf, und ich weinte
> Noch lange bitterlich.
>
> Ich hab' im Traum geweinet,
> Mir träumte, du wärst mir noch gut.
> Ich wachte auf, und noch immer
> Strömt meine Tränenflut.

[In dream I lay a-weeping, / I dreamt, in the grave thou didst lie. / I waked again, and the tear-drops / Still ran from my streaming eye. / In dream I lay a-weeping, / I dreamt thou forsookest me. / I waked again, and awaken'd / Awhile wept bitterly. / In dream I lay a-weeping, / I dreamt thou wert kind to me still. / I waked again, and yet ever / Streams down the deep tear-rill.[17]]

It is difficult to structure a poem in a clearer or more memorable way, difficult to deliver a more straightforward account of this tale of love's endless anguish than Heine does here. Schumann leaves everything as it is, while at the same time turning on its head the traditional aesthetic of the piano-accompanied song. For two of the three verses, the vocal line is unaccompanied:

The opening of "Ich hab' im Traum geweinet" from *Dichterliebe*, op. 48 (1840).

Instead, the piano takes over the role of a fellow conversationalist whose silence is eloquent and who limits himself to helpless gestures in the pauses between the lines of the song. In the final verse the numbness dissolves at the words "strömt meine Tränenflut" (streams down the deep tear-rill), but even then the change is only temporary. Although Schumann brings the vocal line to an end on E-flat — the piece is in E-flat minor — he interprets this note as part of a dissonant six-five chord that then resolves in the direction of A-flat minor, so that voice and piano are again forced apart. Only after the voice has died away does the chord in the piano resolve and produce a consonance.

But this is not the end of the matter, for there follows what the Belgian composer Henri Pousseur has called "one of the longest, emptiest, and most irreconcilable passages in the whole of the classical and romantic repertory, prefiguring sounds that we can find in a good deal of modern music, especially post-Webern."[18] Only superficially is this a postlude in which the hesitant chords in the piano, familiar from earlier, are interrupted by lengthy rests. Or perhaps it would be more accurate to speak of a rest interrupted by hesitant chords.

Since the days of humanism, the *Generalpause* has traditionally been seen as a symbol of the onset of death. In his oratorio, *The Seven Last Words of Christ*, Heinrich Schütz introduces a *Generalpause* into the choral writing after the phrase "and he gave up the ghost," and in his notes on his *Egmont* Overture Beethoven writes: "Death could be expressed by a rest." But few other composers create such a disturbing impact with this stylistic device as Schumann does. Heine experts with an interest in depth psychology have read an unconscious death threat into the line "I dreamt, in the grave thou didst lie," but music lovers generally ignore such thoughts. Are they right to do so? Schumann must have been a hero if his long struggle to win Clara had not acquired aggressive and auto-aggressive aspects. Be that as it may, the "truth of the musical expression"[19] that was so important to Schumann in his song settings undoubtedly extended to the "rare states of mind" that had always animated him as a composer.

In order to do justice to the varied treatment that Schumann lavishes on the subject of unrequited love, we would have to work through *Dichterliebe* song by song, for the composer is forever discovering new aspects of the theme with a rare mixture of boldness and imagination. And if we may compare him with Heine, then his range of expression is far greater than the poet's, for in the Lyrical Intermezzo on which the song cycle is based Heine strikes a sentimental, generally ironical note without exploring the emotional extremes.

In this regard Schumann's music is far more vivid and graphic than Heine's verse. Not only does it create a poetic impression of the "most beautiful month of May, when all the buds were breaking," it also encourages the dolls to dance, most notably in Heine's tale of the young man who loves a young woman who has chosen another man who loves another woman, whereupon the first young woman in her annoyance chooses the first man to come her way. For most of the song, the piano strikes a note of boisterous high spirits appropriate to a wedding, and the voice echoes it almost against its will, at least until we come to a ritardando at the words "the youth is woebegone."

There is also the hint of a minor-key tonality at "anyone who has known it [i.e., this old story]." But by the punch line that follows immediately afterward ("his heart is broken in two"), the old boisterousness has reasserted itself, yet it is now so forced that it is no longer possible to ignore the ambiguities of the song as a whole.

A few years earlier, while discussing the poetry of Byron, Heine, Hugo, and Grabbe, Schumann had written that "for a few brief moments in eternity poetry has donned the mask of irony in order to conceal its anguished features; perhaps a friendly hand will remove it and its wild tears will be seen to have turned into pearls."[20]

Is the composer of *Dichterliebe* an ironist? Perhaps he is merely a humorist in the way that he bathes pain and cruelty in a conciliatory light. This is certainly true of the poetic postlude to the final song, which serves as an epilogue to the cycle as a whole: after the "olden, ugly songs" have been sunk in the sea and, with them, "love" and "pain," Schumann in turn immerses himself in the piano writing in order to explore the art that is genuinely his own and to forget all the emotional confusion that the poet has caused him. Even the performance marking adopts the Italian of professional musicians: "Andante espressivo." We are suddenly among friends. In this context Beate Perrey has spoken of "the ironic glance back."[21]

A great deal of fuss has recently been made about an earlier version of *Dichterliebe* that contains four extra songs and a number of important variant readings. In the early version of the opening song ("Im wunderschönen Monat Mai"), for example, there is no appoggiatura on the syllables "Herzen" and "-gangen"; it was only in the publisher's corrections that Schumann introduced this change. And the same is true of the final line of the song:[22]

The revised (*top*) and original (*bottom*) versions of the line "da ist in meinem Herzen die Liebe aufgegangen" in the opening song, "Im wunderschönen Monat Mai," from *Dichterliebe*, op. 48 (1840).

There is no doubt that at least in the case of *Dichterliebe* these late altera-tions — something that Schumann's publishers feared — are an improvement. What a loss it would have been if it had not occurred to Schumann to add the sob on "Verlangen" (desire) at the last moment! And he evidently had good reason to limit the cycle to the set of sixteen songs familiar to us today, with the result that there is little point in boasting about the "discovery" of an earlier version of the cycle. A discordant note enters the creative process only when there is the danger that audibly inferior alternatives not only elicit a scholarly interest but acquire a patent of nobility by being performed in public.

There are more important things for us to consider — namely, Eichen-dorff's *Liederkreis*. This time it is not love that is the main subject, even though the final song, "Frühlingsnacht" (Spring night), ends with a jubilant outburst innocent of any sense of irony: "And the nightingales repeat it: Yes, she is yours, she is yours!" The few songs in this cycle that deal with love lack all sense of the violent despair and desperate violence that characterizes the relationship in *Dichterliebe* between Heine and Schumann on the one hand and a feminine "you" on the other, culminating in the formers' feeling of rejection by the latter, much as a child might feel rejected by its mother. In the songs that make up the Eichendorff cycle, all this belongs in the past. Time and again the poet's and composer's thoughts wander back in time to the past while ranging far and wide in space. And often enough experiences and impressions are associated with phrases such as "as if." Sometimes the poet seems to watch the world go by with a total lack of interest. The cycle's overarching motto is "I know not where I am."

Schumann was hardly exaggerating when he told Clara that the cycle was "arguably the most romantic of all my works."[23] Readers and listeners inclined to forget that at the turn of the nineteenth century romanticism was discov-ered above all in landscapes will be reminded of that fact by the Eichendorff songs, not one of which is not set in nature or at least redolent of nature. Of course, we are not dealing here with nature as such but with nature as the origin of all things and as the home for which we long but which is repeatedly placed under threat. Schumann succeeds in depicting all this from the most varied perspectives, which sometimes shift even within a single song: seen from close quarters and from a distance, in a past that presents itself to us as the present and in a present that passes us by as if it were the past.

This certainly applies to the song "Auf einer Burg" (In a castle). The "aged knight" should long since have vanished from its ruins, but Schumann al-lows him to live on in his "silent cell" in writing that suggests a rough-hewn hymn tune stretching back to the Middle Ages but enriched with modern harmonies. Finally, something happens in the form of a wedding procession of musicians passing by on the Rhine, animating the musical landscape for little more than a moment. Then everything returns to its former state, and the tears of the beautiful bride that are mentioned in the very last word of all are emphasized by means of an emotionally charged melisma that could come from one of Bach's Passions and sounds, therefore, to come from far away.

To describe the piano writing as "rough-hewn" might be seen as a euphemism, for from an academic point of view the various elements are joined together in ways that are "incorrect." Only within the context of the poem are they "correct." By rejecting the older aesthetic belief that the correct was beautiful and the beautiful correct, Schumann was writing a new chapter in the history of music, though he was still working within the tradition of the late Beethoven. One can sense why his music so unsettled Georgiades, a writer whose thinking was geared to unambiguous semantic structures. Impressive though his comments on Schubert's song cycles may be, the constant shifts in Schumann's Eichendorff *Liederkreis* were bound to leave him feeling bewildered, for whereas the songs that make up *Winterreise* may differ from each other in detail, they are at least seen from the same perspective of the first-person narrator wandering through the winter's cold. In the Eichendorff *Liederkreis*, conversely, the perspective changes constantly between "I" and "you," between the inner world and the outer world, between narrow confines and distant horizons, and finally, between fantasy and reality.

No composer before or since was as adept as Schumann at playing with the possibilities available to him and producing associations and contexts by compositional means, while never becoming insistently illustrative. At the end of the opening song, "In Foreign Lands," a tiny shift to the Phrygian mode at the words "and no one knows me here any more" is enough not only to conjure up the past in general but, more specifically, to recall a chorale such as *Wenn ich einmal soll scheiden*, even if the listener is not conscious of the reference. Conversely, it needs only a few bars at the start of "Moonlit Night" to identify the "magical tone" that is then maintained throughout the song, accompanying the soul on its flight between heaven and earth. Charles Rosen has admired Schumann's ability to conjure up "the erotic vision of a landscape" in this song by means of "absurdly simple forms," while at the same time remaining capable of portraying "the most complex states of feeling."[24]

My concern, of course, is not to insist on any one "authentic" interpretation of "Moonlit Night" but to express astonishment at the fact that music — this music — is capable of offering such a wide range of interpretations while remaining so concentrated upon itself. Titles such as "In Foreign Lands," "Moonlit Night," "In a Castle," and the tenth song, "Twilight," which we shall examine in greater detail in the following Intermezzo, merely indicate certain scenes, without allowing us to experience them with our senses, whereas the music offers us a distinctive taste of all that those titles imply. And at the same time it presents us with the whole: it is the *res ipsa*, as it were, giving us an inkling of what it actually tastes like.[25]

Dichterliebe and the Eichendorff *Liederkreis* may be very different as compositions, but at least their poems share a number of points based on a typically romantic attitude to life. One begins to feel a certain sense of eeriness oneself. Or would it not be better to say: "the man"? From this point of view, it could be argued that Schumann rewards this man — and hence himself — with another important cycle from 1840, *Frauenliebe und -leben* (A woman's love and life) op. 42, the title of which echoes the one that Adelbert von Chamisso had given to a sequence of nine poems published in the *Musenalmanach für das Jahr 1831*. The fact that Schumann set them in their original order underscores their narrative thrust. Chamisso — who amusingly, perhaps, exhibited homoerotic tendencies — describes the journey undertaken by a woman from bashful admirer to beloved, lover, fiancée, wife, mother-to-be, mother, and, finally, widow.

Even Schumann's daughter Eugenie reports on a soprano who struggled to come to terms with the fact that two men could so self-evidently flatter their own sex and place such adulation in the mouth of a woman: "Ever since I saw him, I think that I am blind," the woman announces at the start of the very first song, "him" being "the most glorious of men." Schumann's music offers such enthusiasm an adequate platform, maintaining the same tone throughout the cycle, without attempting to establish any evident sense of objectivity or distance.[26] But as a composer and future husband Schumann had every right to revel in his newfound status, and the reader will surely not begrudge him that. True, the romantic art song would be unbearable if it presented pictures only of women who live for their menfolk alone, and yet this view reflected a profound longing not only on the part of men but also on that of many women at this time — a similar note was struck by Clara Wieck in diary entries (quoted in the last chapter) that drew a line under her life before she struck out in a new direction as Schumann's wife.

Moreover, one of the wonderful things about music is that although it may not demand that we forget the relevant context, it nonetheless enables us as listeners to bring our own contexts to it. When Susanna idolizes her lover in *Le nozze di Figaro* (Figaro's wedding), she is addressing both the count and Figaro in terms of a plot that is already multilayered, but at the same time the music makes it clear that what she is actually hymning is the miracle of love and devotion as such. Much the same is true of Schumann: something would be seriously amiss if—after all the romantically refracted humor of *Dichterliebe* and the Eichendorff *Liederkreis*—pure feeling were not allowed to express itself.

Twilight

"Twilight"

Dämmrung will die Flügel spreiten,
Schaurig rühren sich die Bäume,
Wolken zieh'n wie schwere Träume —
Was will dieses Grau'n bedeuten?

Hast ein Reh du lieb vor andern,
Lass es nicht alleine grasen,
Jäger zieh'n im Wald und blasen,
Stimmen hin und wieder wandern.

Hast du einen Freund hienieden,
Trau ihm nicht zu dieser Stunde,
Freundlich wohl mit Aug' und Munde,
Sinnt er Krieg im tück'schen Frieden.

Was heut' gehet müde unter,
Hebt sich morgen neugeboren.
Manches geht in Nacht verloren —
Hüte dich, sei wach und munter!

[Twilight now her wings is spreading, / Trees are shivering and
sighing, / Clouds like evil dreams are flying; / What the meaning of
my dreading? / If thou hast a darling roe then, / Leave her not alone to
graze; / Huntsmen ride in woodland ways, / Voices echo to and fro
then. / If thou hast a friend, it wise is / At that hour to trust not him; /
Eyes and lips may friendly seem, / War he plans in tricky guises. /
That which sets today in sorrow / Rises new-born on the morrow; /
Many things at night miscarry — / Stand on guard, alert and wary.[1]]

Do you know this provincial word?" Gottfried August Bürger asked his fellow poet, Christoph Martin Wieland, in 1776. "It means the mass of light when day and night part. It precedes dusk."[2] He was referring to the word *Zwielicht* (half-light, or twilight), which was only then gaining acceptance in standard High German. As such, it reflects an attitude to life that was starting to view nature as a mood. The word quickly became a literary metaphor. "I was oppressed by a sense of stagnation in my emotions, an apprehensive twilight zone between bright joy and dark grief," Jean Paul wrote, putting these words in the mouth of one of his first-person narrators who is overwhelmed by romantic impressions in the course of a clandestine journey to the imaginary resort of Waldkappel.[3]

In Eichendorff's *Ahnung und Gegenwart* (Presentiment and presence), the natural phenomenon of dusk is interwoven with the psychological experience of half-light. But Schumann did not need to know Eichendorff's first novel, which had first appeared in print in 1815, for the lines quoted at the start of this chapter also appear in a collection of his poems, albeit without an explanatory context. For readers of the time, this may have represented a loss, but for Schumann it was a welcome invitation to immerse himself in a role that he himself had commended to his own audience: that of the "re-creative" listener.

In May 1840, his struggle to win Clara Wieck's hand in marriage still had some way to run, and Eichendorff's lines about the favorite roe deer that should not be allowed to graze alone will undoubtedly have seemed to reflect his own situation, quite apart from the fact that Clara herself had already copied out these and other lines by Eichendorff for her fiancé. But the couple would have been even more profoundly affected by the next two lines in the poem: "Huntsmen ride in woodland ways, / Voices echo to and fro then." After all, Schumann was familiar with a life filled with fantastical voices of every kind, whether they were interpreted artistically or psychopathologically.

The way in which a composer could deal with such phenomena had become clear to Schumann on seeing a collection of songs by Gottlob Wiedebein that was published in August 1828. As he wrote in an enthusiastic letter to their composer, they had provided him "with many a moment of joy, and it was through them that I learned to understand and decipher Jean Paul's veiled remarks. It was through that magical veiling of your musical creations that Jean Paul's obscure and ghostly sounds finally became bright and clear, more or less revealing how two negatives may become an affirmative."[4] The eighteen-year-old Schumann was presumably referring above all to Wiedebein's setting of an episode from one of his own favorite novels, *Flegeljahre*, in

The opening bars of the autograph manuscript of Schumann's setting of Joseph von Eichendorff's poem "Zwielicht" (Twilight), May 19, 1840. (Courtesy of the Stiftung Preußischer Kulturbesitz, Berlin — Staatsbibliothek. Photograph: bpk, Berlin / Art Resource, NY.)

which Jean Paul writes about Walt's love of Wina: "'Oh, if only I were a star,' thus a voice sang within him."

But we do not need to reconstruct all that the young Schumann found so stimulating in the Braunschweig composer's songs. Far more interesting is the way in which he proclaimed — almost in passing — a whole series of maxims on the aesthetics of lieder writing that he was then to put into practice in his "year of song," for here an "obscure" text becomes "bright and clear" thanks to the "veiling" composition. We do not need to linger over the "obscure" aspects of Eichendorff's poem. But to what extent does the composer of "Zwielicht" operate with "magical veilings"?

If, for a moment, we equate the vocal writing with the "sounds" of the poem (and this appears a legitimate procedure, for the poem is explicitly sung in Eichendorff's novel), then the piano part would be the actual "musical creation." And this veils the singing in the truest sense of the term inasmuch as Schumann uses two compositional devices above all. The first is the Bachian polyphony that is evoked here but which Schumann does not pursue, preferring to allow it to vanish into the darkness. With its voices that literally "echo to and fro," this is combined with an unstable and, indeed, aimless kind of harmonic writing that favors the interval of a tritone, an interval which, three whole tones apart, is regarded as "homeless" within the tonal system.[5]

The second of these compositional devices is the "imprecise unison," a term coined by Adorno and applied to Schumann's song by Reinhold Brink-mann.[6] In other words, the right hand of the piano takes over the notes of the vocal line, but not always simultaneously. Instead, there are often tiny disso-nant shifts that create a sense of puzzlement in the listener, something entirely typical of Schumann and that prove particularly effective in combination with the specific text of this song. Although accurately and objectively notated, they can create a hallucinatory effect, tricking the senses with their intentional insignificance and in that way introducing an element of confusion that lies over the song as a whole, affecting not just its structure but also the way in which the listener perceives it.

Although vocal line and piano accompaniment draw in the main on the same thematic substance, they run along separate lines: the fact that the right hand of the piano paraphrases the vocal line in the way described in the last paragraph may appear to contract this claim, but the contradiction is merely apparent, for the two cannot really agree, and nor are they intended to do so. It is no wonder, then, that with the exception of the final bars, the piano part can often function as an instrumental character-piece. To have the song staged, with the pianist sitting introspectively in the corner of the hall while the singer wanders around, would produce a delightful spectacle. Indeed, we could even go a step further and imagine the scene with Schumann at the piano and Clara as the singer. Certainly, there is talk of marriage in the song: at the words "If thou hast a darling roe then, / Leave her not alone to graze," the notes E–B–E (in German notation, *Ehe* = marriage) appear in the left hand of the piano part, but not at the equivalent point in the other three verses.

It surely requires no further proof that "obscure and ghostly tones" pre-dominate in Eichendorff's poem and that Schumann's setting operates with "magical veilings." It remains only to explain what the two "affirmative nega-tions" make "bright and clear" to the listener. And the answer is provided by Thomas Mann, who struggles to find the superlatives that he needs to praise Schumann's "incredibly inspired" setting of the poem, an encomium he is more than able to justify.[7] Mann, who once famously turned down a request for an opera libretto with the remark that he in any case made "as much music as one can reasonably make *without* music,"[8] felt that as a poet he was inferior to composers. Even the best poetry could speak only in codes and symbols, but music can express this directly through the vibrations of the unconscious.

Referring to the "difficult secret" surrounding the illness and death of young Hanno Buddenbrook, Mann did not even attempt to draw on such codes and symbols, but settled for a secondhand report:

> Hanno had smiled when he heard his voice, though he hardly knew anyone; and Kai had kissed his hands again and again.
> "He kissed his hands?" asked the Buddenbrook ladies.
> "Yes, over and over."
> They all thought for a while of this strange thing, and then suddenly Frau Permaneder burst into tears.[9]

This is all that the reader learns about this "heavy secret."

As a composer, Schumann did not even have to try to fathom the "secret" of Eichendorff's poem. What use to him was the knowledge that in the novel the young Count Friedrich, "utterly alone," hears singing in the nearby forest but is unable to locate its provenance ("Twilight now her wings is spreading")? He did not have to work out in what way Friedrich's existence was fatally bound together by invisible threads. It was enough for him to read the title — missing from the novel — to invoke a twilight that illustrates no external event but is an expression of the "psychological magic" that in Thomas Mann's mind was associated not least with the romantic piano-accompanied songs of composers such as Schubert and Schumann.

God forbid that Schumann's song should ever appear "bright and clear" in terms of its form, its gestural language or its color, for in that case he would have failed in his objective: his concern, after all, was twilight, not brightness and clarity. It is the musical expression of a lack of clarity that this twilight presents in all its transparency. At the same time, the song would not work without its text, the topoi of which offer as much and as little concretization as listeners need to divine a message and to interpret it in their own terms.

All of this takes place against the background of a grandiose dialectic that the young Schumann could vaguely sense but which the Schumann of the "year of song" was able to achieve through his work as a composer. However unambiguous the many weighty words of the poem may appear, each listener will interpret them in different ways and make sense of them as he or she thinks fit. And however diffuse the music, per se, may seem, the audience that hears it in the recital room merges to form a single listener for whom everything momentarily becomes "bright and clear."

Postlude

There is no postlude. In Schumann's works, the postlude often serves to re-solve the interrupted cadence or dissonant chord on which the vocal line has come to rest and in that way ensures that the work ends on a note of reassur-ance. In "Zwielicht," the postlude is replaced by a surprising envoi. The final line, "Hüte dich, sei wach und munter" (Stand on guard, alert and wary), is articulated by the singer in a way suggestive less of a songlike melody than of a heavily accented recitative that is almost literally punched out. After "Hüte dich" and right at the end, the piano intervenes, first with one brief chord, then with three more, placing itself for the first time in the song entirely in the service of the rhetoric associated with the vocal line.

The diffuse twilight mood is now broken, and the warning to be on one's guard emerges, whispered or hissed, from the darkness. Whether the call is addressed to the audience or to the composer, the subject of the song cer-tainly changes its temporal perspective with its final line; ceaselessly circling, ahistorical time now acquires a sense of forward momentum, and a period of waiting "as if from a distance" (one of Schumann's favorite terms) is trans-formed into action of the greatest immediacy.

Eichendorff's poem could have produced such a shift of perspective in each of its earlier verses, but Schumann was a champion of a rigorously con-sistent romantic aesthetic that attached great importance to a higher form of wit. According to the opening sentence of the thirty-fourth of Friedrich Schlegel's Lyceum Fragments, "A witty idea is a disintegration of spiritual substances which, before being suddenly separated, must have been thor-oughly mixed."[10] In this particular case, the wit divides up the diffuse fears that had previously been predominant in order to produce a reality that only the waking, vigilant listener can face.

This is also a political reality. It matters little in which frame of mind Eichendorff may have written his poem, for in 1840 Schumann would have interpreted it within the context of the prerevolutionary period that culmi-nated in the uprisings of 1848 and 1849, a period during which there was every reason to be mistrustful. Schumann was no hero, of course, only a pas-sionate observer of the events that were taking place all around him. But even as a mere observer, he had every reason to undermine the classical ideals of unity and coherence in the service of the truth.

Schumann in 1844. This steel engraving was prepared by Auguste Hüssener after an oil painting by Joseph Matthäus Eigner that is no longer extant. Eigner was a portrait painter in Vienna, and Schumann sat for him several times, wearing the fur coat that he had bought for his visit to Russia between January and March 1844.

(Photograph courtesy of the Robert Schumann Museum, Zwickau.)

CHAPTER 7

Married Life in Leipzig — Visit to Russia (1840–44)

Talents, health, thriving children, sincere affection — this, too, means something and cannot be measured in terms of mere wealth. But of course we must think of this, too, and also of safeguarding my livelihood, that, too, is bound to come.

Robert Schumann, entry in his marriage diary, June 28, 1843

expect you'll then always travel by steam train. But please take extreme care: never look out of the carriage, never stand up, never get out until the carriage has come to a complete standstill. The very idea already makes me feel uneasy."[2] Schumann wrote these lines to Clara while she was staying in Paris in June 1839. It is hard to believe from his warnings that in spite of his fear of heights he was in fact a railway enthusiast — it was as such that he wrote to his sister-in-law Therese on April 28, 1837 on the occasion of the official opening of the Leipzig–Althen stretch of the line from Leipzig to Dresden: "Therese, a glance at the steam train is enough to cure you! Tears came to my eyes in awe at what the human spirit is capable of achieving."[3]

Under the circumstances it is no wonder that Schumann was keen to travel with his wife on the newly completed stretch of line, which he finally did on June 1, 1841. For that reason if for no other, he would have been happy to leave his second-floor apartment in a magnificent new complex of buildings at 5 (now 18) Inselstraße, where he had been living since his marriage on September 12, 1840 (the building has now been successfully restored to all its former glory, inviting visitors to explore the rooms once occupied by the couple).

On their arrival in Dresden, they were delighted by the "beautiful Elbe with its vineyards to one side," Clara wrote in their marriage diary, prompting Schumann to describe his wife as an ideal "traveling companion" and "companion in life," "willing, cheerful, solicitous, and always kind and loving."[4] The marriage diary that they jointly kept from the day on which they married until the end of their visit to Russia in late March 1844 reflects an aim that Schumann had expressed as early as 1839: "Posterity shall see us entirely as a single heart and soul."[5]

In the light of this aim, it is noteworthy that the couple occasionally aired their disagreements in the pages of their diary. They had been married for less than two weeks when Clara noted without further ado: "It's bad that Robert can hear me in his room when I'm playing, so that I can't work during the morning, which is the best time for serious study."[6] But the desire on the couple's part to spare each other's feelings was far more powerful. And so we find Schumann — less and less evident as a diarist — summing up the forty-fifth to forty-seventh weeks of their first year of marriage: "Soon it will be the fifty-second week! What do you think, little Klara [sic]? Do you still like being married? I do — pretty much. We'll always stick together."[7] The phrase "pretty much" was no doubt a comic understatement.

Clara was even more anxious than her husband to keep things on an even keel, a point that she addressed in her very next entry:

I've been feeling really quite dreadful during the last three days! I don't seem to be making any headway at all, and so Robert has to show me some consideration. My most heartfelt prayer to God is that He should never take my Robert away from me — that would be the saddest thing that I could imagine! — I still need lots of time to show Robert all the love that I feel for him — it really is quite infinite![8]

By then Clara was heavily pregnant and needed help herself, but she was still capable of noting that "Robert is so loving and kind, and never looks cross, even when I complain that he's making things too easy for me."[9] This is as good a time as any to ask the obligatory question of whether theirs was a happy marriage.

Even asking the question necessarily means bringing to the discussion our own understanding of what a happy marriage involves. Following Schumann's death, commentators spent the next century hymning an "ideal marriage between two artists." This was undoubtedly true when seen from the standpoint of a man evidently wanting an artist at his side: he could scarcely have done better than Clara Wieck. Familiar with his work from an early age, she was his interpreter, friend, and helpmate all in one. Before and during their marriage she played his piano music whenever it seemed appropriate to do so. The piano music that she studied also served to inspire her husband: they regularly worked through Bach's *The Well-Tempered Clavier*, and even as late as 1845 they were still studying counterpoint together.

Clara was just as impatient as Schumann before the completion of each new composition and prior to its publication would work through every one of his pieces that was written for the piano, encouraging him wherever she could and admiring him as a composer to the point of denying her own abilities in that field. How would he have survived if his genius had not been flattered in this way? And then there were the countless daily chores bound up with their lives as artists: Clara not only worked as an arranger and a copyist but also acted as intermediary between her husband, who was becoming increasingly afraid of contact and conflicts with the outside world, and the ensembles that he had to direct. We shall return to this point in due course.

But how does this "ideal marriage between artists" seem when looked at from Clara's point of view? She clearly played second fiddle, or, to put it another way, in spite of the seven children that she had to bring up, she would undoubtedly have been able to write more music in a more uninhibited way and certainly would have been able to practice more and give more concerts and recitals if she had not had to worry about her husband. On the other hand, Schumann provided her with innumerable artistic ideas, inspiring her and encouraging her to compose.

It was Schumann's idea, for example, to collaborate with Clara on a volume of songs based on poems from Rückert's *Liebesfrühling* (Love's spring), a volume that appeared in print in September 1841. Among Clara's contributions to it is the magnificent setting of "Er ist gekommen in Sturm und Regen." Schumann, too, was highly complimentary about her work. The fact that he declined to include one of her four Rückert settings in the volume had a plausible explanation: presumably the piece was difficult to accommodate within a cycle planned in the form of a dialogue.[10] If we accept this line of argument, then we may also dismiss the recent claim that Schumann could not abide the poem because it failed to reflect his own aesthetic outlook as a lieder composer. While no one would contest the right of the author of *Die andere Clara Schumann* (The other Clara Schumann) to advance such a view, it is impossible to uphold the same writer's unsubstantiated claim that Schumann also removed Clara's song "Er ist gekommen in Sturm und Regen" from their joint collection.[11] This can scarcely be explained as a simple error of fact but is indicative, rather, of the general tendency to give Schumann a raw deal. As such, this raises a further point.

The fact that women composers found life more difficult than their male counterparts in the nineteenth and early twentieth centuries is beyond doubt—Fanny Hensel and Alma Mahler both had a good deal to say on the subject. But whereas Fanny Hensel was kept on a tight rein by her brother and Alma Mahler shocked her husband by telling him that she wanted to write music of her own, we have already seen that Schumann responded with warmth and sincerity to his wife's compositional ambitions. The situation for married artists during this period is clear from the case of the famous soprano Henriette Sontag, who had to abandon the public arena in 1830 and spend the next nineteen years in retirement when it became known that she had married the Sardinian diplomat Count Carlo Rossi. In spite of her seven children, Clara Schumann was in a far more enviable position with her "artists' marriage" to Schumann.

Our present concern, however, is not to play one female artist's career against that of another but to ask if the Schumanns' was a happy marriage. For a difficult man like Schumann, it was no doubt the best solution, and the same was true on a private, personal level—at least to the extent that it is possible to separate man and artist. While it is true that during their engagement he had expressed the wish that Clara should abandon her career and that during their years of marriage he suffered a good deal from his marginal status during her concert tours, it is also the case that there were few things in his life that did not cause him sufferings of one kind or another. It is no accident, therefore, that even as late as September 1852 he wrote to his friend Johann Verhulst in The Hague: "I was pleased to find you as sprightly as of old. Unfortunately, the same cannot be said of me! Perhaps kind spirits will restore me to my former state. I was also pleased to find that you've won for yourself such a dear wife. In that respect we share the same happy lot."[12]

Regardless of the vicissitudes that beset Schumann's marriage and the many psychological crises that did not make married life any easier, we may well be disposed to take this last remark seriously. A handful of writers with an interest in depth psychology have claimed that the couple grew apart during their later years together, although I myself am reluctant to trace such a curve on the basis of the surviving evidence. What seems to me to be more important is the fact that both Schumann and Clara remained convinced from first to last that they were destined for one another.

Clara herself undoubtedly imagined that marriage would be easier than it turned out to be. But, however unfashionable it may be to say this today, there are some marriage partners who do not blame each other for any problems that may arise but prefer to see those difficulties as a part of the fate that they have to deal with together—not that this should prevent us from admiring the resolve that Clara Schumann brought to her marriage and, indeed, to the remainder of her long life.

Particularly remarkable is the moral rigor that Schumann and Clara displayed in demanding of themselves and of each other that they should both lead blameless lives: loving, faithful, enthusiastic, conscious of their duties, hardworking, thrifty, and successful. They were both keen that Schumann should hold a reputable post and that Clara's concerts should be seen as purely in the service of art; as such, their wishes were understandable in the context of their marriage's prehistory, but there was still something almost compulsive about this desire. As for the expense of leading their chosen lives, they sometimes seem to have been more afraid of financial problems than their actual situation gave them cause to be. On a subliminal level they took their cue from the upper-middle-class Mendelssohns and Hensels, two families who seemed to have everything in superabundance and whose everyday lives appeared to run like clockwork.

The constant pressure they placed on themselves is typical of the lower middle classes, but as far as Schumann's music and art in general were concerned, this acted more as a stimulus than as an inhibiting factor. It pleased him to be regarded as a man of action who professionally speaking was abreast of his times and was contributing to an art that he increasingly regarded as quintessentially German. And not least of the virtues of the German artist was tireless industry. He was proud to think that he possessed this quality. If ever he lacked creative ideas as a composer, he could at least write fugues.

But let us return to the Schumanns' first year of marriage. Their lives in the Inselstraße in Leipzig were comfortably middle class. They had a female cook and a chambermaid, although Clara still found herself performing unusual housewifely tasks—during her second week of marriage she describes a supper party in her marriage diary attended by Julius and Emilie Carl, Moritz Emil Reuter, and Ernst Ferdinand Wenzel: "All my anxieties as a housewife robbed me of my appetite, making me fear that the guests would not like the food or that there wouldn't be enough to go round."[13] Schumann himself had reported his delight only a few paragraphs earlier: "First course. Suspense on the faces of the participants. It tasted excellent. [. . .] My Clara is showing every sign of becoming a charming hostess."[14]

Neither initially nor later was there any shortage of housekeeping money, with the result that for the most part Schumann was able to overcome his father-in-law's fears: between 1840 and 1848 he earned between 300 and 600 thalers a year. This was no mean sum. Even so, he had good reason to complain in 1843 that "we are spending more than we're earning."[15] He had to draw on the capital accruing to him from various legacies but was pleased that the couple's visit to Russia, initially undertaken with a distinct lack of enthusiasm, netted a profit of 2,300 thalers. And to Schumann's credit it may be noted that between 1849 and 1853, his income from his compositions rose from 1,300 to 1,900 thalers per annum. At least during his years in Düsseldorf from 1850 to 1854 he was — materially speaking — remarkably successful.

Nevertheless, he needed his annual Düsseldorf salary of 750 thalers to support his large family in the style appropriate to his social standing.[16] When she was seventeen, Clara had told her admirer in no uncertain terms:

> There's one thing I have to tell you — namely, that I cannot be yours until
> circumstances are completely different. I don't want horses and I don't
> want diamonds, I'm happy to be your possession, but I do want to lead a
> life free from care and I know that I wouldn't be happy if I were unable to
> continue working in the field of art — and as for worries about food, no, that
> would be insufferable. I need a lot, and I can see that a lot is needed to lead a
> respectable life.[17]

As far as the financial aspect of these demands was concerned, Schumann was for the most part able to meet them, even though he suspected — perhaps correctly — that the spirit of Friedrich Wieck lay behind them.[18] And to the extent that Clara was obliged to help out, she was undoubtedly pleased to be able to contribute to the family finances by continuing her professional career as a pianist during her years of marriage.

There was certainly plenty for the newlywed Schumann to do. He continued — albeit increasingly reluctantly — to edit his *Neue Zeitschrift*; he took a lively interest in the musical scene in Leipzig; and he applauded his wife when she took part in a performance of Bach's Triple Concerto at the city's Gewandhaus at a soirée organized by Mendelssohn. He also maintained contact with musicians and music lovers, and together with Clara he kept an open house — so much so that it was not long before he was complaining about the "constant interruptions from visitors."[19] He went on tour with Clara and, back at home, he read to her from Rückert's great poem in *terza rima, Edelstein und Perle* (Precious stone and pearl). He also explained Bach's fugues to her. Above all, however, he composed.

By the end of January 1841 he had largely abandoned the world of lieder in order to concentrate on large-scale orchestral works. His first numbered symphony — the *Spring* Symphony in B-flat Major op. 38 — was sketched in the incredibly short space of only four days, but since he still had little experience of instrumentation, it took him rather longer to complete the full orchestral score. Even so, the work received its first performance at the Gewandhaus on March 31, when Mendelssohn conducted from the manuscript score. The concert was mounted as a fundraiser for the orchestra's pension fund and was organized by Clara, who also played the second and third movements of Chopin's Piano Concerto in F Minor. The performances were enthusiastically received by the audience and proved a triumph for the newlywed couple.

Friedrich Wieck is said to have called the *Spring* Symphony a "Symphony of Contradictions," by which he meant that Schumann had written it expressly to contradict him.[20] There may be a grain of truth in this, although few individuals could flaunt a symphony in their father-in-law's face as a token of their rebellion. Conversely, Schumann had good reasons for dedicating the work to King Friedrich August II of Saxony. Only major works are inscribed to potentates — works that can be performed by a court orchestra and that can ideally commend their composer as a candidate for the post of Kapellmeister. (Of course, Schumann's chances of acceding to such a post in Dresden were poor, for Wagner was just beginning his reign in the city, and Mendelssohn had a better hand.)

Be that as it may, Schumann was now resolved to add to his reputation and improve his income by writing large-scale works. Remarkably, he not only aspired to doing so, he actually achieved his aim and wrote several large-scale orchestral works within the space of a year. At the risk of exaggeration, one could argue that Brahms took fourteen years to write his first symphony, which, when it finally appeared, seemed to be carved in stone. Schumann's First Symphony, conversely, creates a more carefree, optimistic, and youthful impression in keeping with the opening line of a poem by Adolf Böttger that provides the piece with its alternative title: "Im Tale blüht der Frühling auf" (In vale and valley spring has come). The meter of the opening line additionally echoes that of the symphony's opening motif.

Schumann was right to claim that this work was "born in an ardent hour."[21] Who would have thought him capable of producing such a positive, large-scale piece that in many respects strikes an almost affirmative note? If he had died before having written it, psychologists interested in the creative process would undoubtedly have had no difficulty in claiming that in the light of his unstable psychiatric state he would never have been able to compose such a work. But the symphony exists, and it may serve as a warning — not as a disincentive to seek to understand Schumann's "rare states of mind" but as a reminder of the dangers of thinking that we know it all.

In the wake of his First Symphony, Schumann wrote his Overture, Scherzo, and Finale op. 52, his Piano Fantasy in A Minor, which he later expanded and turned into his Piano Concerto in A Minor op. 54 (see Intermezzo V), and the first version of his D Minor Symphony, which later became his Fourth Symphony op. 120. A first opus of another kind, the Schumanns' first child, Marie, was born at 10:50 on the morning of September 1, 1841, "to the accompaniment of thunder and lightning."[22] Mendelssohn was the child's godfather. At the end of the year the couple traveled to Weimar, where Schumann was able to hear his First Symphony again and Clara performed Mendelssohn's Capriccio for piano and orchestra.

The following year, 1842, was largely given over to chamber music, which is the subject of our next chapter. We may return, therefore, to our account of a typical day in the life of this liberal-minded and cosmopolitan couple. In February they traveled via Oldenburg and Bremen to Hamburg, where Clara gave a recital and Schumann conducted his First Symphony. They then went their separate ways, albeit only briefly. For Clara, it was an opportunity to visit Copenhagen, and although she had considerable scruples about undertaking the trip, it proved a successful venture and contributed a few hundred thalers to the couple's coffers. Schumann meanwhile returned to Leipzig and struck a reflective note in his marriage diary:

> Our separation has brought home to me our curious and difficult situation. Should I neglect my talent in order to serve as your companion on your travels? And you, should you ignore your own talent because I am fettered to my newspaper and to my piano? At a time when you are young & in your prime? We've found a solution: you took a companion with you, & I returned home to our child & to my work. But what will the world say? And so my thoughts torment me.[23]

Schumann even toyed with the idea of taking soundings in America in the hope of finding better conditions for the couple's artistic coexistence. Meanwhile his *Spring* Symphony was continuing to attract attention, and after a further performance in the Gewandhaus Clara noted in their marriage diary: "It went well and again was well received, but the happiness that I feel on hearing a composition by my Robert is something that no one else can know!"[24] Shortly before that, however, she had reported on her "indescribable sadness": "I feel that you no longer love me as you once did, I often feel so clearly that I'm not good enough for you, and when you're affectionate, I sometimes feel that I must ascribe this to your kind heart."[25]

As time went on, Clara continued to fret about her husband's tendency to withdraw from the world, and each time she blamed herself. When she wrote the foregoing lines, she was pregnant with her daughter Elise, who was born on April 25, 1843, at a time when her husband was again working on a large-scale project, the oratorio *Das Paradies und die Peri* (Paradise and the Peri) op. 50. In the process he was approaching his unspoken goal of drawing on all the relevant musical genres while continuing to operate within the classical tradition. And in this he was successful. During his own lifetime, this full-length work was to be his most popular composition after the B-flat Major Symphony. In April 1848 he was even able to note in his diary: "Time of great excitement — the Peri in New York!"[26]

Back in April 1843, the Schumanns received an unexpected visit from Wagner, who was accompanied by the famous soprano Wilhelmine Schröder-Devrient and who, after his lean years in Paris, was keen to establish himself in Saxony, not least by ingratiating himself with the editor of the *Neue Zeitschrift für Musik*. Writing in his autobiography, Wagner recalled his years in Dresden with his antithetical opposite: "We met from time to time while out walking, and to the extent that it was possible to engage in any kind of conversation with this singularly taciturn man, we exchanged views on many a subject of musical interest."[27] Some years later, Schumann reported on a "chance encounter" with Wagner in the Great Park in Dresden: "He has a tremendous gift of gab and is full of oppressive ideas; it's impossible to listen to him for long."[28] In this respect Clara effortlessly outdid her husband: Wagner, she wrote, "never stops talking about himself, he's insufferably arrogant and is for ever laughing in that lachrymose tone of his."[29]

Paradise and the Peri received its first performance in Leipzig on December 4, 1843. The occasion also marked Schumann's successful debut as a conductor. Although there seem to have been complaints about his excessive laissez-faire attitude during the rehearsals, he would have been in full control of the situation where his own music was concerned. In any event, a performance in the Dresden opera house only three weeks later, again under Schumann's direction, garnered much praise from the local press.

The Dresden performance of *Paradise and the Peri* brought with it a conciliatory letter from Friedrich Wieck, who had in the meantime moved to the city:

Dear Schumann,

Tempora mutantur et nos mutamur in eis [Times change, and we ourselves change with them]. We can no longer stand apart in the eyes of Clara
and the world. You too are now a family man — need I say more? [. . .] It is
with joy that your father awaits you in Dresden, Friedrich Wieck.[30]

They met during the Christmas holidays, thereafter maintaining a respectful distance, a development Clara welcomed with considerable relief, while
Schumann himself preferred to remain aloof, bestirring himself only to report
on his own successes.

One such success was a four-month visit to Russia on which the Schumanns
set out in January 1844. Their two infant daughters, Marie and Elise, spent the
period in Schneeberg with Schumann's brother Carl and his wife, Pauline.
They traveled to Berlin by train, and from there they took the mail coach to
the Baltic resorts which, far from being backward and provincial, were notable centers of music. Even in Königsberg (modern Kaliningrad), where Clara
gave two concerts, Schumann was able to report on various points of interest
in his diary.

It is also worth mentioning in passing that it was in Königsberg that Wagner had landed eight years earlier as the husband of the popular actress Minna
Planer, only for his professional career to founder. Recently married, he and
his wife had so many violent scenes that she returned to her native Germany
in the company of an admirer called Dietrich. In the light of such high drama,
the excitements in the Schumanns' lives seem relatively harmless.

The Schumanns left Königsberg and headed for the Baltic and Russia, at
which point their journey acquired an air of improvisation, the only certainty
being that they had arrived in the middle of a grim Russian winter. How good
it would have been if an agent had been waiting to greet them in every new
town or city, guaranteeing in advance that all doors were open to them and
that they would be performing to full houses! By this date, the internationally celebrated, cosmopolitan figure of Mendelssohn had long since managed
to ensure that he was everywhere welcomed with open arms, whereas it was
only in exceptional cases that advance preparations had been made for the
Schumanns. Arrangements formerly made by Wieck now had to be made
by Clara since her husband was repeatedly overcome by misgivings and was
largely ineffectual as an organizer.

In spite of all this, he took a lively interest in the landscape and population
and in local culture and history, so much so, indeed, that initially at least he

kept a travel diary. Here are the entries for February 5 and 6, 1844:

> 4 in the morning from Tilsit [modern Sovetsk] by post horses — crossing
> the [frozen] Neman somewhat frightening — Russian border — border
> Cossack with pistol — Tauroggen [modern Tauragė] — Russian faces,
> Jews, life on sledges — customs director von Wilken — extremely polite
> treatment and rapid dispatch — Kresslowski [an official], clever fellow in
> a simple coat — excellent inn — leave at 10 with the Russian diligence [a
> public stagecoach] — diligence very comfortable inside — deep snow & slow
> progress — terrible lunch — extremely tedious & tiring journey — Lithuanian
> villages — roads very busy — mostly Jews — long caravans of one-horse
> carriages, 3 in the morning, traveling to Mitau [modern Jelgava] — Mitau,
> capital of Courland — 5 in the morning, the weather even colder — arrival
> at Riga — life on the Dvina — magnificent — terrible jostling & shouting in
> the streets — post — more poor arrangements, no one takes any trouble over
> visitors from abroad — looking for somewhere to stay — terrible room in the
> St. Petersburg [Hotel]. Lutzau [a cellist] helps us — returned to the Hôtel
> de Londres — call on Julius Behrens [a Riga businessman, pianist, and
> composer] — excellent cigars — filthy guesthouse.[31]

It is not hard to imagine that the Schumanns' social contacts would have involved a similarly unpredictable and emotionally draining mixture of friendliness and uncouthness, interesting conversations and "intolerable harassment."[32] Meanwhile Clara was drumming up trade on good and bad pianos in shabby and genteel salons, hoping only that her actual concerts would be a success.

Schumann had fallen behindhand with his plans to complete *Paradise and the Peri*, with the result that although their Russian trip had been planned for some time, they were late in setting out and by the time they reached St. Petersburg and Moscow, other virtuosos had already stolen a march on them, leaving local audiences almost oversated. And yet there were also many triumphs and honors to offset the half-filled halls — the latter a problem that every artist has to face. In St. Petersburg Clara appeared at four major concerts and also took part in soirées and evenings of piano quartets with some of the celebrities on the local musical scene, including counts Mateusz and Michał Wielhorski and the director of the imperial court chapel choir, Aleksey Fyodorovich L'vov.

Clara also played for the tsarina in the Winter Palace and was made an honorary member of the St. Petersburg Philharmonic Society, leaving Schumann — understandably — feeling superfluous; all these aristocrats, generals, diplomats, statesmen, and middle-class property owners wanted Clara as the centerpiece of their salons and soirées, leaving Schumann to hover inconspicuously in the background. By now his wife was so used to his bouts of ill humor that they left her unaffected, although there were also occasions of which she sought to play a more conciliatory role, not only performing some of his piano pieces but also lending luster to a performance of his Piano Quintet op. 44. And Schumann himself was able to conduct a performance of his First Symphony at a soirée at the Wielhorksi Palace, which he later described as "a true cathedral of art."[33]

The couple's subsequent visit to Moscow was less brilliant, not least because the concert season was almost over. Even so, Schumann was fascinated by the city, especially the Kremlin, where the Tsar Bell in particular caught his imagination. Nearly twenty feet high, it is thought to be the biggest bell in the world but was so badly damaged by fire while being cast in 1737 that for almost a century it was left in its mold and not removed until 1836, eight years before the Schumanns' visit. The damaged bell was then placed on a plinth on which it still stands in the Kremlin, at its base a fragment the height of a man that has broken off from its mantle.

Fascinated by this tale, Schumann wrote a long poem in largely unrhymed octosyllabic verse titled "The Bell of Ivan Veliki," describing how a famous bell-caster was hoist by the petard of his own vanity when he tried to cast a bell of unprecedented size and beauty for the Ivan Veliki Belfry. The poem's central section tells of the failed attempt to free the bell from its mold:

Nun ist's vollbracht, die Form gefüllt,
Nun kühle sich die gähr'nde Masse,
Die Bilder, die der Künstler schuf
In reiner Treue aufzunehmen.
Und bald in allvereinter Kraft
Rühr'n sich die Hände, Flaschenzug
Und Hebel greifen ineinander.
Von ihrer Stelle, daß sie schwebe,
Die ries'ge Glocke fort zu rücken.
Nun hebt sie sich, der Knopf zuerst
Mit schön gewund'nen Tragebändern —
Doch um des Meisters Sinne dunkelt's,
Das Erz, es deckt ein fahles Grau
Und halb erkenntlich springen die
Gebilde auf der Fläche vor,

Und nun zur Hälfte in die Höh'
Die Glocke weiter aufgezogen —
Ganz nahe des Erlösers Bild.
Es klafft ein Sprung, es fehlt ein Stück,
Und unbeweglich in der Tiefe
Ein Rest bleibt stehn — Entsetzen
Faßt rings das Volk und faßt den Meister.
Und wie er trauernd seine Augen
Abwendet, das Gesicht verhüllt,
Das Schreckliche nicht mehr zu schau'n —
Die Mutter, die im stummen Schmerz
Das todtgeborne Kind betrachtet,
Ihr Antlitz mag nicht schmerzensvoller sein —
Da drängt ein Mann sich im Talar
Zu ihm und spricht:
Du hast versucht, was du nicht solltest,
Mit Heil'gem nied'ren Sinn beschönt:
Nicht Gott ist's, dem du dienen wolltest,
Der Eitelkeit hast du gefrönt:
So sei dein Nam' fortan verhöhnt,
Du, tausend And'ren gleich vergessen.
Soll Dir ein Werk mit Gott gelingen,
Lern' erst zur Demuth dich bezwingen.
Und schweigend hört's der Künstler an,
Und wie die Menge sich verlor,
Verlor er mit sich im Gedränge.[34]

[It's finished now, the mold is filled, / Now let the yeasting liquid cool / And reproduce the pictures that / The artist made so true to life. / And then with one accord all hands / Bestir themselves, and pulley blocks / And levers are engaged to hoist / The massive bell and lift it up / Until it seems to float in space. / And now it rises up, the top / Emerges first, beribboned — but / The master's senses start to reel: / The metal's veiled in pallid gray, / The letters on the surface seem / Inchoate and too vague to read. / By now the bell is raised to half / Its massive height and rests quite close / To where our Savior's likeness hangs. / A crack appears, a piece falls off, / A section, motionless, remains / Embedded in the mold. Alarm / Transfixes all, the Master too. / And as he turns his eyes away / In sadness, covering his face, / The better to avoid the sight — / No mother racked by silent grief / As she beholds her stillborn child / Could be as wrought by pain as he — / A robèd figure's forced his way / To him and speaks the words: / "You tried to do what no man ought— /It was with baseness that you sought/To justify a sacred thought./It was not God you served but naught/Save your own vanity. And so/Your name shall henceforth be accursed,/Like countless others that you know./If God shall bless your work, then first/You have to learn humility."/The artist silently gave ear,/And as the crowd dispersed, he too / Was lost among the milling throng.]

It is possible that Schumann saw this poem as the basis of a future composition, for in May 1844 we find him writing to his father-in-law: "For the present, a poetic greeting from Moscow—I don't trust myself to hand it to you in person. It is hidden music as there was no time or leisure for composition."[35] And until such time as new material presents itself, we may not go far wrong in assuming that Schumann found the hubris motif not in Russian legends but in his own imagination.

In any event, the subject fascinated him to such an extent that while he was in Moscow he also wrote a poem about Napoleon's hubristic plan to conquer Russia. A few years later he explored an identical theme in his choral ballad *Das Glück von Edenhall* (The good fortune of Edenhall) op. 143, based on a poem by Ludwig Uhland. On this occasion the starting point was not a cracked bell but a priceless piece of glass on which the weal and woe of an aristocratic family hangs. In a fit of high spirits, the young lord breaks it, and with that his rule comes to an end.

The events just described are among the minor miracles in Schumann's life and works: although he often felt unwell in Moscow and suffered attacks of dizziness that sometimes left him unable to see, he was fond of walking in the grounds of the Kremlin and would "return home utterly enchanted."[36] He turned the tale of the Tsar Bell into a legend about human hubris, a theme he also explored with reference to Napoleon. Although he did not work straightaway on the music that was "hidden" in his poem, he returned to the subject nine years later in the political context of the revolutions of 1848. Now everything came together—panic attacks and the thrill of discovery, crises of self-esteem and creative enthusiasm, feelings of horror and the power of the imagination, the fear of hubris and confidence in his own artistic abilities. What finally emerged was a work independent of its prehistory and yet permeated by that same past history.

In Moscow, the Schumanns attended a wearisomely lengthy Russian Orthodox service with "terrible singing."[37] Clara also played at an orphanage, "where everything was immaculate."[38] They then returned to St. Petersburg, where Schumann noted in his marriage diary on a rainy day in May:

In the morning we went to the Zoological Museum with Madame Henselt and Doctor Schulz. We got into a cab, but Madame Henselt and Dr. Schulz preferred to cross the Neva by boat, when they were surprised by a terrible downpour. We met up again at the Museum.[39]

This diary entry makes the museum visit sound harmless, but it appears from a letter that the aforementioned Dr. Georg von Schulz wrote to his mother that behind it lay a miniature drama:

> Our tour of the city ended, unfortunately, on a discordant note. I had suggested that we might visit the imperial vault in the Cathedral of Saints Peter and Paul, but Schumann could not be persuaded by his wife's encouragements and entreaties to climb into the little boat that was to take us across the Neva to the island fortress. And so we had to abandon the idea. The most remarkable thing of all was that from then on Schumann became monosyllabic and very bad-tempered. As a doctor I was strangely moved by this expression of an almost morbid fear.[40]

From St. Petersburg they traveled by steamship to Swinemünde (modern Świnoujście), then by mail coach to Leipzig and finally went to collect their children in Schneeberg. In his letter thanking his brother, Schumann wrote from Leipzig on June 3, 1844:

> Marie kept wanting to return "to Schneeberg;" she really didn't seem to know where she actually lived. Here the children were received in triumph by half the Inselstraße; they had decorated their little desk with flowers and presents; the little ones enjoyed themselves enormously, just as everyone was delighted by them, by their cheerful and attractive appearance and behavior.[41]

At the beginning of 1844 Schumann left his study in Leipzig only with great reluctance, yet writing retrospectively about his trip to Russia, he was able to describe it as "not without its exertions, but interesting from start to finish."[42] After all, he had managed to make a virtue of a necessity and had mobilized his interest in the country's history and people. On one occasion, he even toyed with the idea of settling in Moscow. He may well have recalled this idea when, on his return to Leipzig, he took out his pencil sketch of the Kremlin. It is his only surviving drawing outside his travel diaries.

Schumann's pen drawing of the Kremlin, April or May 1844.
(Photograph courtesy of the Robert Schumann Museum, Zwickau.)

The Magic of Allusions

A brief tutti chord in the full orchestra serves as the starting pistol for three bars of cascading quarter- and eighth-notes in the piano. As such, this passage harkens back to the traditional opening gesture of a baroque overture, while the interval of a minor second around which the passage is centered has always been associated with the idea of a sigh. Eight bars of a lyrical first subject are entrusted to the woodwinds and horns, after which the piano adds a further eight bars of its own to produce a sixteen-bar period. Far from pausing to rest, the composer then continues to spin out the musical argument in a passage in which the piano's baritone register assumes the lead, while accompanied by filigree quintuplets in the right hand. But this is not just *Fortspinnung* in the sense defined by Wilhelm Fischer: it is also an "answer" with its own thematic significance. The "answer" expands to the accompaniment of a growing involvement of the orchestra to which the piano briefly abandons the melodic line, itself assuming the function of a bass. And so the musical argument proceeds, intricately interwoven, until a liberating six-four chord on G provides the first subject with a platform on which to build in the key of C major: the heavens appear to stand open before us.

It is impossible within the space available to describe all the musical and metrical subtleties that make this movement what it is: a piano-symphonic miracle occupying a position between Beethoven and Brahms. And if *their* concertos are more solid in form and character, then Schumann's undoubtedly possesses a greater sense of poetry. In any discussion of nineteenth-century works still indebted to the earlier tradition, the use of terms such as "opening ritornello," "solo exposition," "first subject-group," "bridge passage," "second subject-group," "exposition," "development section," and "recapitulation" is already problematical, but in Schumann's case it amounts

The opening bars of the Concerto for the Pianoforte (1841), the forerunner of the opening movement of the Piano Concerto in A Minor op. 54. (Photograph courtesy of the Heinrich Heine Institute of the Regional Capital of Düsseldorf.)

to an insult. The miracle of the Piano Fantasy in A Minor — only later turned into the opening movement of Piano Concerto op. 54 — is that it manages to escape from the rules that inform such works and does so, moreover, with sovereign ease. While avoiding impressionist diffuseness, this fantasy refuses to be pinned down to any of the usual categories of musical form but demands to be judged in terms of its narrative qualities.

Narrativity does not mean that Schumann is telling a story here. After all, he had no time for the Lisztian symphonic poem. What it does mean is that the floodtide of the music is like the flow of a narrative. This has nothing to do with symmetry. In the case of a real river, too, there is a constant shift between stronger and weaker currents, between surging waves and tiny eddies, and between passages that are now calm, now more agitated, quite apart from the changing landscape on the riverbank. But the simile does throw light on the procedures of a composer who allows himself to be carried along by an initial idea as if it were the subject of a conversation maintained over an entire movement. The sense is not that of a motific development planned in advance, but of a willingness to go where the spirit takes him.

Even so, this willingness to be driven in disparate directions is by no means lacking in a plan, a point that becomes clear when the movement reaches its slow middle section, an Andante espressivo. No matter how brief it may be, this is the spiritual heart of the piece. We are in A-flat major, light-years away from the opening key; and the main idea now appears in a gently rocking 6/4 meter, albeit foreshortened to one and a half bars. This type of narrative mode was much favored by Schumann — at the equivalent place in the C Major Fantasy op. 17 he added the marking "In the Tone of a Legend." It emerges even more forcefully from the original version of the piece, even if the surviving evidence allows us to reconstruct this version only in part. Here a thunderous transitional passage lasting twenty-two bars in missing, Schumann having decided to introduce it only in the definitive version of the three-movement concerto. Only by the later date had he begun to take a greater interest in structural stability.

For unbiased listeners, narrativity means immersing ourselves in a gripping and nuanced performance whose train of ideas may not all be ultimately intelligible — nor is there any obligation on us to understand them — but whose ideas convince us through their charm and organic flow. And those of us who listen to the Piano Fantasy against the background of our knowledge of the Schumanns' lives will hear in it a regular story that we can leaf through as if it were a book.

The story begins with Schumann writing his A Minor Fantasy in response to a piano concerto in the same key that Clara had written as her op. 7 between her thirteenth and seventeenth birthdays. Schumann had helped her with the instrumentation of its final movement and in his own piece he took over a motif from the earlier work. But with the exception of this reminiscence, his fantasy is in fact more of a rejoinder to Clara's op. 7. Although the skill with which the young artist was able to write a virtuoso concerto tailored to existing models deserves our admiration, when compared with the specific magic of Schumann's composition, her concerto seems no more than an empty stage designed to display her own talents.

Clara would have been the last person to disagree with this assessment of the two works, and she never again played her own piano concerto after she married Schumann. By way of compensation, Schumann honored her in his own composition: the motif of a descending third, C–B–A–A, which permeates his fantasy from beginning to end, is a coded version of Chiara, the name Clara was given as a member of the League of David. Even more significantly, a sketch has recently come to light for a duet based on a poem by Friedrich Rückert. The woman begins: "I am your tree, O gardener, whose faithfulness maintains me in love's care and keeping." To which the man replies: "I am your gardener, O tree of faithfulness, I feel no jealous desire for any other happiness."[1] This duet was originally intended for *Liebesfrühling* op. 37, a collaboration between husband and wife, but in the end it was omitted as the main idea had in the meantime found a niche for itself in the Piano Fantasy as the musical motif of the central Andante espressivo. First stated by the piano before being taken up by the clarinet, where it is transposed by the same interval of a second as that found in the duet, this motif can be underlaid with the words "Ich bin dein Baum, o Gärtner, dessen Treue" (I am your tree, O gardener, whose faithfulness . . .). Both pieces — the original sketch for the duet and the Andante espressivo of the Piano Fantasy — are in 3/4 time. And both are in A-flat major. It is as if Schumann regarded this key as somehow off limits and sacrosanct "in order to compose a concerto in A minor around it."[2]

But there is even more to this "magic of allusions": from the musical quotation of "You are my tree," a journey takes us back in time to a passage in A-flat major in Beethoven's *Fidelio* — namely, the opening line of Florestan's aria, "In des Lebens Frühlingstagen," which goes on to describe his vision of his wife, Leonore, coming to console him in the guise of an angel. Throughout the difficult years of their engagement, Schumann and Clara had seen themselves in the roles of Florestan and Fidelio/Leonore: on November 29, 1837, for example, Schumann had written to her from Vienna: "I kiss you with heartfelt love. — Adieu, my Fidelio in the form of Julius Kraus. Be faithful to me as Leonore was to her Florestan."[3] (Julius Kraus was the name that Clara used to collect her post, turning herself into a man in the same way that Leonore had done when assuming the identity of Fidelio.)

Peter Gülke's comment that Schumann's music is all about Clara[4] applies with particular force to the Piano Fantasy in A Minor, which also contains allusions to Clara's *Soirées musicales* op. 6 and to her Romance op. 11, no. 2, as well as to the *Grande sonate* op. 3 by Ludwig Schuncke, a composer with whom Schumann was friendly until his premature death in 1834.[5] And Schumann also plays with different layers of time: when the original form of the opening motif is "unveiled" in the Andante espressivo, it turns out that Schumann was working toward this moment as a pointer to the past — namely, as a reference to Beethoven and to a fateful period in the couple's lives.

We do not need to know all of this in order to love Schumann's Piano Fantasy, but there is no doubt that we can love it even more if we are aware of this background, for these little secrets are not extrinsic to the work but are so intricately interwoven with it that they represent a vital thread. As a composer of piano concertos, Schumann cannot be compared with Beethoven or Brahms, both of whom set out from a basic conceptual structure that imposes a sense of order on the individual musical ideas. Rather, Schumann shares with other romantic artists the belief that a work's raw material is too impoverished to allow him to achieve his aim, which is to present his listener with a notion of the transcendental. Against this background romantic artists were constantly reflecting on ways of transcending both material reality and their own temporality in an attempt to reach beyond themselves.[6]

But this will work only if the artist reflects on his or her own existence and seeks to channel the narrative flow along lines that are based on that life. To Beethoven and Brahms, this would have seemed hubristic. For them, the essence of a piano concerto was to be found in the interplay between orchestra and soloist, the former representing the "public" sphere, the latter its "private" equivalent. Together they constitute an example of social order. Schumann subverts this idea, for his thinking is entirely grounded in the piano, which incorporates the orchestra to the extent that it results in a single body of sound — *his* body of sound. In doing so he was following a course that he had already charted two years earlier in his concerto movement in D minor — albeit — to quote Claudia Macdonald — "in a very different guise."[7]

If Liszt's witticism is true when he claimed that Schumann had written a "concerto without a piano," then this might be seen as a compliment. (Liszt was, of course, also alluding to Schumann's *Concert sans orchestre* op. 14.) The resultant work is not a concerto for a keyboard virtuoso but one in which the omnipresent sound of the piano merges with that of the orchestra to create a single entity — it was in this sense that the composer hoped to merge with his interpreter, Clara, who even helped him in writing out the score.

The interpreter in question was not only an accomplished virtuoso but also a profoundly artistic woman, and so she was fully able to judge what her husband had produced after he had pondered the question at length and after a complex compositional process — and in every case he had discussed these matters with her. Only someone who is not only a feminist but also an artist can say what happiness she must have felt on seeing the finished work. It is a happiness she must have continued to feel on every subsequent occasion when she performed it.

At the time, critics praised the work for its "vigor and impassioned strength" and spoke of "interiority and truth of feeling." The most famous of them, Eduard Hanslick, compared the A-flat major episode with a "little lake, as bright as a mirror, between dark rocks and trees."[8] Such images do not provide us with an explanation but are like a love letter sent to the work in question. And what is there that is more beautiful than a love letter? The more infrequently we write them in real life, the more willingly we address them to music.

Lithograph of Schumann, after a portrait painted by the distinguished portraitist Eduard Kaiser in Vienna in January 1847, during a visit to the city by the composer and his wife. "During the morning sittings for Kaiser," we read in their housekeeping book for January 13, 1847. In the event, it was not until some ten years later that lithographs were prepared from his portrait at the request of the Viennese art dealer Friedrich Paterno. Conversely, a double portrait of Schumann and Clara that was also painted by Kaiser in 1847 appeared on the market in the form of a lithograph later that same year. (Photograph courtesy of the Robert Schumann Museum, Zwickau.)

CHAPTER 8

Schumann as a Public Figure in the Years before the March Revolution of 1848

What one would like to call Schumann's secret idea — namely, the desire to permeate classical forms with romanticism or, if one prefers, to capture the spirit of romanticism within a classical circle.

Franz Liszt in his article "Robert Schumann" for the *Neue Zeitschrift für Musik*, 1855[1]

Within the framework of his own aesthetic outlook, Liszt's comment on Schumann was meant to be more skeptical than it sounds when quoted out of context. However well disposed he may have been toward him as a person, he doubted if, of all his contemporaries, Schumann was the one who would be capable of squaring the circle, as it were. Instead, he preferred to privilege his own symphonic poems and Wagner's music dramas, placing them at the top of his agenda. For him, there was ultimately only one question: who was the worthy successor of the "classical" Beethoven, the giant forever looking over his successors' shoulders? Was it the champions of "absolute" music or the New Germans who banked on the clarity of extra-musical programs or on the Wagnerian total artwork?

Both "parties" — and the term is entirely legitimate from the 1850s onward — could adduce valid arguments of their own. There was a Beethoven who turned the symphony's traditional four-movement form into the yardstick by which everything else was measured and who was unimpressed by the question of whether it was possible to tell a credible story within the straitjacket of this four-movement form. This Beethoven not only set store by the structural force that lay within a symphony's four different types of movement but, more generally, he believed that the "meaning" of a work was revealed above all by the immanent motific and thematic processes that the composer set in motion and guided through the work. More than any other composer, it was Brahms who was heir to this particular Beethoven — no matter what scruples he may have felt at assuming that role.

By contrast, the "New German" party celebrated Beethoven as an artist who traded in ideas and whose symphonies and piano sonatas invariably revealed that music not only consists of what Hanslick termed "forms animated by musical sounds" but conveyed emotions, moods, and ethical attitudes that could assume highly concrete forms, notably in the case of Prometheus/Napoleon in the *Eroica*, the question of "fate" in the Fifth, and the "Awakening of Feelings of Joy on Arriving in the Countryside" in the *Pastoral* Symphony. With his final symphony — the Ninth — Beethoven, or so the New Germans triumphantly declared, argued that ideas previously discernible only indirectly in music could now be declaimed with greater clarity. It was no longer sufficient to revel in "joy" in purely orchestral sounds, no longer enough for all men to become brothers against the background of those sounds. No, the word alone could offer total clarity.

Liszt and Wagner were determined that even if they had to fight their battles independently, they would ultimately triumph together and fall heir to Beethoven's mantle. Liszt used words to sketch out "programs" for symphonic poems such as *Mazeppa* and *Prometheus*, but after his initial successes he encountered difficulties in this field, and his heroic poems failed to recreate the impression of the epic songs on which they were modeled. Wagner was more successful in this regard. By banking on an ancient theatrical tradition he created the total artwork in which the principal medium was music, with its immediate appeal to the emotions, while the libretto — or "poem," as Wagner liked to call it — carried the action forward and ensured that the myth acquired a visual form onstage.

And it is myth that is the keyword in terms of the factional conflict between the two parties — a conflict that was political in the wider sense of the term. The question was no longer who was composing the more beautiful music but who had the better concept for positioning music within society. Writing in the wake of Kant and Schiller, the adherents of the theory of "absolute" music, who — at the risk of oversimplification — may be placed in the conservative camp, drew a distinction between the "realm of necessity" and the "realm of freedom." Whereas the material and, specifically, the economic constraints that obtained in the "realm of necessity" could be dismantled only piecemeal at best, art could present the world with a "realm of freedom" in which people could do as they liked—assuming that art demanded no influence on the "realm of necessity."

But it was precisely this influence that the members of the progressive "New German school" demanded for themselves. Since his youth, Liszt had been a Saint-Simonian and a social revolutionary whose virtuosic piano piece *Lyon* commemorated an uprising by that city's silk weavers in 1831, a revolt that had had to be put down by twenty thousand government soldiers. Although his symphonic poems were written almost twenty years later in neoclassical Weimar, they are no less politically engaged. Liszt was even willing to pay the price of being the lesser composer if in the process he was able to proclaim ideas of humanity, dignity, and heroism that he was determined should not remain in the "realm of freedom" but should prepare for a revolution in the "realm of necessity."

It is no wonder, then, that Liszt provided shelter for Wagner when the latter fled to Weimar after his active involvement in the failed revolution in Dresden in May 1849. By that date only a fraction of the libretto of the *Ring* had been completed, but Liszt nevertheless must have suspected what was at stake for his future son-in-law: Wagner was throwing down a tremendous challenge to the ruling classes, which he still needed to implement his ideas: "Not like this," he hurled in their faces. When money and power were all that counted, then society was doomed to perish.

"Prophets to the right and prophets to the left, the child of the world in the middle"—Goethe's lines from 1774 could well be applied to the Schumann of the 1840s. Goethe certainly did not want to present himself as a nonbeliever when describing himself in this way, and it would be equally wrong of us to use this characterization to deny Schumann all his ideals. Even so, these ideals were not set in stone. The hypothetical alternatives of "art must remain what it always was" and "art must achieve something completely different" could be offset with a third artistic credo: "the artist must remain true to himself."

How could Schumann hope to achieve this aim when in 1841 he suddenly switched from writing piano pieces and songs to symphonic works, a switch from works that were felt to be highly "subjective" to others which were committed to "objectivity" and universal intelligibility not least because they were intended to be performed in public? Critics were often only half-hearted in their praise, since they felt that he had failed to heed their demand that "the composer's self must assume a form of expression in which others can instantly recognize their own selves."[2] But Schumann did not care to play off the subjective against the objective; for him, all genres must be permeated by a musical poetry for which the composer took personal responsibility — even at the risk of not being universally understood.

The significance of this is immediately clear from Schumann's First Symphony, in which he sensibly took his cue neither from the formal rigor of a Beethoven symphony nor from the formal liberties of Berlioz's *Symphonie Fantastique*. Instead, his guardian angel ensured that he was introduced just in time to Schubert's *Great* C Major Symphony, in which he found all that he needed. First and foremost he discovered a poetic motto that placed its seal on the symphony as a whole; that, at least, is how Schumann interpreted the horn call with which Schubert had launched his own symphony. And in that spirit he refashioned it as his own motto and did so in such a way that — as we have noted — it can be sung to the words "Im Tale blüht der Frühling auf." But Schumann also learned from Schubert's ingenious ability to write in a manner that was both formally fixed and novelistically free. Finally, he allowed himself to be inspired by Schubert's musical poetry: "Here there is not only a masterful musical technique but also life in every fiber, the most subtly shaded colors, significance everywhere, the keenest expression on points of detail, and the whole work imbued with a romanticism familiar from many other works by Schubert."[3]

Even though Schumann had described himself in his youth as a "brave epigone,"[4] it seems inappropriate to judge his First Symphony in B-flat Major by the standards of Schubert's C Major Symphony. Nonetheless, the work was such a success with its early audiences that between 1841 and 1852 he was able to record no fewer than forty-three performances on the front endpaper of his autograph copy of the score. Even so, there is an evident sense of effort in his handling of large-scale form that can be discerned behind the ease with which he explores the theme of spring. This was bound up, of course, with the symphonic situation at this time — we find much the same in Mendelssohn's *Italian* Symphony, a work which in spite of its various revisions its composer refused to publish.

Fired by the success of his First Symphony, Schumann followed it up with three further large-scale orchestral works between April and September 1841 — an astonishingly short space of time. These were his Overture, Scherzo, and Finale op. 52; the A Minor Piano Fantasy described in detail in Intermezzo V; and a second symphony which, following a series of revisions, became the Fourth Symphony in D Minor op. 120. In the case of the op. 52, writers have found it difficult to resist the temptation to indulge in a note of mockery by quoting a passage from Schumann's *Neue Zeitschrift* of July 1839:

For the most part the newer symphonies have sunk to the level of overtures, especially their opening movements; the slow movements are there only because they cannot be allowed to go missing; the scherzos are scherzos in name alone; and the final movements have no idea what the earlier ones contained.[5]

Certainly, the Overture, Scherzo, and Finale leaves an ambivalent impression, even though Schumann had originally planned it as a relatively lightweight "sinfonietta." The poetic idea implied by the opening motto is not carried through; and the orchestral fireworks set off especially in the Finale remain conventional. Schumann himself was, of course, satisfied and so it was with a correspondingly positive feeling that he moved on to one of the high points of his career as a composer: the Fantasy in A Minor. After that there was to be another major symphony, and in order to avoid the impression of randomness that the sequence of movements of the Sinfonietta op. 52 might have left, he fell back on a device that was then becoming fashionable and allowed the movements to pass into each other without a break. In the opening movement, moreover, he dispensed with a recapitulation, ensuring that the transition to the second movement could be as informal as possible. The result is a work that can legitimately be described as a symphonic fantasy, a description that Schumann in fact envisaged for the revised version, even though this version is less deserving of such an appellation. True, both versions contain long sections of a wildly impassioned or melancholy minor-key character that provide a sense of unity sufficient to suggest associations with the still to be invented genre of the symphonic poem. It is interesting that in 1841 listeners were clearly overtaxed by the work's apparently improvisatory features, whereas the situation had changed completely within only ten years, when the conservative critic Ludwig Bischoff praised the revised version of the D Minor Symphony as a piece whose formal cohesion allowed it to stand out to its own advantage from what he called the "bunglings" of the current New German school of composers such as Berlioz, Liszt, and Wagner.

Even for those of us with a good understanding of the historical situation, it is often difficult to say why a particular work should go down well with its audiences at a certain point in time, while another work fails to find favor. Why, for example, was the Gewandhaus concert on December 6, 1841, when the Sinfonietta op. 52 and the D Minor Symphony both received their first performances, no more than a limited success? Perhaps the concert was simply poorly planned. To the Schumanns' delight, Liszt had declared his willingness to appear onstage with Clara at the end of the evening and play works for two pianos, but their joint appearance seems to have eclipsed the rest of the program.

Negotiations with the publishing house Breitkopf & Härtel likewise came to nothing, and so for now Schumann locked away the D Minor Symphony and turned to a field that he had not previously tilled: chamber music. At the aforementioned "quartet mornings" that took place at his home in the late 1830s, the concertmaster Ferdinand David recalled that he generally "sat in the furthest corner of the room, saying little but exuding the happiest of moods" and afterward offering his guests glasses of champagne.[6] By now Schumann had not only assimilated the quartets of his avowed models, Beethoven and Mendelssohn, he had also studied in detail those of Haydn and Mozart. The three String Quartets op. 41 can certainly stand comparison with those of their dedicatee, Mendelssohn.

Some years earlier Schumann had reviewed a chamber work by George Onslow in his *Neue Zeitschrift für Musik*, in the course of which he noted that "a true quartet is one in which everyone has something to say— it is an often genuinely beautiful, often strangely and unclearly convoluted conversation between four people, where the spinning out of the threads" creates an attractive impression.[7] In writing this, Schumann was consciously introducing a note of fantasy to Goethe's famous definition of the string quartet as a conversation between four intelligent people—and this was the direction that Schumann himself now took. His quartets are arguably more exciting than the contemporary works by Mendelssohn, but they are also less accessible and less memorable. Or, rather, they do not necessarily make sense at an initial hearing, since the four voices are regularly treated as obbligato instruments. It comes as no surprise, therefore, to learn that decades later Theodor Billroth—a leading physician, friend of Brahms, and passionate recitalist—wrote in his book *Who Is Musical?* that "in my enthusiasm I was happy to go along with Mendelssohn and Chopin, because the musical training that I had acquired until then was sufficient; but for Schumann and Brahms I needed guides."[8]

In a brilliant study of the opening movement of the String Quartet op. 41, no. 3, Peter Gülke has spoken of the "ingenious solutions" forced on the composer by his thoughtless choice of themes, and he accuses Schumann of "increasingly intense impatience" whenever he fails to "concentrate on formalities" and acts in opposition to "his picture of what he suspects as being neoclassical."[9] Of course, contemporary audiences were attracted less to Schumann's string quartets than to two chamber works written with Clara in mind: the Piano Quartet op. 47 and, above all, the Piano Quintet op. 44. The opening movement of this last-named work begins with an Allegro brillante as energetic as the double fugue at the end of its final movement, which combines this movement's main idea with the opening movement's first subject, while additionally quoting an episode from the slow movement. Marked "In modo d'una marcia," this dark-toned slow movement is the heart of the Piano Quintet (and will be discussed in greater detail in Intermezzo VI).

But it was with a large-scale vocal work that Schumann enjoyed his greatest public success in the 1840s, *Paradise and the Peri*. He refused to describe it as an oratorio, preferring to ascribe it to a "new genre,"[10] and insisting that it was intended "not for the oratory but for cheerful souls."[11] On completing the work in June 1843, he wrote to his friend Johann Verhulst: "A piece like this involves a good deal of work—it's really only then that you learn what it means to write more such works—like Mozart, for example, writing eight operas in such a short space of time." And again: "The story of the peri [...] comes from Thomas Moore's *Lalla Rookh* and might almost have been written for music. The idea underlying the work as a whole is so poetic and so pure that it really inspired me."[12]

In spite of his admiration for Bach's Passions and Mendelssohn's *St. Paul*, Schumann had no desire to write a traditional ecclesiastical work, still less a Christian piece in the narrower sense of that term. Instead, he set out to produce something more original combining the religious traditions of three different culture groups, Indian, Egyptian, and Muhammadan, in a single coherent action centered around the figure of the peri, while at the same time hinting at Christian symbols. The peri is a half-human, half-celestial figure and can enter Paradise only by offering a gift that Heaven finds pleasing. The peri's first two sorties take her halfway around the world. She returns from the first with the blood of a young hero and from the second with the sighs of a virgin who sacrificed her life for her bridegroom. But Heaven acknowledges only the tears of remorse shed by a man who, laden with sin, sets eyes on a pure child.

In alighting on the figure of the peri, Schumann chose well. The subject was so popular at this time that it could reckon on the interest of the choral societies that decided the fate of such works. But the subject was also supremely well suited to Schumann himself, a point noted by an anonymous contemporary critic, who claimed that the composer's decision to tackle it was the fruit of "acute self-awareness and understanding of his own character and strengths."[13]

As we observed at the start of the present study, the phrenologist Richard Noel was struck by a number of Schumann's characteristics at more or less this time: a great love of the truth, great honesty, great benevolence, emotionality through and through, a genuine appreciation of formal structures, and modesty. We do not need to invest this characterization with an undue degree of mystique to see that it was admirably suited to a composer who was enthusiastic about the peri as a subject. Schumann did not choose a hero, a prophet or a saint, whether male or female, nor did he select a creature whose only function was to be sacrificed. Instead, he opted for a character who, humble to the core, accepts personal responsibility for her own salvation and finds Paradise through her encounter with love, kindness, devotion, and repentance.

Of course, Schumann was not the only artist at this time to find spiritual inspiration in legend and fairytale. But for an artist who invariably felt guilty through no fault of his own, this road to redemption must have seemed particularly inviting. This also explains why Schumann initially felt remote from *Tannhäuser*, on which Wagner was working at a time when Schumann was putting the finishing touches to *Paradise and the Peri*. In Wagner's case, a not-dissimilar subject is treated in a far more graphic manner; from a compositional point of view, there was something distinctly "materialistic" about Wagner's treatment of his subject, an approach that contemporaries regarded with praise or censure depending on their point of view.

Schumann's work begins with the peri motif, which wafts down from Heaven before combining with a passage of gentle counterpoint and finally leads directly into the opening scene. This is both more organic and more subtle in its impact than Wagner's approach in his *Tannhäuser* overture, which operates on the level of powerful stimulants and stark contrasts, to say nothing of the final apotheosis, which tests the patience of even the most committed Wagnerian, for here Wagner combines a much expanded *fortissimo* statement of the motif associated with divine clemency with endlessly descending scales of sixteenth notes that Wagner himself said expressed "the seething and swelling of every pulse of life in a chorus of redemption."[14]

Schumann's overture to *Paradise and the Peri* even emerges with credit from a comparison, not with *Tannhäuser*, but with Mendelssohn's *St. Paul*, a popular, oft-performed oratorio at this period. In the course of its overture the chorale *Wachet auf, ruft uns die Stimme* is presented in a magnificent orchestral garb as a symbol of the unshakable Protestant faith. So great is the composer's contrapuntal artistry, moreover, that it is impossible to overlook the affinities between Bach and his later imitator.

With regard to the finished works, too, it is gratifying that there is an alternative to *Tannhäuser* on the one hand and to *St. Paul* on the other. It was an alternative that in the eyes of contemporary critics not only laid the foundations for a "new genre" located midway between sacred oratorio and opera,[15] but also was capable of lending distinctive new features to opera. On a formal level this novelty consists in an increasing tendency to move in the direction of through-composition, a trend scarcely less advanced in *Paradise and the Peri* than it was to be only a few years later in Schumann's own opera *Genoveva* and Wagner's *Lohengrin*. Aesthetically speaking, there is also something novel about the idea of a unified "tone," which — borrowing a term from one of the performance markings in the Piano Fantasy op. 17 — we could call a "legendary tone." Such a tone embraces a whole range of color from sheer delight to mystic darkness, while avoiding triumphalist screams and extended portrayals of horror. In spite of its historically charged images, touching strophic songs, and vivid individual scenes, *Paradise and the Peri* gives the impression of a work in which action and music eschew excessive climaxes and contrasts as they move toward the peri's apotheosis at the words, "My work is done."

It is almost certainly no accident that in departing from his source, Thomas Moore's *Lalla Rookh*, Schumann chose not to include the name of a person in first position in his title, but preferred to describe a state — namely, the state that mankind has forfeited and to which we long to return with every fiber of our being. This is also one of the reasons he succeeds in avoiding the shows of strength traditional in oratorios and operas in the form of emotionally charged arias, agitated ensembles, monumental choral fugues, and melodramatic finales.

Schumann's contemporaries were able to appreciate this quality — after all, there were enough works at this time that relied on drama and strident colors to achieve their impact. Here one thinks of Friedrich Schneider's oratorio *Das Weltgericht* and Meyerbeer's opera *Les Huguenots*, for example. If today's listeners are inclined to mock the long stretches of parched arioso rather than admire the work's lyrical subtleties, they have every right to do so, and yet the world would be a poorer place without this bold and innovative work in the field of symphonic vocal music.

In order to assess two works that are associated with Schumann's public persona and which, dating from the period before March 1848, belong in the present chapter, I need to anticipate his time in Dresden. The first is the Piano Concerto in A Minor op. 54 that Schumann completed in the summer of 1845, when he added a second and a third movement to the Piano Fantasy of

1841 discussed in Intermezzo V. Although some years were to pass before this became one of the most popular piano concertos in the classical repertory, it met with a positive response from the outset, Schumann having succeeded in gaining acceptance among increasingly neoclassically minded music critics with a work that abandons none of the romanticism of the fantasy on which it was based but retains its thematic material even in the movements that were added later.

Less unequivocal was the contemporary reaction to the C Major Symphony op. 61 that Mendelssohn introduced to his Gewandhaus audiences in November 1846. Within a year Mendelssohn was dead, and so for a brief period Schumann himself came to represent German musical culture in the spirit of the older classicism — this, at least, is how he was viewed in the current debate on musical aesthetics. But such an honor brings with it its own burden of responsibilities, begging the question whether Schumann could assume this new function with this particular piece. In Leipzig's two leading music journals, the *Allgemeine musikalische Zeitung* and the *Neue Zeitschrift für Musik*, Alfred Dörffel and Eduard Krüger both struck a charitable note when claiming that Schumann had survived his "fermentation process" and for the most part managed to ensure that the "objective and subjective elements" — in other words, the powers of representation and imagination — were now "in the right relationship from a neoclassical standpoint."[16]

But however well-respected and committed these two critics may have been, they had clearly failed to listen properly to the piece. While Schumann had plainly returned to the traditional four-movement form of the Beethovenian symphony and was keen to make a fine-sounding symphonic noise, the situation is in fact more complicated than it appears to be at first sight, for in the summer of 1846, after completing his C Major Symphony, he noted that "from 1845 onward I started to develop a completely different way of composing, for it was then that I began to think everything up and work it all out in my head."[17] There seems little doubt that he had the C Major Symphony in mind when he wrote these lines. Be that as it may, it is evident that he has created a far denser web of motific and thematic relationships than he had done in his earlier symphonies and that these relationships extend beyond the individual movements to embrace the work as a whole. It was for this reason that he encouraged one connoisseur among his listeners to pay particular heed to not only the poetic idea but also the "musical framework," a phrase comparatively unusual with Schumann.[18]

Although the C Major Symphony positively flaunts the effort that has gone into it and—to the extent that the fanfare motif heard at the start of the symphony may be said to hold its own right through to the final movement—may be regarded as a work in which that final movement is the goal toward which the symphony as a whole aspires, there are no rigorous motivic and thematic processes in the sense in which Beethoven understood that term. Instead, Schumann seems repeatedly to become lost in the dense undergrowth of his musical textures, ultimately succeeding in escaping from them only by dint of an act of violence that consists in the fact that in the final movement it is not Schumann who triumphs, but Beethoven. As in the C Major Piano Fantasy op. 17, Beethoven appears here in the form of the theme "Nimm sie hin denn, diese Lieder," which, for Peter Gülke, represents an "explicit musical presentation" of the symphony to Clara and at the same time an astonishing act of "breaking free from all the existing rules."[19]

The fact that in the course of the final movement Schumann is by no means sparing in his repeats of his Beethoven reminiscence need not diminish the work in our eyes. Even the "sounds of anguish" for which he cites the Adagio with its "melancholic bassoon"[20] can be accommodated within a symphony whose home key is for long periods obscured so that only in the course of the final movement does the work strike the note of optimism traditionally associated with the key of C major. (It may be added parenthetically that even after his conversion to the Wagnerian cause, Hans von Bülow still claimed that whenever he heard the aforementioned Adagio he wanted to "sink to his knees in prayer."[21])

More problematical is the fact that the musical language is excessively coded. The C Major Symphony evokes not only Beethoven but Bach, too, for in the second movement's second trio, Schumann uses the B–A–C–H motif, while the Adagio includes a reminiscence of the Trio Sonata from the *Musical Offering*, to say nothing of a possible echo of Haydn in the opening fanfare motif. When combined with the movement's motivic density, such foreign allusions are likely to confuse impartial listeners who may suspect that such references are present but be unable to identify them. And this problem is exacerbated by the fact that the melodic writing does not have the vividness and verve that listeners would admire only a few years later in the *Rhenish* Symphony. Of course, none of this should prevent us from taking the work seriously; not only did the composer have to struggle hard to create it, but it was wrung, so to speak, from the musico-aesthetic discourse of the time. The question that was in the air in the years leading up to the revolution of March 1848 also left its mark on the C Major Symphony: "Should the old head-in-

In modo d'una marcia

In June 1848, Liszt turned up unexpectedly in Dresden and let it be known that he would be calling on the Schumanns. Unfortunately his visit caused something of an incident when he arrived two hours late, by which time the chamber music that had been arranged in his honor and that included a performance of Beethoven's Piano Trio in D Major op. 70, no. 1 (*Ghost*) was almost over. Although Liszt professed to like Schumann's new Piano Trio op. 63, which was presumably performed from the manuscript parts, he is said to have found the Piano Quintet op. 44 of some years earlier too "*leipziger-isch*" — too typical of the city of Leipzig. And when he then had the effrontery to champion Meyerbeer at the expense of Mendelssohn — the latter had been in his grave for less than eight months — Schumann seized him by the shoulders in a state of some agitation: "Meyerbeer is a pygmy next to Mendelssohn, who as an artist worked not just in Leipzig but for the whole world, and Liszt would do better to hold his tongue" — or so we read in Clara's diary.[1]

Liszt sought to play down the matter and in a subsequent conversation with Wagner tried to see the funny side of it, but Schumann had been goaded beyond reason, and a year later, when Liszt expressed an interest in the Scenes from Goethe's *Faust* on which Schumann was currently working, the latter wrote to him, barely concealing his sarcasm:

> But, my dear friend, don't you think you'll find the piece too "leipzigerisch"? Or do you regard L[eipzig] as a miniature Paris where something might yet be achieved? But to be serious — I really would have expected someone who knows so many of my compositions to have acted differently and not to have passed judgment, lock, stock, and barrel, on an entire artist's life. If you were to look at my compositions in more detail, you would find a fair variety of views in them, just as I have always tried to express something different in each of my compositions — and not just in terms of their form.[2]

The autograph of the opening bars of the second movement (*Un poco largamente. In modo d'una marcia*) of the Piano Quintet in E-flat Major op. 44 (1842). (Photograph courtesy of the University and Regional Library, Bonn.)

What exactly was at stake here? This was a time when Liszt was trying to put behind him his career as a pianist and was teeming with ideas for symphonic poems, hoping to create a kind of music that would reflect "society's spirit and sentiments, its lives and ideals."[3] This society — and here it is the Saint-Simonian and popular educator we hear speaking — should aspire to a higher form of existence, which it could do by means of an art that amounted to more than mere empty virtuosity on the one hand and formal games on the other but which should seek to convey ideas of genuine substance. Against this background — and in spite of a certain sympathy with its representatives — he was bound to see the "Leipzig school" of composers like Mendelssohn and Schumann as occupying an ivory tower: art for art's sake with a tendency toward the conventional. Liszt was enough of a musician to find Schumann's music attractive, but he expected more than that.

As a result, Liszt may have been critical of the fact that at the chamber recital at the Schumanns' house, the formal exercise of the Piano Trio op. 63 was immediately followed by a similar exercise in the guise of the Piano Quintet, which operates along identically predictable lines — the opening Allegro brillante, for example, is cast in regular first-movement sonata form, its exposition featuring a typical cantabile theme on the dominant that takes its textbook place on the tonic in the recapitulation. And there is a development section between the exposition and recapitulation. In Liszt's eyes this itself was reactionary in the extreme and, more particularly, typical of Schumann's embarrassment at having to "say something specific" in such a passage. (Mahler was later to say exactly the same about the development sections of both Mendelssohn and Schumann.)

If we also recall that the last thing that Liszt heard ringing in his ears was the double fugue with which Schumann ends the final movement of his piano quintet, it becomes easy to understand his reaction. At the same time, Schumann was right to be annoyed. Not only did he not see a neoclassical command of formal structures as regressive, he regarded such a device as a compositional gain. As we have already noted, he had informed his colleague Carl Koßmaly on May 5, 1843, four months after the piano quintet received its first performance at a Gewandhaus concert: "Man and musician have always sought to express themselves simultaneously with me, and I expect that it is exactly the same now, when I have, of course, learned to exercise greater control in my art."

Implicit in this remark is the conviction that even though Schumann's chamber music may strike a more neoclassical note than his early piano music or his songs, this does not mean that it is not equally pervaded by personal experience. As our brief glance at his string quartets should have indicated, not only is the formal organization of these chamber works innocent of all neoclassical glibness — at least as soon as we examine the original details of their internal structure — but many of these details are eloquent in a way that goes far beyond all generalized emotions. Even Donald Francis Tovey, a veteran of music criticism, wrote of this work that "every note tells, and the instruments are vividly characterized in spite of the preponderance of the pianoforte throughout."[4]

Schumann's constant quest for striking motifs emerges with particular force from a letter that he addressed to Mendelssohn on September 20, 1845:

Dear Mendelssohn,

When we recently said our goodbyes to each other, you really must have thought me insane for paying you such a hideous compliment, especially after you had just played me your charming song in E and were bound to assume that it was to this song that I was referring. What I meant by this and by the "Eichendorff" was the one in D minor ♩♪♫♩. It seemed to come to me as from an ancient chronicle, when the town players announced the tournament and the knights refused to appear and the musicians became impatient and so on. Tell me, am I missing the point? Or did you really have something like that before your mind's eye?[5]

Schumann's question was posed against the following background. Mendelssohn had been a guest of the Schumanns in Dresden the previous month and had played one of his *Songs Without Words* in E Major — presumably the "Cradle Song" op. 67, no. 6 — in addition to the "Horseman's Song" in D minor. Both were still unpublished at this date. Schumann seems to have been particularly taken by the "Horseman's Song" and to have thought of Eichendorff and of a medieval scene. The eight-note motif that he jotted down in his letter evidently conjured up these associations for him in a particularly impressive manner.

It is interesting that Schumann did not quote the opening of the "Horseman's Song," even though he may still have had this in his mind's ear. What he noted down instead is a brief motif that could certainly be interpreted as a signal or horn call and that Schumann soon invested with a concrete meaning. This was his way of listening to music. And on this occasion he was so convinced by his own aural impression that he needed to know if the composer had had a similar image in mind.

But Mendelssohn could not be so easily coerced into offering a programmatical interpretation of his *Songs Without Words*: "If I love a piece of music," he told Marc-André Souchay, his cousin by marriage,

> then what it tells me is not ideas too *vague* to be put into words, but ideas that are too *definite*. If you ask me what I was thinking about in the case of individual numbers [i.e., in the *Songs Without Words*], I would have to say that it was the song exactly as it stands there. And if I had in mind a particular word or words when writing this or that piece, I do not care to tell anyone what it was because only the song itself can say the same thing to one person as it does to another and awaken the same feeling in both of them — a feeling that is not, however, expressed by the same words.[5]

From this point of view, Schumann's question cannot have filled Mendelssohn with any great enthusiasm, even though he confirmed his correspondent's association of ideas in his reply. Perhaps he was just being polite.

The two composers were not in fact very far apart in terms of their aesthetic principles, and yet their methods of composition differed on one essential point, a point that Schumann illustrated particularly clearly when he argued that every phrase in a piece of music was "eloquent." It was a point on which he insisted to an extent that the strict adherents of "absolute" music found almost unsettling. A comparison between Mendelssohn's *Songs Without Words* and Schumann's *Kinderscenen* makes this difference clear, for the *Songs Without Words* are dominated by a kind of uniform process to which the individual phrases conform. At the risk of sounding polemical, we could say that Mendelssohn speaks in generalities rather than specifics. For Schumann, the situation was very different. Whether we take "Dreaming" or "The Poet Speaks" from the *Kinderscenen*, every phrase, no matter how brief, is fully articulated, leading a life of its own and contributing something specific to the overall narrative context. The reader may care to recall the metrical patterns at the start of "Dreaming," with their "deeply felt" sequence of 5/4, 3/4, 2/4, 2/4, and 4/4 time signatures. Mendelssohn would never have written anything like this.

This brings us back to Liszt's reproach that Schumann's works were all too typical of the Leipzig school and Schumann's indignation at his comment. If the criticism had been directed at Mendelssohn, one might be inclined to accept it. But Schumann could rightly claim that in each of his compositions he had "brought something different to light — and not just in terms of its form." And this is true not only of the work or of the movement as a whole but also of its individual details. From this point of view, we may take a closer look at the second movement of the Piano Quintet op. 44, which is marked "In modo d'una marcia" and is generally regarded as the heart of the work.

It is a funeral march and as such it has a number of prominent predecessors in the nineteenth century, including the slow movements of Beethoven's *Eroica* Symphony and of Chopin's Piano Sonata op. 35, which struck Schumann — astonishingly — as exaggeratedly "somber" and even "repellent."[7] Also worth mentioning here is Mendelssohn's *Song Without Words* op. 62, no. 3, which adopts the language of a funeral march and is traditionally referred to as such. A comparison between the funeral marches of Schumann and Mendelssohn offers us a good opportunity to draw a distinction between the Leipzig styles of them both.

As listeners, we are astonished first and foremost by the fact that Schumann's march, which lasts around three and a half minutes in performance, is only a little longer than Mendelssohn's, even though it contains substantially more information. Mendelssohn begins with a signal-like introduction, the triplet rhythm of which is already found in the *Eroica*, where it serves the same genre-specific function. The *Song Without Words* as a whole is divisible into three groups of 16 + 12 + 16 bars and comprises an introduction, a middle section and a slightly modified repeat of the introduction, A–B–A'. Although Mendelssohn could never be accused of schematicism, he remains in the home key of E minor, with only minor harmonic deviations. Metrically speaking, the work is clearly made up of symmetrical structures, each of which is 4 bars long, while it draws its melodic life from its opening theme.

The clear formal structure and memorable design of Mendelssohn's "Funeral March" are typical of his *Songs Without Words* in general, ensuring that this particular piece was so popular in middle-class salons in the nineteenth century that Strindberg could assume a knowledge of it in his three-part drama *To Damascus* and use it as a leitmotif: scraps of the music are heard as the expression of a constant threat on street corners, at the doctor's, in the hotel, on the open road, and so on.

Mendelssohn was successful in writing a genre piece, which, in spite of the initial stimulus of its rapid triplets, is essentially songlike in character. Within these narrow, self-imposed limits he avoids introducing anything unduly "personal." The result is funeral music that maintains its sense of decorum, which is why it was also appropriate for it to be performed at his funeral service in Leipzig's University Church. Could the march from the piano quintet have been played at Schumann's obsequies?

Of course, it could have been played, but it would have honored an artist in whose works personal passion invariably triumphs over the pure genre piece. Not that genre-like elements are missing from Schumann, for even the march in the piano quintet draws its strength above all from its ability to tap into our preconceptions of the archetypal funeral march. And its gestural weight is further underlined by the fact that the march disappears for a time before returning as the "unchangeable." Writers on the theory of musical form speak dispassionately here of a rondo in A–B–A–C–B–A form. But for Schumann, this form has a very specific function: the "shock" triggered by the march theme is something that can briefly be shaken off, but it cannot be exorcised for good.[8]

It would be wrong, therefore, to dismiss Schumann's recourse to traditional rondo form as neoclassical and hence as "typical of Leipzig" in the sense intended by Liszt. But it is equally important to note that Schumann's funeral march differs from those of Beethoven, Chopin, and Mendelssohn in that it does not speak the language of noble tragedy, a language that acquires a certain bitterness, if at all, through the piercing accents in the accompanying voices. Rather, there is something hesitant even about the melodic writing, investing it with a quality that is hard to associate with sublime grief or with the memory of a hero. We are reminded instead of a funeral procession whose swaying figures advance only with some difficulty. Symptomatic of this is the small step out of line descending to the subdominant at the end of the opening phrase and robbing the melodic line of its straightforwardness from the very outset.

We may perhaps extend the image of the funeral procession and turn it into a scene from a film: the two "episodes" that are inserted between the blocks of the rondo recall a camera panning to events on the edges of the main action. At the performance marking "espressivo ma sempre p," we may imagine a small group of singers intoning a gently ecstatic hymn, and at the "Agitato" passage in the second episode we may think of a man gesticulating wildly in his desperate grief but being swallowed up by the funeral procession even as he does so.

Even if we were to disregard Tchaikovsky's yet more flowery description of Schumann's "marcia," according to which the three main motifs embody "tragedy," "a selfless willingness to endure the inevitable blows of fate," and "rebellion on the part of a passionate soul shaken by the death of a much-loved friend,"[9] such wordy explanations are bound to be embarrassing, not least because they ignore the compositional characteristics of the piece — in other words, those features that make it unique. On the other hand, they offer us a welcome lifeline, because everyone tolerably familiar with the encodings of classical music will perceive something vaguely similar and will therefore be able to conclude that even without an explicit program the movement is not an example of some academic art for art's sake as defined by Liszt but follows a coherent narrative concept.

From the outset, the inspired main idea guarantees the movement's narrativity. As we have already noted, this idea does not entirely meet the expectations that we bring to a typical funeral march, the usual characteristics of which are rendered so unrecognizable by Schumann that the listener reacts to the movement with apprehension and uncertainty. When the "marcia" motif finally collapses in on itself, exhausted, at the end, it becomes clear that we have been following a line of argument with narrative qualities to it.

The opening (*top*) and closing (*bottom*) passages in the first violin line in the second movement of the Piano Quintet in E-flat Major op. 44 (1842).

This runs counter to the movement's underlying structure inasmuch as the rounded parataxis of its rondo form is turned into a narrative process. The German musicologist Hans Kohlhase has spoken, moreover, of the "imaginary simultaneities of impressions and emotions" that constitute the compositional "idea" behind the "marcia."[10] This aim is achieved by the work's multiple perspectives, for Schumann not only evokes the idea of a funeral procession going its gloomy way, he also explores the individual anguish to which the mourners are abandoned, which he does in the form of the head motif of the C major episode:

The head motif in the first violin part in the C major episode from the second movement of the Piano Quintet in E-flat Major op. 44 (1842).

Schumann uses this motif more than twenty times within a very short space and at the same time makes it unequivocally clear that here, too, he is not playing any navel-gazing games with "neutral" musical material but heaving a series of recognizable sighs that pass from instrument to instrument like real human voices.

This procedure recalls elements in the works of Bach and Beethoven, Schumann's self-declared models. They too were repeatedly successful at creating musical textures in which "objective" and "subjective" perspectives, the "universal" and the "particular," and "form" and "content" asserted themselves in turn. If Liszt was not entirely wrong to regard Mendelssohn's music as "typical of Leipzig," he was doing Schumann's piano quintet a disservice by attempting to tar it with the same brush. Helpless writers in the field of the aesthetics of music tend to locate Schumann's outlook between "absolute music" and "program music." But whereas the word "between" implies the idea of a compromise, Schumann may feel that in the case of his own compositions he inhabited a world beyond the categories of "absolute" music on the one hand and program music on the other.

A daguerreotype of Schumann, taken in the Hamburg studio of the photographer Johann Anton Völlner in March 1850 at the request of publisher Julius Schuberth. Three daguerreotypes were taken on this occasion. They represent our only surviving photographic record of the composer. Clara spoke in this context of a "glorious likeness" (Litzmann 2:208). She later loaned the original to the artist Eduard Bendemann, with whom she was friendly, and he prepared a charcoal drawing from it. Schumann is depicted here in a melancholic attitude — the sort of attitude that had become a topos with Dürer's famous copper engraving *Melencolia I.* It would be interesting to know if it was Schumann himself who chose to adopt this posture in Völlner's studio or whether it was suggested to him by the photographer. Whatever the answer, the image was soon being reproduced in all manner of different media, with the result that from an early date it left its mark on public perceptions of Schumann as a "melancholy" figure. (Photograph courtesy of the Robert Schumann Museum, Zwickau.)

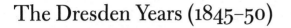

CHAPTER 9

The Dresden Years (1845–50)

*Ah yes — to tell my music all about the anguish and joy that animate
this age of ours is a gift which I feel has been conferred on me rather
than on many others. And the fact that you sometimes inform people of
the extent to which my music is rooted in the present and that it seeks
anything but euphony and pleasant entertainment pleases me and
encourages me to aspire to higher things. [. . .] I have worked a very
great deal throughout this whole period; never have I felt more impelled
to do so, never was it so easy for me. But it was my most recent marches
[op. 76] that gave me the greatest pleasure.*

Schumann to Franz Brendel, June 17, 1849[1]

Following his return from Russia in May 1844, Schumann found himself unable to settle in Leipzig, which no longer felt like home to him. Against this background, the fact that he soon gave up the editorship of the *Neue Zeitschrift für Musik* may not be particularly significant, for the move was long overdue. Yet it seems to have rankled with him that in spite of his successes with his First Symphony and *Paradise and the Peri* he was not considered a serious candidate to replace Mendelssohn at the Gewandhaus. In any event, however, it was none of these factors that persuaded him to move from Leipzig but an acute physical and mental crisis that became worse during a visit to Dresden in October 1844. "Robert couldn't sleep at all," Clara noted in her diary. "His imagination painted the most terrible pictures, in the morning I generally found him sobbing, he'd given up completely."[2] Since the couple's return to Leipzig would have brought only further agitation, they agreed to settle in Dresden for the time being and rented a ground-floor apartment at 6 Waisenhausstraße.

A farewell concert for the couple took place at the Gewandhaus on December 8, 1844, when the Piano Quartet op. 47 received its first performance, with Clara at the piano. We do not know who else was involved. Conversely, surviving records indicate that the quasi-public concerts that formed part of the examinations at the Leipzig Conservatory that Mendelssohn had helped to establish in 1843 and where Schumann himself taught the piano part-time for several months were attended by as many as eight hundred people, an indication of the outstanding role that music played at this time in public awareness in the city.

Since even serious writers on Schumann sometimes give the impression that things were generally more "difficult" in Dresden and the couple's marriage came under strain, it is worth casting a look at the family's situation at this time. During the Schumanns' five years in Dresden, four children were born to them: Julie, Emil, Ludwig, and Ferdinand. Although Schumann's diary entries are not the best guide to the atmosphere within the family, they nevertheless attest to the fact that he devoted his love and attention to his growing brood of children.

He related to his eldest daughter best: "In the afternoon with Marie to the Linkesches Bad — happy with the child," he noted on March 19, 1845.[3] "A volume of 'Children's Melodies' for piano solo for Marie," a second entry reads, this one dated early April 1846 and already adumbrating the later *Album für die Jugend*.[4] The entry for Easter Day 1845 reads: "First shoots of green grass — the cherry trees already in blossom — in my hand a nestling child — we had a really enjoyable walk. In the wood there were beautiful butterflies; I caught a few Camberwell beauties for M[arie], but then we let them go again. The happy days of childhood — one relives them in one's children."[5] "Went for a walk to the Prater with Marie,"[6] we read in December 1846 in the context of Schumann's visit to Vienna. "In the afternoon with the children to the Hegereiter [a local hostelry]," runs the entry for April 14, 1847.[7]

The family went on regular walks to the great park that lay close to their Dresden apartment. They also rode the carousel on the Vogelwiese and took boat rides on the Elbe. And as soon as the younger children could walk they were taken sledging and encouraged to go on country walks to pick flowers.[8] Their birthdays were marked in various ways. And shortly before they moved to Düsseldorf they watched the English balloonist Henry Coxwell descend to earth by parachute.

Throughout their time in Dresden, Clara was almost constantly pregnant, adding to Schumann's worries, but in spite of his own problems he was always able to prove an attentive husband. His housekeeping book includes a detailed note of all that he bought for her twenty-seventh birthday: "1 silk-lace shawl, 1 handkerchief, 6 bottles of eau de Cologne, 3 tablets of soap, 1 purse, 1 bottle of sauce, 1 melon, flowers, 1 bottle of Lößnitz champagne, ice cream, medallion, cake."[9]

For her part, Clara continued to bestow tokens of her affection on her husband. On one occasion she surprised him by presenting him with a copy of a painting that had caught his attention during a visit to Berlin: a portrait of Princess Elisa Radziwill as a winged peri painted by Mendelssohn's brother-in-law, Wilhelm Hensel. "For as long as I can remember, the picture stood on Mother's piano,"[10] Eugenie recalled, her reminiscences centering for the most part on Clara's years of widowhood.

In the Waisenhausstraße in Dresden, a female cook and a nursery maid helped with the household chores, which included entertaining the more than two hundred visitors who called on the Schumanns over the years and whose names are recorded in their Dresden diaries. Occasionally there was a party atmosphere. The Leipzig concertmaster Ferdinand David recalled one such evening:

> Johannisberger and Marcobrunner wine flowed freely. Madame Schumann was forever dragging in bottles, Schumann gestured to us that we should drink, while he himself set the best possible example, and we all followed his lead. It was great fun, a genuine Schumannesque evening which, once all the ladies apart from Mme Schumann had left, finally ended amid a great deal of cigar smoke at half past two in the morning.[11]

But Clara's role was not limited to that of a housewife and mother in thrall to her family, for she continued to support her husband in his own artistic endeavors, even though he rarely revealed what he was currently working on. In the spring of 1845, when he was practicing organ playing on the pedal pianoforte that he had built from his existing grand piano by adding a rented pedal-board, Clara followed suit, at least for a time. And last but not least, she also composed: her Preludes and Fugues op. 16 were the product of a lengthy period of intensive study of counterpoint, while her Piano Trio op. 17 was the high point of her chamber output. On October 2, 1846, she was happy to note in her diary: "There is nothing more enjoyable than to have composed something oneself and then to hear it played. There are a few attractive passages in the Trio and I think that formally too it is quite successful."[12]

Clara continued to make frequent appearances in the concert hall and also performed at soirées both in Dresden and in neighboring Leipzig. There were additionally concert tours of greater or lesser duration that she undertook during her early years in Dresden, which included visits not only to central and northern Germany but also — in the winter of 1846–47 — to Vienna, Brno, Prague, and Berlin.

The fact that travel is in itself an education does not need to be emphasized here, but it is worth recalling the many well-educated and artistically interesting men and women that Clara met through her husband. Apart from Meyerbeer, who was a red flag to a bull where the Schumanns were concerned, there was scarcely an eminent musician with whom they did not dine. Schumann's encounters with writers such as Eichendorff, Freytag, Geibel, Grillparzer, Gutzkow, Hebbel, Hoffmann von Fallersleben, Reinick, Rückert, Stifter, and Auerbach generally included his wife, and in many cases it was she herself who made the arrangements. And then there were all the painters in Dresden and Düsseldorf, to whom we shall return in due course.

"Otherwise there are very few artists here,"[13] Schumann complained to Mendelssohn six or so months after his arrival in Dresden. But by December 18, 1845, we find him writing to his friend: "We get together every week — Bendemann, Rietschel, Hüb[ner], Wagner, Hiller — Reinick."[14] Yet it is no accident that among the individuals named here Bendemann, Rietschel, and Hübner were painters or sculptors, while Reinick represented a cross between an artist and a poet.

One of the few musicians who was friendly with the Schumanns was Ferdinand Hiller, but he left for Düsseldorf in 1847, with the result that Schumann's feelings of isolation were not entirely unfounded. In Leipzig, Mendelssohn had set the tone and helped the Schumanns to the best of his abilities, whereas the musical life of Dresden was dominated by the Court Opera, where Wagner held noisy sway. Although Wagner was fond of entering into long and even stimulating discussions with Schumann on questions of politics and the aesthetics of opera, he was ultimately unwilling to tolerate a rival on his own particular patch of turf.

In Leipzig — a city famous for its publishing houses — Schumann had occupied a key position as the editor of his own journal. Once he resigned that post, his wife was forced to realize that although Dresden enjoyed an international reputation as a city of the visual arts, it had neither a regular concert hall nor a symphony orchestra capable of standing comparison with that of the Leipzig Gewandhaus. This also made it more difficult to perform Schumann's large-scale works, a point confirmed by the statistics for this period, which demonstrate that by the end of the century, Schumann's symphonies had received around a hundred performances in Leipzig, but only around thirty-five in Dresden. On the other hand, these figures reveal that Schumann was not entirely ignored in Dresden, where he enjoyed considerable success with his First Symphony, Piano Quintet op. 44, and *Paradise and the Peri*. It was in Dresden, moreover, that his Piano Concerto in A Minor received its brilliant first performance on December 4, 1845, in the Hôtel de Saxe. The complete program of the concert, which took place under Ferdinand Hiller's direction, was as follows:

Hiller's Overture to a Comedy
Schumann's Piano Concerto, with Clara Schumann as the soloist
An aria performed by Louise Franchetti
Chopin's Ballade in A-flat Major played by Clara Schumann
Schumann's Overture, Scherzo, and Finale
Mendelssohn's Allegro brillante op. 92 for four hands, played from the
    autograph score by Hiller and Clara Schumann
Two Schumann lieder, "The Lotus Flower" and "The Nut Tree," sung by
    Louise Franchetti
A Bach fugue, Adolf Henselt's "Cradle Song," and one of Mendelssohn's
    Songs Without Words played by Clara Schumann

The program for this concert — entirely typical of its period in terms of its random sequence of items — may serve to refute the view that for Schumann the year 1845 was a time of unmitigated disaster, as his diary entries might suggest. Rather, it is clear that in spite of his problems, Schumann continued to live his life and write music. He had learned to live with his crises — not until the very end was he to fail in this. Even so, the sheer number of emotional shocks he suffered during his early period in Dresden was nothing short of alarming. "What a terrible winter I've had and what total lassitude I've felt so that I was assailed by terrible thoughts and reduced to virtual despair," he told Mendelssohn on July 17, 1845, while preferring not to go into detail. Instead, he reported that the situation was now looking "more favorable again," perhaps as a result of his doctor's advice to bathe in the Elbe.[15] Within two weeks, however, his diary, which was increasingly assuming the function of a daily medical bulletin, was recording a "tendency to dizziness. Anxiety & restlessness, especially in my hands & feet — ragings in my limbs — not much appetite — pulse weak, easily agitated — pain in various places in my head — not violent but worrying."[16]

A visit to Bonn that had been planned at a time of high spirits had to be canceled, preventing Schumann from attending the celebrations accompanying the unveiling of the monument to Beethoven that had been masterminded by Liszt. Instead, the couple remained in Saxony, and, in an attempt to distract Schumann, they traveled to Leipzig, Weimar, Rudolstadt. Schwarzburg, Saalfeld, Gera, Zwickau, Schneeberg, and Chemnitz. Back in Dresden, Schumann worked with Hiller on a scheme to establish a series of subscription concerts modeled on those in Leipzig: "Every year *one* Beethoven symphony, and decorations to the chapel ad libitum — more isn't possible. Will the people in Leipzig ever support us?"[17] This was the question that he put to Mendelssohn, and even though the project never really got going, it says much for Schumann's initiative at this time that he was still prepared to make the effort.

And in spite of the "somber moods" that he felt were blighting his work as a composer in 1845 and 1846, his output remained respectable. As we have already noted, he began "by conceiving everything and working it out" in his head. It was a "very different way of composing" that he tried out first of all on piano pieces based on strict contrapuntal procedures.[18] His great model was Bach, who in view of his own weaknesses was able to serve as a kind of character reference. As early as 1832 he had told his piano teacher Johann Gottfried Kuntsch that studying *The Well-Tempered Clavier* had a "morally invigorating impact on the whole person, for Bach was a man through and through; with him, there were no half measures, nothing sickly, everything was written as if for all eternity."[19]

Meanwhile Schumann had not only made *The Well-Tempered Clavier* his constant companion, he also had written out *The Art of Fugue* and studied *The Musical Offering.* He was also familiar, of course, with Mendelssohn's piano fugues, which he had praised in highly poetical terms in his *Neue Zeitschrift,* only to dismiss them in his marriage diary a few years later as "impoverished" in comparison to those of Bach.[20] Having acquired a copy of Cherubini's *Cours de contrepoint et de fugue* and rented a pedal-board, he studied fugue technique with Clara, then fired off a whole series of works. In April and May 1845, for example, he completed six Studies for the Pedal Pianoforte op. 56, four (noncontrapuntal) Sketches for the Pedal Pianoforte op. 58, and Six Fugues on the Name BACH for Organ or Pianoforte with Pedal op. 60.

We would not be doing their creator an injustice by seeing these studies first and foremost as a successful attempt at self-assurance on Schumann's part: he was able to function as a composer and could invent things "in his head," with the result that he was not dependent on ideas that might or might not strike him at the piano, depending on the mood of the moment. He himself regarded his op. 60 fugues as the work that was most likely to survive him. In any event, he was by no means alone in writing such works but was part of a wider trend, for fugues were not only test pieces in conservatories but also could be offered to connoisseurs, who would use them as a means of stocking up on their musical education. Finally, later composers as distinguished as Bizet and Debussy considered the op. 56 Studies worth arranging. Bizet made an arrangement of them for piano duet in 1872, while Debussy's version for two pianos dates from 1891. In the present writer's view, these works create a somewhat blurred impression when played on the organ—the original sound of the pedal pianoforte is better suited to making them seem interesting in terms of domestic music-making. Unfortunately, pedal pianofortes are nowadays hard to find.

One such instrument was standing in the Schumanns' music room when they received a visit on August 29, 1846, from the then–twenty-year-old Eduard Hanslick—later to become famous as a music critic. In view of the halting conversation, their visitor was clearly relieved when Clara played something from the op. 56 Studies for the Pedal Pianoforte. Hanslick was then invited to accompany the family on a walk through the great park. Emil, who was only six months old and who did not survive infancy, was entrusted to a wet-nurse on this occasion. Hanslick latter recalled:

> Clara went on ahead with the oldest girl, Schumann led the second one by
> the hand, and I took the youngest, Julie, an exceptionally beautiful child
> whom Schumann jokingly called my bride. [...] I was now able to observe
> him as a family man, contented and tender by turns. Here, too, however, he
> said but little, and yet his friendly, almost childlike eyes and smiling lips,
> which seemed pursed as if he were about to start whistling, struck me as
> uniquely and touchingly eloquent.[21]

That same evening, Schumann and Hanslick attended a performance of *Tannhäuser* under Wagner's own direction, prompting Schumann to write to Mendelssohn: "*I have to take back many of the things* I said to you after reading through the score; from the stage everything looks very different. I was very affected by much of it."[22]

In September 1846 the Schumanns moved to 26 Reitbahnstraße, and on November 5, Mendelssohn conducted the first performance of the still-unpublished C Major Symphony in the Gewandhaus. The Schumanns and their eldest children then traveled to Vienna, hoping the new symphony would prove to be the unqualified success there that it had failed to be in Leipzig — a success necessary if Schumann was to be restored to an even keel.

Events conspired against him, and the performances of the piano concerto and C Major Symphony, both of which Schumann conducted himself, encountered little response. Even Clara's own recitals were only moderately successful, for she apparently played "pieces that were too good and that the audience didn't understand."[23] Her diary entry for Christmas Eve strikes a correspondingly despondent note:

> We lit a tree and gave the children a few trifles, but Robert and I were unable to give each other presents as we'd earned nothing whatsoever! In my heart of hearts I was very sad, it was the first Christmas when I'd not been able to give my dear Robert any pleasure but had brought him only unhappiness.[24]

Clara's final concert in Vienna featured two very demanding pieces: Beethoven's *Appassionata* Sonata and her own arrangement of Bach's Organ Prelude in A Minor. Fortunately, it was sold out and proved sufficiently profitable for the couple to return to Dresden with a net profit of three hundred thalers. Even so, their pleasure was marred by the fact that they owed it above all to Jenny Lind, who with her usual kindness had agreed to share the platform at Clara's concert, prompting the latter to note in her diary: "I could not resist the most embittered feeling that a single song by Lind achieved more than I could ever do with all my playing."[25] Otherwise, the couple's contacts with the "divine" Jenny Lind were a source of unalloyed delight both artistically and personally; how good it was that in spite of all the pressure under which they always placed themselves, they could still enthuse about others!

They had also enthused about Mendelssohn, whose premature death in November 1847 was a bitter blow for them both. After all, they could hardly have found a more affable patron. As a composer, too, Schumann saw Mendelssohn as a great model. That his admiration could also give rise to self-doubt is clear from his work in the field of the piano trio, a genre to which Mendelssohn had made two important contributions in the form of his opp. 49 and 66, both of which had set such high standards that Schumann struggled to match them.

During his "chamber music year," 1842, he had, it is true, written four movements for piano, violin, and cello, but these struck him as so untypical of the medium of the piano trio that it was not until eight years later that he published them under the noncommittal title of Fantasy Pieces. In 1847 he wrote two "proper" trios in D Minor op. 63 and F Major op. 80. In terms of the design and sequence of their movements, Schumann produced some extremely solid work here, even if, for some listeners, he indulged in excessively complex polyphonic procedures. But equally striking is the fact that for the first time in his chamber output he used German performance markings, which he did for a very good reason.

The movements of the first trio are headed "Mit Leidenschaft und Energie" (With passion and resolve), "Lebhaft, doch nicht zu rasch" (Lively, but not too fast), "Langsam, mit inniger Empfindung" (Slow, with heartfelt emotion), and "Mit Feuer" (With fire). As such, they are an appeal to performers and listeners alike not to be so distracted by the work's elaborate artistry that they lose sight of the fact that the composer is speaking through the voices of a Florestan and a Eusebius, "as in olden times." The way in which the differing elements of polyphonic procedures and eloquent emotionality can be intertwined is well illustrated by bars 11–20 in the slow movement, which is cast in the form of a set of variations. In the first variation the cello leads us deep inside a style of writing which even before had been metrically and harmonically complex but which now acquires an almost impenetrable opaqueness. Of course, even this music "sounds," yet it tells not of neoclassical structures but of "rare states of mind," and it already reveals some of the extremism of modern avant-garde music. It is striking that Schumann did not repeat this episode when taking up the opening section but ended the movement in a bright A major. Here we see an example of his sense of form, which never allowed him to lose his way completely. As such, this may warn us against thinking that music can be interpreted as a literal record of a composer's state of mind.

When Hiller moved to Düsseldorf at the end of 1847, Schumann inherited the Dresden Liedertafel and immediately devoted all his energies to it. It was for this organization that he wrote his Three Songs for Male-Voice Choir op. 62 to words by Eichendorff, Rückert, and Klopstock: "Der Eidgenossen Nachtwache" (The confederates' night-watch), "Freiheitslied" (Freedom song), and "Schlachtgesang" (Battle song). And he expended considerable effort on finding a publisher who would bring out these songs "as a nice Christmas present for Prince Metternich" — the universally hated representative of the reactionary League of Princes that was an increasing focus of anger on the eve of the bourgeois revolution for which Schumann, too, could hardly wait. In particular the Eichendorff setting, which tells of "the victories of free old Switzerland," could not be "better suited to present conditions" but must "be published without delay," if it was to have any effect.[26]

In point of fact it was not until February 1848 that these songs finally appeared in print, by which time Schumann's housekeeping book was reporting on "terrible events," "tremendous political agitation," "street fighting," and so on.[27] Schumann was in fact initially shocked by this violent turn of events, whereas Clara quickly made it clear where her loyalties lay. Unlike Wilhelmine Schröder-Devrient, a singer whom she greatly admired, she did not — it is true — call on her fellow citizens to march on the Dresden Castle during the May uprising in 1849, but a diary entry of March 13, 1848, reads, "In the evening the most dreadful news from Berlin, the king refuses to yield, the people are fighting terribly with the military." And a few days later: "Over 1,000 people are said to have been killed, what must a king like that have on his conscience!" Clara was an ardent champion of the freedom of the press, so that following an argument with a woman from Berlin we find her confiding in her diary: "It is sad to see how few genuinely liberal people there are among the educated classes." And although the Schumanns were on friendly terms with the Dresden artist Julius Hübner, their visits to the Hübner household were by no means uncontentious: "I called on Madame Hübner and had a regular row with her — about politics, would you believe it! [. . .] These people are not in the least bit liberal in their beliefs."[28]

Schumann was by no means inactive throughout this period but wrote a series of freedom songs whose political tendencies were plain to see. They would, he hoped, be performed in public by male-voice choirs in Dresden: "Zu den Waffen" (To arms), "Schwarz-Rot-Gold" (Black, red, and gold), and "Deutscher Freiheitsgesang" (German freedom song).[29] In any rate, he gave up the directorship of his Liedertafel after barely a year, as he found "too little real musical ambition" among its members: "And when I've spent the whole day making music on my own, these endless six-four chords of the male-voice choral style are really not to my liking."[30]

He preferred to be drawn into conversation with Wagner. On January 20, 1848, for example, his diary entry reads: "1.45 in the morning a little boy" — this is all he has to say on the subject of the birth of his son Ludwig, after which he continues with an account of the rest of the day's events: "In the morning to Rietschel's studio — bust of Mendelssohn — in the afternoon R. Wagner called on me."[31] Entries for May and June 1848 include the following: "Wagner's Lohengrin," "Saw Wagner in the morning — his theater republic," "Visit from Wagner — his political poem," "R. Wagner's political coup."[32] We may assume that Schumann would have been astonished at Wagner's revolutionary views as retailed to him in person or gleaned from the pages of local newspapers, which carried reports on essays and poems with titles such as "Draft for the Organization of a German National Theater for the Kingdom of Saxony," "Greetings from Saxony to the Viennese," and "How Do Republican Aspirations Stand in Relation to the Monarchy?"

Although Schumann would have followed all these events with interest and presumably even with sympathy, he was not someone who carried on as a revolutionary. Even so, he championed music that was "rooted in the present"—and not just in the form of pithy male-voice choruses. Rather, he toyed with the idea of a subject such as "The German Peasants' War" and he set an Advent Song op. 71, which starts with the words "Your king comes in lowly garments." Within the contemporary political context these words could be inflammatory, and that is how they were intended. While the king of Prussia had contemptuously rejected the crown that had been offered to him by his people within the framework of a constitutional monarchy, the biblical Jesus in Rückert's hymn was "a powerful ruler with no armies" and a "prince of peace of great power."

Even the *Album für die Jugend* (Album for young people) op. 68 for piano that Schumann wrote in the fall of 1848 reflected the spirit of the times. If the *Kinderscenen* of 1838 had been the "reflections of an older man for older people," the new album—which was successful from the very outset—tended to contain "prefigurations, presentiments, future states for younger people."[33] In this respect, Schumann was no backward-looking romantic keen to glorify childhood; rather, he was a father who had taken a keen interest in his children's everyday lives: "I wrote the first pieces in the album for our eldest child on her birthday, and the others were gradually added afterwards."[34]

"Der kleine Morgenwanderer" (Little morning wanderer), no. 17, refers to Marie's first day at school; "Ein Stückchen" (A little piece), no. 5, was originally called "Nach vollbrachter Schularbeit" (On completing one's homework); and "Erster Verlust" (literally, "First loss," but more usually translated as "First sorrow"), no. 16, was initially known as "Kinder-Unglück" (Children's unhappiness), an allusion to the death of a bird of which the children had been very fond but which their father had killed by feeding it too many bone-marrow dumplings. The "Reminiscence" of Mendelssohn's death was written in the style of Mendelssohn's *Songs Without Words* and deserves its place in the collection, at no. 28, because Mendelssohn was Marie Schumann's godfather.[35]

The poetic element is never eclipsed by didactic concerns, although it is no longer poetry for adults but for children. Any reader who grew up playing

"Der fröhliche Landmann" (The happy farmer) will recall not so much the off-beat eighth notes in the right hand that make the piece sound uncannily like a study as the rollicking melodic line that leads with such feeling to the diminished seventh at the double bar line and then proceeds to repeat the melodic line with an added third: this is enough for a child to enter another world, if only for a few brief moments.

The *Waldszenen* (Forest scenes) op. 82 for piano that Schumann wrote during the winter of 1848–49 picks up where the *Album für die Jugend* left off. True, these beautiful and expressive pieces are intended for adults, and yet here, too, a realistic element is clearly identifiable: there are no reflections of an inner fantasy world but in its place a loving engagement with nature. The nine numbers are headed "Eintritt" (Entrance), "Jäger auf der Lauer" (Hunter lying in wait), "Einsame Blumen" (Solitary flowers), "Verrufene Stelle" (Place of ill repute), "Freundliche Landschaft" (Friendly landscape), "Herberge" (Shelter), "Vogel als Prophet" (Bird as prophet), "Jagdlied" (Hunting song), and "Abschied" (Farewell). None of them is illustrative in character but for the most part is an example of highly reflective musical poetry. Although we know that at the time he was working on these pieces Schumann had numerous paintings of woodland scenes hanging in his apartment, the music goes far beyond a mere depiction of nature. "Verrufene Stelle," for example, is inspired by Hebbel's poem "Böser Ort" (An evil place), which is permeated by somber symbolism, and the work that Schumann was moved to write is reminiscent, in its cryptic way, of Bach's *The Well-Tempered Clavier*.

Of course, a political impulse did not prevent Schumann from continuing to work on large-scale compositions during 1848, compositions which even less than those just mentioned can be reduced to their contemporary context. Two of them — *Genoveva* and *Manfred* — will be dealt with in Intermezzos VII and IX, leaving us in the present chapter to examine only the Scenes from Goethe's *Faust*.

Schumann had considered writing an opera on the subject of Faust as early as 1840, but it was during his visit to Russia in 1844 that he began to sketch an oratorio[36] based on the final scene from part 2 of Goethe's play. Conceived under the title "Faust's Transfiguration," it was designed as a setting of the entire final scene, which takes place in a mountain gorge and runs from "Waldung, sie schwankt heran" (Woods, hither wavering) to "Das Ewig-Weibliche zieht uns hinan" (Eternal womanhood draws us on high). But then the project stagnated. On September 24, 1845, for example, Schumann wrote to Mendelssohn: "The scene from *Faust* is resting in a drawer of my desk; I'm really afraid of looking at it again. I was so moved by the sublime poetry of the ending that I felt emboldened to start work on it; but now I don't know if I shall ever publish it."[37]

But he was then indeed emboldened to complete "Faust's Transfiguration," and the scene received its first performance in Cosel's Palace in Dresden on June 15, 1848, proving so successful that Schumann was encouraged to add two further sections during the time that remained to him in the city. The first was a group of three scenes from part 1 of *Faust* ("Scene in the Garden," "Gretchen Before the Image of the Mater Dolorosa," and "Scene in the Cathedral"), while the second comprised three scenes from part 2 ("Ariel: Sunrise," "Midnight," and "Faust's Death"). In Düsseldorf, finally, Schumann added an overture. But it was not until after his death that all three parts were performed for the first time in the Gürzenich Hall in Cologne on January 14, 1862.

At the time, the work was regarded above all as an "educational oratorio" and as an attempt "to understand art through art."[38] That was also how Schumann himself saw it, although he also had to reckon on being criticized: "Why write music to such consummate poetry?"[39] Certainly, he felt such profound respect for his hallowed source that in contradistinction to his usual practice he did not alter a single phrase but followed it so slavishly, word for word, that even Goethe's strophic structure was of only secondary importance to him.

This approach encouraged a certain monotony — a reproach that has often been leveled at the work. Although such a criticism may well be exaggerated, it is nonetheless beyond doubt that the juxtaposition of all three sections has resulted in a sequence of scenes lacking in any dramatic concept. If we may believe Schumann's early biographer, Wilhelm Joseph von Wasielewski, on this point, then Schumann encouraged such a criticism when he remarked that he could imagine a complete performance "as a curiosity at best."[40] Of course, these scenes are not entirely lacking in an overriding idea, for they are imbued with the concept of a mystic release from various earthly entanglements, a concept typical of the composer.

In composing this work, Schumann drew on the world of Christian symbolism that he had avoided in the case of *Paradise and the Peri*. In this he seems to have been inspired by Goethe, who had struck an astonishingly sober note when discussing the subject with Johann Peter Eckermann:

You will confess that the conclusion, where the redeemed soul is carried up, was difficult to manage; and that I, amid such supersensual matters, about which we scarcely have even an intimation, might easily have lost myself in the vague, if I had not, by means of sharply-drawn figures, and images from the Christian Church, given my poetical design a desirable form and substance.[41]

For the first performance of "Faust's Transfiguration" in Dresden, Schumann placed his trust in the massed ranks of the Dresden Choral Society, but for his particular favorites he used his own Society for Choral Singing with which he could "perform all the music I love in the proper way, to my heart's content."[42] The association met for the first time in the Garden Room of the Harmony Society—the former Hoym Palace—on January 5, 1848. Fifty or sixty singers were involved. They began with a Bach chorale, and the choir's minutes go on to record rehearsals of motets by Palestrina, Felice Anerio, and Giovanni Maria Nanino, among others. But they also worked their way through the later repertory, exploring Bach's motets and the final chorus from the same composer's *St. John Passion*, Handel's *Jephtha*, Beethoven's *Missa solemnis*, Cherubini's Mass in C Minor, and Schubert's setting of the twenty-third psalm. For a time, the choir also took an interest in Schumann's own works: the enchanting Romances and Ballads opp. 67, 75, 145, and 146 and the Romances for women's voices opp. 69 and 91 were all written with his own choral society in mind.

This was the situation when the political spotlight was turned on Dresden in the spring of 1849. On April 30, King Friedrich August II of Saxony dissolved both houses of parliament and triggered the Dresden Uprising. Prussian troops were called in to put it down and were not slow to act. Schumann seems to have been taken by surprise by the rapid turn of events and noted in his diary on May 4: "Revolution—walk with K[lara]—dead bodies in the street—the Brühl Terrace—through the town in the evening—state of revolution."[43]

Clara left a more detailed account, remaining an accurate chronicler even in the face of the confused situation around her:

Thursday the 3rd. Went for lunch to the villa in the Plauen Valley and reveled in the beauties of the natural world—of course, we had no idea what was going on in the city in the meantime. We had been home for barely half an hour when drums sounded a general alarm, bells rang from every tower, and it wasn't long before we heard shooting. [. . .] On Friday the

4th we found all the streets barricaded when we went into the city, and on the barricades stood men armed with scythes and republicans who made them build the barricades higher and higher, everywhere there was the utmost lawlessness, hatches and paving stones had been torn up, as well as the cobbles from the streets, and were turned into barricades; in the town hall the democrats gathered together and elected a provisional government, the king having fled to Königstein during the night; they were soon issuing proclamations of every kind as part of their war on the soldiers who were encamped with cannon in front of the castle and in the New Town. As we walked through the city we saw the terrible sight of fourteen dead bodies, men who had fallen the previous day and now lay in dreadful array in the hospital forecourt as a warning to others.[44]

Within two days it was no longer safe to leave the house: "A security patrol was formed in our street, and they wanted Robert to join. After I had twice denied that he was in, they threatened to search the house: we escaped with Marie by the garden gate to the main station."[45] From there the Schumanns and their daughter made their way by a circuitous route to the country estate of Major Friedrich Serre, a friend of theirs who lived at Maxen. But their younger children, including the fifteen-month-old Ludwig, remained behind in Dresden in the care of their nanny, and so Clara returned to the city the following day and after a particularly difficult and dangerous journey managed to reach the Reitbahnstraße. She snatched the sleeping children from their beds and took them, together with their nanny, to Maxen, where Robert was still waiting, having heard that all the men in Dresden were being forcibly recruited into the rebel army.

Unlike Wagner, who was seized by revolutionary fervor, Schumann had no desire to become actively involved in the uprising, and after returning briefly to the devastated capital, the couple sought refuge in nearby Kreischa, which was "much more pleasantly situated and has a milder climate."[46] Opinions were divided at this time, and the liberal Schumanns found themselves caught between two opposing camps, although on balance their sympathies lay with the rebels rather than those still loyal to the crown, and so we find Clara critical of some of the members of the aristocracy who had also come to Kreischa and who "spoke of the people merely as *canaille* and rabble, till it made one quite uncomfortable."[47] Again it is Clara who reports on events in detail and helped to save the family from imminent danger — and this in spite of the fact that she was seven months pregnant.

Schumann regained his spirits only when a copy of the *Augsburger Allge-*

meine Zeitung allowed him to form a picture of the situation in Dresden. He devoured the newspapers while also finding time for composition, including the *Liederalbum für die Jugend* (Lieder album for young people) op. 79, which Clara was soon trying out on the piano of the Kreischa choirmaster. Other works dating from this time are the *Lieder und Gesänge aus Goethes "Wilhelm Meister"* (Lieder and songs from Goethe's *Wilhelm Meister*) op. 98a and the motet *Verzweifle nicht im Schmerzenstal* (Do not despair in this vale of tears) op. 93, the latter a setting of a text from Friedrich Rückert's *Makamen des Hariri* with which he had long been familiar. It appears there under the heading "Der Krankenbesuch" (Visiting the sick).

By the middle of June the family was back in Dresden, where Schumann wrote his Four Marches op. 76 in quick succession: "No old Dessau marches, only republican ones," he told his publisher Friedrich Whistling, on June 17, 1849. "I could think of no better way of venting my agitation — they were written in a veritable frenzy of enthusiasm."[48] He insisted that they must be published without delay, and they duly appeared in print the following month. Their titles — "Mit größter Energie" (With the greatest resolve), "Sehr kräftig" (Very powerful), "Lager-Szene" (Camp scene), and "Mit Kraft und Feuer" (With force and fire) — give no indication of the difficult situation in Dresden at this time, where the townspeople were groaning beneath the yoke of billeted Prussian troops financed by a levy on the population. Clara was indignant: "First they come and shoot down the townsfolk who have done nothing to them, and then we have to give them food and drink for free — it's humiliating!"[49]

Her husband, conversely, was positively euphoric. Once the real revolution had failed, it continued to be fought in the provinces of the mind, and this was something to which Schumann could relate. In spite of recurrent bouts of melancholy, he used the Goethe celebrations of 1849 to present himself to the world as the precursor of a solidly authentic German art that would be effective in the public arena. On July 28, 1849, for example, he wrote to his publisher Hermann Härtel in the run-up to a performance of the final part of the Scenes from Goethe's *Faust* that took place on August 29 as part of the celebrations marking the centenary of the playwright's birth:

> The concert should take place in the palace in the Great Park and should include [Mendelssohn's] *Walpurgis Night*. At the same time — or more especially *after* this performance — there should be singing, music, and celebrations at various points in the park; one would like a kind of fairground atmosphere, unless the rain god decrees otherwise.[50]

Schumann's *Faust* music was also performed at more or less the same time as part of the celebrations accompanying the Goethe centenary in Leipzig and Weimar, so Schumann had every reason to regard himself at this period as Germany's leading composer, especially since Mendelssohn was now dead and Wagner had been forced to flee into exile in Switzerland. Would he be able to succeed Wagner as Kapellmeister to the royal court of Saxony? But before his friends and patrons could adopt a clear strategy in what—if the truth be told—was a hopeless situation, a new door opened in Düsseldorf.

Before that, however, one of Schumann's dreams came true with a production of his opera *Genoveva*.

Genoveva Is Not *Lohengrin*

I t's quite true about my grand opera: I'm all fire and flame, and I spend the whole day reveling in sweet and fabulous sounds. The opera is called 'Hamlet,' the thought of fame and immortality is giving me strength and firing my imagination."[1] Schumann was twenty when he wrote these lines to his mother in 1830, presumably well aware that at this date he was not remotely capable of writing an opera. Although this situation changed with the passage of time, one problem remained: a libretto.

There are two basic types of opera composer. First, there are those who choose their librettos without subscribing to the views that those texts contain. In setting them, they are like good actors consumed by their roles without ever becoming identified with them in the longer term. Mozart, Verdi, and Richard Strauss belong in this group, as do Rossini and Meyerbeer. The members of the other group would be happiest if they could bond forever with their heroes and with the plots of their operas. As such, they form a minority: Beethoven with *Fidelio*, Wagner with everything that he wrote after *Rienzi*, and Schumann with *Genoveva*, a work that remains largely unknown even if it has recently been rather more widely discussed than it used to be.

Schumann had already toyed with around fifty different operatic subjects before things finally worked out for him with *Genoveva*. After stumbling upon Friedrich Hebbel's tragedy of the same name on Maundy Thursday 1847, he immediately drafted the overture and then began to refashion Hebbel's play, while also drawing on Ludwig Tieck's tragedy *Leben und Tod der heiligen Genoveva* (Life and Death of St. Genovefa).

"Do you know my morning and evening prayer as an artist?" he had asked Carl Koßmaly five years earlier. "It is German opera."[2] The word "German" not only referred to the language in which the work would be sung, but it also was a pointer to the nationalist cause. In international circles, there were really only two types of opera at this time: Italian *opera seria* and *opera buffa*, and French grand opera. The works that German composers had succeeded in writing were no longer singspiels, it is true, but they rarely commanded attention. As always, it is the exceptions that confirm the rule: Mozart's *Die Zauberflöte* (The Magic Flute), Beethoven's *Fidelio*, Weigl's *Die Schweizer-familie* (The Swiss Family), Weber's *Der Freischütz* and *Euryanthe*, Spohr's *Jessonda*, Marschner's *Der Vampyr* and *Hans Heiling*, and Lortzing's *Zar und Zimmermann* (Tsar and Carpenter).

Of these last-named composers, only Mozart, Beethoven, and Weber commanded Wagner's respect. The works of all the others were lumped together as a type of "German opera music" that he likened to a "prude," a kind of woman who fills us "with feelings of revulsion and horror." Or so he wrote in *Opera and Drama*, a polemical, programmatic work that was to create a stir only months after Schumann's *Genoveva* had received its first performance. NonGerman composers suffered just as badly at Wagner's hands: Italian opera was said to resemble a "prostitute" who "never loses control and never sacrifices herself except when she herself wants to feel pleasure or gain an advantage." But at least she exercised the "sensual functions of the feminine sex," whereas French opera was a "coquette" who sought only "joy for herself and satisfaction for her vanity."[3] For Wagner there was only one cure: himself.

But apart from Wagner, what was it that inspired German composers of the 1840s, such as Schumann and Mendelssohn? Borne aloft by their sense of a cultural mission, they sought librettos that took as their starting point a popular theme from German myth or history and at the same time encapsulated ethical values that were also valid in their own day.

Even in the nineteenth century, the popular medieval legend of St. Genovefa had lost none of its appeal and remained a suitable topic for treatment, most notably in the modern versions by Hebbel and Schumann. When one of Charles Martel's followers, Siegfried, Count Palatine, goes to war against the Moors in order to check their northward advance from Spain into France, he commends his wife, Genoveva, to the care of a trusted friend, Golo, who has remained behind at court. Urged on by the wicked witch Margaretha, Golo falls victim to Genoveva's charms and sues for her hand in marriage. Incandescent with rage at his rejection, he hatches a plot whereby Genoveva is exposed as an adulteress and sentenced to death. Margaretha admits to her complicity in the plot, preparing the way for a happy ending.

Clara knew and loved the legend, which may well have confirmed her husband in his choice of the subject and certainly contributed to the fact that in

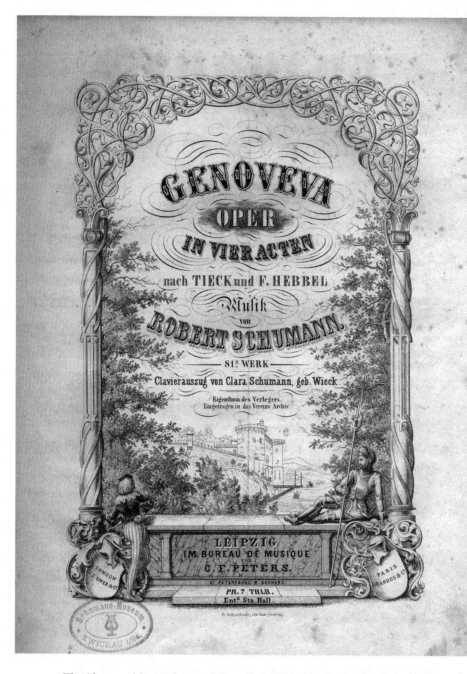

The title page of the vocal score of *Genoveva,* published by C. F. Peters of Leipzig in 1851. (Photograph courtesy of the Robert Schumann Museum, Zwickau.)

his adaptation of the material he played down the elements of "black" romanticism that had been germane to the original action, with the result that Golo now appears less in a sinister light than as a figure driven by forces beyond his control. But the "white" romanticism, too, had its brightness dulled. "I shall sing you a song of sorrow"—this was the message that the critic Eduard Krüger heard in the overture, which anticipates the action not in any programmatic way but in terms of its atmosphere and emotions. Was there substance here for an opera? Schumann's pupil Louis Ehlert later claimed that the work contained "glorious details, [. . .] a soul-stirring orchestra, in reality an underhand continuous overture, the highest nobility of intention and of choice of material, all that one might desire; but it was no opera."[5]

At about the same time, Wagner, writing in his own periodical, the *Bayreuther Blätter*, adopted a note of sneering contempt in recalling that Schumann had had no hesitation in declaring that the libretto of *Lohengrin* could never be set to music, while refusing point-blank to rewrite the "lamentably foolish third act" of *Genoveva*: "He took offense and was convinced that in offering him my advice I was wanting to spoil his very best effects. For effect was precisely what he aimed at: everything 'German, chaste, and pure,' but with a piquant dash of mock unchastity."[6]

Wagner missed any sense of straightforwardness and immediacy in the libretto. But Schumann was capable of writing only a drama in which the inner lives of his characters were explored in detail, rather than creating a plot that was propelled forward with all the subtlety of poster art. Not only did Wagner himself expect such an approach, so too did the spirit of the age. True, interested groups were waiting expectantly for a German opera from Schumann, and yet what they wanted was no psychological navel-gazing but due regard for positive values that would bring together the people, or *Volk*. In a word, they wanted positive encouragement, not dark and beetle-browed brooding.

Against this background, the first performance of *Genoveva* in Leipzig on June 25, 1850, was relatively well received—the friendliness of the response being directed as much at Schumann as at his work—but there was also a degree of criticism that proved just short of fatal in the longer term. One writer wondered "why the genuinely vivid and at the same time dramatic course of the old and eerie legend" had not been preserved, and he slated the "insipid world-weariness" and "tormented characterization à la Hebbel." Ernst Kossak, a journalist often hailed as the first feature writer in Berlin, did not even shy away from attacking Schumann in highly personal terms; the composer's talent, he claimed, was "going downhill because of an unfortunate pathological mixture: this opera—assuming we want to retain the name that the composer has given to it—is the culmination of this evil admixture of creative imagination, sentiment, and a completely uneducated judgment. The question is whether his doctor's advice is more needful than that of the philosopher."[7]

But when Kossak also complained that the opera was really "instrumental music accompanied by human voices," he was articulating a response that, dictated by aesthetic and generic considerations, remains valid to this day. It was not just malice that persuaded two of the nineteenth century's leading literary figures to heap mockery on the work. While Hanslick saw "the singer disappear from sight in a fold of the inflated orchestra,"[8] Bernard Shaw, who attended a student performance of the opera at London's Royal College of Music in 1893, felt that the symphonic style of the work was "only tolerable on condition of dismissing as so much superfluous rubbish all of the actual drama shewn on the boards."[9]

For a conductor as fond of experimentation as Nikolaus Harnoncourt, such a shortcoming is actually an advantage. Referring to the opera in the context of performances he conducted at the Zurich Opera in 2008, he spoke enthusiastically not just of a psychological drama but of "a single great symphony—the whole work is built up of a delicate web of leitmotifs." These do not characterize the characters onstage but represent "attitudes, parts of a personality, facets of an individual person"—a person in whom we are intended to recognize not only the historical Schumann but also ourselves.[10]

The nineteenth century had a word for this: "tone poem." And there is no doubt that two things come together in *Genoveva*. On the one hand, Schumann was unable to conceive of music that was not poetic or at least poetically inspired, in the widest sense of that term. And on the other hand, this conviction could never produce program music or opera music in the narrower sense. Whereas Wagner was born to write music for the stage, Schumann declined to share his contemporary's view that music was a woman who gave birth to the musical drama. For him, it was a force *sui generis*—autonomous and subservient to no one.

During the weeks when *Genoveva* was being politely applauded by the good people of Leipzig and encountering only skepticism in the wider world, the rest of the musical scene was looking forward with feverish excitement to a rather different event: the world premiere of Wagner's *Lohengrin*, which was unveiled in Weimar in August 1850 under the direction of Franz Liszt, a man who at that time regarded himself, not without good reason, as a friend of both Wagner and Schumann. He had attended the first performance of

Genoveva in Leipzig, as had Louis Spohr, Ferdinand Hiller, Ignaz Mosche-les, and Niels Gade. But not even *they* could compete with the roster of dis-tinguished musicians who attended the first night of *Lohengrin* two months later. Not only was the great Meyerbeer curious to know what his erstwhile protégé had produced, but literary figures such as Karl Gutzkow and Bettina von Arnim were anxious not to miss Wagner's latest work. And music critics came from as far afield as London and Paris. And all of this was for a com-poser who was living in Switzerland as a political exile and who celebrated the first performance of his latest opera by accomplishing a personal feat of his own and scaling the Rigi.

Genoveva and *Lohengrin* have a remarkable number of points in common, starting with the national romanticism of their subject matter and continuing with the compositional method employed by both composers. Both men felt a common hatred of the hugely successful Meyerbeer and, turning their backs on number opera, took their first steps in the direction of the musical drama, in both cases incurring the wrath of conservative critics. Both *Lohengrin* and *Genoveva* were condemned for containing too few beautiful tunes and too much symphonic ballast.

But there are also differences between the two works, which help to ex-plain why only one of their two composers acquired the status of a hero in the field of opera. In his search for a suitable libretto, Schumann saw himself as a reader burrowing his way through all manner of literary texts and finally set-tling on one of them. However much it may have appealed to him, it was still the work of another. If Schumann had been an opera composer of the stamp of Mozart or Strauss and kept his distance, this would not have mattered. But he was the sort of composer who needed to identify with his libretto just as surely as he had done with the poems that he had set as a lieder composer, and this was bound to cause him problems: he had to serve the different charac-ters whether he liked them or not.

Even Beethoven had had difficulties with this problem in *Fidelio*. Ul-timately, the only characters who mattered to him were the heroic couple of Florestan and Leonore. The rest of the characters — above all, the jailer Rocco, who is really a figure out of a singspiel — remain musically colorless. For his part, Schumann had difficulty breathing life into Genoveva, Siegfried, Golo, and Margaretha. It was easiest for him to identify with Genoveva her-self, but the fact that he felt nothing for any of her three antagonists left its mark on the title role, too. In the final analysis, Genoveva is lacking in any distinctive dramatic profile.

But this was not Wagner's way. He, too, began with a detailed study of literary texts, but he then moved away from them in order to create his own Lohengrin myth with striking scenes of archetypal power and characters whom — musically and dramatically — he was able to imagine from the outset as his own. And since he wanted not only to retrace the outlines of a legend but also to convey a message all of his own, he was more successful than Schumann in bringing out semantically clear strands in the action: on the one hand we have the positive pairing of Lohengrin and Elsa, on the other the two conspirators, Telramund and Ortrud. It is for this reason that the musical leitmotifs that can be identified in both operas are more striking and compelling in Wagner's case than in Schumann's.

When Liszt wrote enthusiastically that "a single chord brings us closer together than any number of phrases,"[11] he was referring not to Schumann but to Wagner and to the bewitching chord that is heard just before Lohengrin's words "Das süße Lied verhallt" (The sweet song has died away). However enthusiastic Nikolaus Harnoncourt may be about the "song of sorrow" at the start of the *Genoveva* overture, it was not this overture that changed the course of musical history but the beguiling sonorities of the prelude to the first act of *Lohengrin*.

In his libretto for an "opera for piano," titled *Schumann, Schubert und der Schnee* (Schumann, Schubert, and snow), the opera director Hans Neuenfels has Schubert say to Schumann in "an aggressive, almost contemptuous tone":

> That's why our operas were bound to fail, Schumann. To write operas, you have to love people openly or hate them just as openly, you have to stand up to society while spoiling for a fight, you have to seek out conflict and want to stretch your powerful ego to breaking point, so that it is broken down into many different pieces, you have to risk making designs on the world when your only safeguard is your own enthusiasm for yourself.

To which Schumann replies: "No, Schubert, we're not like that."[12]

Is there any point to such comparisons? Of course, we have the right to rehabilitate *Genoveva*, but there is no obligation on us to do so. All of us who demand that musical theater should involve drama are not insisting on superficialities but want music that is propelled by the action to achieve things of which it would otherwise be incapable. The fact that Mozart's *La clemenza di Tito* (The clemency of Titus) is unlikely to achieve the popularity of *Le nozze di Figaro* has nothing to do with any falling off in the level of composition but with the inferior quality of the plot. In the case of the later *opera seria*, music and action remain at a respectful distance from one another, whereas in that of the *opera buffa* the plot makes the music its accomplice, inspiring it to play ever more insane tricks on us.

None of this should prevent self-declared lovers of Schumann's music from preferring *Genoveva* to *Lohengrin*. In this, they could claim the support of Mozart's biographer Otto Jahn, who in 1854 wrote of *Lohengrin*: "Instead of artistic form and structure being used to produce true characterization, we find only raw materialism of the most superficial kind."[13]

Fortunately, no important composer has yet succeeded in writing in ways demanded of him by his critics — if he had done, what would be left of his music?

The only photographic double portrait of Robert and Clara Schumann was taken in Johann Anton Völlner's Hamburg studio in March 1850. A steel engraving based on the daguerreotype was already widely available in Schumann's day. Daguerreotypes represent their subjects the wrong way around, and so this image has been reversed in order to ensure that the couple appear as they did in real life. (Photograph: Réunion des Musées Nationaux / Art Resource, NY.)

CHAPTER 10

Director of Music in Düsseldorf (1850–54)

Relocation costs & travel

Transportation of all effects by train from Dresden	132. 7. –
3 people to help with unpacking here at 20 gr.	2. 16. –
To Herr Disch at the inn in Düsseldorf	55. 15. –
Hired servants	1. 15. –
Sundries	– 28. –
Fare for 4½ tickets	58. 15. –

Schumann's housekeeping book, entry for September 1850, following his move to Düsseldorf[1]

Schumann's new post as municipal director of music in Düsseldorf was worth seven hundred and fifty thalers a year. By midcentury, the city had some forty-five thousand inhabitants, many of whom were proud of its large Prussian garrison, while the rest preferred its Academy of Arts. Schumann's preference naturally lay with the latter and he soon became a member of the Paint-Box Society of Artists that was formed in 1848 and made up of members of the academy and freelance artists. The society had originally seen its aim as encouraging the republican aspirations of the bourgeois revolution of 1848–49, but after the failure of that movement it struck out in a new direction and from then on it regarded itself as artistically progressive in its rejection of both outdated romanticism and bloodless neoclassicism, while pinning its colors to the mast of the new "realism" in art. There was a factional thrust to this last-named movement inasmuch as it attacked social inequality in the spirit of the French artist Gustave Courbet, but it was also apolitical, seeking to depict humankind and nature without false pathos and in so doing to examine things that had previously been viewed as unworthy of artistic attention.

In the course of his years in Düsseldorf Schumann assimilated many of the ideas promoted by the city's school of painting, but for the present he was confronted by the sort of everyday musical concerns that he had largely been spared in Dresden. He had to conduct the choral society once a week and give ten concerts a year with the municipal orchestra, together with four major musical events in the city's two main churches, St. Lambert's and St. Maximilian's. The choir was made up of around 120 amateurs, although this number would often be increased for special occasions, while the string section of the orchestra comprised a mixture of around 30 professional and amateur musicians. The wind players were mostly from the local garrison, with only a handful of amateurs — the second oboist, for example, was Wilhelm Wortmann, a member of the city council who went on to become the local mayor.

Such conditions were typical of the period — only in Leipzig were they any better. It was the task of the city's music director to forge his motley troops into a coherent army and turn the situation to as good an advantage as possible. Schumann was fortunate to find in Düsseldorf a musical landscape well cultivated by three of his predecessors: Mendelssohn, Julius Rietz, and Ferdinand Hiller.

It was Hiller who, on moving to Cologne, had commended Schumann to the General Music Society that determined Düsseldorf's musical fate. Schumann hesitated to accept the post, as he did not want to abandon prematurely the vague hope that he might succeed Wagner at the Dresden Court Opera. But he finally reached the point when Dresden struck him as just one more city whose dust he would be happy to shake off from his feet. And Düsseldorf had much to offer; he had just turned forty, and for the first time in his career was now a city's director of music. It was also the first time that he had had a regular salary, meaning greater financial security for Clara, who on December 1, 1851, was to bring another daughter into the world, Eugenie.

The Schumanns' move to Dresden passed uneventfully, unmarked by any public or private celebrations, but when the family arrived at the main station in Düsseldorf at seven o'clock on the evening of September 2, 1850, on the new train from Cologne to Minden, they were greeted by an impressive welcoming committee. The local glee club then serenaded Schumann at the elegant Hotel Breidenbach. Five days later, an official concert was held in the city's Geisler Hall to welcome Schumann to the city. If the surviving parts can be trusted, some 370 singers were involved. To Schumann's surprise, the program included the *Genoveva* overture and the second part of *Paradise and the Peri.* According to Clara's diary, the ensuing reception was notable for its numerous long speeches and shortage of food.

By the following day the couple was brought back to the grim reality of the cares and concerns that beset them, including acute financial worries. Their move to Düsseldorf had proved expensive, and their hotel bill was so exorbitant that they moved as quickly as possible to rooms with a Fräulein Schön on the corner of Alleestraße and Grabenstraße, although this turned out to be a bad move, and Schumann was reduced to "a highly nervous, agitated, and excitable state" by the "constant noise on the main road—barrel organs, screaming children, carriages, and so on." Clara herself was "unable to play on account of all our domestic chores, also I really can't allow myself to be seen among the lower orders here, almost all of whom are coarse, insolent, and pretentious." In short, "I feel like weeping all day!"[2]

Fortunately the society ladies with whom Clara came into contact proved friendly and willing to help, even if their informal and cheerful manner sometimes seemed "to exceed the bounds of femininity and decency." "Married life is supposed to be more frenchified and more frivolous here," she confided in her diary.[3] Instead she clung to the doctor, poet, and writer of music Wolfgang Müller von Königswinter and his wife, who by all accounts were a laudable exception to the rule. The couple maintained even closer contacts with Richard Hasenclever, a physician and aesthete, and the artist Theodor Hildebrandt, who was Eugenie's godfather. This little group of artists also included Carl Sohn, Christian Köhler, and Carl Friedrich Lessing. Other acquaintances were Wilhelm von Schadow, the director of the Düsseldorf Academy of Art and a former friend of Mendelssohn, and Joseph Euler, a local notary with an interest in music. On September 15, the young violinist and later Schumann biographer Wilhelm Joseph von Wasielewski arrived in Leipzig as concertmaster of the orchestra. It was not long before he also assumed the function of Schumann's right-hand man.

Schumann's first appearance as a conductor at the subscription concert on October 24, 1850, was an outright success, not least as a result of Clara's contribution in the form of a brilliant rendition of Mendelssohn's Piano Concerto in G Minor. This was also the first time for many years that she had played from memory. But when she was given a little basket of flowers instead of a fee, she wrote indignantly to Hiller: "It is completely inconceivable that these gentleman should think I'll play at their concerts for nothing, nor can I understand their lack of delicacy in even demanding such a thing! Do they think we're well off?"[4]

The fact that the ten subscription concerts that took place in the course of this first season were essentially a success was due not least to Schumann's ambitious programming: among the works he conducted were Handel's *Israel in Egypt* and Bach's *St. John Passion*, numerous orchestral pieces by Beethoven and, of course, music by Schumann himself, including his *Rhenish* Symphony, which was repeated very soon after its acclaimed first performance on February 6, 1851. On the other hand, the Cello Concerto in A Minor op. 129 that Schumann wrote in October 1850 remained unperformed, at least for the time being, as the cellist Robert Emil Bockmühl for whom it was intended raised a number of persistent and petty objections to the solo part.

The eighth concert of the opening season was devoted almost exclusively to works by Schumann. In spite of the participation of Clara and the popular contralto Sophie Schloß, it was coolly received by its audience — an early sign of the difficulties from which the Schumanns were soon to suffer. Schumann felt persecuted, and for the most part Clara shared that view. As always, there are two sides to the coin. On the one hand, we need to remind ourselves that Schumann had little experience as a conductor and above all he had been dealt a poor hand. If he was prevented from rehearsing a work — as often happened with guest appearances — he would fight back, but if he had to ensure disciplined rehearsals and motivate a possibly unenthusiastic ensemble, he tended to run away rather than try to inspire his forces. When conducting his own compositions, he occasionally seems to have listened to them with his inner ear rather than following what was actually taking place in the concert hall.

Shortly after Schumann took up his new post, the singer Friederike Altgelt reported:

> He is a real character, eccentric but good-natured, silent, often one
> doesn't know whether to laugh at him or become angry. *She is an angel*,
> delightful, kind, childishly cheerful. [. . .] He is an exacting director with
> a keen ear, but he wields his baton in a rather irregular way. *She* directs
> everything — wherever you look, it's *her*. She sets the tone, helps you when
> you get stuck, and always plays the piano for the choral society.[5]

Schumann soon became resigned when things did not go the way he wanted and was either unwilling or unable to intervene decisively and impartially in the many arguments that any leader of a large and motley ensemble almost always has to face. And so we find the pianist and composer Louise Japha complaining after the second concert of the 1851–52 winter season:

It's a pity that a large part of the local public is against Sch[umann]
and listens to all his works in a prejudicial frame of mind; it is easy to
grow impatient when you see how many people — otherwise highly
cultured — have absolutely no idea about Sch[umann] and wish that their
former music director, Hiller, would come back because "he conducts much
better and is much kinder, a man truly at home in the salon."[6]

During his second season in Düsseldorf, Schumann nonetheless introduced local audiences to Handel's *Jephtha* and Bach's *St. Matthew Passion*,
Schubert's C Major Symphony (*Great*), Gade's B-flat Major Symphony,
Mendelssohn's A Major Symphony, and Chopin's Piano Concerto in F Minor. He himself contributed to the proceedings with performances of his own
oratorio *Der Rose Pilgerfahrt* (The pilgrimage of the rose) op. 112 and choral
ballad *Der Königssohn* (The king's son) op. 116. Reporting on the success of
the last work, Clara informed her friend in Dresden, Marie von Lindemann,
in May 1852:

The audience was very enthusiastic, at least to the extent that they are
able to be so here, for it is difficult to find a colder audience in the whole
of Germany; they have absolutely no idea how lucky they are to have
my husband, just as they had no idea with their previous conductors,
Mendelssohn, Rietz, and Hiller. As soon as an opportunity presents itself,
we'll be leaving Düsseldorf.[7]

At the end of 1852, three members of the board of directors of the General
Music Society openly demanded that Schumann curtail his activities as a conductor or even end them completely. The resultant conflict was resolved when
numerous members of the society came out in support of Schumann, but the
corrosive effect of the dispute continued to make itself felt throughout the
1852–53 season, even though there were again important first performances
to celebrate: this time the works included such impressive pieces as the great
choral ballad *Des Sängers Fluch* (The minstrel's curse) op. 139, a cycle of four
shorter ballads titled *Vom Pagen und der Königstochter* (The princess and the
page) op. 140, two movements of the Mass op. 147 and the revised version of
the Symphony in D Minor op. 120.

The situation finally came to a head at the start of the 1853–54 season with
a disastrous performance of Moritz Hauptmann's Mass in G Minor in St.
Maximilian's Church. Schumann's assistant, Julius Tausch, had rehearsed
the work and conducted the final rehearsal. In spite of this, Schumann — evi-

dently energized by the presence in the city of Brahms, Joseph Joachim, and Bettina von Arnim — insisted on conducting the public performance, which was given as part of the official celebrations marking the Feast of St. Maximilian. The performance turned into a fiasco, after which the choir refused to sing Mendelssohn's *First Walpurgis Night* under Schumann's direction at the first subscription concert of the new season. As a result, Tausch conducted the work on October 27, 1853, although at the same concert Schumann himself took the baton for the first performance of his Violin Fantasy op. 131, with Joachim as the soloist. And yet, not even this was what Schumann had in fact wanted, for the fantasy was a late replacement for his new violin concerto, which the directors of the General Music Society had banned outright.

The situation was hopeless. The directors of the society suggested that in future Schumann might conduct only his own works and leave everything else to Tausch, but Schumann indignantly turned down their proposal. The resultant "letters of ultimatum"[8] that Schumann wrote amounted to a resignation that no one on the committee showed any inclination to decline. Even so, it was not until October 1, 1854, that the contract was finally canceled. Until then, Schumann continued to be paid.

The Schumanns again discussed the idea of moving to Vienna or Berlin, reviving plans that they had already mooted and abandoned. For the present they turned their backs on the now-hated city of Düsseldorf only for a short period in the weeks leading up to Christmas 1853. A four-week conducting tour of the Netherlands was intended as a distraction, with Johann Verhulst — now court music director in The Hague — ensuring that it was a success: "Schumann found the concerts well prepared and needed only to stand on the podium in order to conduct," the critic of the *Signale für die musikalische Welt* informed his readers in the context of the concerts in Utrecht, The Hague, Rotterdam, and Amsterdam, concerts that on the whole passed off very well.

In Rotterdam, Schumann conducted his *Rhenish* Symphony and Clara played his piano concerto. After the concert, a large crowd gathered outside his hotel and in spite of the extreme cold, a wind band and a hundred torch-bearing singers performed the Forest Chorus from *Der Rose Pilgerfahrt* and a "birthday march" — presumably an arrangement of Schumann's op. 85, no. 1. Verhulst conducted both works. Clara also performed at court, where Prince Friedrich of the Netherlands turned to her husband and asked what was presumably the obligatory question: "Are you musical, too?"[10] But in general, Schumann was honored not only as a composer but also as a conductor, and it was with some satisfaction, therefore, that he was able to take his leave of the "pig-headed monster,"[11] which is how he had once described the institution of the orchestra. As it turned out, it was to be his definitive farewell.

But Schumann was not only a music director, he was also a composer, and we must now turn our attention to that aspect of his life in Düsseldorf. I have already mentioned the success of his *Rhenish* Symphony, about which I shall have more to say in Intermezzo VIII. There followed the oratorio *Der Rose Pilgerfahrt* op. 112, which had its unofficial first performance in the Schumanns' new home on the Kastanienallee, into which they moved in July 1851. (The street was renamed the Königsallee in 1854.) Here there was a salon that could seat up to sixty people and was admirably suited to a performance of the work's more intimate version with piano accompaniment.

According to the reminiscences of the tenor Ernst Koch, Clara's playing was "wonderfully poetic," while Schumann sat beside her, conducting from the autograph score, "blissfully dreaming."[12] Here, surrounded by a small group of selected professional and amateur singers, including the aforementioned contralto Sophie Schloß as the Elfin Queen, he felt more at his ease than in front of a sometimes alarmingly large ensemble in the Geisler Hall. He could also reckon on greater interest and attention.

Schumann used the second half of 1851 to work on various pieces, including the two Violin Sonatas opp. 105 and 121, the Piano Trio op. 110 and the second version of his Symphony in D Minor. Nor should we forget his overture to Goethe's *Hermann und Dorothea* op. 136 or his choral ballad *Der Königssohn*. We have already had occasion to refer to some of the works from 1852: the choral ballads *Des Sängers Fluch* and *Vom Pagen und der Königstochter*, the Mass op. 147 and the Requiem op. 148. The mass, which Schumann felt was "just as well suited to church as to the concert hall,"[13] is an example of church music that is both elaborately artistic and practicable but even today it remains unjustly ignored. In addition to its rapt melodic writing, it also uses contrapuntal procedures that are never an end in themselves but used for expressive purposes. He later added an offertory, "Tota pulchra es, Maria" (You are all beautiful, Mary), that represents the Protestant composer's contribution to the cult of the Virgin Mary. It is hard to conceive of a more heartfelt piece. As such, it is another example of Schumann's desire to be understood and appreciated by the citizens of Düsseldorf.

Among the works that Schumann wrote in 1853 are his *Drei Klaviersonaten für die Jugend* (Three piano sonatas for young people) op. 118, the overture to the Scenes from Goethe's *Faust*, the Introduction and Allegro for piano and orchestra op. 134, the Violin Fantasy op. 131, the Violin Concerto in D Minor, the *Gesänge der Frühe* (Songs of dawn) op. 133, and the Third Violin Sonata in A Minor (which, as we shall see toward the end of this chapter, represents a reworking of the *F–A–E* Sonata).

As a prophet in his own country, Schumann may not have been held in very high esteem at this time, but his fame continued to grow away from home. It was no accident that he was an honorary member of various societies and institutions, including the Salzburg Mozarteum, the Vienna Academy of Music, the Viennese Gesellschaft der Musikfreunde (Society of Friends of Music), the London Musical Institute, and the Dutch Society for the Promotion of Music. Although publishers may not have been beating down his door, they were still occasionally interested in his works. A typical day in Düsseldorf might well find Schumann fully occupied negotiating with publishers, preparing new works for the printer, arranging piano reductions of large-scale orchestral pieces, or superintending new editions of older compositions. In 1852, he was additionally occupied with a major literary project in the form of a new edition of the articles that he had written for the *Neue Zeitschrift für Musik*. It appeared in 1854 under the title *Gesammelte Schriften über Musik und Musiker* (Collected writings on music and musicians). Its four volumes are a miracle of originality in their ability to explore the subject of music criticism from a multiplicity of perspectives. And yet Schumann did not merely want to set up a literary memorial to himself, he also planned to collect together what others had said about music in the guise of a "garden of musical poets." The project was largely completed, though it had to wait until relatively recently to see the light of day. From Endenich, Schumann wrote to Bettina von Arnim to explain the project:

> In 1853 I thought that under the title "Poets' Garden for Music" I would round off all that can be read in the first poets about music and how it affects them — affects them wondrously like a heavenly language. The finest and most glorious contributions are those of Martin Luther, Shakespeare, Jean Paul, and Rückert.[14]

To this end Schumann paid repeated visits to the Royal Library in Düsseldorf and read Greek and Latin authors, Goethe, Schiller, Heinse, and the Bible in his quest for suitable quotations. We should not see his activities as a collector as a substitute for any flagging interest in composition. Rather, his search was the fulfillment of a long-held and deeply felt wish to authenticate the art of music by means of philosophy and poetry. For him, the ideas found here reflected the range of emotional states that music is capable of expressing. This was a long-standing theme of his: by dint of its union with poetry and thinking, music would gain in effectiveness and meaning.

Although Schumann never abandoned his former habit of immersing himself in the world of his own imagination, he remained receptive to outward stimuli. In the summer of 1851, for example, the Schumanns traveled to southern Germany and Switzerland, a journey described by Clara as "the most beautiful that Robert has undertaken with me. [. . .] Even in Bonn, where we boarded the boat and where there were crowds of boisterous students, the sky looked so clear, the Rhine so green, and, throughout it all, such cheerful music that Robert, too, cheered up and remained so."[15] They also visited Heidelberg, where Schumann was reminded of his student days, after which they traveled on to Basel and Geneva and thence to Chamonix. From their room in the Hôtel Royal they could see Mont Blanc "just as if the good Lord had placed it there for us."[16]

Schumann was then asked to judge a competition for male-voice choirs in Antwerp, an invitation that Clara described as a "curious postlude." He complained about having to work a twelve-hour day and vilified the French choirs, "all of which sang only the worst possible stuff." But a few free days following the competition allowed him to admire Antwerp's art treasures, "especially Rubens," and, in Brussels, to see the "funny little Mannikin." He also bought some lace as a gift for Clara.[17]

Back in Düsseldorf, the Schumanns received some unexpected visitors on September 1, 1851, as Clara noted in her diary:

> 5 in the afternoon, Liszt arrived with the Princess Wittgenstein (whom he intends as his future wife), together with her fourteen-year-old daughter [Marie] and governess. We were surprised to find the princess a somewhat matronly woman who can fascinate Liszt only by her kindness and wit and refined culture, which she possesses in the truest sense of the term.

A children's party planned for Marie's birthday had to be called off, and instead they played an arrangement of Schumann's Symphony in C Major for piano eight hands that existed in manuscript form, and at the end Liszt dazzled his listeners with a new concert work: "As always, he played with truly demonic bravura, his command of his instrument is positively devilish (there's no other word for it), but, ah! the works themselves are such wretched stuff!" Although Liszt felt apparent consternation at his listeners' silence, Clara felt that it was better to say nothing "when one is so deeply offended."[18]

Fortunately, Liszt bore no grudges and was happy to perform Schumann's *Manfred* op. 115 in Weimar on June 13, 1852.

In April 1852, the Schumanns moved to the Herzogstraße for six months, not finding a permanent place to stay in the town until September 1852, when they rented property at 1032 (now 15) Bilker Straße. Shortly before that, Clara suffered a miscarriage and as a result was "in considerable pain," as Schumann noted in his diary.[19] Since the early summer, he himself had been suffering from insomnia, depression, and a speech impediment. By November his hearing was "strangely affected."[20] And on December 27, 1852, he summed up his condition with the words: "For almost half the year I've been laid low with a profound nervous disorder."[21]

In spite of this, he did all he could to get through each day. "His home life," reports Wasielewski, who was an important eyewitness of the composer's final years,

> was regular to the point of monotony. He would work every morning until noon. He would then go for a walk, usually in the company of his wife or one or other of his closer acquaintances. At 1 o'clock he dined, then, after a brief rest, he would work till 5 or 6. At that point he often visited some public place or the private society of which he was a member in order to read the papers and drink a glass of beer or wine. He normally returned home at 8 for his evening meal.[22]

Although Schumann also attended some of the celebrations organized by local artists, he felt more comfortable in the company of friends and acquaintances, enjoying a cigar — he called them "little devils" — or drinking a glass of beer or champagne. He continued to take a lively interest in outstanding natural phenomena. On April 27, 1852, for example, he read in the paper that the respected director of the Düsseldorf Observatory, Robert Luther, had discovered the asteroid Thetis. By the following evening he had turned up at the observatory in person in order to see the phenomenon for himself.

Otherwise Schumann took regular walks through the Hofgarten and, further afield, to some of the local forests and the grounds of Benrath Castle. His eldest daughter, Marie, later told her younger sister Eugenie about family life in Düsseldorf:

> Before we left for school, we used to say "Good morning" to our father — our parents breakfasted alone. We did not see him again until lunchtime, when he sometimes chatted with us but often remained silent or spoke to our mother. [...] After lunch we returned to school and saw our father

again only in the evening when he stopped working—by then it was already growing dark. But it was wonderful when this happened for he then devoted himself to us entirely. When we were small, he would let us ride on his knees, reciting a little poem, or he played a game with us that he called "Bread in the baker's oven" and which involved his taking one of us by the hands and sliding us between his legs.[23]

The children were sometimes included whenever their father pursued one of his new spiritualist interests, about which Clara reports candidly and with a certain indulgence. "When he starts his table-rapping, he is completely relaxed and agreeably excited," she described a meeting in the Schumanns' home during the Thirty-First Lower Rhineland Music Festival in May 1853. Shortly beforehand Schumann himself had written to Hiller in Paris:

> We tried out table-rapping for the first time yesterday. A wonderful power! Just imagine: I ask the table to tell me the rhythm of the first two bars of the C Minor Symphony! It hesitated longer than usual before answering— but finally it started: ⁊ ♫ | ♩ | —only a little on the slow side. When I said: "But the tempo is faster, my dear table!" it made haste to beat the right time.[25]

We do not need to interpret such actions as harbingers of Schumann's mental breakdown but may regard them, rather, as a meaningful attempt at self-help—perhaps he was trying to find a harmless escape value for all the worries with which he was obsessed. It was harmless to the extent that table-rapping was then regarded as a piquant social pastime with no obloquy attached to it. In this context it is worth recalling an entry in Cosima Wagner's diary for April 1, 1872, describing a visit by Nietzsche: "Yesterday we tried without success to make a table move; we had spoken about it at lunchtime. R[ichard] explains it as a matter of will power, I as fraud."[26]

Schumann's pleasure in being able to add a touch of art to his everyday existence emerges from a short piece for vocal quartet and piano to which Clara gave the title: "On 13 September 1853, composed by Robert for Klara [*sic*] on the gift of a grand piano." It opens with the lines "Die Orange und Myrthe hier, / Und rings der Blumen Zier" (The orange and the myrtle here / And all around the flowers dear). Clara naturally recalled the time thirteen years earlier when her husband had given her her first piano as a bridal gift and added the lines about orange and myrtle. In 1853, to mark her birthday, he secretly bought a new instrument from the Düsseldorf piano maker Johann Bernhard Klems and also lined up four singers who surprised Clara with a setting of the familiar words as she entered the apartment. "It may sound arrogant when I say it, but isn't it true that I'm the happiest woman alive?" she asked her diary after they had tried out Schumann's latest works on the new piano.[27]

Clara was thirty-four when she wrote these lines. Meanwhile, the twenty-year-old Johannes Brahms was on a walking tour of the Rhine valley, starting out from Mainz. He had previously given recitals in several towns and cities in northern Germany. In Hanover he was introduced to Joseph Joachim, Schumann's twenty-two-year-old protégé, and in Weimar he met Liszt. In Bonn, finally, he encountered Schumann's former concertmaster Wasielewski, so that there were now no fewer than three musicians to draw his attention to Schumann. Of these three, Wasielewski was particularly insistent that he should call on Schumann in Düsseldorf.

Like Schumann, Brahms was a great admirer of the writings of E. T. A. Hoffmann — so much so, indeed, that in the autograph score of his Piano Sonata op. 1, he attributed the piece to "Johann Kreisler junior," alluding to the fictional character whom Schumann had already honored in his *Kreisleriana*. Of Schumann's compositions, he knew only *Carnaval* but did not think very highly of it, no doubt because he found it too illustrative in character. In order for Brahms to demonstrate greater appreciation of Schumann's music, he first needed to spend some time on the Mehlem estates of the Cologne financier Wilhelm Ludwig Deichmann, a visit organized by Wasielewski. Here there were scores aplenty; here local and foreign artists would often meet to make music in sociable surroundings; and it was here, finally, that Brahms decided to call on Schumann in Düsseldorf, announcing his visit for September 30.

The composer and conductor Franz Wüllner later recalled that in 1853 there was almost universal enthusiasm for the "slim youth with long blond hair and a veritable head of John the Baptist, from whose eyes flashed energy and wit."[28] But this was only the start, for when Brahms arrived in Düsseldorf, Schumann acquired an heir in spirit, and Clara a friend for life. Brahms remained in Düsseldorf for over a month. Writing when the visit was already over, Clara recalled:

> this month introduced us to a quite wonderful person in the twenty-year-old composer Brahms from Hamburg. Here is another of those people who seems positively God-sent! He played us sonatas, scherzos, etc. of his own composition, all of them showing exuberant imagination, depth of feeling, and mastery of form. Robert says that there was nothing that he could tell him to take away or to add. [. . .] He has a great future before him, for he will first find the true field for his genius when he begins to write for the

orchestra! Robert says that one can only hope that heaven may keep him fit and well![29]

This was a ray of light in the darkness surrounding the arguments over the post of music director, arguments that were eating away at Schumann's self-esteem. It was not that he felt that he had burned himself out as a composer or that he could already foresee his own premature end, but there were times when he doubted whether there was any point to what he was doing: he missed his comrades from Leipzig — in other words, the members of the League of David. But now a new community of artists was opening its arms to him and telling him that his work was not in vain but that there were young people able to carry forth his message into the world. This group of artists, which had been summoned into existence in so wondrous a way, included not only Schumann, Clara, and Brahms but now also the young Joseph Joachim and the twenty-five-year-old Albert Dietrich, who was then living in Düsseldorf as Schumann's pupil.

In the middle of October Joachim announced that he would be coming from Hanover to visit them, prompting the three composers in Düsseldorf to surprise him with a sonata for violin and piano based on the three notes F–A–E, the initials of Joachim's motto in life, *Frei, aber einsam* (free but solitary). Schumann wrote the second and fourth movements, Dietrich the opening movement, and Brahms the Scherzo, albeit without reference to the motto, which Brahms was later to appropriate in the form *Einsam, aber frei* (solitary but free). The joint piece was intended to demonstrate that the old Schumannesque spirit was still alive and well: the poetic symbol guaranteed that the work as a whole would have a deeper meaning, one that its compositional structure on its own was unable to provide.

Brahms had been in Düsseldorf for less than two weeks when Schumann wrote his famous essay "New Paths" and published it overnight in the *Neue Zeitschrift für Musik*, even though he had not been actively involved with the paper for the last ten years. He spoke of the fulfillment of his Messianic hopes of a man who was "fated to give expression to the times in the highest and most ideal manner."[30]

It would be wrong to dismiss the hymnlike tone of this article as mawkish sentimentality on the part of a man bruised and battered by fate, for the essay, which appeared on the paper's front page, was intended to create a splash that would provoke tremors among initiates. True, Franz Brendel, who was now the paper's editor and who had in the meantime switched his allegiance from

Schumann to Wagner and Liszt, unceremoniously dismissed his predecessor's aesthetic credo as representing an "outdated standpoint,"[31] but he was unwilling to deny Schumann a platform. There is a certain irony, then, to the fact that in a journal that was awaiting a Messiah by the name of Wagner and that was biding its time by opening its columns to Liszt's ideas on educating the masses, Schumann should speak of hopes very different from those of its editor. Schumann, after all, was hoping for "a secret alliance of kindred spirits" that would perpetuate a type of music that was not "absolute" in the spirit of a dogmatic writer like Hanslick but "poetic" in the sense understood by Bach and Beethoven and by their spiritual successors, Kreisler, Florestan, and Eusebius.

The Road to Freedom

F riedrich Nietzsche was not only musically literate, he could also write eloquently on the subject of music. He praised Beethoven for "the invention of the grand form for the expression of passion" and criticized Beethoven's successors for having failed in their attempt to imitate their model:

> That is why the symphony after Beethoven is such a strangely confused affair, especially when in its individual parts it still stammers the language of Beethovenian pathos. The means are not appropriate to the objective, and the objective as a whole is not at all clear to the listener because it was never clear to the composer either.[1]

By demanding a clarity that cannot exist in purely instrumental music, Nietzsche was hoping to break a lance for the Wagnerian musical drama, but at the same time he found the Achilles heel of the post-Beethovenian symphony—for however much composers may have wanted to equal their great model in matters of ethos and pathos they had signally failed to produce any works of comparably concentrated power.

Beethoven's symphonies are like major public buildings: imposing but without any false monumentality, well constructed but elastic, presenting us with an overall structure but evincing loving detail. Quite how Beethoven achieved this remains his secret—in spite of considerable advances in professional musical analysis. How, for example, does such an approach explain the compelling logic of the sequence of ideas in the Allegretto of the Seventh Symphony? To all appearances, this is a harmless set of variations. But which other composer would have succeeded within this straightforward form in conveying what one commentator has called the "sense of a mounting development, the impression of a building rising ever higher"?[2] And which other composer would have managed the transition from measured steps to hymn-like singing so that listeners do not know what is happening to them and yet have the feeling that what is happening is nonetheless inevitable?

Not even Mendelssohn and Schumann — the leading representatives of the generation after Beethoven and Schubert in the field of the German symphony — could do this. Although they had poetic ideas, rousing mottos, and the will to create Nietzsche's "grand form for the expression of passion," they found it hard to reconcile these two elements. Beginning with his *Spring* Symphony, Schumann's symphonies offer a cornucopia of memorable motifs and beautiful melodies that fill the listener with very real pleasure each time that they appear, but, formally speaking, we still ask ourselves: why this particular transition? Why this element in the development section? And where is the consistent attempt to guide the listener's expectations?

The objection that it is wrong to judge Schumann by Beethovenian standards and that formal rigor should not be used as a criterion by which to assess the excellence of romantic music is valid to only a limited degree, simply because as a symphonist Schumann applied Beethovenian criteria to himself. Indeed, there are times when even more than his model he strove on the one hand to unify the thematic material and on the other to achieve multilayered textures. There are also many hidden relationships and cross-references that invest his symphonies with the kind of musical poetry that permeates almost every one of his works.

In short, the problem is not that these works lack complexity but that they lack straightforwardness. In view of the fact that their message is sometimes excessively coded, Schumann himself seems to have felt himself a stranger within own symphonic structures. As we have already noted, he was assailed by self-doubts on completing his Third Symphony and wondered if "anyone would like it," suggesting that he was then struggling to come to terms with his own introvert neoclassicism.

In terms of the "grand form for the expression of passion," the litmus test for any composer came above all in the final movement of his symphonies. Could he finally harvest the fruits of his labors? Had he worked sufficiently hard in the previous movements to be able to bring in a harvest at all? This was the central problem of idealistic music aesthetics — one that in the generation before Schumann had been handled by Beethoven on the very highest level. In their very different ways, Beethoven's first eight symphonies all provide an answer to the question of how the final movement can provide the most compelling distillation of all that has gone before it. Only in the final

The autograph score of the opening bars of the first movement of Schumann's
Third Symphony in E-flat Major (*Rhenish*) op. 97 (1850). (Courtesy of the
Stiftung Preußischer Kulturbesitz, Berlin — Staatsbibliothek. Photograph:
bpk, Berlin / Art Resource, NY.)

movement of the Ninth did he then capitulate in the face of his own demands. Here it is impossible for musical logic alone to give meaning to that movement. Rather, the composer requires a *deus ex machina* in the guise of Schiller's "Ode to Joy."

Wagner regarded the Ninth Symphony's solution to the problem posed by the final movement as a challenge: from then on musical ideas would have to be expressed not through the medium of the symphony but through that of the musical drama. Schumann's various solutions to the problem of the symphonic finale, conversely, appeal to the "classical" Beethoven of the first eight symphonies. But with what results! In the final movement of the Symphony in C Major, it is not one of Schumann's motifs that triumphs but one taken over from Beethoven in a spirit of reverence. As we observed in an earlier chapter, when we quoted Peter Gülke on the subject, this is an astonishing example of a composer breaking free from the rules.

But it was in his final symphony, the *Rhenish*, that Schumann achieved an even more amazing, not to say pioneering, feat of breaking free from these rules. The opening of the first movement in the autograph score is reproduced here. Over the symphony as a whole it is no longer Beethoven who hovers as a superego but Schubert, who functions as a benevolent spirit with his Symphony in C Major (*Great*). Without being intimidated by him, Schumann celebrates in this work the "novelistic character" that reminded him of Vienna — "Vienna with its spire of St. Stephen's Cathedral, its beautiful women, its public splendor, and the way in which it is girded by the Danube as if with countless ribbons, stretching out into the blossoming plain that gradually rises to ever greater heights."[3]

Schumann could not have written in such a relaxed way about one of Beethoven's symphonies. But he was willing to take this risk in the case of Schubert, and he chose the C Major Symphony as the model for his *Rhenish*. When he did so a good ten years after his first encounter with it, it was not in the spirit of a stylistic copy. Rather, Schubert's music was like one of Jean Paul's novels in that its function was to open up new worlds to his imagination.

Schumann did not depart from his usual method of interweaving themes and motifs or of pointing up their relationships and of using assonance as a compositional device.[4] But all of this remains in the background and at least for the unprejudiced listener plays no part in the listening process, since such listeners perceive the symphony above all as a sequence of events which, viewed from a Beethovenian standpoint, are juxtaposed in an almost insolent manner. It is not the architectural form but the narrative element that occupies the forefront of the listener's attention.

As a result, an early review of the symphony — presumably based on hints handed out by Schumann's close circle of friends — speaks of a work in which "a scene from Rhineland life unfolds with cheery joviality," while the second movement recalls "beautiful boat rides between grape-green hills and the grape pickers' welcoming celebrations." In the third movement, the "tone poet leans his head in thought against the old castle window" before "the subtle sounds of natural horns" recall him to the present.[5]

This is admirably in tune with Schumann's rapturous description of Schubert's symphony, and it also reflects the impression that is left on listeners. It is no accident that for many years the main themes of the first two movements were used as signature tunes for two programs broadcast by the former North-West German Radio, their characteristic local color designed to drum up trade for the programs in question. Of course, the *Rhenish* Symphony and a "Rhineland character" are not the same thing, but it is nonetheless true that Schumann's music has a quality that makes the "re-creative" listener think that such attributions are meaningful.

From the fourth movement of the *Rhenish* Symphony onward, Schumann adopts a concept that on a formal and narrative level differs in fundamental ways from the one that Schubert had used. Instead of steering toward the final movement, he interpolates a movement that introduces what in the context of traditional four-movement form can only be described as an irregularity. In the printed score this movement is headed "Feierlich" (solemn), but at the first performance it was marked "In the character of the accompaniment to a solemn ceremony."[6] Schumann's early biographers claim that the composer was inspired by the elevation of Archbishop Johannes von Geissel to the rank of cardinal in Cologne Cathedral.

But details such as these do not matter. Rather, what concerns us is the novelty of the composer's narrative strategy, which no longer allows him to follow up a third movement occupying the place of a Scherzo with a finale — whether he was motivated by a conscious awareness of the tradition in which he was working or by mere naïveté is irrelevant here. Instead, this final movement is "staged" in an extremely reflective way. In his fourth movement, Schumann not only departs from the largely jovial character of the three preceding movements, he also changes the narrative level in not insubstantial ways: much as E. T. A. Hoffmann and Jean Paul do in their novels, he spends a whole chapter directing his gaze at the past and in doing so enters a world of mystical darkness that fills him — and us — with awe and apprehension. From a musical point of view, Schumann uses layers of fourths to erect the monumental façade of a gloomy building inside which may be heard the sounds of individual anguish inspired by Bach's chromatic counterpoint. In this context, R. Larry Todd has drawn attention to the C-sharp Minor Fugue from part 1 of *The Well-Tempered Clavier*.[7]

There is no compelling logic to all this. Rather, it is based on narrative calculation: before "everyone runs outside," to quote from the aforementioned critic's account of the final movement,[8] listeners are led inside a locked and darkened room. And before they can abandon themselves to the cheerful present, of which the first three movements have already given them a taste, they are first confronted by the splendor but also by the sorrows of the past.

Only then may we cheerfully cast aside all unwanted baggage and strike out on the road to freedom once and for all. But this brings us back to the problem of the idea underpinning the final movement, a problem that Schumann proceeds to solve in an altogether virtuosic way. In the final movement of the *Rhenish* Symphony he may play with the device of bringing together thematic threads that he has woven in the previous movements, but at the same time he has glimpsed an alternative solution, a third way between a finale that promises grand solutions to all the problems previously raised and a finale that regards itself as a simple envoi heedless of all that has gone before it.

This third solution is the road to freedom, and it suggested itself to Schumann because it leads out of the darkness and oppressive confines of the locked space. The fact that he found this exit at all is in itself sufficient grounds for celebration — nothing more is needed to legitimize the final movement. As listeners we may enjoy our present lives — thus runs the symphony's message.

There are good reasons the final movement begins with the performance marking "Dolce" (sweetly): the less bombast a conductor brings to it, the more he or she will be able to demonstrate to an audience the ease with which Schumann can promulgate a festive atmosphere. There are times when we may even be reminded of a fairground, notably in the context of the spirited trumpet signal that repeatedly asserts itself from bar 60 onward or the witty way in which the basses pluck up courage in bars 244–46 before launching into the final jubilation in bar 255.

In spite of these popular elements, the movement is far from wholly innocent in character. Toward the end of what we may perhaps be permitted to call its development section, for example, Schumann produces a veritable stroke of genius. Starting in bar 130, the horns suddenly expound a jubilant fanfare motif in B major. Following a bold harmonic shift, this motif is then transposed to B-flat major and from there it modulates to the home key of E-flat major. This in itself is enough to create the effect of a sophisticated compositional triumph on the completion of a particularly difficult feat. And yet the punch line is still to come. As the consequent phrase of the fanfare motif, Schumann conjures up the main theme of the final movement and introduces a kind of recapitulation at a totally unexpected point in the musical argument. Two armies that had previously operated on their own close ranks in a striking manner in order to march together in joint formation toward the hymnlike closing celebrations. For me, this passage always has a feeling of déjà vu to it in the sense that although I know what to expect, I still feel a thrill of excitement when that moment finally arrives.

Peter Gülke has called the *Rhenish* Symphony a "solitary work."[9] His aim is not to deny the work's communicative qualities, which audiences have always been able to appreciate. Rather, his position is that of a historian aware that between 1824 and 1876 — the dates of the first performances of Beethoven's Ninth and Brahms's First — there was no significant symphony that was not more emphatic in its rejection not only of traditional four-movement form but also of obvious links between its movements,[10] to say nothing of idealistic weight and German interiority. "Folk-like elements had to prevail," Schumann told Wasielewski.[11] And this is also the message of the *Rhenish* Symphony. If we may ignore the specific function of the fourth movement, the work is sparing in its use of musical metaphysics and of pointers to ideas that might lie hidden behind the actual sound of the music. And it also eschews Nietzsche's demand for a "grand form for the expression of passion" in favor of a more instantly accessible narrativity. While professing his faith in the "grand symphony," Schumann manages to make do without grand gestures and problematical promises of happiness. At least within the German tradition, this is practically unique.

The only bust of Schumann to be made during his lifetime is this plaster bust by the Düsseldorf sculptor Johann Peter Götting. An entry in the Schumanns' housekeeping book for March 2, 1852, reads simply, "Sitting for a sculptor" (*Tagebücher* 3/2:587). The original — now in the Schumann Museum in Zwickau — is almost life-size but has been reproduced in many smaller formats. (Photograph courtesy of the Heinrich Heine Institute of the Regional Capital of Düsseldorf.)

CHAPTER 11

The Late Works

> *The task of formulating a new aesthetic is like trying to square the*
> *circle. There is always an infinite gap between theory and practice,*
> *between the rule and its example, and between laws and freedom. But*
> *perhaps this gap is more important than the whole.*
>
> Schumann's note in his collection of mottos[1]

Schumann had copied out this passage from Wolfgang Menzel's article "Aesthetics" in the early 1830s. Two decades later it had lost none of its relevance for him but continued to encapsulate his constant attempt to strike a balance between what he wanted to achieve in terms of the aesthetics of art and what he actually did accomplish as a composer.

Schumann and Wagner were the only nineteenth-century composers to underwrite their activities with a permanent series of reflections on the philosophy of art. By the early 1850s, Schumann had concrete reasons for doing so inasmuch as his works had become central to contemporary discourse on musical thinking. On the admittedly relatively small stage that was then seeking to raise the profile of German musical culture, the question was forever being asked: was Schumann the great hope for the future, or did he represent an "outmoded standpoint"? As we have already observed, even his successor as the editor of the *Neue Zeitschrift für Musik* reproached Schumann for clinging to the past, by which he meant that against the background of the bourgeois revolution music could no longer muddle along as a separate, special art but must open itself up to the great questions of the day and in that way contribute to social renewal. In the political realm this process had failed with the violent suppression of the revolutions of 1848 and 1849, with the result that all hopes were now placed in the cultural "superstructure." Progressive contemporaries banked on the idea of a utopian "total artwork" in which all desires and hopes would be subsumed, as in the symphonic poems of Liszt and the future music dramas of Wagner.

The goals of the "realists" were less high-flown. Theirs was a movement promoted above all by the journal *Die Grenzboten*, which drew most of its support from literature and the visual arts while also influencing discussions in the field of music. Although there were lines of communication between Liszt and Wagner on the one hand and the partisans of *Die Grenzboten* on the other, the differences between the two factions were more striking. Whereas Wagner and Liszt had grand utopian ideas aimed at amelioration, the champions of realism, at least as far as its German variant were concerned, were satisfied with rather less than that. For them, it was enough if the arts reported positively on the present rather than trying to escape from the world by seeking refuge in a romantic past. This also allowed them to avoid any unduly harsh critique of prevailing conditions. The family paper *Die Gartenlaube* shared *Die Grenzboten*'s views and was initially progressive in tone. It was here, for example, that Berthold Auerbach's *Dorfgeschichten* (Village stories) was published alongside reproductions of socio-critical genre scenes that were part of the repertory of Düsseldorf's "realistic" school of painters at this time.

With his lively interest in current affairs, Schumann was familiar with all of this. For him, it was partly living history, partly the actual present. In his youth he had championed romanticism, before sympathizing with the bourgeois revolution. He had spoken frequently to Liszt and Wagner and as a result he knew their own positions. He also met Auerbach on many occasions in Düsseldorf, and he was a regular visitor to the Düsseldorf studios of the city's various painters. Now he had to define — or redefine — his own standpoint.

On the occasion of the publication of his collected writings in 1854, Schumann was pleased to note that he had no reason to take back any of the views on musical aesthetics that he had expressed in his articles for his *Neue Zeitschrift für Musik*. He had remained the tone poet that he had always been. The only difference was that depending on the situation his tone poetry had tended more in the direction of romanticism, more in that of neoclassicism, and more toward the popularity of folk music — assuming that it did not embrace all three of them at once.

Schumann did not reject the cultural and political programs of Wagner and Liszt, nor was he opposed in principle to new genres such as the musical drama and the symphonic poem. After all, he had struck out on the road to music drama with his opera *Genoveva* and had created a whole new genre with his choral ballads, while *Manfred* had brought new luster to the melodrama. And in a letter to Liszt he was sufficiently fair-minded to describe Wagner's artistic creed, as expressed in *Opera and Drama*, as "very significant."[2] No, the dividing line lay elsewhere and affected one of Schumann's most sacrosanct concerns, the creative act itself.

Each of these three composers required an outside impetus to begin work on a new piece. But whereas Liszt in his symphonic poems and Wagner in his music dramas set out from lofty concepts such as myth, which they sought to present to their listeners' emotions with the help of their music, Schumann drew his inspiration from whatever he found in his everyday life: "It can be a flower or a poem that is all the more spiritual in consequence, an instinctual drive in raw nature or a work of poetic awareness." We have already quoted the continuation of this credo:

I am affected by everything that happens in the world: politics, literature, people — I think about everything in my own way, and this then seeks to vent itself and find an outlet through music. That is why many of my compositions are so difficult to understand because they relate to remote interests, including even significant ones, and because everything remarkable that happens in this age moves me and I then have to express it in my music.[3]

This marks the dividing line between the two approaches. Whereas music was a means to an end for Liszt and Wagner, it was the one and only truth for Schumann. Of course, it was "truth" as it appeared to the romantic artist within the confines of his own existence, whether in the form of his daily routine or of some particularly gripping reading matter. For Schumann it was an absolute sacrilege to use music in a rational way to implement ideas. When music and ideas met, it was ultimately music alone that had any permanence: it was divine and nondisposable, whereas ideas were mutable and a product of human agency. In February 1854, Schumann spelled out this point in a letter to the writer on music Richard Pohl, whose early admiration for the composer was later to turn to criticism: "Do not look for it [i.e., a politically correct definition of music] in philosophical expressions or in subtle distinctions. The fellow with an open mind and heartfelt emotions understands music more profoundly than the keen-thinking Kant."[4]

The German musicologist Bernhard Appel knows as much as anyone about Schumann. In conversation he once spoke of the composer's "spiritual homelessness," pointing out that although he was a baptized and confirmed Protestant, Schumann was not a committed Christian. But as the plentiful quotations contained in his "Poet's Garden" indicate, Schumann certainly believed in art in a way that makes Liszt and Wagner seem positively godless — godless in the sense that they sought to steer the compositional process along rational lines in furtherance of their own desires and aims, whereas Schumann continued to believe that it was inspiration that guided his pen as a composer. And *that* was something godlike.

Of course, these traces of metaphysics in Schumann's thinking about music should not mislead us into imputing to him an understanding of "absolute" music of the kind propagated by Hanslick in his book *Vom Musikalisch-Schönen* (The beautiful in music), which first appeared in print at this time. Ideally Hanslick wanted a composer who produced "regularly beautiful bodies of sound" beyond all extra-musical insinuations. Listeners could assimilate these works only in the guise of "pure contemplation." As such, Hanslick's attitude comes suspiciously close to that of Plato's theory of ideas — and Plato, as we know, was famously skeptical about music.[5]

Schumann, by contrast, espoused a kind of "poetic realism" — to use Ulrich Tadday's felicitous phrase.[6] As we have already observed, Schumann saw music not as an art concerned with ideas that could be reduced to categories and concepts but as a "philosophy of the mind."[7] To that extent a work of music was based on the experience and communication of specific states of mind. Although these states of mind may have all manner of different causes, they are also produced by external stimuli and are therefore real. In other words, they are not due to the mere contemplation of pure ideas. Whereas this aspect of Schumann's thinking flew in the face of Hanslick's views on aesthetics, the category of the poetic also represented a repudiation of Wagner and Liszt. Realistically experienced states of mind were merely the starting point and were poeticized in the act of composition and raised from the personal to the universal. As Schumann put it in his letter to Pohl, this process resulted in "spiritual beauty in its most beautiful form."[8]

In short, Schumann's music was not a continuation of his diary entries using the resources of music but an attempt to invest a diffusely experienced reality with meaning. His message to his fellow fighters might run as follows: "We experience the moments of pleasure and anxiety within the reality of this world more intensely than others and we do everything in our power to turn the water of our daily experiences into the wine of an artistic experience." And Schumann felt particularly happy that at the end of his own creative life he had met the young Brahms, in whom he saw another such fellow fighter in an altogether ideal guise. Here was a member of the League of David who on the one hand knew how to write believable music based on profound personal experience and at the same time was able to channel the floodtide of sounds along such poetic lines that listeners could think only of music. Brahms was the true Messiah, whereas Liszt's "Weimar gospels," as Schumann ironically called them,[9] proclaimed tidings that could just as well be peddled without the need for music.

This does not mean that Schumann's music was lacking in a political message. But it is a message that cannot be pinned down to a few republican marches and freedom songs. Rather, such a message was more general in character and only latently present. Moreover, Schumann was part of the radical change — or paradigm shift — that was marked in the political realm by the bourgeois revolution of 1848 and 1849. In his early piano works, he had tended to be *against* something — the *juste milieu* of the philistines — whereas after the revolution he was now *in favor of* popular education in a nationalist spirit. This was a reflection of the credo of realism, although Schumann put it into practice in only *some* of his post-1848 compositions — in particular the choral ballads and large sections of the late chamber works and the pieces written for domestic consumption. The *Rhenish* Symphony may also be included under this heading.

Of course, Schumann did not have to demonstrate any greater degree of national consciousness after 1848 since he had always championed a specifically German musical culture. But there is perhaps a sense in which toward the end of his career he fought more vigorously for the national inheritance than he had done at an earlier date. In support of this suggestion is his dismissive response to Richard Pohl in February 1854 after Pohl had proposed a toast to Liszt and Wagner as two "musicians of the future": "What you regard as musicians of the future, I regard as musicians of the present, and what you claim as musicians of the past (Bach, Handel, and Beethoven) strike me as the best musicians of the future."[10]

By generally upholding older German values, Schumann may have been in tune with the spirit of the times, but by continuing to criticize prevailing political conditions, by setting ballads by Ludwig Uhland, who sat on the far left in the Frankfurt National Assembly, and by writing to the extreme left-wing poet Hermann Rollett on February 7, 1854 and asking him for the text for a new choral ballad, Schumann also served notice of his credentials as a militant republican.

Those elements that were aimed at instructing the nation and that are found more especially in the composer's choral ballads inevitably raise the question whether this music should be regarded as a means to an end in the same way that Liszt's symphonic poems and Wagner's music dramas were a means to an end. By the same token, Liszt could also claim that with *Les préludes* and *Mazeppa* he had written orchestral music that was accessible to listeners even without a knowledge of his program of "national education." And in the case of *Tristan und Isolde*, Wagner could draw his listeners' attention to a motific fabric that would be a credit to any symphony. Here we are dealing with the deliberate drawing of clear-cut boundaries at the edge of the respective composer's works, rather than with any appreciable differences. For both parties it was a question of character: either they decided to champion the magic of musical poetry or they espoused the dramaturgy of the total artwork.

Even if the term "poetic realism" is a suitable key with which to gain access to the works that Schumann composed in Düsseldorf, those works are nonetheless remarkable for their astonishing heterogeneity. While Schumann's musical handprint is everywhere in evidence, there are far greater stylistic differences than we find, for example, in Mendelssohn's works, which almost all remain committed to an intellectually based neoclassical romanticism. Brahms's works, too, are far more stylistically consistent than the later Schumann felt was necessary, to say nothing of Wagner, for whom such questions became irrelevant as soon as he pinned his colors to the mast of the musical drama. And as for Bruckner, we are reminded of the wit who once claimed — not entirely unjustly — that the Austrian composer wrote the same symphony nine times in all.

By contrast, the range of Schumann's Düsseldorf works is vast: at one end of the scale are the intentionally popular choral ballads and the oratorio *Der Rose Pilgerfahrt* (The pilgrimage of the rose), at the other the hermetic violin sonatas and the *Songs of Dawn*. Between these two extremes are the songs for voice and piano, the Mass and Requiem, and the three symphonic works: the *Rhenish* Symphony and the cello and violin concertos. Yet not even these last three works present a uniform picture, for whereas the symphony is remarkably forward-looking, the Cello Concerto in A Minor op. 129 is neoclassical in character, with its typically Schumannesque ideas and beautiful solo writing, but also a stereotypical formal structure. The violin concerto, finally, reveals a completely different side of Schumann as an orchestral composer breaking free from generic conventions, for all that relics of those conventions continue, of course, to be present.

During his earlier period, Schumann had composed his music and written his articles with a striking degree of careful planning: first there was the piano music, then the songs for voice and piano, after which came the orchestral works, then chamber music, and finally a great oratorio. During his years in Düsseldorf, conversely, Schumann seems to have been keen to demonstrate a more general side of his nature. In order to avoid the concert-guide approach of discussing one work after another, the present writer prefers to offer a tour d'horizon that will, however, linger at rather greater length over a few of these works — for the most part the ones that are relatively unknown.

The three choral ballads after poems by Ludwig Uhland are rarely performed today. Schumann set them to music in a dramatized form prepared by Richard Pohl. Scored for large-scale forces of solo voices, chorus, and full orchestra, they were written with the aim of providing amateur choirs with works that, however ambitious, were not too difficult to perform. Dramaturgically compelling, they explore themes that were very much in the air at this time.

To put it crudely, the new genre seemed to audiences to be ballads dressed in particularly luxurious musical garb. Such works have obvious parallels with the tableaux vivants presented at the Düsseldorf Academy of Art even during Mendelssohn's time in the city, when they were regularly accompanied by music. Handel's oratorios, too, are a distant part of the same picture — not stylistically, but in terms of their popular monumentality. Here one thinks especially of Schumann's setting of Uhland's *Des Sängers Fluch* (The minstrel's curse) op. 139, which tells the old tale of a harper and his son. At court they sing of "spring and love, of a blissful golden age, of freedom, manly virtue, troth and righteousness," moving the exquisitely sensitive queen to tears, while her mistrustful consort suspects betrayal and in his fury strikes down the younger minstrel with his sword. The father thereupon curses the "proud halls," which promptly crumble to the ground.

While dramatizing the poem, Pohl — undoubtedly with Schumann's agreement — added considerably to the libretto's political thrust. In his version, the two minstrels sing "the German anthem, a freedom song from ages past," which contains the following lines:

Wenn "Freiheit! Vaterland!" ringsum erschallet,
Kein Sang tönt schöner in der Männer Ohren;
Im Kampfe, wo solch heilig Banner wallet,
Hat sich der Mann das schönste Loos erkoren.
Dem Volke Heil, wo dieses Lied erschallet!

Dem Helden Preis, der diesem Volk geboren!
Bald blüht der Frühling, bald der gold'ne Friede,
Mit mildern Lüften und mit sanftem Liede.

[When "Freedom! Fatherland!" rings out around, / No song in menfolk's
ear doth fairer sound; / In battle where this sacred banner flies / No man
could choose a fairer fate than this. / All hail the nation where this song is
sung! / All hail the hero from this nation sprung! / The spring will come and
bring a golden peace / With milder breezes and a song's release.]

Elsewhere in his libretto Pohl refers explicitly to "Master Uhland" in order to
ensure that there is no doubt that the "freedom song from ages past" actually
applies to the present day, a telescoping of timelines intended as a tribute to a
pioneer of the bourgeois revolution who had in the meantime withdrawn into
himself without, however, accepting the prevailing conditions. At a time when
Schumann was writing his choral ballads, Uhland was refusing to accept either the Prussian order Pour le mérite or the Bavarian Order for Science and
Art, arguing that he had no desire to emerge from the bankruptcy of German
hopes weighed down with princely baubles.

Writers on Schumann have regularly praised *Des Sängers Fluch*. One of
the composer's contemporaries, the Leipzig poet and writer Peter Lohmann,
for example, claimed that "every character is worked out in vivid detail, right
down to individual features, while the orchestra is treated in an endlessly
subtle and meaningfully nuanced way and the choruses explore the whole
gamut of the life of the emotions."[11] And Michael Struck, a Schumann scholar
of the present day, has admired the "high level of differentiation" that the
composer has brought to the "motific and thematic writing, as well as to the
use of harmony and sonority."[12] At the same time, it has to be admitted that
Schumann's choral ballads have failed to survive the test of time, a situation
that their praiseworthy political impulse has been unable to alter. Within the
shadow of the Wagnerian music drama, the genre of the choral ballad has
been unable to shake off its reputation for mere worthiness.

Schumann's decision not to pursue his goal of writing an oratorio on the
subject of Martin Luther may not represent a particularly grave loss to the
world of music, even though we should dearly like to know how he would
have depicted this "great man of the people" in a way that would have been
intelligible to "peasants and burghers" alike. In a letter that he wrote to Pohl in
June 1851, Schumann explained that he would "strive" to strike a similar note
in his music, which would "avoid artificiality, complexity, and counterpoint

as far as possible and be simple and memorable, preferring to create its impact by means of rhythm and melody."[13] Perhaps he was thinking of Ludwig Börne's parable *Le rocher et l'éponge* (The rock and the sponge), in which Luther the "rock" was played off against Heinrich Heine, the "sponge."

In the event Schumann preferred to turn to a typically romantic subject, the story of a rose that takes on human form to enjoy the pleasures and sufferings of the children of this earth. A setting of a poem by the Chemnitz court official Moritz Horn, it was given the title *Der Rose Pilgerfahrt* by Schumann, who described it as a "fairytale" related to the earlier *Paradise and the Peri* "in terms of its form and expression, but more rustic and more German."[14]

Schumann himself proposed the ending whereby the rose is raised to a higher existence, an ending that reflects his fondness for parables of redemption:

> How would it be if after Rosa's death an angelic choir were to strike up:
> Rosa has not been turned back into a rose but into an angel. [. . .] The
> ascent from rose to young woman and thence to angel strikes me as poetic
> and also points to that doctrine about the higher transformations of
> creatures to which we are all so attached.[15]

The effusively sentimental words of *Der Rose Pilgerfahrt* may be on a lower level than the texts of the choral ballads, which are based for the most part on Uhland's pithy poems, and yet the music still has something to offer us even today: performances given in an intimate setting make it clear that Schumann's musical language is not indebted to the bourgeois world of Biedermeier art but evinces a wealth and range of expression that does not need to fear comparison with ostensibly more advanced music of the period. Listeners willing to treat *Der Rose Pilgerfahrt* as a series of numbers imbued with the spirit of a choice lieder recital and happy to dispense with any sense of drama will find Schumann at his best here.

For Schumann, 1851 was an exceptionally productive year, including, as it did, three purely orchestral works of a distinctly popular stamp: the overtures to Schiller's *Die Braut von Messina* (The bride of Messina) op. 100, Shakespeare's *Julius Caesar* op. 128, and Goethe's *Hermann und Dorothea* op. 136. Schumann wanted to offer the subscribers of his orchestral concerts repertory works that would be easier for them to grasp than symphonies, while not forgoing his claims to want to educate them. The overture to *Hermann und Dorothea* is famous enough but tends to be undervalued on account of its somewhat garish colors. It includes — for the third and last time in its composer's career — a quotation of the *Marseillaise*, here evidently intended as an ironic allusion to the recent news of Louis-Napoléon's coup d'état in France. Only the most alert of listeners will appreciate how original this overture is in its ability to negotiate a path between the poles of topicality and universal validity.

There is no one who can compare with Schumann in this regard — in part because few others have achieved this balancing act, and certainly not, as Schumann did, within the space of only five days, and in part because we now live in an age when "serious" composers are eager from the outset to create a monument to themselves, precluding distractions of any kind. Even Brahms considered himself too good to curry favor with his public — his Academic Festival Overture op. 80, which was written to thank the University of Breslau for conferring an honorary doctorate on him and which is a loosely structured work based in part on student songs, is the arguably inevitable exception to this rule. Schumann, conversely, needed no external incentive to write his popular *Fest-Ouvertüre mit Gesang über das Rheinweinlied* (Festival overture with singing on the Rhine wine song) op. 123, which was performed at the conclusion of the 1853 Lower Rhineland Music Festival. On that occasion sections of the audience seem to have taken seriously the soloist's invitation "O add your voices" and, thinking that it applied to themselves, joined in the singing, so that in this case we may well speak of a genuine "folk chorus" from the composer's pen.

In the field of the piano-accompanied song, too, Schumann wrote works that were both political and popular in character. It is no accident that in January 1851 he set a text by Johann Gottfried Kinkel for the first and last time in his career: the song in question was the *Abendlied* (Evening song) op. 107, no. 6. Kinkel was a revolutionary who had been sentenced to life imprisonment for his part in the Baden Uprising, but — as Schumann may have heard — he had just escaped from Spandau Prison and fled to England. Perhaps the composer smiled or at least drew his own conclusions when setting the lines "O hear, cast aside what offends you and all that makes you afraid."

In general, Schumann took a remarkable interest in the fate of his fellow human beings during his years in Düsseldorf. His opp. 103 and 104 songs, for example, are settings of poems by Elisabeth Kulmann, who had died in 1824 at the age of only seventeen. He was profoundly touched by the way in which so young a woman had reflected in verse on her short life, and he prefaced each of the op. 104 songs with a commentary of his own. The fact that he took these poems seriously as literary artifacts has been interpreted as a symptom of his waning critical faculties, although it has to be said that he had always been enthusiastic about second-rate writers, so that his admiration for Elisabeth Kulmann is not particularly exceptional.

The subject of a valediction to the world is by no means confined to Elisabeth Kulmann's verse, for the Poems of Mary Stuart op. 135, which Schumann found in an anthology of early English poetry, revolve around the same theme. Behind the Four Hussar Songs op. 117 that are settings of poems by Nikolaus Lenau is an outspoken critique of the business of killing, while the melodrama, "Die Ballade vom Haideknaben" (Ballad of the boy on the heath) op. 122, no. 1, describes a boy's cruel murder.

Of course, death is not the only subject in which Schumann took an interest during his years in Düsseldorf, but it is striking that death now entered the world of ideas that had previously been centered on love and nature, not least in the lieder written during the "year of song" in 1840. The proverbial "lyrical self" that had set the tone in the Eichendorff and Heine cycles was starting to fall silent and was being replaced by a greater number of poems of a more sententious kind. Even nature is conjured up in what Reinhard Kapp has called "politically charged metaphors" rather than in more immediately empirical ways: "Spring," "Streams," "Storm," Cloudless Sky," "Morning," "Forest," and "Hunt."[16]

As for the music itself, a comparison between the songs of the Düsseldorf period and those from 1840 reveals an absence of the great cyclical outpourings inspired by Kerner, Eichendorff, Heine, Rückert, and Chamisso, but the range of expression is greater, the gestural language either more emotional or more naïve — in each case intentionally so. If Schumann had effectively been singing to himself in 1840, he was now singing for others. And yet Schumann the tone poet has by no means disappeared. The music of the Kulmann settings is touching, and the songs of the Mary Stuart cycle — Schumann's swansong in the field of the piano-accompanied solo song — can easily stand comparison with the earlier anthologies in terms of their intensity, an intensity fuelled by the composer's ability to develop these songs from the speech rhythms of the poems. The composer Aribert Reimann was so impressed by the concentrated simplicity with which Schumann treated the theme of a farewell to the world that in 1988 he prepared a version of these songs for mezzo-soprano and chamber ensemble.

The songs for voice and piano that Schumann wrote in Düsseldorf straddle the boundary between the political and popular on the one hand and the elitist on the other, whereas the three late violin sonatas, the violin concerto, and the *Songs of Dawn* are unashamedly elitist. A new recording of the three violin sonatas (in A Minor, op. 105; D Minor, op. 121; and A Minor, with no opus number) by Carolin Widmann and Dénes Várjon reveals their hidden qualities for neither performer attempts to impose any neoclassical suavity on them, but instead they explore their elements of brooding and forlornness, while bringing both passion and countless interpretive refinements to their reading.

A comparison between Schumann's late chamber music and his early piano pieces reveals an identical impulse against a different background, a background that is no longer the masked ball at which Florestan and Eusebius meet Vult and Wina but the empty vessel of sonata form. But it was still a question of translating "rare states of mind" into the language of poetry. And if we examine the three sonatas in the order in which they were written, we shall observe an increasing tendency on Schumann's part to move in the direction of what we might call a "noble decadence" — it will be recalled that Baudelaire was working at this time on *Les fleurs du mal* (The flowers of evil). In short, "decadence" is not to be equated with personal decline, although listeners who think they can identify this quality in the final sonata can certainly appeal to much later remarks by Clara and Joseph Joachim. On the other hand, those same listeners will find it impossible to adduce any technical criteria that are of any real use in this context.

Rather, the term "decadence" should be taken to mean Schumann's increasing willingness to allow hints of gloom, forlornness, abruptness, and even absence to infiltrate his music. Although the A Minor Sonata op. 105 begins with a movement that remains entirely within the tradition of the romantic and neoclassical Schumann with its performance marking of "with an impassioned expression," the final movement already starts to play up: "I was unable to bring to it enough of the restive, surly tone of the piece," Wasielewski reported after playing through the piece with Clara Schumann on September 16, 1851.[17] She, too, spoke of a "rather less graceful and more recalcitrant movement."[18] Schumann must have deliberately turned his back on the traditional idea of a hymnlike or carefree ending, an idea virtually indispensable in music designed to be effective in public.

Schumann's next contribution to the medium, the D Minor Violin Sonata op. 121, begins by striking a note that is neither emphatic nor ingratiating but features a neobaroque dialogue between violin and piano that is brusque and somber by turn. Its thematic writing truly makes sense only to the listener who knows that the work was dedicated to the violinist Ferdinand David, whose surname is the starting point for the series of notes D–A–F [for "v"]–D that figures prominently in the piece. Schumann had long been familiar with such a device, but in the present case it is also symptomatic of what Hans Kohlhase has called a "kaleidoscope technique"[19] involving motific and thematic procedures and ultimately concerned with brooding and with marking time. No less unusual is the way in which piano and violin communicate with one another: on the one hand there are passages in which the two instruments pursue their own separate interests with a degree of independence that suggests that they are neither willing nor able to listen to one another, while on the other hand they are constantly drawn together by the D–A–F–D motif. A partnership as dissociative and at the same time as associative as this is unique in the history of music.

The final work in this group of three is the A Minor Sonata WoO that started life as the *F–A–E* Sonata written jointly by Schumann, Brahms, and Dietrich in October 1853. Schumann now proceeded to expand his own two-movement contribution by adding a further two movements. It is difficult not to be struck by the uncensored juxtaposition of heterogeneous elements. The earlier period is recalled by the high-flown tone and cascading scales that seem to have been written with Clara in mind. At the same time there is a tendency to impose a sense of unity on the motific material by means of the F–A–E motif and a second three-note "nuclear" motif. [20] In the final movement in particular the sheer persistence of the motific writing is hard to beat. Finally there are mannerisms such as those that take the form of traditional violinistic figures like the ones that Schumann had used when arranging Bach's sonatas for unaccompanied violin and in his more recent adaptation of Paganini's Caprices. Most striking of all are the interruptions to the narrative flow. All in all, it is a magnificent piece of chamber music as long as the listener does not expect stylistic purity or hard-won climaxes but is willing to countenance the idea of individual tirades.

Qualities that may work in the intimate context of a chamber sonata may not be as effective in a rather more public arena. We should not accuse Clara, Joachim, and Brahms of inconsistency for adopting a positive attitude to the Violin Concerto that Schumann worked on at almost the same time as the final movements of the *F–A–E* Sonata, while locking it away after his death. There is, after all, a difference between studying a work in close contact with its creator and in full knowledge of his aims and fretting over the question of how an audience avid for sensation might react to such a composition. Would they discover early signs of Schumann's impending breakdown in the piece?

Some eighty-four years were to pass before posterity had a chance to judge for itself. Yehudi Menuhin was asked by the publishing house of Schott to give the work's posthumous first performance in New York and wrote enthusiastically to the conductor Vladimir Golschmann on July 22, 1937:

> This concerto is the missing link of the violin literature; it is the bridge between the Beethoven and the Brahms concertos, though leaning more towards Brahms. Indeed, one finds in both the same human warmth, caressing softness, bold manly rhythms, the same lovely arabesque treatment of the violin, the same rich and noble themes and harmonies.[21]

Although one cannot help but wonder why Menuhin does not mention Mendelssohn's Violin Concerto — a work of which he was immensely fond — as the "missing link" between Beethoven and Brahms, there is no doubt from his comments that he felt that Schumann's concerto was worth an airing. In fact, it was not Menuhin who gave the work its first performance, but the German violinist Georg Kulenkampff, who performed the piece in the Deutsche Oper in Berlin on November 26, 1937, under the baton of Karl Böhm. Menuhin had to wait until ten days later, when he performed the piece with piano accompaniment in New York's Carnegie Hall. Kulenkampff, it should be added, played the solo part from a version prepared by Paul Hindemith, whose contribution remained anonymous after he had been ostracized by the National Socialists. Menuhin himself had been banned from giving the work's first performance after the National Socialists' cultural bureaucrats discovered that Schott had acquired the publishing rights to the work, the autograph score of which was preserved in the State Library in Berlin. Instead, they demanded it back for the nation: as a Jew, Menuhin was not to be allowed to perform it. The work was especially welcome to the National Socialists as a substitute for the now proscribed Violin Concerto by the Jewish Mendelssohn. At a conference organized jointly by the Reich Culture Chamber and the Nazi association Strength Through Joy, the influential critic Walter Abendroth presumed to declare that although the concerto's "fragmentary, sketch-like design" meant that it was hardly "a revelation of sensational significance," it was nonetheless "German through and through."[22] More recently, Gidon Kremer has observed that its "naked ideas or naked impulses are so brilliant that they are sometimes more powerful than the most carefully composed piece of music by Brahms."[23]

It is, of course, impossible to pass objective aesthetic judgment on works that attest to a high degree of compositional reflection while at the same time refusing to conform to any traditional model. Reinhard Kapp has analyzed the first forty-four bars of the concerto — in other words, its orchestral introduction alone — in the course of a charitable assessment that extends to twenty-three closely printed pages, arguing that this detail may be interpreted one way, that detail another way.[24] This makes sense. And it is undoubtedly impressive. But the work will never be a crowd-pleaser. And it is far too resistant to attempts to judge it by traditional generic criteria. One would like to listen to the work in as open-minded a way as possible, but, as Laura Tunbridge has noted: "With the Violin Concerto we are so aware of the work's reception history that we cannot but listen to it as a late work."[25]

There remain the *Songs of Dawn* op. 133, a set of five relatively short piano pieces. These are the last piano works whose publication Schumann himself superintended from his asylum at Endenich. As such, the work is surrounded by a very particular aura, not least because for a long time Schumann considered calling it "Diotima: Songs of Dawn." He was no doubt thinking of Hölderlin's figure of Diotima and was equally certainly affected not only by the character herself but also by the fate of her creator: we have already referred to the "feelings of awe" with which he spoke about Hölderlin, who from 1806 to 1843 lived in a tower in Tübingen, plagued by mental illness.

Schumann's project book for the period between 1849 and 1851 already mentions plans for the *Songs of Dawn*. But there is something strangely touching about the way in which work on a project with such an optimistic subject as dawn could be slipped into his schedule — reconstructed from his housekeeping book for the autumn of 1853 — between his daily concerns and the (undisclosed) fiasco surrounding the performance of Moritz Hauptmann's Mass in St. Maximilian's Church:

> 15 [October]: Sat for a second time for [the French painter Jean-Joseph-Bonaventure] Laurens. Very attractive picture. Idea for a sonata for Joachim [*F-A-E* Sonata]. *Diotima.*
> 16 [October]: [...] *Diotima.* — 5 o'clock music. Laurens for the last time. — Gift of manuscripts to him & Brahms.
> 17 [October]: Busy. — Failed attempt at spirit-rapping.
> 18 [October]: Completed "Songs of Dawn." — Rhenish Antiquarian.[26]

(The last two words of this entry relate to the first two volumes of a major publication that was then in the process of appearing. According to its title page, it contained "the most important and most agreeable geographic, historical, and political curiosities along the whole of the River Rhine.")

A few days before he threw himself into the Rhine, Schumann wrote to the publisher Friedrich Wilhelm Arnold, describing the *Songs of Dawn* as "pieces depicting the emotions on the approach & waxing of morning, but more an expression of feeling than painting."[27] This explanation clearly recalls Beethoven's famous comment on his *Pastoral* Symphony ("more an expression of feeling than painting"). Nor was it chosen at random. For even more clearly than the piano works from Schumann's earlier years, the *Songs of Dawn* eschew programmatic and poetically associative elements, preferring instead to explore characteristic differences in terms of their form and design, so much so, indeed, that we may be inclined to echo Michael Struck and speak of different types of "instrumental song": "chorale," "duet," "song with instrumental accompaniment," and "hunting song with horn writing."[28] Listeners would have to decide for themselves whether to relate Schumann's ideas on the subject of dawn to Hölderlin's poem "To Diotima," to the same writer's fragmentary novel *Hyperion*, to the more general idea of newly awakening life, or to the specific image of a new dawn in nature. Schumann himself may have remembered that he had already set the words "When, O when will morning come, when, O when?" in his *Spanisches Liederspiel* op. 74, where the setting, however powerful, appears under the title "Melancholia."

A "Sugary Saxon"?

Born in 1788, Lord Byron was a legend in his own lifetime, albeit less so in his native England, which sought, rather, to outlaw him on account of what was regarded as his scandalous lifestyle, than in Continental Europe, where he became a leading figure in the world not only of poetry but also of politics as a result of his passionate support for the Greek War of Independence. Goethe raised a monument to him in the figure of Euphorion in the second part of *Faust*. Byron, who died of cholera in the Greek town of Missolonghi at the age of only thirty-six, was regarded by European intellectuals as the embodiment of youth and of a generation that refused to accept that the ideals of the French Revolution had been compromised and ultimately destroyed first by political atrocities and then by the violent restoration of the ancien régime.

In German-speaking countries, Byronism found its most powerful echo within the literary movement known as "Young Germany," whose supporters regarded the poet as the expression of a modern view of the world: convinced that their own fates were exceptional, they sought to lead lives that were a mixture of grandiosity, world weariness, lovesick repining, disgust with life, and an entanglement with black magic. Nowadays we might be inclined to dismiss all of this as a sign of protracted puberty, but Byron was able to articulate it in poems that swept younger readers off their feet and left few composers untouched. Of the countless Byron settings, three have remained in the repertory: Berlioz's four-part *Harold en Italie*, Tchaikovsky's *Manfred* Symphony, and Schumann's *Manfred* op. 115.

In the course of his life Schumann took many literary figures to heart: E. T. A. Hoffmann's Kapellmeister Kreisler in his *Kreisleriana*; Vult, Walt, and Wina from Jean Paul's *Flegeljahre* in *Papillons*; Goethe's Mignon in his Wilhelm Meister Songs op. 98a and in his Requiem for Mignon op. 98b;

and Faust in his Scenes from Goethe's *Faust*. But none of these characters includes as many Schumannesque elements as Byron's Manfred: a dark sense of guilt that weighs down on the hero; a lifelong fascination with his one and only love, Astarte; a striving for the grandiose; loneliness and existential anxieties; a search for hidden knowledge involving the use of magic; and, finally, the attempt to end his own life. Although these elements cannot be applied without further ado to Schumann himself, the more somber aspects of his character do appear to be reflected here as if in a mirror, albeit invested with a sublime and grandiose dimension. Even the loneliness of the high mountains in which the action of *Manfred* is set—like the world of the gods in Wagner's *Ring*—gives the work an air of tragic grandeur that one also senses in John Martin's watercolor *Manfred on the Jungfrau* (reproduced on p.243).

The young Schumann was able to read some of Byron's poems in a German translation in his father's library. An entry in his student diary for March 26, 1829, reads: "Agitated state of mind—bedtime reading: Byron's Manfred—terrible night." Three days later another entry runs: "Childe Harold in bed—terrible night disturbed by dreams about death."[1] A number of the impressions that Schumann wrote down during his tour of the Alps that year also echo Byronic phrases.

It was not until 1848 that Schumann felt bold enough to tackle a project based on Byron's *Manfred*. Evidently it needed the impetus of the revolution for him to approach a poem that struck him and many of his contemporaries as the embodiment of grandeur. In August 1848, immediately after he had completed *Genoveva*, he was seized by what he himself described as a very real "enthusiasm for Manfred."[2] His grandson Ferdinand recalled that "My grandmother Clara told me in 1895 that my grandfather read to her from Byron's *Manfred* while they were sitting in a field one evening, and by the end she was in tears."[3] When he subsequently read to his wife from the poem in Düsseldorf, "his voice suddenly broke off, tears poured down his face, and such emotion seized hold of him that he was unable to go on reading."[4]

Schumann wrote the overture, followed by fifteen other numbers, during the second half of 1848, his aim being to turn Byron's "theater of the mind" into a theatrical event that would raise the subject of Manfred in public awareness. The purely instrumental numbers tend in the main to underscore the dialogue spoken by Manfred and the other participants in the drama, and to that extent Schumann's setting is a melodrama. But there are also songs and choruses for the spirits and "monastic chanting" that is heard in the distance.

Schumann described the work, which lasts some eighty minutes in per-

John Martin, *Manfred on the Jungfrau*, 1837. (© Birmingham Museums and Art
Gallery. Photograph courtesy of The Bridgeman Art Library.)

formance, as a "Dramatic Poem in Three Parts with Music." He had to wait
almost four years for a performance, which he ultimately owed to the commit-
ment of Franz Liszt, who conducted the world premiere in a fully staged version at the Weimar Court Theater on June 13, 1852. The work was frequently
performed thereafter—in 1855, Brahms organized a concert performance in
Hamburg, and Munich audiences heard the piece in 1868 when Ernst Possart
took the leading role in what was to prove an important step on his career as a
famous actor and, later, a theater director.

Staged during the reign of King Ludwig II, this successful production in
Munich coincided with Wagner's heyday in the Bavarian capital, indicating
that Schumann's music was not felt to be in the least provincial but was regarded as an example of a substantial kind of art that traded in ideas. It undoubtedly went down just as well with a cultured audience as Liszt's *Mazeppa*
and *Tasso*, two symphonic poems likewise inspired by Byron.

But how are we to interpret Schumann's remark to the effect that "I have
never abandoned myself to a composition with the love and expenditure of
effort that I did in the case of Manfred"?[5] After all, this is a work that privileges the spoken word, obliging him as a composer to play second fiddle. Of
course, there are classic precedents, such as Beethoven's incidental music to

Egmont, but whereas the music to *Egmont* serves no more than an ancillary function during performances of Goethe's tragedy, Schumann envisaged a total artwork featuring highly heterogeneous musical elements which, admittedly, were fully attuned to the spoken word and onstage action but which could never be judged by the aesthetic standards of "absolute" music.

The answer to our question takes two forms. First, Schumann's identification with his subject was so extreme in the present case that there was a significant difference between his own approach and Beethoven's; second, his music serves far more than a mere ancillary purpose, for ultimately the music alone can bring to light all that lies hidden in the poem. On its own, it has little value, of course, which is why Schumann was so annoyed with his publisher when the latter brought out a vocal score of *Manfred* in which the poem was reproduced at the beginning rather than being set between the individual numbers: "The music will remain a puzzle to anyone unfamiliar with its connection with the poem."[6] Schumann was concerned less with his own work as such than with the bigger picture, and there is no doubt that he could enlist his contemporaries' support in this regard, for they too viewed art as a holistic experience and were presumably not unhappy with programs in which symphonies and arias were not simply juxtaposed but language and music helped to enhance one another.

Today's listeners appear to find Byron's overwrought poetry almost unbearable, but they still have the overture: an opening bar of Beethoven, 11 closing bars of Mendelssohn, but between them 296 bars of uniquely distinctive Schumann. It matters little whether *Manfred* is generally closer to the aesthetic of the New German school, for which Schumann really had little time for all that he was closer to it than he realized. No, what matters is that no other composer can hold a candle to this overture: not Beethoven, not Mendelssohn, not Liszt, not Wagner. For which other composer could present such a credible portrait of a character like Manfred in the constant vicissitudes of his passions and in his inner conflict between heroic bombast, his desire for love, and a sense of profound depression, churned up, as he is, by the somberly sublime signals issuing from Ariman's realm of the dead? Who could turn all of this into a work that makes sense on its own terms and needs no program for the listener to understand it?

All of his hero's "rare states of mind" that are so convincingly depicted here by Schumann are reflected in the musical structure in which the drama of the unfolding events is mirrored. The way in which the motifs are torn apart, expanded, and woven together again is an accurate reflection of Manfred's complex state of mind, and the same is true of the disjointed nature of the musical argument, of the passage in bars 104–109 that suggests a state of total disorientation, and of the fact that it is not until the end of the overture, in bars 258–73, that we hear a self-contained sixteen-bar period that might express any sense of reassurance. All of this may be interpreted as an expression of Manfred's inner landscape, while retaining its status as "absolute" music and, as such, eliciting Brahms's unconditional admiration. Although Brahms once whimsically remarked that all he had ever learned from Schumann was how to play chess, he was so fascinated by *Manfred* in general that when he came to write the opening movement of his First Symphony he included a clear echo of the motif associated not only with Astarte's love but also — in Brahms's mind — with Clara:

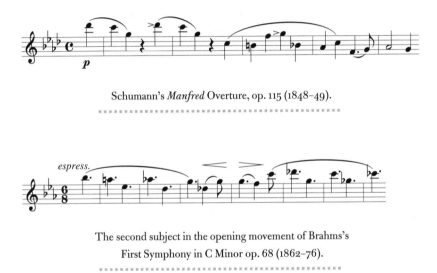

Schumann's *Manfred* Overture, op. 115 (1848–49).

The second subject in the opening movement of Brahms's
First Symphony in C Minor op. 68 (1862–76).

Schumann himself reintroduces this motif in his final scene as the echo of a "requiem" sung by a "choir in the distant monastery" as Manfred lies dying. Byron's hero dies without the consolation of the Christian faith, "cold — cold — even to the heart," whereas Schumann adopts a more conciliatory ending: the "Requiem aeternam dona eis" (give them eternal rest) is heard in the form of a double canon, conveying the idea of calm expectation and implying that Manfred, too, may find peace in death. The final lines of the monks' chanting incorporate the motif associated with Astarte's love, and in doing so they also recall the appearance of a motif traditionally described as "redemption through love" in the final bars of Wagner's *Götterdämmerung*

(Twilight of the gods). Where words would be spoken in vain, music may offer us a glimmer of hope.

Unlike Wagner, however, Schumann has to answer to a librettist — in this case Byron, who would have had no time whatsoever for a conciliatory ending. It comes as no surprise, therefore, to discover that one of Byron's admirers, Friedrich Nietzsche, who was familiar with large sections of Schumann's music and even worked through them at the piano, had harsh words to say about *Manfred* in *Ecce homo*:

> I must be profoundly related to *Byron's* Manfred: I discovered all these abysses in myself — I was ripe for this work at thirteen. [. . . But] the Germans are *incapable* of any conception of greatness: proof Schumann. Expressly from wrath against this sugary Saxon, I composed a counter-overture to Manfred, of which Hans von Bülow said he had never seen the like on manuscript paper: it constituted a rape on Euterpe.[7]

Although Nietzsche's implied reproach that Christianity has no scope for genuine tragedy is certainly worth noting, his reference to his own *Manfred* overture suggests nothing so much as a satyr play following on from a tragedy. Here the philosopher, who lacked any sense of musical form, for all that his compositions are of a decent amateur quality, is guilty of a certain grotesqueness. Admittedly, he was sufficiently self-critical to describe his own *Manfred Meditation* of 1872 as a "piece for four hands expressive of the darkest pathos and made up of nothing but incantatory phrases."[8] And in a second letter to his friend Gustav Krug, he explained that he would find it "harmful to lie on my stomach in such a musically melancholy manner like a bear on its bear skin" and to be preoccupied with such "crass matters and with such awkward fortissimos and tremolandos."[9]

But Nietzsche should have known better than to remain attached to his *Manfred Meditation*. Expectantly he wrote to Bülow, begging him to pass judgment on the piece, and when Bülow's verdict turned out to be annihilating, he turned to a higher authority: Bayreuth. Not a year had passed since the Wagners, at that date still at Tribschen on Lake Lucerne, had had fun at the expense of the philosopher's *Echo of New Year's Eve*, which was a kind of preliminary draft for his *Manfred Meditation*. True, they kept their feelings to themselves and said nothing to Nietzsche, a frequent and welcome visitor to whom they were grateful for the Wagnerian *Birth of Tragedy*. But following her husband's break with Nietzsche, Cosima Wagner was pleased to confide in her diary the extent to which the couple had had to suppress their laughter in 1872. Hans Richter, who was present on this occasion, recalled Wagner's mocking, if not entirely uncharitable, remark: "You spend eighteen months in regular contact with a person without suspecting anything like this; and now he comes along, insidiously hiding a score in his clothes."[10]

Nietzsche asked Wagner to back him in his argument with Bülow, prompting Wagner to explain in as friendly a way as he could that on a recent visit his father-in-law Liszt had found Bülow's condemnation "fairly extreme,"[11] making Nietzsche think that Liszt had "expressed an entirely favorable opinion" about the piece, as he claimed in a letter to his sister.[12] As a result, he continued with his determined attempt to enlist the support of others for his *Manfred Meditation*.

It is perhaps worth ending this intermezzo by recalling the title of the chapter in *Ecce homo* in which Nietzsche, a writer whose views on music were actually extremely astute, poured out his contempt for Schumann's *Manfred*: it is headed "Why I Am So Clever."

A colored drawing of Schumann by the French artist Jean-Joseph-Bonaventure Laurens, now in the Heinrich Heine Institute in Düsseldorf. Schumann was in regular contact with the painter, who was a great admirer of his music. When Schumann sat for him three times in his apartment in October 1853, Laurens was struck by the "abnormal dilation" of Schumann's pupils, whereupon Clara — in a state of "great concern" — confided that her husband was "ill" (*Briefe. Neue Folge* 530). Laurens produced a total of four drawings of Schumann. None of them enjoys a particularly high reputation among writers on the composer, even though Clara described one of them as "wonderfully fine" (Litzmann 2:283). Schumann's own entry in his housekeeping book for October 15, 1853, reads, "Sat for Laurens for a second time. Very attractive portrait" (*Tagebücher* 3/2:639). (Photograph courtesy of the Heinrich Heine Institut, Düsseldorf.)

CHAPTER 12

Endenich (1854–56)

*Your paper's cultural journalism — the more of it there is, the worse
it gets. As soon as one enters into the ideological simplifications and
biographical reductivism of cultural journalism, the essence of the
artifact is lost. Your cultural journalism is tabloid gossip disguised as
an interest in "the arts," and everything that it touches is contracted
into what it is not. Who is the celebrity, what is the price, what is
the scandal? What transgression has the writer committed, and not
against the exigencies of literary aesthetics but against his or her
daughter, son, mother, father, spouse, lover, friend, publisher, or pet?*

Philip Roth, *Exit Ghost*[1]

The foregoing philippic is taken from a fictional letter written to the
New York Times by one of the characters in a Philip Roth novel. By
the same token, any Schumann biographer would surely have to reproach himself for approaching the final years of his subject's life with a cold
or even malicious glint in his eye, an approach for which there are — unhap-
pily — many precedents. Whereas Nancy B. Reich, in her 1990 article "Clara
Schumann and Johannes Brahms," maintains a decorous distance from all
idle speculation,[2] Eva Weissweiler, whose three-volume edition of the correspondence between Schumann and his wife would otherwise entitle her
to be regarded as a serious Schumann scholar, adopted a positively libelous
tone that very same year when describing the couple's final years of marriage.
Evidently fired by her love of sensationalism and flying in the face of all the
historical evidence, she claimed that Clara was unwilling to visit her husband
at the asylum in Endenich in order not to spoil the "happiness" inspired by
her "love" for Brahms.[3] The fact that in this context she peddles the old wives'
tale about the couple's eldest son Felix, claiming that his father was in fact

Brahms and that in her diary, in order to divert attention from this, Clara deliberately gave the wrong date for the discovery of her pregnancy[4] represents an act of particularly brazen effrontery, for by the time that her biography of Clara had appeared in print, the couple's housekeeping books had been available for eight years, making it clear beyond peradventure that Schumann discovered that his wife was pregnant on October 3, 1853, and that he had sex with her that very same day. Brahms did not arrive in Düsseldorf until four days later.

These acts of meanness and malice cannot simply be ignored, for they found an avid audience among the tabloid journalists invoked by Philip Roth and even today continue to be bandied about in the guise of cultural gossip. But such reports can at least be countered by an account of a marriage based on love that was capable of withstanding the extreme pressures that were placed upon it. In order to provide this account, we do not need to place an unduly sentimental interpretation on the vast amount of surviving evidence. It is enough to examine this material in a spirit of impartiality. Even so, the events that we shall be describing remain inescapably and undeniably tragic.

Until February 1854, when his illness finally erupted with such devastating consequences, Schumann fought an impressive battle against the psychological problems that were a permanent part of his life. Above all, his varied work as an artist helped him to forget even the professional altercations in which he became embroiled. But from February 1854 onward, he found himself suffering increasingly from difficulties speaking and auditory problems. On February 17, Clara noted in her diary that her husband thought that he could hear the voices of angels that soon turned into "demonic voices attended by terrible music" and proclaiming that "he was a sinner whom they planned to cast down into Hell."[5] At the same time, however, Schumann was also able to cast a critical eye over the proofs of his cello concerto and to note down his *Geistervariationen* (Ghost, or spirit, variations), a simple piano piece based on a theme from the violin concerto but, its simplicity notwithstanding, worth taking seriously as a work. Clara ensured that he had constant medical care and remained at his side day and night. But Schumann, dressed only in a dressing gown and slippers, still managed to slip out of the house at two in the afternoon on February 27. It was raining heavily and was bitterly cold, but there was a carnival atmosphere in the town — it was the day before Shrove Tuesday — and his strange appearance excited no further notice. He ran to the nearby bridge over the Rhine and gave the attendants his handkerchief instead of the toll they demanded. From the middle section of the bridge he threw himself into the river but was rescued by some fishermen, who had observed the scene from the riverbank. They pulled him into a boat, although he again tried to jump back into the ice-cold water. "I dreamt that I drowned in the Rhine," he had noted in 1829 at the time of a boat trip on the river,[6] although on that occasion, of course, he had been writing in the spirit of the sentimental romanticism inspired by the Rhine as a symbol of all that was German.

"His journey home must have been terrible," the young musician Ruppert Becker wrote in his diary, "he was transported by eight men, while a crowd of plebs made fun of him in the only way they knew how."[7] On March 4, on the advice of his doctors and also at his own request, Schumann was taken to an institution at Endenich outside Bonn that was run by the psychiatrist Franz Richarz. According to his medical records, the reason for his immurement was "melancholia with delusions." It was presumably only after Schumann's death that a note was added in pencil: "Paralysis."[8]

"Melancholia" and "paralysis" — the latter the final stage of syphilis — are the two words that continue to bedevil discussions on the cause of Schumann's death. But his medical records, including his autopsy report, support the idea of a progressive psychological degeneration without any incidence of syphilis. None of the surviving documents gives a single indication of the symptoms of such an illness. Writers on medical history wanting to give the cause of death as the final stages of syphilis are thrown back above all on Schumann himself as their crown witness — and yet such appeals are ultimately lacking in plausibility. For the painful "wound" that he mentions in the 1831 diary entry from which we have already quoted and which appears in close proximity with the name "Christel" is relatively untypical of the early stages of syphilis. And the feelings of guilt that Schumann expressed at that time may have been of a more general kind.

Even the entry in the Endenich records for September 12, 1855 — "In 1831 I was syphilitic and cured with arsenic"[9] — does not necessarily get us any further, for quite apart from the fact that treatment with arsenic was by no means usual at that time, we may well be dealing here with the patient's febrile fantasies. There is only one thing that we can assert with any certainty: throughout his life Schumann suffered from pronounced feelings of guilt, which became worse at Endenich and assumed the signs of a religious mania. Nor is it entirely clear from his records what symptoms his doctors were trying to treat. The fact that the word "paralysis" was added only belatedly means that it was evidently not until the time of his death that his doctors settled on this as a diagnosis. But not even *this* can tell us very much, since the link between "paralysis" and syphilis had not been established at that time. In his study of Schumann, Peter Ostwald draws a distinction between "mental disorder," "personality disorder," and "physical disorders." He declines to speculate needlessly on the unexplained physical causes of Schumann's death, but concludes, "Prolonged isolation at Endenich was Schumann's nemesis. It destroyed what was left of his marriage, made it impossible for him to return to his former status as a writer or musician, and confirmed his deepest dread and suspicions about being mad."[10]

The Endenich clinic was a private institution with some thirty patients who were housed in a pleasant-looking building that had been built as a manor house at the end of the eighteenth century. It now houses the municipal music library and a Schumann museum. Schumann was probably not housed in "a couple of attractive rooms on the ground floor," as Clara initially thought,[11] but almost certainly had only a single room. However, he also had use of a communal room large enough to accommodate a grand piano, which he often used. His wife paid six hundred thalers a year for him to stay in the clinic. Although this bought her husband only a modest level of care, it was still almost as much as he had been earning as director of music in Düsseldorf.

Would it be macabre to quote at this point from a letter that Schumann wrote to his predecessor in Düsseldorf, Ferdinand Hiller, on December 3, 1849, expressing an interest in the post?

> There's one more thing: I was recently looking in an old atlas for some information on Düsseldorf, and I came across the following curiosities: three convents and a madhouse. I'm happy to put up with the convents, but I felt uncomfortable reading about the madhouse. I'll tell you why. A few years ago, you'll recall that we were living in Maxen. I discovered that the main view from my window was of the Sonnenstein [the asylum at Pirna]. In the end I found this outlook a real problem; indeed, it ruined the whole of my stay in the town. And so I thought that the same might be true of Düsseldorf. But perhaps the entire note is wrong and the asylum is just a hospital of the kind found in any town or city. I really have to be on my guard against melancholy impressions of this kind.[12]

The Endenich clinic was run according to the latest medical findings and offered its patients a chance to engage in activities of their own choosing. They were even allowed to undertake long walks in the company of an attendant. Even so, the clinic's annexes included a section for more disturbed patients, and it seems likely that Schumann was occasionally taken there. An entry in his medical records for April 20, 1854—a time when he was particularly disturbed—reads: "At noon yesterday he promised to stay calm in bed without being restrained, but he failed to keep his word, later he was calm in his jacket. At noon he had some soup, half a portion of meat and wine, stewed fruit, in the evening he ate almost everything placed in front of him but only when forced to do so."[13]

Between April 1854 and the early summer of 1855, Schumann's symptoms do not appear to have grown any worse. Although he expressed a number of delusional ideas, he continued to lead his life as best he could, reading newspapers and perusing atlases and textbooks on geography. In August 1855, Franz Richarz, who was responsible for his treatment, noted, "At visiting time he pored over the map, muttering to himself and saying with a laugh that he was always traveling on it." On another occasion, Richarz's assistant, Eberhard Peters, recorded that "during the visit" Schumann was "preoccupied with the atlas and when asked what he was doing said that he was sailing in the polar sea."[14]

Schumann also played dominos and after studying an English book on chess expressed his delight "at having solved a number of unsolved games."[15] But over and above these "useful" activities, which he was recommended to pursue in the main as a way of passing his time, he also corrected the proofs of his latest works and at least until April 1855 corresponded "rationally" with his publishers, while demanding to be kept in the picture and asking for music manuscript paper. The last surviving piece in his own hand is a simple chorale setting of Nicolaus Herman's sixteenth-century hymn "Wenn mein Stündlein vorhanden ist" (When my hour has come) and an untexted fragment that may be a chorale based on Luther's "Mitten wir im Leben sind von dem Tod umfangen" (In the midst of life we are in death).

Schumann developed an interest in his family's welfare only after his wedding anniversary on September 12, 1854, but from then on he insisted on being given regular news on the subject, and when Clara wrote, he replied by return:

> Beloved Clara,
>   What tidings of joy you have again brought to me when informing me
> that in June Heaven sent you a splendid boy and that to your surprise and
> mine dear Marie and Elsie played to you from the *Bilder aus Osten* (Pictures
> from the East) [op. 66] on your birthday, also that Brahms, to whom you
> were going to give my friendly greetings and best regards, has moved to
> Düsseldorf for good—that's excellent news! I'm sure you can guess what

my favorite name is: the Unforgettable [Mendelssohn]! I was delighted to hear that my collected writings have appeared in their entirety, likewise the Cello Concerto, the Violin Fantasy that Joachim played so magnificently, and the Fughettas. Could you send me one or other of them, as you kindly offered to do? [...]

8 o'clock in the evening. Just got back from Bonn, where, as always, I saw the Beethoven statue and was enchanted by it. While I was standing in front of it, someone started to play the organ in the Minster Church. I'm now much stronger and look much younger than in Düsseldorf. There's something I'd like you to do for me: would you mind writing to Dr. Peters and asking him to give me as much money as I want, which you'll then reimburse? Poor people often ask me for money, and I feel sorry for them. Otherwise my life isn't as turbulent as it used to be. How different it once was! But do give me news about the lives of our relatives and friends in Cologne, Leipzig, Dresden, and Berlin, about Woldemar, Dr. Härtel, you know them all. I'd now like to remind you of something, of the happy times we spent together, of our visit to Switzerland, Heidelberg, Lausanne, Vevey, Chamouny [i.e., Chamonix], then of our visit to The Hague, where you achieved the most amazing things. [...] Do you still have the small double portrait (by Rietschel in Dresden) [see p. 202]. You'd make me very happy if you were able to send it to me. I'd also like to ask you to let me know the dates of the children's birthdays, they were in the little blue book. I now intend to write to Marie and Elise, who sent me such a nice letter. Farewell, dearest Clara. Don't forget me, write soon. Your Robert.[16]

Clara did as she was asked, encouraging Schumann to send her a further list of questions, all of which attest to his mental alertness: "Thank you for letting me have a note of the years in which our dear children were born. Which godparents are you planning to choose, dear Clara, and in which church will he [Felix] be baptized?"[17] As he had promised, he wrote to his eldest daughters:

Dearest Marie and Elise,

How pleased I was to receive your letters and to know that you're working so hard, and that you played the pieces from my *Pictures from the East* for Mama on her birthday. I was very surprised by this. Do you remember how happy we were a year ago in Benrath, do you remember Vienna, where you once got lost, Marie, and also Prague and how you both sang in the steam train? Or have you forgotten? Have you written any more poems, Marie? Who's your teacher now? I've nothing but praise for the fact that you're playing such delightful and difficult pieces as Beethoven's A-flat

Major Sonata, Mendelssohn-Bartholdy's *Songs Without Words*, the Haydn sonata, my Gathering of the Grapes [from the *Album for young people*], and Cramer's studies. Every good wish to Bertha. Love and kisses to you both as well as to Julie, Ludwig, Ferdinand, and Eugenie. Your papa Robert.[18]

It is heartrending to read lines such as these in which Schumann expresses his desire to see his wife and family again after he himself had insisted on being locked up in the clinic, so afraid was he that he might turn violent and harm Clara. Scarcely less moving, of course, is Clara's own situation. Her husband's doctors had issued strict instructions that she was not to be allowed to visit him at Endenich as they claimed that such visits would leave him more agitated than ever. She heeded their advice in the expectation that his condition would soon improve and instead sent relatives, friends, and pupils to the clinic with presents and useful items, hoping that they would return with as favorable news as possible.

On May 21, 1854, she wrote to her friend Henriette Reichmann: "No woman can have loved and possessed a man like him and have called him her own without being destroyed by his loss. No one knows what a wonderful man he is! What a disposition, what a mind!" She was heavily pregnant at this time: "What I feel when I think about this is something I can't describe! His child, and yet not to have him here with me, perhaps not even in his thoughts!"[19]

With the birth of Felix on June 11, 1854, she had seven children to look after. Apart from a wet nurse, there were also two female servants. And Julie, the third-eldest child, had gone to stay with Clara's mother, Marianne Bargiel, in Berlin, while her two eldest daughters, whom Brahms had previously taken under his wing, were sent to boarding school in Cologne. Even so, it required tremendous strength to deal with each day as it came, not least because she increasingly had to stand up for her husband in her dealings with society at large and attempt to refute the stories that were circulating in the newspapers.

In this respect, admonitions from female friends abroad to bear her cross with equanimity were of little practical help: "I'm trying to perform my duties, trying to bear my misfortune as best I can, but not through praying and reading sacred texts, only through activity and working for others! Only here do I find the strength and courage to go on!"[20] In order to raise the money that she needed to pay for her husband's medical bills at the clinic and to support her family, she undertook an extended tour of northern and central Germany at the end of 1854. The following year she gave concerts in the Netherlands,

Berlin, Danzig (modern Gdańsk), Elberfeld, Leipzig, and elsewhere. And in early 1856 she even traveled as far afield as Austro-Hungary and then for several months to England.

Throughout her husband's illness Clara collected flowers and pressed them into the pages of an enchanting volume to which she gave the title *Blumenbuch für Robert/in der Krankheit vom März 1854 bis July 1856/angelegt von seiner Clara. Den Kindern aufbewahrt* (Flower book for Robert during his illness from March 1854 to July 1856 designed by his Clara. Preserved for their children). Published in a bibliophile edition by Gerd Nauhaus and Ingrid Bodsch in 2006, it is the fulfillment of an idea that occurred to Clara during her first concert tour, according to which she would "devote a flower" to her husband from every town or city where she stayed.[21] The first was a rose, which Clara pressed into the book in Leipzig on October 25, 1854; the last little nosegay was added in Richmond on June 15, 1856, and comprised a dwarf rose, thyme, and forget-me-not, three plants that Marie and Elise picked on their father's birthday and sent to Clara in England. The last four of the total of fifty-four pressed flowers date from the final days of Schumann's life and are headed: "Ludwig for Papa on 26 July 1856," "Picked in Endenich on 28 July 1856 — flowers of sorrow," "Picked in Endenich on 28 July 1856. In deepest sorrow!" and "Leaves from my Robert's grave. — From the wreath that Johannes carried and placed on the coffin. — From the wreath from Concordia. — From Johannes's wreath."[22]

It must be admitted that between 1857 and 1859 Clara also made a book of pressed flowers for Brahms, albeit one that was less ambitious in scope. We may perhaps regard it as a sequel to the diary that she kept for Schumann; it certainly says much for the profound affection that they felt for each other at this time. Brahms supported Clara from the time of Schumann's breakdown, continuing to make entries in the housekeeping book and helping her in everyday matters. Much later, when he was fifty-three, he explained that "I think she'd have gone mad if she'd not had me — the only man among all those women — to talk her out of all that nonsense."[23] Although Brahms was referring only to the way in which he protected Clara from unwelcome advice, his comment throws light on the situation in general.

At the same time, Brahms was hopelessly in love with Clara and even lived in the same house following her move to the Poststraße in Düsseldorf in the middle of 1855. They attended a performance of Beethoven's *Missa solemnis* in Cologne and in July 1855 stayed together on the Rhine while undertaking a joint concert tour. But Clara traveled with a female companion, so any suggestion of a relationship that went beyond an intense friendship between kindred souls or a love that was suppressed is bound to remain mere speculation. Clara had not exactly been cosseted by life, and one can understand why she might warm to the love of a man fourteen years her junior and feel helpless during the times when he was absent. Nor should we forget that she held his genius in almost as high a regard as that of her husband, whom she now sorely missed as an artist.

She received Schumann's last surviving letter in May 1855. After that date he was no longer willing or able to write, in spite of her entreaties that he might do so. In general, his mental reserves seem to have started to fail him during his second year at Endenich, although it must remain an open question to what extent this was due to his worsening illness or to his hospitalization. Wasielewski reports that by the summer of 1855 Schumann's improvisations at the piano had become "unendurable."[24] And on April 25, 1856, Brahms wrote to his friend Joachim:

> How he's changed! He received me as joyfully and as cordially as ever, but it chilled me through and through — I couldn't understand a word he said. We sat down, the situation grew increasingly painful for me, my eyes were brimming over, he kept talking, but I still didn't understand a word. I looked down at what he was reading. It was an atlas, and he was busy copying out parts of it, but they were just childish scrawls, of course.[25]

On July 23, an alarmist telegram brought Clara to the clinic, but on the advice of Brahms and the doctor, she did not make direct contact with her husband. Four days later she saw him again for the first time in more than two years:

> I saw Him, it was between 6 and 7 in the evening. He smiled at me and threw his arm around me with a great effort as he could no longer move his limbs — I shall never forget it. [...] He was still talking a lot with the spirits, it seemed, and wouldn't let anyone stay with him for long, otherwise he became agitated, but you could barely understand anything any longer.[26]

Her diary goes on:

> For weeks he has had nothing but wine and jelly — today [July 28] I gave it to him, and he took it with the happiest expression on his face and with real haste, slurping the wine from my finger — he knew it was me ... On Tuesday the 29th he was to be released from his sufferings, at 4 in the afternoon he slipped quietly away. His final hours were calm, and so he fell asleep completely unnoticed, no one was with him at the time.[27]

Schumann was buried in the municipal cemetery at Bonn at seven o'clock in the evening on July 31. Clara did not follow the coffin to the grave but remained behind in the chapel:

> I could hear the funeral music, he was then lowered into the earth, but I had the clear feeling that it wasn't him but only his body — his spirit was high above me — I don't think I have ever prayed more fervently than I did at that moment. May God give me the strength to live without him. Johannes and Joachim walked ahead of the coffin, which was carried by some of the members of the Concordia Society who had once performed a serenade for him in Düsseldorf. It was their way of showing how much they honored him. The mayors were there, too, Hiller had come from Cologne, but otherwise there were none of our friends. I hadn't made any announcement as I didn't want them to come. His dearest friends were at the front, I brought up the rear (unnoticed), which was best — certainly it was in his spirit![28]

The poet Klaus Groth had traveled to Bonn with Brahms and recalled:

> The little procession moved peacefully and silently until the road widened and the tolling of the bells grew louder in the marketplace as we drew closer. But lo! people poured out of the narrow streets as if to see a prince's royal progress. [...] Within minutes the marketplace was packed, and in the neighboring streets people crowded to their windows, the cortege scarcely able to maintain a measured step and pass through the sympathetic crowd. As we left the place, the crowd surged all around us as if half the town had come out. The beautifully situated graveyard was black with people.
>
> It was the burial of a prince of art.[29]

The children of Robert and Clara Schumann. Ambrotype by Wilhelm Severin, taken in Düsseldorf in 1854. This is the only known copy of this image, which Clara presumably sent to Schumann in Endenich at Christmas 1854. From left to right, Ludwig, Marie with Felix in her lap, Elise, Ferdinand, and Eugenie. Missing from the family portrait is Julie, who was then staying with her grandmother in Berlin.

(Photograph courtesy of the Robert Schumann Museum, Zwickau.)

Epilogue

Schumann was forty-six when he died in 1856. Clara Schumann (1819–96) survived him by a further forty years. She began a second — and internationally successful — career as a virtuoso. After his death she wrote little new music of her own but took a correspondingly intense interest in cultivating his artistic legacy, which she did as a pianist, as his executrix, and as the editor of his works. She did not remarry but maintained a lifelong friendship with Brahms that survived all manner of complications. From 1878 she taught at the Hoch Conservatory in Frankfurt, the city in which she died on May 20, 1896.

Her daughter Marie (1841–1929) looked after and assisted her mother, including helping her with her daily chores. She was an excellent pianist and took over some of her mother's pupils. She additionally did what she could to keep her brothers and sisters together. She spent her declining years at Interlaken in the Bernese Oberland.

Elise Schumann (1843–1928) earned a living as a piano teacher in Frankfurt. Then, in 1877, she and her husband, the businessman Louis Sommerhoff, went to America for six years, after which she returned to Frankfurt. Her descendants still live in the United States.

Julie (1845–72) enjoyed the affection of Brahms but in 1869 she married an Italian count with the fine-sounding name of Vittorio Amadeo Radicati di Marmorito. She died giving birth to their third child.

Ludwig (1848–99) was a problem child. Physically attractive, he was educationally subnormal and found it difficult to complete any formal training. Following a nervous breakdown in 1870 he was placed in a private asylum in Pirna but was then moved the following year to the regional asylum at Colditz, where he died, blind and mentally deranged.

Ferdinand (1849–91) became a banker in Berlin and in the face of Clara's wishes married Antonie Deutsch, who bore him seven children. After he became dependent on drugs, Clara largely assumed responsibility for his family, taking complete care of two of her grandchildren.

Eugenie (1851–1938) spent her early years in boarding schools and then, until 1891, lived with her elder sister Marie and their mother. Later she traveled to England with the singer Marie Fillunger and for the next two decades worked there as a piano teacher. She published her memoirs in German in 1925 (an English translation appeared two years later), and a reminiscence of her father in 1931.

Felix (1854–79) never saw his father but followed in his footsteps as a jurist, musician, and poet. He died from tuberculosis. Brahms set three of his poems to music.

Notes

PROLOGUE

1. Robert Schumann, *Tagebücher*, ed. Georg Eismann and Gerd Nauhaus (Basel and Frankfurt: Stroemfeld and Roter Stern, 1971–82), 2:401 (entry of June 1, 1846).
2. Ibid., 3/1:281 (entry of June 1, 1846).
3. Béla Hamvas, "Korruptheit und Moral: Über die Kapitulation des Gewissens und die Brutstätte der Rebellion." *Lettre international* 84 (2009): 65.
4. *Neue Zeitschrift für Musik* (hereafter, *NZfM*) 12 (1840): 82.
5. On the link between the "inner voice" and a novelistic motif in Jean Paul, see Erika Reiman, *Schumann's Piano Cycles and the Novels of Jean Paul* (Rochester, NY: University of Rochester Press, 2004), 181–83.
6. Robert Schumann, *Briefe. Neue Folge*, 2nd ed., ed. F. Gustav Jansen (Leipzig: Breitkopf & Härtel, 1904), 227 (letter to Carl Koßmaly, May 5, 1843).
7. Roland Barthes, *The Preparation of the Novel*, trans. Kate Briggs (New York: Columbia University Press, 2011), 314.
8. Hans-Georg Gadamer, *Truth and Method*, trans. W. Glen-Doepel, rev. Joel Weinsheimer and Donald G. Marshall (London: Continuum, 2004), 7, 15.
9. Thus the title of the 1981 study by Julius Alf and Joseph A. Kruse, *Robert Schumann: Universalgeist der Romantik* (Düsseldorf: Droske, 1981).

CHAPTER 1

1. Robert Schumann, *Tagebücher*, ed. Georg Eismann and Gerd Nauhaus (Basel and Frankfurt: Stroemfeld and Roter Stern, 1971–82), 1:30 (entry of January 24, 1827).
2. *NZfM* 2 (1835): 3.
3. Ludwig van Beethoven, *Briefwechsel*, ed. Sieghard Brandenburg (Munich: G. Henle, 1996–98), 4:298; 2:822 (in translated volume) (letter to Archduke Rudolph, July 29, 1819).
4. Robert Schumann, *Briefe. Neue Folge*, 2nd ed., ed. F. Gustav Jansen (Leipzig: Breitkopf & Härtel, 1904), 321 (letter to Eduard Krüger, November 29, 1849).
5. *NZfM* 2 (1835): 153–54.
6. Ernst Burger, *Robert Schumann: Eine Lebenschronik in Bildern und Dokumenten* (Mainz: Schott, 1999), 32.
7. Ibid.
8. Ibid.

9. Ibid., 33.

10. Ibid.

11. Georg Eismann, *Robert Schumann: Ein Quellenwerk* (Leipzig: Breitkopf & Härtel, 1956), 1:23.

12. Ibid., 1:65.

13. Clara Schumann, ed., *Jugendbriefe von Robert Schumann: Nach den Originalen mit-getheilt* (Leipzig: Breitkopf & Härtel, 1885), 117 (letter to Christiane Schumann, July 30, 1830).

14. Ibid., 128–30 (letter to Christiane Schumann, November 15–16, 1830).

15. Ibid., 232 (letter to Christiane Schumann, March 19, 1834).

16. Clara Schumann and Robert Schumann, *Briefwechsel: Kritische Gesamtausgabe*, ed. Eva Weissweiler (Frankfurt: Stroemfeld, 1984–2001), 1:20; 1:18 (in translated volume) (letter from Clara Wieck to Robert Schumann, February 13, 1836).

17. Eugenie Schumann, *Robert Schumann: Ein Lebensbild meines Vaters* (Leipzig: Koehler & Amelang, 1931), 115.

18. *NZfM* 3 (1835): 1.

19. Schumann, *Tagebücher*, 2:402 (undated entry [June 1846]).

20. Robert Schumann, *Neue Ausgabe sämtlicher Werke*, ed. Akio Mayeda et al. (Mainz: Schott, 1991–), 3/1/1:133.

21. Corinna Wenke, "Aspekte zu Robert Schumanns Entwicklung" (PhD diss., University of Leipzig, 1987), 75.

22. Emil Flechsig, "Erinnerungen an Schumann. Aus dem Manuskript erstmals vollständig veröffentlicht von seiner Urenkelin Hilde Wendler," *Neue Zeitschrift für Musik* 117 (1956): 392–96.

23. Schumann and Schumann, *Briefwechsel*, 1:125; 1:128 (in translated volume) (letter from Robert Schumann to Clara Wieck, March 19, 1838) and Schumann, *Tagebücher*, 1:82 (undated entry before May 27, 1828).

24. Schumann, *Jugendbriefe*, 16 (letter to Emil Flechsig, March 17, 1828).

25. Aigi Heero, *Robert Schumanns Jugendlyrik* (Sinzig: Studio, 2003), 259.

26. Schumann, *Jugendbriefe*, 12 (letter to Emil Fleschsig, December 1, 1827).

27. Gerd Nauhaus, "Robert Schumann: Jünglingswallfahrten," in *Zwischen Poesie und Musik: Robert Schumann—früh und spät*, edited by Ingrid Bodsch and Gerd Nauhaus (Bonn: Stroemfeld, 2006), 44.

28. The incident is fully documented, with a commentary, in Gerd Nauhaus and Ulrich Tadday, ed., *Prosa und Poesie: Robert Schumanns Schulaufsätze* (Sinzig: Studio, 2010).

29. Schumann, *Tagebücher*, 1:77 (undated entry [1827]).

30. Siegfried Kross, ed., *Briefe und Notizen Robert und Clara Schumanns* (Bonn: Bouvier, 1982), 18–21 (letter to Eduard Moritz Rascher, June 16, 1828).

INTERMEZZO I

1. Elisabeth Eleonore Bauer, "Beethoven — unser musikalischer Jean Paul: Anmerkungen zu einer Analogie," in *Beethoven: Analecta varia*, ed. Heinz-Klaus Metzger and Rainer Riehn (Munich: text + kritik, 1987), 88.
2. Jean Paul, *Sämtliche Werke: Historisch-kritische Ausgabe*, ed. Eduard Berend (Weimar: Preußische Akademie der Wissenschaften, 1925-64), 1/10:169.
3. Ibid., 1/10:181.
4. Ibid., 1/10:425.
5. Robert Schumann, *Tagebücher*, ed. Georg Eismann and Gerd Nauhaus (Basel and Frankfurt: Stroemfeld and Roter Stern, 1971-82), 1:97 (undated entry [before July 22, 1828]).

CHAPTER 2

1. Clara Schumann, ed., *Jugendbriefe von Robert Schumann: Nach den Originalen mitgetheilt* (Leipzig: Breitkopf & Härtel, 1885), 34 (letter to Christiane Schumann, August 31, 1828).
2. Ibid., 19 (letter to Julius Schumann, April 25, 1828).
3. Robert Schumann, *Tagebücher*, ed. Georg Eismann and Gerd Nauhaus (Basel and Frankfurt: Stroemfeld and Roter Stern, 1971-82), 1:64 (entry of May 8, 1828).
4. Schumann, *Jugendbriefe*, 22 (letter to Christiane Schumann, May 21, 1828).
5. Ibid., 27 (letter to Christiane Schumann, June 29, 1828).
6. Ernst Burger, *Robert Schumann: Eine Lebenschronik in Bildern und Dokumenten* (Mainz: Schott, 1999), 75, 101.
7. Schumann, *Tagebücher*, 1:323.
8. Georg Eismann, *Robert Schumann: Ein Quellenwerk* (Leipzig: Breitkopf & Härtel, 1956), 1:43.
9. Eugenie Schumann, *Robert Schumann: Ein Lebensbild meines Vaters* (Leipzig: Koehler & Amelang, 1931), 72.
10. Wilhelm Joseph von Wasielewski, *Schumanniana* (Leipzig: Breitkopf & Härtel, 1883), 90-91.
11. Ibid., 91-92.
12. Schumann, *Tagebücher*, 1:97 (undated entry [before July 22, 1828]).
13. *Allgemeine musikalische Zeitung* 33 (1831): 808.
14. *NZfM* 4 (1836): 138.
15. Schumann, *Tagebücher*, 1:147 (entries of November 21 and 22, 1828).
16. Ibid., 1:97 (undated entry [between July 22 and 29, 1828]).
17. Schumann, *Jugendbriefe*, 105 (letter to Christiane Schumann, February 24, 1830).
18. Ibid., 53-54 (letter to Christiane Schumann, May 25, 1829).
19. Robert Schumann, *Briefe. Neue Folge*, 2nd ed., ed. F. Gustav Jansen (Leipzig: Breitkopf & Härtel, 1904), 99 (letter to Johanne Christiane Devrient, September 15, 1837).
20. Schumann, *Tagebücher*, 1:222 (entry of January 24, 1830).

21. Ibid. (entry of January 26, 1830).

22. Martin Kreisig, ed., *Gesammelte Schriften über Musik und Musiker von Robert Schumann*, 5th ed. (Leipzig: Breitkopf & Härtel, 1914), 1:1, 2:106.

23. Schumann, *Tagebücher*, 1:226 (entry of February 8, 1830).

24. Berthold Litzmann, ed., *Clara Schumann: Ein Künstlerleben. Nach Tagebüchern und Briefen*, 6th ed. (Leipzig: Breitkopf & Härtel, 1920), 1:21–22; 1:18 (in translated volume [emended]) (letter from Friedrich Wieck to Christiane Schumann, August 9, 1830).

25. Siegfried Kross, ed., *Briefe und Notizen Robert und Clara Schumanns* (Bonn: Bouvier, 1982), 28.

26. Schumann, *Jugendbriefe*, 140–41 (letter to Christiane Schumann, February 18, 1831).

27. Burger, *Robert Schumann*, 101.

28. Schumann, *Tagebücher*, 1:386 (entry of May 7, 1832).

29. Schumann, *Jugendbriefe*, 188 (letter to Christiane Schumann, August 9, 1832).

30. Ibid., 210 (letter to Christiane Schumann, June 28, 1833).

31. Ibid., 209 (letter to Christiane Schumann, June 28, 1833).

32. Eckart Altenmüller, "Focal Dystonia: Advances in Brain Imaging of Fine Motor Control in Musicians," *Hand Clinics* 19 (2003): 1–16.

33. Schumann, *Tagebücher*, 1:416 (entry of October 7, 1833).

34. Schumann, *Jugendbriefe*, 227–28 (letter to Christiane Schumann, November 27, 1833).

35. Schumann, *Tagebücher*, 1:419 (undated entry [1833]).

36. Ibid., 1:330 (entry of May 12, 1831).

37. Ibid., 1:412 (entry of July 13, 1832).

38. Clara Schumann and Robert Schumann, *Briefwechsel: Kritische Gesamtausgabe,* ed. Eva Weissweiler (Frankfort: Stroemfeld, 1984–2001) 1:7; 1:5 (in translated volume [emended]) (letter from Robert Schumann to Clara Wieck, July 13, 1833).

39. Ibid., 1:8; 1:6 (in translated volume [emended]) (undated letter from Clara Wieck to Robert Schumann [July 1833]).

40. Ibid., 1:13–14; 1:11–12 (in translated volume [emended]) (letters from Clara Wieck to Robert Schumann, June 8, 1834, and from Robert Schumann to Clara Wieck, July 10, 1834).

41. Ibid., 1:15–16; 1:14 (in translated volume [emended]) (letter from Robert Schumann to Clara Wieck, July 10, 1834).

INTERMEZZO II

1. Clemens Brentano, *Werke*, ed. Friedhelm Kemp (Munich: Carl Hanser, 1963), 2:882.

2. Ibid., 2:900.

3. E. T. A. Hoffmann, *Sämtliche Werke*, ed. Gerhard Allroggen et al. (Frankfurt: Deutscher Klassiker Verlag, 1985–2006), 6:389; see also Jürgen Link, "Empirisch-transzendentale Objekte in der Romantik und die empirisch-transzendentale Dublette

Mensch," in *Schläft ein Lied in allen Dingen? Romantische Dingpoetik*, ed. Christiane Holm and Günter Oesterle, 43–54 (Würzburg: Königshausen & Neumann, 2011).

4. Jean Paul, *Sämmtliche Werke* (Berlin: Reimer, 1826–28), 15:569.

5. Heinrich Heine, *Sämtliche Schriften*, ed. the Nationale Forschungs- und Gedenkstätten der klassischen deutschen Literatur in Weimar and the Centre National de la Recherche Scientifique in Paris (Berlin: Akademie-Verlag, 1970–), 2:253.

6. *NZfM* 2 (1835): 116.

CHAPTER 3

1. *NZfM* 2 (1835): 3.

2. Robert Schumann, *Tagebücher*, ed. Georg Eismann and Gerd Nauhaus (Basel and Frankfurt: Stroemfeld and Roter Stern, 1971–82), 1:344 (entry of July [2,] 1831).

3. Robert Schumann, *Briefe. Neue Folge*, 2nd ed., ed. F. Gustav Jansen (Leipzig: Breitkopf & Härtel, 1904), 78 (letter to Heinrich Dorn, September 14, 1836).

4. Martin Kreisig, ed., *Gesammelte Schriften über Musik und Musiker von Robert Schumann*, 5th ed. (Leipzig: Breitkopf & Härtel, 1914), 2:260–61 (italics in original).

5. Ibid., 2:262.

6. Ibid., 2:268.

7. Eduard Hanslick, *Aus meinem Leben*, 4th ed. (Berlin: Allgemeiner Verein für Deutsche Literatur, 1911), 1:72.

8. *NZfM* 3 (1835): 70.

9. *NZfM* 1 (1834): 38.

10. [Ludwig Rellstab], "Ueberblick der Erzeugnisse," *Iris im Gebiete der Tonkunst* 4 (1833): 110–12.

11. *NZfM* 2 (1835): 163.

12. *NZfM* 4 (1836): 69.

13. Siegfried Kross, ed., *Briefe und Notizen Robert und Clara Schumanns* (Bonn: Bouvier, 1982), 41.

14. *NZfM* 6 (1837): 29.

15. Johann Wolfgang von Goethe, *Sämmtliche Werke* (Stuttgart: Cotta, 1840), 2:208; 235 (in translated volume [trans. Edgar Alfred Bowring as *The Poems of Goethe*]).

16. *NZfM* 2 (1835): 197.

17. *NZfM* 1 (1834): 1. The lines are taken from *King Henry the Eighth*, a play now attributed to Shakespeare and Fletcher.

18. *NZfM* 1 (1834): 89.

19. *NZfM* 1 (1834): 93.

20. *NZfM* 3 (1835): 29.

21. Friedrich Gustav Jansen, *Die Davidsbündler: Aus Robert Schumanns Sturm- und Drangperiode* (Leipzig: Breitkopf & Härtel, 1883), 12.

22. *NZfM* 1 (1834): 73.

23. *NZfM* 1 (1834): 153.

24. *NZfM* 2 (1835): 116.

25. Ibid.

26. Hans-Georg Gadamer, *Truth and Method*, trans. W. Glen-Doepel, rev. Joel Weinsheimer and Donald G. Marshall (London: Continuum, 2004), 186.

27. *NZfM* 2 (1835): 117.

28. Friedrich Schlegel, "Athenaeums-Fragmente," *Kritische Schriften* (Munich: Carl Hanser Verlag, 1964), 25–88, esp. 38–39.

29. *NZfM* 1 (1834): 7.

30. *NZfM* 5 (1836): 112–13.

31. *NZfM* 5 (1836): 135.

32. *NZfM* 5 (1836): 135–36.

33. *NZfM* 3 (1835): 182.

34. Leon B. Platinga's 1967 study, *Schumann as Critic* (New Haven, CT: Yale University Press), still offers the best overview of Schumann's *Neue Zeitschrift für Musik*.

35. *NZfM* 10 (1839), 1–2.

CHAPTER 4

1. Clara Schumann and Robert Schumann, *Briefwechsel: Kritische Gesamtausgabe*, ed. Eva Weissweiler (Frankfurt: Stroemfeld, 1984–2001), 1:146; 1:150 (in translated volume [emended]) (letter from Robert Schumann to Clara Wieck, April [15,] 1838).

2. Peter Gülke, quoted in Ulrich Tadday, *Schumann Handbuch* (Stuttgart: Bärenreiter, 2006), 33.

3. Schumann and Schumann, *Briefwechsel*, 2:368; 2:32 (in translated volume [emended]) (letter from Robert Schumann to Clara Wieck, January [26,] 1839).

4. Max Kalbeck, *Johannes Brahms*, 2nd ed. (Berlin: Deutsche Brahms-Gesellschaft, 1908–14), 3/1:165.

5. Martin Kreisig, ed., *Gesammelte Schriften über Musik und Musiker von Robert Schumann*, 5th ed. (Leipzig: Breitkopf & Härtel, 1914), 1:22.

6. Ibid., 1:343.

7. *NZfM* 7 (1837): 135.

8. *NZfM* 8 (1838): 22.

9. *NZfM* 7 (1837): 135–36.

10. *NZfM* 3 (1835): 208.

11. Robert Schumann, *Tagebücher*, ed. Georg Eismann and Gerd Nauhaus (Basel and Frankfurt: Stroemfeld and Roter Stern, 1971–82), 1:339 (entry of June 8, 1831).

12. Ibid., 1:361 (entry of August [14,] 1831).

13. Ibid., 2:402 (undated entry [June 1846]).

14. Kreisig, *Gesammelte Schriften*, 1:18.

15. Clara Schumann, ed., *Jugendbriefe von Robert Schumann: Nach den Originalen mitgetheilt* (Leipzig: Breitkopf & Härtel, 1885), 158 (letter to Christiane Schumann,

November 25, 1831).

16. Helmut Loos, *Robert Schumann: Interpretationen seiner Werke* (Laaber: Laaber-Verlag, 2005), 1:3.

17. Ignaz Moscheles, *Aus Moscheles' Leben. Nach Briefen und Tagebüchern* (Leipzig: Duncker & Humblot, 1872–73), 2:15.

18. Schumann, *Tagebücher*, 1:399 (entry of May 28, 1832).

19. Schumann, *Jugendbriefe*, 174 (letter to Christiane Schumann, May 8, 1832).

20. Kreisig, *Gesammelte Schriften*, 2:24.

21. Schumann, *Jugendbriefe*, 167–68 (letter to Ludwig Rellstab, April 19, 1832).

22. Ernst Burger, *Robert Schumann: Eine Lebenschronik in Bildern und Dokumenten* (Mainz: Schott, 1999), 103.

23. Kreisig, *Gesammelte Schriften*, 1:18.

24. *NZfM* 12 (1840): 120.

25. *NZfM* 3 (1835): 50.

26. Schumann and Schumann, *Briefwechsel*, 1:42; 1:40 (in translated volume [emended]) (letter from Robert Schumann to Clara Wieck, November 8, 1837).

27. Schumann, *Tagebücher*, 1:407 (entry of June 9, 1832).

28. Schumann and Schumann, *Briefwechsel*, 2:367; 2:31 (in translated volume [emended]) (letter from Robert Schumann to Clara Wieck, January [26,] 1839).

29. Robert Schumann, *Briefe. Neue Folge*, 2nd ed., ed. F. Gustav Jansen (Leipzig: Breitkopf & Härtel, 1904), 170 (letter to Heinrich Dorn, September 5, 1839).

30. Ibid., 290 (letter to Carl Reinecke, October 4, 1848).

31. Schumann, *Tagebücher*, 2:34 (undated entry [July 1837]).

32. Schumann and Schumann, *Briefwechsel*, 2:368; 2:31 (in translated volume [emended]) (letter from Robert Schumann to Clara Wieck, January [26,] 1838).

33. Ibid., 1:127; 1:130 (in translated volume [emended]) (letter from Robert Schumann to Clara Wieck, March 19, 1838).

34. Ibid., 1:219, 121; 1:225, 123 (in translated volume [emended] (letters from Robert Schumann to Clara Wieck, August 3, 1838 and March 19, 1838).

35. Ibid., 2:458; 2:127 (in translated volume [emended]) (letter from Clara Wieck to Robert Schumann, March 24, 1839).

36. *NZfM* 7 (1837): 70.

37. Schumann and Schumann, *Briefwechsel*, 1:153; 1:157 (in translated volume [emended]) (letter from Robert Schumann to Clara Wieck, April 20, 1838).

38. Kreisig, *Gesammelte Schriften*, 2:361.

39. Schumann, *Tagebücher*, 1:112 (entry of August 14, 1828).

40. *NZfM* 2 (1835): 202.

41. Hans Pfitzner, *Die neue Ästhetik der musikalischen Impotenz: Ein Verwesungssymptom?* (Munich: Süddeutsche Monatshefte, 1920), 65.

42. Peter Gülke, quoted in Tadday, *Schumann Handbuch*, 69.

43. Ulrike Kranefeld, *Der nachschaffende Hörer: Rezeptionsästhetische Studien zur Musik Robert Schumanns* (Stuttgart: J. B. Metzler, 2000), 176–77. Goethe's comments on

Runge were first published in the second volume of his *Ueber Kunst und Alterthum in den Rhein und Mayn Gegenden* (Stuttgart: Cotta, 1817), 46.

44. Ludwig Wittgenstein, *Werkausgabe* (Frankfurt: Suhrkamp, 1984–88), 5:280.

45. Umberto Eco, *Die Grenzen der Interpretation*, trans. Günter Memmert (Munich: Carl Hanser Verlag, 1992), 202; on the themes of brevity and wit, see also John Daverio, "Schumann's Systems of Musical Fragments and *Witz*," in *Nineteenth-Century Music and the German Romantic Ideology*, 49–86 (New York: Schirmer Books, 1993).

46. *NZfM* 2 (1835): 156.

47. Roland Barthes, *The Responsibility of Forms: Critical Essays on Music, Art, and Representation*, trans. Richard Howard (New York: Hill and Wang, 1985), 295–96.

48. Hans Joachim Köhler, *Robert Schumann: Sein Leben und Wirken in den Leipziger Jahren* (Leipzig: Peters, 1986), 42.

49. See Martin Geck, *Von Beethoven bis Mahler: Leben und Werk der großen Komponisten des 19. Jahrhunderts* (Reinbek: Rowohlt, 2000), 139–42 ("Komponieren am Klavier").

50. Schumann, *Briefe. Neue Folge*, 76 (letter to Ignaz Moscheles, July 30, 1836).

51. Schumann and Schumann, *Briefwechsel*, 1:126 (where the word is wrongly transcribed as "Raffiniertestes"); 1:129 (in translated volume) (letter from Robert Schumann to Clara Wieck, March [19,] 1838).

52. Ibid., 2:495; 2:166 (in translated volume [emended]) (letter from Robert Schumann to Clara Wieck, April 22, 1839).

53. For a comparison of the motifs, see Linda Correll Roesner, "The Chamber Music," in *The Cambridge Companion to Schumann*, ed. Beate Perrey (Cambridge: Cambridge University Press, 2007), 129.

54. See Peter Schleuning, "'Ein einziger Liebesschrei' — 'an die ferne Geliebte.' Der erste Satz von Schumanns Klavierfantasie op. 17," in *Musik, Deutung, Bedeutung: Festschrift für Harry Goldschmidt zum 75. Geburtstag*, ed. Hanns-Werner Heister and Hartmut Lück (Dortmund: Edition V im Pläne-Verlag, 1986), 80–85.

INTERMEZZO III

1. Roland Barthes, "Rasch," in *The Responsibility of Forms: Critical Essays on Music, Art, and Representation*, trans. Richard Howard (New York: Hill and Wang, 1985), 299.

2. E. T. A. Hoffmann, *Poetische Werke*, ed. Klaus Kanzog (Berlin: Walter de Gruyter, 1957–62), 9:270.

3. See Meiki Becker-Adden, *Nahtstellen: Strukturelle Analogien der "Kreisleriana" von E. T. A. Hoffmann und Robert Schumann* (Bielefeld: Transcript, 2006).

4. Julia Kristeva, *Revolution in Poetic Language* (New York: Columbia, 1984), 16.

5. Florens Christian Rang, *Historische Psychologie des Karnevals*, ed. Lorenz Jäger (Berlin: Brinkmann & Bose, 1983), 23. Although written in 1909, Rang's text was not published until 1983.

6. See in particular Dieter Schnebel, "Rückungen — Ver-rückungen: Psychoanalytische

Betrachtungen zu Schumanns Leben und Werk," in *Sonderband Robert Schumann I*, ed. Heinz-Klaus Metzger and Rainer Riehn (Munich: text + kritik, 1981), 43–54; and Stephan Münch, "'Fantasiestücke in Kreislers Manier': Robert Schumanns 'Kreisleriana' op. 16 und die Musikanschauung E. T. A. Hoffmanns," *Die Musikforschung* 45 (1992): 255–75.

7. See Martin Geck, *Von Beethoven bis Mahler: Leben und Werk der großen Komponisten des 19. Jahrhunderts* (Reinbek: Rowohlt, 2000), 137–54 ("Absolute Poesie in den *Kreisleriana*").

8. Jean Paul, *Vorschule der Ästhetik*, ed. Norbert Miller (Munich: Hanser, 1974), 110.

9. Clara Schumann and Robert Schumann, *Briefwechsel: Kritische Gesamtausgabe*, ed. Eva Weissweiler (Frankfurt: Stroemfeld, 1984–2001), 1:219; 1:225 (in translated volume [emended]) (letter from Robert Schumann to Clara Wieck, August 3, 1838).

10. Ibid., 1:138; 1:141–42 (in translated volume [emended]) (letter from Robert Schumann to Clara Wieck, April 13, 1838).

11. Ibid.

12. Julius Becker, *Der Neuromantiker: Musikalischer Roman* (Leipzig: Weber, 1840), 1:93–95.

13. Hugo Riemann, *Geschichte der Musik seit Beethoven* (Berlin: Spemann, 1901), 442.

14. Theodor W. Adorno, "Klangfiguren," in *Gesammelte Schriften*, ed. Rolf Tiedemann (Frankfurt: Suhrkamp, 1997), 199–200; 171 (in translated volume).

15. Jürgen Link, "Metamorphosen der romantischen Kulturrevolution," *Kulturrevolution* 12 (1986): 51.

16. Martin Geck, *Zwischen Romantik und Restauration: Musik im Realismus-Diskurs 1848–1871* (Stuttgart: J. B. Metzler, 2001), 108–10.

17. Friedrich Schlegel, "Athenaeums-Fragmente," *Kritische Schriften* (Munich: Carl Hanser Verlag, 1964), 25–88.

18. Walter Benjamin, *Der Begriff der Kunstkritik in der deutschen Romantik*, ed. Hermann Schweppenhäuser (Frankfurt: Suhrkamp, 1973).

19. Umberto Eco, *The Middle Ages of James Joyce: The Aesthetics of Chaosmos*, trans. Ellen Esrock (London: Hutchinson Radius, 1989), 76.

20. Slavoj Žižek, "Die abwesende Melodie," *Die Zeit*, December 6, 2007, 62.

21. Jean Genet, *Le condamné à mort et autres poèmes* (Paris: Gallimard, 1999), 110.

CHAPTER 5

1. Robert Schumann, *Briefe. Neue Folge*, 2nd ed., ed. F. Gustav Jansen (Leipzig: Breitkopf & Härtel, 1904), 83 (letter to Therese Schumann, December 31, 1836).

2. Berthold Litzmann, ed., *Clara Schumann: Ein Künstlerleben. Nach Tagebüchern und Briefen*, 6th ed. (Leipzig: Breitkopf & Härtel, 1920), 1:69; 1:61 (in translated volume [emended]).

3. Ibid., 1:74 (this passage is not included in the English translation).

4. Ibid. (this passage is not included in the English translation).

5. Clara Schumann and Robert Schumann, *Briefwechsel: Kritische Gesamtausgabe*, ed. Eva Weissweiler (Frankfurt: Stroemfeld, 1984–2001), 1:95–96; 1:97 (in translated volume [emended]) (letter from Robert Schumann to Clara Wieck, February 11, 1838).

6. Robert Schumann, *Tagebücher*, ed. Georg Eismann and Gerd Nauhaus (Basel and Frankfurt: Stroemfeld and Roter Stern, 1971–82), 1:421 (undated entry [late 1835]).

7. Schumann and Schumann, *Briefwechsel*, 1:96; 1:98 (in translated volume [emended]) (letter from Robert Schumann to Clara Wieck, February 11, 1838).

8. Litzmann, *Clara Schumann*, 1:59; 1:53 (in translated volume).

9. Ibid., 1:81; 1:68 (in translated volume [emended]).

10. Schumann and Schumann, *Briefwechsel*, 1:79; 1:80 (in translated volume [emended]) (letter from Clara Wieck to Robert Schumann, January 18, 1838).

11. Ibid., 1:138; 1:142 (in translated volume [emended]) (letter from Robert Schumann to Clara Wieck, April 13, 1838).

12. Translated by Edgar Alfred Bowring.

13. Ibid., 1:75; 1:76 (in translated volume [emended]) (letter from Robert Schumann to Clara Wieck, January 5, 1839).

14. Ibid., 1:203; 1:209 (in translated volume [emended]) (letter from Robert Schumann to Clara Wieck, July 13, 1838).

15. Ibid., 1:207; 1:213 (in translated volume [emended]) (letter from Clara Wieck to Robert Schumann, July 14, 1838).

16. Ibid., 1:265; 1:274 (in translated volume [emended]) (letter from Clara Wieck to Robert Schumann, October 17, 1838).

17. Ibid., 1:244–45; 1:252–53 (in translated volume [emended]) (letter from Clara Wieck to Robert Schumann, September 22, 1838).

18. Ibid., 1:245; 1:253 (in translated volume [emended]) (letter from Robert Schumann to Clara Wieck, September 24, 1838).

19. Martin Kreisig, ed., *Gesammelte Schriften über Musik und Musiker von Robert Schumann*, 5th ed. (Leipzig: Breitkopf & Härtel, 1914), 2:12.

20. See Friederike Preiß, *Der Prozeß: Clara und Robert Schumanns Kontroverse mit Friedrich Wieck* (Frankfurt: Peter Lang), 2004.

21. Ibid., 315.

22. Litzmann, *Clara Schumann*, 1:430; 1:299 (in translated volume) (diary entry of September 12, 1840).

23. Schumann, *Tagebücher*, 3/1:161 (entry of September 10, 1840).

24. Litzmann, *Clara Schumann*, 1:430–31; 1:300 (in translated volume) (diary entry of September 12, 1840).

25. Schumann and Schumann, *Briefwechsel*, 1:169–70; 1:174–75 (in translated volume [emended]) (letter from Robert Schumann to Clara Wieck, May 11, 1838).

26. Anonymous, untitled review, *Blätter für Musik und Literatur* 1 (October 1840): 14.

27. Carl Koßmaly, "Ueber Robert Schumann's Claviercompositionen," *Allgemeine musikalische Zeitung* 46 (1844): 20; 310 (in translated volume).

28. Schumann, *Briefe. Neue Folge*, 235 (letter to Carl Koßmaly, January 25, 1844).

29. Ibid., 227 (letter to Carl Koßmaly, May 5, 1843).

30. *NZfM* 3 (1835): 151. Firlenz was the name that the members of the League of David gave to the city of Leipzig.

31. Robert Schumann, *Erinnerungen an Felix Mendelssohn Bartholdy*, ed. Georg Eismann (Zwickau: Predella-Verlag, 1948), 43–44.

32. Ibid., 44.

33. Schumann, *Tagebücher*, 2:50 (entry of January 29, 1838).

34. Ibid., 2:27 (entry of September 23, 1836).

35. Ibid. (entries of September 26 and 27, 1836).

36. Ibid., 2:55 (entry of May 13, 1838).

37. Hans Joachim Köhler, *Robert Schumann: Sein Leben und Wirken in den Leipziger Jahren* (Leipzig: Peters, 1986), 40.

38. Friedrich Gustav Jansen, *Die Davidsbündler: Aus Robert Schumanns Sturm- und Drangperiode* (Leipzig: Breitkopf & Härtel, 1883), 62.

39. Leander Hotaki, *Robert Schumanns Mottosammlung* (Freiburg im Breisgau: Rombach, 1998), 156.

40. "Projectenbuch" (project book), unpublished manuscript, Robert Schumann Museum, Zwickau.

41. *NZfM* 12 (1840): 82.

42. Schumann, *Tagebücher*, 2:96 (undated entry [February 1840]).

CHAPTER 6

1. Robert Schumann, *Briefe. Neue Folge*, 2nd ed., ed. F. Gustav Jansen (Leipzig: Breitkopf & Härtel, 1904), 158 (letter to Hermann Hirschbach, June 30, 1839).

2. Robert Schumann, *Tagebücher*, ed. Georg Eismann and Gerd Nauhaus (Basel and Frankfurt: Stroemfeld and Roter Stern, 1971–82), 1:417 (undated entry [1833]).

3. Ibid., 2:59 (entry of June 25, 1838).

4. Clara Schumann and Robert Schumann, *Briefwechsel: Kritische Gesamtausgabe*, ed. Eva Weissweiler (Frankfurt: Stroemfeld, 1984–2001), 3:942; 3:102 (in translated volume [emended]) (letter from Robert Schumann to Clara Wieck, February 22, 1840).

5. Ibid., 3:947; 3:107 (in translated volume [emended]) (letter from Robert Schumann to Clara Wieck, February 24, 1840).

6. Christiane Tewinkel, quoted in Ulrich Tadday, *Schumann Handbuch* (Stuttgart: Bärenreiter, 2006), 409.

7. *NZfM* 19 (1843): 35.

8. Ibid.

9. *NZfM* 11 (1839): 71.

10. *NZfM* 8 (1838): 86.

11. Translated by Sir Robert Randolph Garran.

12. Thrasybulos Georgiades, *Schubert: Musik und Lyrik* (Göttingen: Vandenhoeck & Ruprecht, 1967), 134.

13. Lawrence Kramer, *Music and Poetry: The Nineteenth Century and After* (Berkeley: University of California Press, 1984), 146.

14. Translated by Sir Robert Randolph Garran.

15. Heinrich Heine, *Sämtliche Schriften*, ed. the Nationale Forschungs- und Gedenkstätten der klassischen deutschen Literatur in Weimar and the Centre National de la Recherche Scientifique in Paris (Berlin: Akademie-Verlag, 1970–), 20:21.

16. Thus my university teacher, Werner Korte: Korte, *Robert Schumann* (Postdam: Athenaion, 1937), 76.

17. Translated by Sir Robert Randolph Garran.

18. Henri Pousseur, "Schumann ist der Dichter: Fünfundzwanzig Momente einer Lektüre der Dichterliebe," in *Sonderband Robert Schumann II*, ed. Heinz-Klaus Metzger and Rainer Riehn (Munich: text + kritik, 1982), 92.

19. *NZfM* 13 (1840): 119.

20. *NZfM* 3 (1835): 50–51.

21. Beate Perrey, *Schumann's "Dichterliebe" and Early Romantic Poetics: Fragmentation of Desire* (Cambridge: Cambridge University Press, 2002), 208.

22. A facsimile of the first version may be found in Rufus Hallmark, *The Genesis of Schumann's "Dichterliebe"* (Ann Arbor: UMI Research Press, 1979), 37.

23. Schumann and Schumann, *Briefwechsel*, 3:1043; 3:201 (in translated volume [emended]) (letter from Robert Schumann to Clara Wieck, May 22, 1840).

24. Charles Rosen, *The Romantic Generation* (Cambridge, MA: Harvard University Press, 1995), 694.

25. On the reception of the Eichendorff *Liederkreis*, see David Ferris, *Schumann's Eichendorff* Liederkreis *and the Genre of the Romantic Cycle* (Oxford: Oxford University Press, 2000), 208–10.

26. On the tension between the sexes, see Robert Samuels, "Narratives of Masculinity and Femininity: Two Schumann Song Cycles," in *Phrase and Subject: Studies in Literature and Music*, ed. Delia da Sousa Correa (Oxford: Legenda, 2006) 137–40.

INTERMEZZO IV

1. Translated by Sir Robert Randolph Garran.

2. Gottfried August Bürger, *Briefe von und an Gottfried August Bürger*, ed. Adolf Strodtmann (Berlin: Gebrüder Paetel, 1874), 1:369.

3. Jean Paul, *Werke* (Berlin: Hempel, 1870–78), 5:25.

4. Robert Schumann, *Briefe. Neue Folge*, 2nd ed., ed. F. Gustav Jansen (Leipzig: Breitkopf & Härtel, 1904), 6 (letter to Gottlob Wiedebein, July 15, 1828).

5. See the fascinating harmonic analysis in David Ferris, "'Was will dieses Grau'n bedeuten?' Schumann's 'Zwielicht' and Daverio's 'Incomprehensibility Topos,'" *Journal of Musicology* 22 (2005): 131–53.

6. Reinhold Brinkmann, *Schumann und Eichendorff: Studien zum Liederkreis opus* 39 (Munich: edition text + kritik, 1997), 49–51.

7. Thomas Mann, *Gesammelte Werke*, ed. Hans Bürgin et al. (Berlin: S. Fischer, 1960–74), 10:922.

8. Thomas Mann, *Große kommentierte Frankfurter Ausgabe: Werke — Briefe — Tagebücher*, ed. Eckard Heftrich et al. (Frankfurt: S. Fischer, 2002–), 21:378.

9. Thomas Mann, *Buddenbrooks*, trans. H. T. Lowe-Porter (London: Vintage Books, 1999), 603.

10. Friedrich Schlegel, *Lucinde and the Fragments*, trans. Peter Firchow (Eugene, OR: Wipf & Stock, 1971), 146.

CHAPTER 7

1. Robert Schumann, *Tagebücher*, ed. Georg Eismann and Gerd Nauhaus (Basel and Frankfurt: Stroemfeld and Roter Stern, 1971–82), 2:266 (entry of June 28, 1843).

2. Clara Schumann and Robert Schumann, *Briefwechsel: Kritische Gesamtausgabe*, ed. Eva Weissweiler (Frankfurt: Stroemfeld, 1984–2001), 2:604; 2:281 (in translated volume [emended]) (letter from Robert Schumann to Clara Wieck, June 27, 1839).

3. Kazuko Ozawa, "Merkwürdige Zeiten: Bemerkungen zu Schumanns Neugier," in *Robert Schumann und die Öffentlichkeit: Hans Joachim Köhler zum 70. Geburtstag*, ed. Helmut Loos (Leipzig: Schröder, 2007), 271.

4. Schumann, *Tagebücher*, 2:171, 173 (entries of July 1 and July 4–11, 1841).

5. Schumann and Schumann, *Briefwechsel*, 2:571; 2:246 (in translated volume [emended]) (letter from Robert Schumann to Clara Wieck, June 13, 1839).

6. Schumann, *Tagebücher*, 2:103 (entry of September 20–27, 1840).

7. Ibid., 2:178 (entry of July 18–August 8, 1841).

8. Ibid., 2:182 (entry of August 18, 1841).

9. Ibid., 2:183 (entry of August 21, 1841).

10. Joachim Draheim and Brigitt Höft, ed., *Clara Schumann: Sämtliche Lieder* (Wiesbaden: Breitkopf & Härtel, 1990–92), 1:6.

11. Veronica Beci, *Die andere Clara Schumann* (Düsseldorf: Droste, 1997), 98.

12. Robert Schumann, *Briefe. Neue Folge*, 2nd ed., ed. F. Gustav Jansen (Leipzig: Breitkopf & Härtel, 1904), 359 (letter to Johann Verhulst, September 8, 1852).

13. Schumann, *Tagebücher*, 2:103 (entry of September 20, 1840).

14. Ibid., 101 (entry of September 14, 1840).

15. Berthold Litzmann, ed., *Clara Schumann: Ein Künstlerleben. Nach Tagebüchern und Briefen*, 6th ed. (Leipzig: Breitkopf & Härtel, 1920), 2:59; 1:353 (in translated volume [emended]).

16. See Schumann, *Tagebücher*, 3/1:10–11.

17. Schumann and Schumann, *Briefwechsel*, 1:46; 1:45 (in translated volume [emended]) (letter from Clara Wieck to Robert Schumann, November 24, 1837).

18. Ibid., 1:47; 1:46 (in translated volume [emended]) (letter from Robert Schumann to

Clara Wieck, November 28, 1837).

19. Schumann, *Tagebücher*, 2:107 (entry of September 27–October 4, 1840).

20. Ibid., 2:164 (entry of May 10–22, 1841).

21. Schumann, *Briefe. Neue Folge*, 209 (letter to Robert Griepenkerl, October 31, 1841).

22. Schumann, *Tagebücher*, 2:184 (entry of September 17, 1841).

23. Ibid., 2:206 (entry of March 14, 1842).

24. Ibid., 2:252 (entry of November 3, 1842).

25. Ibid., 2:251 (undated entry [before November 3, 1842]).

26. Ibid., 3/2:449 (entry of December 30, 1847).

27. Richard Wagner, *Mein Leben* (Munich: List, 1976), 332; 319 (in translated volume).

28. Schumann, *Tagebücher*, 2:398 (entry of March 17, 1846).

29. Ibid., 2:257 (entry of February 12, 1843).

30. Litzmann, *Clara Schumann*, 2:13; 1:311 (in translated volume [emended]) (letter from Friedrich Wieck to Robert Schumann, December 15, 1843).

31. Schumann, *Tagebücher*, 2:280–81 (entries of February 5 and 6, 1844).

32. Ibid., 2:281 (entry of February 8, 1844).

33. Mikhail Saponov, "Schumann im Kreml," in *Robert Schumann und die Öffentlichkeit: Hans Joachim Köhler zum 70. Geburtstag*, ed. Helmut Loos (Leipzig: Schröder, 2007), 112.

34. Schumann, *Tagebücher*, 2:377–78 (undated entry [1844]).

35. Schumann, *Briefe. Neue Folge*, 239 (undated letter to Wieck [mid-May 1844]).

36. Schumann, *Tagebücher*, 2:351 (entry of April 9, 1844).

37. Ibid., 2:366 (entry of May 4, 1844).

38. Ibid., 2:360 (entry of April 28, 1844).

39. Ibid., 2:368–69 (entry of May 14, 1844).

40. Ibid., 2:546; Schulz's account was published in his *Briefe eines baltischen Idealisten an seine Mutter 1833–75*, ed. Johannes Werner (Leipzig: Koehler & Amelang, 1934), 88.

41. Schumann, *Briefe. Neue Folge*, 240 (letter to Carl Schumann, June 3, 1844).

42. Olga Lossewa, *Die Russlandreise Clara und Robert Schumanns* (Mainz: Schott, 2004), 81.

INTERMEZZO V

1. Thomas Synofzik, "Ein Rückert-Kanon als Keimzelle zu Schumanns Klavierkonzert op. 54," *Die Musikforschung* 58 (2005): 28–32.

2. Ibid., 32.

3. Clara Schumann and Robert Schumann, *Briefwechsel: Kritische Gesamtausgabe*, ed. Eva Weissweiler (Frankfurt: Stroemfeld, 1984–2001), 1:53; 1:52 (in translated volume [emended]) (letter from Robert Schumann to Clara Wieck, November 29, 1837).

4. Peter Gülke, quoted in Ulrich Tadday, *Schumann Handbuch* (Stuttgart: Bärenreiter, 2006), 38.

5. Arnfried Edler, *Robert Schumann und seine Zeit*, 3rd ed. (Laaber: Laaber-Verlag,

2008), 167–68.

6. Marc A. Weiner, "Reading the Ideal," *New German Critique* 69 (1996): 60.

7. Claudia Macdonald, *Robert Schumann and the Piano Concerto* (New York: Taylor and Francis, 2005), 196.

8. August Gerstmeier, *Robert Schumann: Klavierkonzert a-Moll, op.* 54 (Munich: Fink, 1986), 41–43.

CHAPTER 8

1. *NZfM* 42 (1855): 136.

2. *NZfM* 26 (1847): 17.

3. Martin Geck, "Der Weg ins Freie: Die Überwindung der traditionellen Viersätzigkeit in Schumanns *Rheinischer Symphonie* zugunsten eines neuen, narrativen Symphonietypus," in *Robert Schumann und die große Form: Referate des Bonner Symposions 2006,* ed. Bernd Sponheuer and Wolfram Steinbeck (Frankfurt: Peter Lang, 2009), 96–97.

4. Robert Schumann, *Tagebücher,* ed. Georg Eismann and Gerd Nauhaus (Basel and Frankfurt: Stroemfeld and Roter Stern, 1971–82), 2:74 (undated entry [between October 3 and 15, 1838]).

5. *NZfM* 11 (1839): 1.

6. Friedrich Gustav Jansen, *Die Davidsbündler: Aus Robert Schumanns Sturm- und Drangperiode* (Leipzig: Breitkopf & Härtel, 1883), 76.

7. *NZfM* 8 (1838): 182.

8. Theodor Billroth, *Wer ist musikalisch?,* ed. Eduard Hanslick., 2nd ed. (Berlin: Gebrüder Paetel, 1896), 177.

9. Peter Gülke, quoted in Ulrich Tadday, *Schumann Handbuch* (Stuttgart: Bärenreiter, 2006), 65–66.

10. Robert Schumann, *Briefe. Neue Folge,* 2nd ed., ed. F. Gustav Jansen (Leipzig: Breitkopf & Härtel, 1904), 226 (letter to Carl Koßmaly, May 5, 1843).

11. Ibid., 228 (letter to Eduard Krüger, June 3, 1843).

12. Ibid., 229–30 (letter to Johann Verhulst, June 19, 1843).

13. Gerd Nauhaus, quoted in Helmut Loos, *Robert Schumann: Interpretationen seiner Werke* (Laaber: Laaber-Verlag, 2005), 1:323.

14. Richard Wagner, *Gesammelte Schriften und Dichtungen.* 4th ed. (Leipzig: C. F. W. Siegel, 1907), 5:179.

15. *Allgemeine musikalische Zeitung* 45 (1843): 955.

16. Geck, "Der Weg ins Freie," 101.

17. Schumann, *Tagebücher,* 2:402 (undated entry [after June 1, 1846]).

18. Arnfried Edler, *Robert Schumann und seine Zeit,* 3rd ed. (Laaber: Laaber-Verlag, 2008), 183.

19. Peter Gülke, quoted in Henriette Herwig, *Übergänge zwischen Künsten und Kulturen: Internationaler Kongress zum 150. Todesjahr von Heinrich Heine und Robert Schumann* (Stuttgart: J. B. Metzler, 2007), 679.

20. Schumann, *Briefe. Neue Folge*, 300 (letter to Georg Dietrich Otten, April 2, 1849).
21. Reinhard Kapp, quoted in Loos, *Robert Schumann*, 1:396.
22. Ulrich Tadday, *Das schöne Unendliche: Ästhetik, Kritik, Geschichte der romantischen Musikanschauung* (Stuttgart: J. B. Metzler, 1999), 176–78.
23. Berthold Litzmann, ed., *Clara Schumann: Ein Künstlerleben. Nach Tagebüchern und Briefen*, 6th ed. (Leipzig: Breitkopf & Härtel, 1920), 2:127; 1:400 (in translated volume [emended]) (diary entry of January 18, 1849).
24. Schumann, *Briefe. Neue Folge*, 347 (letter to Adolf Schubring, September 22, 1851).

INTERMEZZO VI

1. Berthold Litzmann, ed., *Clara Schumann: Ein Künstlerleben. Nach Tagebüchern und Briefen*, 6th ed. (Leipzig: Breitkopf & Härtel, 1920), 2:221; 1:395 (in translated volume [emended]).
2. Wolfgang Seibold, *Robert und Clara Schumann in ihren Beziehungen zu Franz Liszt* (Frankfurt: Peter Lang, 2005), 2:59–60.
3. Franz Liszt, *Gesammelte Schriften*, ed. La Mara and Lina Ramann (Leipzig: Breitkopf & Härtel, 1880–83), 1:163.
4. Donald Francis Tovey, *Essays in Musical Analysis: Chamber Music* (London: Oxford University Press, 1944), 151.
5. Robert Schumann, *Briefedition*, ed. Thomas Synofzik et al. (Cologne: Dohr, 2008–), 2/1:223 (letter to Felix Mendelssohn, September 20, 1845).
6. Felix Mendelssohn, *Briefe aus den Jahren 1830 bis 1847*, ed. Paul and Carl Mendelssohn Bartholdy (Leipzig: Hermann Mendelssohn, 1870), 482 (letter to Marc-André Souchay, October 15, 1842).
7. *NZfM* 14 (1841): 40.
8. On the early form of the marcia, see John Daverio, *Robert Schumann: Herald of a "New Poetic Age"* (New York: Oxford University Press), 256.
9. Pyotr Ilyich Tchaikovsky, *Erinnerungen und Musikkritiken*, ed. Richard Petzoldt and Lothar Fahlbusch (Leipzig: Reclam, 1974), 160.
10. Hans Kohlhase, "Robert Schumanns Klavierquintett," in *Sonderband Robert Schumann I*, ed. Heinz-Klaus Metzger and Rainer Riehn (Munich: text + kritik, 1981), 154.

CHAPTER 9

1. Robert Schumann, *Briefe. Neue Folge*, 2nd ed., ed. F. Gustav Jansen (Leipzig: Breitkopf & Härtel, 1904), 306–7 (letter to Franz Brendel, June 17, 1849).
2. Berthold Litzmann, ed., *Clara Schumann: Ein Künstlerleben. Nach Tagebüchern und Briefen*, 6th ed. (Leipzig: Breitkopf & Härtel, 1920), 2:76; 1:366 (in translated volume [emended]).
3. Robert Schumann, *Tagebücher*, ed. Georg Eismann and Gerd Nauhaus (Basel and Frankfurt: Stroemfeld and Roter Stern, 1971–82), 3/1:383 (entry of March 19, 1845).

4. Ibid., 2:399 (undated entry [between April 1 and 6, 1846]).

5. Ibid., 2:400 (entry of April 13, 1846).

6. Ibid 3/1:337 (entry of December 20, 1846).

7. Ibid., 3/1:346 (entry of April 14, 1847).

8. Ibid., 3/2:493 (entry of May 31, 1849).

9. Ibid., 3/1:291 (entry of September 12, 1846).

10. Ernst Burger, *Robert Schumann: Eine Lebenschronik in Bildern und Dokumenten* (Mainz: Schott, 1999), 246.

11. Arnfried Edler, *Robert Schumann und seine Zeit*, 3rd ed. (Laaber: Laaber-Verlag, 2008), 302.

12. Litzmann, *Clara Schumann*, 2:139; 1:410 (in translated volume [emended]) (diary entry of October 2, 1846).

13. Robert Schumann, *Briefedition*, ed. Thomas Synofzik et al. (Cologne: Dohr, 2008–), 2/1:212 (letter to Felix Mendelssohn, July 17, 1845).

14. Ibid., 2/1:257 (letter to Felix Mendelssohn, December 18, 1845).

15. Ibid., 2/1:211 (letter to Felix Mendelssohn, July 17, 1845).

16. Schumann, *Tagebücher*, 2:396 (entry of August 2, 1845).

17. Schumann, *Briefedition*, 2/1:237 (letter to Felix Mendelssohn, October 22, 1845).

18. Schumann, *Tagebücher*, 2:402 (undated entry [after June 1, 1846]).

19. Clara Schumann, ed., *Jugendbriefe von Robert Schumann: Nach den Originalen mitgetheilt* (Leipzig: Breitkopf & Härtel, 1885), 187 (letter to Johann Gottfried Kuntsch, July 27, 1832).

20. Schumann, *Tagebücher*, 2:105 (entry of September 20–27, 1840).

21. Eduard Hanslick, *Aus meinem Leben*, 4th ed. (Berlin: Allgemeiner Verein für Deutsche Literatur, 1911), 1:72.

22. Schumann, *Briefedition*, 2/1:252 (letter to Felix Mendelssohn, December 12, 1845). (The date given in Schumann, *Briefe. Neue Folge*—November 12, 1845—is incorrect.)

23. Litzmann, *Clara Schumann*, 2:144; 1:413–14 (in translated volume [emended]).

24. Ibid.; 1:414 (in translated volume).

25. Ibid., 2:146; 1:416 (in translated volume).

26. Schumann, *Briefe. Neue Folge*, 451 (letter to Friedrich Kistner, December 9, 1847).

27. Schumann, *Tagebücher*, 3/2:454–55 (entries of March 2, 5, and 15, 1848).

28. Litzmann, *Clara Schumann*, 2:178–79; 1:443–44 (in translated volume [emended]).

29. See John Daverio, "Einheit—Freiheit—Vaterland: Imitations of Utopia in Robert Schumann's Late Choral Music," in *Music and German National Identity*, ed. Celia Applegate and Pamela Potter (Chicago: University of Chicago Press, 2002), 61–63.

30. Schumann, *Briefe. Neue Folge*, 294 (letter to Johann Verhulst, November 4, 1848).

31. Schumann, *Tagebücher*, 3/2:451 (entry of January 20, 1848).

32. Ibid., 3/2:460–63 (entries of May 11, 15, and 20, and June 19, 1848).

33. Schumann, *Briefe. Neue Folge*, 290 (letter to Carl Reinecke, October 6, 1848).

34. Ibid.

35. Bernhard R. Appel, *Robert Schumanns "Album für die Jugend": Einführung und Kommentar* (Mainz: Schott, 1998).

36. Schumann, *Briefe. Neue Folge*, 244 (undated letter to Eduard Krüger [October 1844]).

37. Schumann, *Briefedition*, 2/1:229 (letter to Felix Mendelssohn, September 24, 1845).

38. Edda Burger-Güntert, *Robert Schumanns "Szenen aus Goethes Faust": Dichtung und Musik* (Freiburg im Breisgau: Rombach, 2006), 197.

39. Schumann, *Briefe. Neue Folge*, 285 (letter to Franz Brendel, July [5,] 1848).

40. Wilhelm Joseph von Wasielewski, *Robert Schumann: Eine Biographie*, 4th ed. (Leipzig: Breitkopf & Härtel, 1906), 434.

41. Johann Peter Eckermann, *Gespräche mit Goethe in den letzten Jahren seines Lebens*, ed. H. H. Houben (Leipzig: F. A. Brockhaus, 1939), 400; 554 (in translated volume) (entry of June 6, 1831).

42. Schumann, *Briefe. Neue Folge*, 302 (letter to Ferdinand Hiller, April 10, 1849).

43. Schumann, *Tagebücher*, 3/2:490 (entry of May 4, 1849).

44. Litzmann, *Clara Schumann*, 2:185–86; 1:449–50 (in translated volume [emended]) (entries of May 3 and 4, 1849).

45. Ibid., 2:186; 1:450 (in translated volume [emended]) (entry of May 5, 1849).

46. Ibid., 2:190; 1:454 (in translated volume [emended]) (entry of May 10, 1849).

47. Ibid., 2:188; 1:452 (in translated volume [emended]) (entry of May 8, 1849).

48. Schumann, *Briefe. Neue Folge*, 461 (letter to Friedrich Whistling, June 17, 1849).

49. Litzmann, *Clara Schumann*, 2:193; 1:456 (in translated volume [emended]).

50. Schumann, *Briefe. Neue Folge*, 308–9 (letter to Hermann Härtel, July 28, 1849).

INTERMEZZO VII

1. Clara Schumann, ed., *Jugendbriefe von Robert Schumann: Nach den Originalen mitgetheilt* (Leipzig: Breitkopf & Härtel, 1885), 133 (letter to Christiane Schumann, December 12, 1830).

2. Robert Schumann, *Briefe. Neue Folge*, 2nd ed., ed. F. Gustav Jansen (Leipzig: Breitkopf & Härtel, 1904), 220 (letter to Carl Koßmaly, September 1, 1842).

3. Richard Wagner, *Gesammelte Schriften und Dichtungen*. 4th ed. (Leipzig: C. F. W. Siegel, 1907), 3:317–18.

4. Hansjörg Ewert, *Anspruch und Wirkung: Studien zur Entstehung der Oper Genoveva von Robert Schumann* (Tutzing: Hans Schneider, 2003), 304.

5. Louis Ehlert, *From the Tone World: A Series of Essays*, trans. Helen D. Tretbar (New York: Charles F. Tretbar, 1885), 226.

6. Wagner, *Gesammelte Schriften*, 10:170.

7. Hansjörg Ewert, "'Genoveva' im Spiegel der Kritik," in *Genoveva: Programmbuch des Opernhauses Zürich* (February 2008). For all other references, see Ewert, *Anspruch und Wirkung*, 96–97.

8. Eduard Hanslick, *Die moderne Oper* (Berlin: Allgemeiner Verein für deutsche Literatur, 1885), 260.

9. Bernard Shaw, *Shaw's Music: The Complete Musical Criticism of Bernard Shaw*, ed. Dan H. Laurence (London: The Bodley Head, 1989), 3:63.

10. Quotations from Ewert, "'Genoveva' im Spiegel der Kritik."

11. Erich Kloss, ed., *Briefwechsel zwischen Wagner und Liszt*, 3rd ed. (Leipzig: Breitkopf & Härtel, 1912), 1:197 (letter from Liszt to Wagner, December 27, 1852).

12. Hans Neuenfels, *Wie viel Musik braucht der Mensch?* (Munich: Bertelsmann, 2009), 137.

13. Martin Geck, *Von Beethoven bis Mahler: Leben und Werk der großen Komponisten des 19. Jahrhunderts* (Reinbek: Rowohlt, 2000), 322.

CHAPTER 10

1. Robert Schumann, *Tagebücher*, ed. Georg Eismann and Gerd Nauhaus (Basel and Frankfurt: Stroemfeld and Roter Stern, 1971–82), 3/2:538 (entry of September 13, 1850).

2. Berthold Litzmann, ed., *Clara Schumann: Ein Künstlerleben. Nach Tagebüchern und Briefen*, 6th ed. (Leipzig: Breitkopf & Härtel, 1920), 2:227; 2:4–5 (in translated volume [emended]) (entry of October 1, 1850).

3. Ibid., 2:228; 2:5 (in translated volume [emended]) (entry of October 21, 1850).

4. Irmgard Knechtges-Obrecht, "Robert Schumann in Düsseldorf," in *Zwischen Poesie und Musik: Robert Schumann—früh und spät*, ed. Ingrid Bodsch and Gerd Nauhaus (Bonn: Stroemfeld, 2006), 130.

5. Bernhard R. Appel, "Robert Schumann als Dirigent in Düsseldorf," in *Robert Schumann: Philologische, analytische, sozial- und rezeptionsgeschichtliche Aspekte*, ed. Wolf Frobenius et al. (Saarbrücken: Saarbrücker Druckerei & Verlag, 1998), 122.

6. Ibid., 123.

7. Knechtges-Obrecht, "Robert Schumann in Düsseldorf," 131.

8. Schumann, *Tagebücher*, 3/2:642 (entry of November 19, 1853).

9. *Signale für die musikalische Welt* 11 (1853).

10. Litzmann, *Clara Schumann*, 2:286; 2:47 (in translated volume).

11. Martin Kreisig, ed., *Gesammelte Schriften über Musik und Musiker von Robert Schumann*, 5th ed. (Leipzig: Breitkopf & Härtel, 1914), 2:141.

12. Gerd Nauhaus, "Der Rose Pilgerfahrt op. 112: Schumanns Abschied vom Oratorium," in *Schumann in Düsseldorf: Werke—Texte—Interpretationen*, ed. Bernhard R. Appel (Mainz: Schott, 1993), 185.

13. Robert Schumann, *Neue Ausgabe sämtlicher Werke*, ed. Akio Mayeda et al. (Mainz: Schott, 1991–), 4/3/2:XXIV.

14. Bernhard R. Appel and Inge Hermstrüwer, ed., *Robert Schumann und die Dichter: Ein Musiker als Leser* (Düsseldorf: Droste, 1997), 167.

15. Litzmann, *Clara Schumann*, 2:261; 2:24 (in translated volume [emended]).

16. Ibid., 2:262; 2:25 (in translated volume [emended]).

17. Ibid., 2:262–63; 2:26 (in translated volume [emended]).

18. Ibid., 2:263–64; 2:26–27 (in translated volume [emended]).

19. Schumann, *Tagebücher*, 3/2:607 (entry of November 2, 1852).

20. Ibid., 3/2:608 (entry of November 21, 1852).

21. Robert Schumann, *Briefe. Neue Folge*, 2nd ed., ed. F. Gustav Jansen (Leipzig: Breitkopf & Härtel, 1904), (letter to Richard Pohl, December 27, 1852).

22. Wilhelm Joseph von Wasielewski, *Robert Schumann: Eine Biographie*, 4th ed. (Leipzig: Breitkopf & Härtel, 1906), 503.

23. Eugenie Schumann, *Robert Schumann: Ein Lebensbild meines Vaters* (Leipzig: Koehler & Amelang, 1931), 355–56.

24. Litzmann, *Clara Schumann*, 2:254 (this passage is not included in the English translation).

25. Schumann, *Briefe. Neue Folge*, 370–71 (letter to Ferdinand Hiller, April 25, 1853).

26. Cosima Wagner, *Die Tagebücher*, ed. Martin Gregor-Dellin and Dietrich Mack (Munich: Piper, 1976–77), 1:506; 1:472 (in translated volume) (entry of April 1, 1872).

27. Litzmann, *Clara Schumann*, 2:277; 2:40 (in translated volume [emended]) (diary entry of September 13, 1853).

28. Max Kalbeck, *Johannes Brahms*, 2nd ed. (Berlin: Deutsche Brahms-Gesellschaft, 1908–14), 1/1:104.

29. Litzmann, *Clara Schumann*, 2:280–81; 2:42–43 (in translated volume [emended]).

30. *NZfM* 39 (1853): 185.

31. Martin Geck, *Zwischen Romantik und Restauration: Musik im Realismus-Diskurs 1848–1871* (Stuttgart: J. B. Metzler, 2001), 85.

INTERMEZZO VIII

1. Friedrich Nietzsche, *Sämtliche Werke: Kritische Gesamtausgabe*, ed. Giorgio Colli and Mazzino Montinari (Munich: Deutscher Taschenbuch Verlag and Walter de Gruyter, 1988), 1:492–93 ("Richard Wagner in Bayreuth"). Translated by R. J. Hollingdale as *Untimely Meditations* (Cambridge: Cambridge University Press, 1983), 241–42.

2. Peter Gülke, "Zur Bestimmung des Sinfonischen bei Beethoven," in *Deutsches Jahrbuch der Musikwissenschaft für* 1970 (Leipzig: Peters, 1971), 68.

3. *NZfM* 12 (1840): 82.

4. See the analyses in Reinhard Kapp, *Studien zum Spätwerk Robert Schumanns* (Tutzing: Hans Schneider, 1984), and Peter Gülke, "Robert Schumanns 'Rheinische Sinfonie,'" in *Die Sprache der Musik: Essays von Bach bis Holliger* (Stuttgart: J. B. Metzler, 2001).

5. Kapp, *Studien zum Spätwerk Robert Schumanns*, 189.

6. Ibid., 179.

7. R. Larry Todd, "On Quotation in Schumann's Music," in *Schumann and His World*, ed. R. Larry Todd (Princeton, NJ: Princeton University Press, 1994), 99.

8. Kapp, *Studien zum Spätwerk Robert Schumanns*, 189.

9. Gülke, "Robert Schumanns 'Rheinische Sinfonie,'" 290.

10. But see Reinhard Kapp, "Über Satzanschlüsse beim (nicht nur) späten Schumann,"

in *Der späte Schumann*, ed. Ulrich Tadday (Munich: text + kritik, 2006), 156–57.

11. Wilhelm Joseph von Wasielewski, *Schumanniana* (Leipzig: Breitkopf & Härtel, 1883), 456.

CHAPTER 11

1. Leander Hotaki, *Robert Schumanns Motosammlung* (Freiburg im Breisgau: Rombach, 1998), 409. In spite of Hotaki's claims to the contrary, a further mention of this same passage also dates back to Schumann's early years.

2. Robert Schumann, *Briefe. Neue Folge*, 2nd ed., ed. F. Gustav Jansen (Leipzig: Breitkopf & Härtel, 1904), 351–52 (letter to Franz Liszt, December 6, 1851).

3. Clara Schumann and Robert Schumann, *Briefwechsel: Kritische Gesamtausgabe*, ed. Eva Weissweiler (Frankfurt: Stroemfeld, 1984–2001), 1:146; 1:150 (in translated volume [emended]) (letter from Robert Schumann to Clara Wieck, April [15,] 1838).

4. Ulrich Tadday, *Das schöne Unendliche: Ästhetik, Kritik, Geschichte der romantischen Musikanschauung* (Stuttgart: J. B. Metzler, 1999), 178.

5. Martin Geck, *Zwischen Romantik und Restauration: Musik im Realismus-Diskurs 1848–1871* (Stuttgart: J. B. Metzler, 2001), 174.

6. Ulrich Tadday, *Schumann Handbuch* (Stuttgart: Bärenreiter, 2006), 129–35.

7. Robert Schumann, *Tagebücher*, ed. Georg Eismann and Gerd Nauhaus (Basel and Frankfurt: Stroemfeld and Roter Stern, 1971–82), 1:96 (undated entry [between July 13 and 22, 1828]).

8. Geck, *Zwischen Romantik und Restauration*, 85.

9. Schumann, *Briefe. Neue Folge*, 361 (letter to Julius von Bernuth, October 17, 1852).

10. Geck, *Zwischen Romantik und Restauration*, 85.

11. Ibid., 83.

12. Michael Struck, "Kunstwerk-Anspruch und Popularitätsstreben: Ursachen ohne Wirkung? Bemerkungen zum *Glück von Edenhall* op. 143 und zur *Fest-Ouvertüre* op. 123," in *Schumann in Düsseldorf: Werke — Texte — Interpretationen*, ed. Bernhard R. Appel (Mainz: Schott, 1993), 277.

13. Schumann, *Briefe. Neue Folge*, 344 (letter to Richard Pohl, June 25, 1851).

14. Schumann, *Briefe. Neue Folge* (the quotation appears only in the 1886 edition, p. 293).

15. Gerd Nauhaus, quoted in Helmut Loos, *Robert Schumann: Interpretationen seiner Werke* (Laaber: Laaber-Verlag, 2005), 2:208.

16. Reinhard Kapp, "Schumann nach der Revolution: Vorüberlegungen, Statements, Hinweise, Materialien, Fragen," in *Schumann in Düsseldorf: Werke — Texte — Interpretationen*, ed. Bernhard R. Appel. (Mainz: Schott, 1993), 358–60.

17. Wilhelm Joseph von Wasielewski, *Aus siebzig Jahren* (Stuttgart: Deutsche Verlagsanstalt, 1897), 125.

18. Berthold Litzmann, ed., *Clara Schumann: Ein Künstlerleben. Nach Tagebüchern und Briefen*, 6th ed. (Leipzig: Breitkopf & Härtel, 1920), 2:265; 2:28 (in translated volume

[emended]) (entry of October 16, 1851).

19. Hans Kohlhase, *Die Kammermusik Robert Schumanns: Stilistische Untersuchungen* (Hamburg: Wagner, 1979), 1:203.

20. Michael Struck, *Die umstrittenen späten Instrumentalwerke Schumanns* (Hamburg: Wagner, 1984), 530.

21. Ibid., 342.

22. Ibid., 349.

23. John Daverio, "Songs of Dawn and Dusk: Coming to Terms with the Late Music,"in *The Cambridge Companion to Schumann*, ed. Beate Perrey (Cambridge: Cambridge University Press, 2007), 286.

24. Reinhard Kapp, *Studien zum Spätwerk Robert Schumanns* (Tutzing: Hans Schneider, 1984), 79–101. For Peter Gülke's balanced assessment, see Tadday, *Schumann Handbuch*, 72–73.

25. Laura Tunbridge, *Schumann's Late Style* (Cambridge: Cambridge University Press, 2007), 128.

26. Schumann, *Tagebücher*, 3/2:639 (entries of October 15–18, 1853).

27. Struck, *Die umstrittenen späten Instrumentalwerke*, 469.

28. Ibid., 481.

INTERMEZZO IX

1. Robert Schumann, *Tagebücher*, ed. Georg Eismann and Gerd Nauhaus (Basel and Frankfurt: Stroemfeld and Roter Stern, 1971–82), 1:183–84 (entries of March 26 and 29, 1829).

2. Ibid., 3/2:466 (entry of April 5, 1848).

3. Ibid., 3/2:769.

4. On Schumann's identification with the figure of Manfred, see Laura Tunbridge, "Schumann as Manfred," *Musical Quarterly* 87 (2004): 546–69.

5. Wilhelm Joseph von Wasielewski, *Robert Schumann: Eine Biographie*, 4th ed. (Leipzig: Breitkopf & Härtel, 1906), 248.

6. Hermann Erler, "Zwei ungedruckte Briefe von Robert Schumann," *Die Musik* 2 (1902/3): 28.

7. Friedrich Nietzsche, *Sämtliche Werke: Kritische Gesamtausgabe*, ed. Giorgio Colli and Mazzino Montinari (Munich: Deutscher Taschenbuch Verlag and Walter de Gruyter, 1988), 6:286–87 ("Ecce homo"). Translated by R. J. Hollingdale as *Ecce homo* (London: Penguin Books, 1988), 58.

8. Friedrich Nietzsche, *Sämtliche Briefe: Kritische Studienausgabe*, ed. Giorgio Colli and Mazzino Montinari (Munich: Deutscher Taschenbuch Verlag, 1986), 3:319 (letter to Gustav Krug, May 2, 1872).

9. Ibid., 4:29 (letter to Gustav Krug, July 24, 1872).

10. Martin Gregor-Dellin, *Richard Wagner: Sein Leben, sein Werk, sein Jahrhundert* (Munich: R. Piper & Co., 1980), 651 (this passage is not included in the 1983 trans-

lated volume).

11. Elisabeth Förster-Nietzsche, *Wagner und Nietzsche zur Zeit ihrer Freundschaft* (Munich: Georg Müller, 1915), 130 (letter from Wagner to Nietzsche, October 24, 1872).

12. Nietzsche, *Sämtliche Briefe*, 4:74 (letter to Elisabeth Nietzsche, October 26, 1872).

CHAPTER 12

1. Philip Roth, *Exit Ghost* (London: Vintage Books, 2008), 182.

2. Nancy B. Reich, "Clara Schumann and Johannes Brahms," in *Brahms and His World*, ed. Walter Frisch and Kevin C. Karnes, rev. ed. (Princeton, NJ: Princeton University Press, 2009), 57–71.

3. Eva Weissweiler, *Clara Schumann: Eine Biographie* (Hamburg: Hoffmann und Campe, 1990), 341.

4. Ibid., 290.

5. Berthold Litzmann, ed., *Clara Schumann: Ein Künstlerleben. Nach Tagebüchern und Briefen*, 6th ed. (Leipzig: Breitkopf & Härtel, 1920), 2:297; 2:56 (in translated volume [emended]) (entry of February 17, 1854).

6. Robert Schumann, *Tagebücher*, ed. Georg Eismann and Gerd Nauhaus (Basel and Frankfurt: Stroemfeld and Roter Stern, 1971–82), 1:51 (entry of May 13, 1829).

7. Gerd Nauhaus and Ingrid Bodsch, ed., *Clara Schumann: Blumenbuch für Robert* (Frankfurt: Stroemfeld, 2006), 213.

8. Bernhard R. Appel, *Robert Schumann in Endenich (1854–1856): Krankenakten, Briefzeugnisse und zeitgenössische Berichte* (Mainz: Schott, 2006), 18–19.

9. Ibid., 326, where Appel sets out the latest medical findings.

10. Peter Ostwald, *Schumann: The Inner Voices of a Musical Genius* (Boston: Northeastern University Press, 1985), 303–6.

11. Litzmann, *Clara Schumann*, 2:303 (this passage is not included in the English translation).

12. Robert Schumann, *Briefe. Neue Folge*, 2nd ed., ed. F. Gustav Jansen (Leipzig: Breitkopf & Härtel, 1904), 323 (letter to Ferdinand Hiller, December 3, 1849).

13. Appel, *Robert Schumann in Endenich*, 96 (entry of April 20, 1854).

14. Ibid., 322 (entries of August 23 and 26, 1855).

15. Schumann, *Briefe. Neue Folge*, 401 (letter to Clara Schumann, October 12, 1854).

16. Ibid., 398–99 (letter to Clara Schumann, September 18, 1854).

17. Ibid., 400 (letter to Clara Schumann, September 26, 1854).

18. Appel, *Robert Schumann in Endenich*, 144 (letter to Marie and Elise Schumann, September 18, 1854).

19. Ibid., 109 (letter from Clara Schumann to Henriette Reichmann, May 21, 1854).

20. Litzmann, *Clara Schumann*, 2:321 (this passage is not included in the English translation).

21. Nauhaus and Bodsch, *Clara Schumann: Blumenbuch für Robert*, 9.

22. Ibid., 214–26.

23. Max Kalbeck, *Johannes Brahms*, 2nd ed. (Berlin: Deutsche Brahms-Gesellschaft, 1908–14), 1/1:163.

24. Wilhelm Joseph von Wasielewski, *Robert Schumann: Eine Biographie*, 4th ed. (Leipzig: Breitkopf & Härtel, 1906), 497.

25. Appel, *Robert Schumann in Endenich*, 373 (letter from Brahms to Joachim, April 25, 1856).

26. Litzmann, *Clara Schumann*, 2:414; 2:138–39 (in translated volume [emended]) (entry of July 27, 1856).

27. Ibid., 2:415; 2:139 (in translated volume [emended]) (entries of July 28 and 29, 1856).

28. Ibid., 2:416; 2:140 (in translated volume [emended]) (entry of July 31, 1856).

29. Nauhaus and Bodsch, *Clara Schumann: Blumenbuch für Robert*, 226.

I should like to take this opportunity to thank Gerd Nauhaus, the long-standing director of the Robert Schumann Museum in Zwickau, for casting a critical eye over the German typescript and for offering me his authoritative advice. —M. G.

Bibliography

Adorno, Theodor W. "Klangfiguren." In *Gesammelte Schriften.* 20 vols., edited by Rolf Tiedemann, 16:7–248. Frankfurt: Suhrkamp, 1997. Translated by Rodney Livingstone as *Sound Figures.* Stanford, CA: Stanford University Press, 1999.

Alf, Julius, and Joseph A. Kruse, eds. *Robert Schumann: Universalgeist der Romantik: Beiträge zu seiner Persönlichkeit und seinem Werk.* Düsseldorf: Droste, 1981.

Altenmüller, Eckart. "Focal Dystonia: Advances in Brain Imaging of Fine Motor Control in Musicians." *Hand Clinics* 19 (2003): 1–16.

Appel, Bernhard R. "Robert Schumann als Dirigent in Düsseldorf." In *Robert Schumann: Philologische, analytische, sozial- und rezeptionsgeschichtliche Aspekte,* ed. Wolf Frobenius et al., 116–37. Saarbrücken: Saarbrücker Druckerei & Verlag, 1998.

———. *Robert Schumann in Endenich (1854–1856): Krankenakten, Briefzeugnisse und zeitgenössische Berichte.* Mainz: Schott, 2006.

———. *Robert Schumanns "Album für die Jugend": Einführung und Kommentar.* Mainz: Schott, 1998.

Appel, Bernhard R., and Inge Hermstrüwer, eds. *Robert Schumann und die Dichter: Ein Musiker als Leser.* Düsseldorf: Droste, 1991.

Barthes, Roland. *The Preparation of the Novel,* translated by Kate Briggs. New York: Columbia University Press, 2011.

———. "Rasch." In *The Responsibility of Forms: Critical Essays on Music, Art, and Representation,* translated by Richard Howard, 299–312. New York: Hill and Wang, 1985.

Bauer, Elisabeth Eleonore. "Beethoven — unser musikalischer Jean Paul: Anmerkungen zu einer Analogie." In *Beethoven: Analecta varia,* edited by Heinz-Klaus Metzger and Rainer Riehn, 83–105. Munich: text + kritik, 1987.

Beci, Veronica. *Die andere Clara Schumann.* Düsseldorf: Droste, 1997.

Becker-Adden, Meike. *Nahtstellen: Strukturelle Analogien der "Kreisleriana" von E. T. A. Hoffmann und Robert Schumann.* Bielefeld: Transcript, 2006.

Becker, Julius. *Der Neuromantiker: Musikalischer Roman.* 2 vols. Leipzig: Weber, 1840.

Beethoven, Ludwig van. *Briefwechsel.* 7 vols. Edited by Sieghard Brandenburg. Munich: G. Henle, 1996–98. Translated by Emily Anderson as *The Letters of Beethoven.* 3 vols. London: Macmillan Press, 1961.

Benjamin, Walter. *Der Begriff der Kunstkritik in der deutschen Romantik.* Edited by Hermann Schweppenhäuser. Frankfurt: Suhrkamp, 1973.

Billroth, Theodor. *Wer ist musikalisch?* Edited by Eduard Hanslick. 2nd edition. Berlin: Gebrüder Paetel, 1896.

Brentano, Clemens. *Werke.* 4 vols. Edited by Friedhelm Kemp. Munich: Carl Hanser, 1963.

Brinkmann, Reinhold. *Schumann und Eichendorff: Studien zum Liederkreis opus 39.* Munich: edition text + kritik, 1997.

Burger, Ernst. *Robert Schumann: Eine Lebenschronik in Bildern und Dokumenten.* Mainz: Schott, 1999.

Bürger, Gottfried August. *Briefe von und an Gottfried August Bürger.* 4 vols. Edited by Adolf Strodtmann. Berlin: Gebrüder Paetel, 1874.

Burger-Güntert, Edda. *Robert Schumanns "Szenen aus Goethes Faust": Dichtung und Musik.* Freiburg im Breisgau: Rombach, 2006.

Daverio, John. *Robert Schumann: Herald of a "New Poetic Age."* New York and Oxford: Oxford University Press, 1997.

——. "Einheit — Freiheit — Vaterland: Intimations of Utopia in Robert Schumann's Late Choral Music." In *Music and German National Identity*, edited by Celia Applegate and Pamela Potter, 59–77. Chicago: Chicago University Press, 2002.

——. "Schumann's Systems of Musical Fragments and *Witz.*" In *Nineteenth-Century Music and the German Romantic Ideology*, 49–86. New York: Schirmer Books, 1993.

———. "Songs of Dawn and Dusk: Coming to Terms with the Late Music." In *The Cambridge Companion to Schumann*, edited by Beate Perrey, 268–91. Cambridge: Cambridge University Press, 2007.

Draheim, Joachim, and Brigitt Höft, eds. *Clara Schumann: Sämtliche Lieder.* 2 vols. Wiesbaden: Breitkopf & Härtel, 1990–92.

Eckermann, Johann Peter. *Gespräche mit Goethe in den letzten Jahren seines Lebens.* Edited by H. H. Houben. Leipzig: F. A. Brockhaus, 1939, translated by John Oxenford as *Conversations of Goethe with Eckermann.* London: G. Bell and Sons, 1913.

Eco, Umberto. *Die Grenzen der Interpretation*, translated by Günter Memmert. Munich: Carl Hanser Verlag, 1992.

——. *The Middle Ages of James Joyce: The Aesthetics of Chaosmos*, translated by Ellen Esrock. London: Hutchinson Radius, 1989.

Edler, Arnfried. *Robert Schumann und seine Zeit.* 3rd ed. Laaber: Laaber-Verlag, 2008.

Ehlert, Louis. *From the Tone World: A Series of Essays*, translated by Helen D. Tretbar. New York: Charles F. Tretbar, 1885.

Eismann, Georg, ed. *Robert Schumann: Ein Quellenwerk über sein Leben und Schaffen.* 2 vols. Leipzig: Breitkopf & Härtel, 1956.

Erler, Hermann. "Zwei ungedruckte Briefe von Robert Schumann." *Die Musik* 2 (1902/3): 26–30.

Ewert, Hansjörg. *Anspruch und Wirkung: Studien zur Entstehung der Oper Genoveva von Robert Schumann.* Tutzing: Hans Schneider, 2003.

——. "'Genoveva' im Spiegel der Kritik," in *Genoveva: Programmbuch des Opernhauses Zürich* (February 2008).

Ferris, David. *Schumann's Eichendorff Liederkreis and the Genre of the Romantic Cycle.* Oxford: Oxford University Press, 2000.

———. "'Was will dieses Grau'n bedeuten?' Schumann's 'Zwielicht' and Daverio's 'Incomprehensibility Topos.'" *Journal of Musicology* 22 (2005): 131–53.

Flechsig, Emil. "Erinnerungen an Schumann. Aus dem Manuskript erstmals vollständig veröffentlicht von seiner Urenkelin Hilde Wendler." *Neue Zeitschrift für Musik* 117 (1956): 392–96.

Förster-Nietzsche, Elisabeth. *Wagner und Nietzsche zur Zeit ihrer Freundschaft.* Munich: Georg Müller, 1915.

Gadamer, Hans-Georg. *Truth and Method*, 2nd rev. ed. Translated by W. Glen-Doepel, revised by Joel Weinsheimer and Donald G. Marshall. London: Continuum, 2004.

Geck, Martin. *Von Beethoven bis Mahler: Leben und Werk der großen Komponisten des 19. Jahrhunderts.* Reinbek bei Hamburg: Rowohlt, 2000.

———. "Der Weg ins Freie: Die Überwindung der traditionellen Viersätzigkeit in Schumanns *Rheinischer Symphonie* zugunsten eines neuen, narrativen Symphonietypus." In *Robert Schumann und die große Form: Referate des Bonner Symposions 2006*, edited by Bernd Sponheuer and Wolfram Steinbeck, 93–110. Frankfurt: Peter Lang, 2009.

———. *Zwischen Romantik und Restauration: Musik im Realismus-Diskurs 1848–1871.* Stuttgart: J. B. Metzler, 2001.

Genet, Jean. *Le condamné à mort et autres poèmes.* Paris: Gallimard, 1999.

Georgiades, Thrasybulos. *Schubert: Musik und Lyrik.* Göttingen: Vandenhoeck & Ruprecht, 1967.

Gerstmeier, August. *Robert Schumann: Klavierkonzert a-Moll, op.* 54. Munich: Fink, 1986.

Goethe, Johann Wolfgang von. *The Poems of Goethe*, translated by Edgar Alfred Bowring Chicago: Belford, Clarke & Company, [1874].

———. *Sämmtliche Werke.* 40 vols. Stuttgart: Cotta, 1840.

Gregor-Dellin, Martin. *Richard Wagner: Sein Leben, sein Werk, sein Jahrhundert.* Munich: R. Piper & Co., 1980. Partial translation by J. Maxwell Brownjohn as *Richard Wagner: His Life, His Work, His Century.* London: Collins, 1983.

Gülke, Peter. "Robert Schumanns 'Rheinische Sinfonie.'" In *Die Sprache der Musik: Essays von Bach bis Holliger.* Stuttgart: J. B. Metzler, 2001.

———. "Zur Bestimmung des Sinfonischen bei Beethoven." In *Deutsches Jahrbuch der Musikwissenschaft für 1970*, 57–95. Leipzig: Peters, 1971.

Hallmark, Rufus. *The Genesis of Schumann's "Dichterliebe."* Ann Arbor, MI: UMI Research Press, 1979.

Hamvas, Béla. "Korruptheit und Moral: Über die Kapitulation des Gewissens und die Brutstätte der Rebellion." *Lettre international* 84 (2009): 62–65.

Hanslick, Eduard. *Aus meinem Leben.* 4th ed. 2 vols. Berlin: Allgemeiner Verein für Deutsche Literatur, 1911.

———. *Die moderne Oper.* Berlin: Allgemeiner Verein für deutsche Literatur, 1885.

Heero, Aigi. *Robert Schumanns Jugendlyrik.* Sinzig: Studio, 2003.

Heine, Heinrich. *Säkularausgabe.* 30 vols. Edited by the Nationale Forschungs- und

Gedenkstätten der klassischen deutschen Literatur in Weimar and the Centre National de la Recherche Scientifique in Paris. Berlin: Akademie-Verlag, 1970–.

———. *Sämtliche Schriften.* 7 vols. Edited by Klaus Briegleb. Munich: Deutscher Taschenbuch Verlag, 2005.

Herwig, Henriette et al., eds. *Übergänge zwischen Künsten und Kulturen: Internationaler Kongress zum 150. Todesjahr von Heinrich Heine und Robert Schumann.* Stuttgart: J. B. Metzler, 2007.

Hoffmann, E. T. A. *Poetische Werke*, edited by Klaus Kanzog. 10 vols. Berlin: Walter de Gruyter, 1957–62.

———. *Sämtliche Werke.* 6 vols. Edited by Gerhard Allroggen et al. Frankfurt am Main: Deutscher Klassiker Verlag, 1985–2006.

Hotaki, Leander. *Robert Schumanns Mottosammlung.* Freiburg im Breisgau: Rombach, 1998.

Jansen, Friedrich Gustav. *Die Davidsbündler: Aus Robert Schumanns Sturm- und Drangperiode.* Leipzig: Breitkopf & Härtel, 1883.

Jean Paul. *Sämmtliche Werke.* 60 vols. Berlin: Reimer, 1826–28.

———. *Sämtliche Werke: Historisch-kritische Ausgabe.* 33 vols. Edited by Eduard Berend. Weimar: Preußische Akademie der Wissenschaften, 1927–64.

———. *Vorschule der Ästhetik.* Edited by Norbert Miller. 2nd ed. Munich: Hanser, 1974.

———. *Werke.* 60 vols. Berlin: Hempel, 1870–78.

Jost, Peter. "Schumanns und Wagners Opernkonzeptionen: Genoveva versus Lohengrin." In *Der späte Schumann*, edited by Ulrich Tadday, 133–52. Munich: text + kritik, 2006.

Kalbeck, Max. *Johannes Brahms.* 2nd ed. 4 vols. Berlin: Deutsche Brahms-Gesellschaft, 1908–14.

Kapp, Reinhard. "Schumann nach der Revolution: Vorüberlegungen, Statements, Hinweise, Materialien, Fragen." In *Schumann in Düsseldorf: Werke — Texte — Interpretationen*, edited by Bernhard R. Appel, 315–415. Mainz: Schott, 1993.

———. *Studien zum Spätwerk Robert Schumanns.* Tutzing: Hans Schneider, 1984.

———. "Über Satzanschlüsse beim (nicht nur) späten Schumann." In *Der späte Schumann*, edited by Ulrich Tadday, 153–61, 216. Munich: text + kritik, 2006.

Kloss, Erich, ed. *Briefwechsel zwischen Wagner und Liszt*, 3rd ed. 2 vols. Leipzig: Breitkopf & Härtel, 1912.

Knechtges-Obrecht, Irmgard. "Robert in Düsseldorf." In *Zwischen Poesie und Musik: Robert Schumann — früh und spät*, edited by Ingrid Bodsch and Gerd Nauhaus, 121–42. Bonn: Stroemfeld, 2006.

Köhler, Hans Joachim. *Robert Schumann: Sein Leben und Wirken in den Leipziger Jahren.* Leipzig: Peters, 1986.

Kohlhase, Hans. *Die Kammermusik Robert Schumanns: Stilistische Untersuchungen.* Hamburg: Wagner, 1979.

———. "Robert Schumanns Klavierquintet." In *Sonderband Robert Schumann I*, edited by Heinz-Klaus Metzger and Rainer Riehn, 148–73. Munich: text + kritik, 1981.

Korte, Werner. *Robert Schumann.* Potsdam: Athenaion, 1937.

Koßmaly, Carl. "Ueber Robert Schumann's Claviercompositionen." *Allgemeine musikalische Zeitung* 46 (1844): 1–5, 17–21, 33–7. Translated by Susan Gillespie as "On Robert Schumann's Piano Compositions (1844)." In *Schumann and His World*, edited by R. Larry Todd, 303–16. Princeton, NJ: Princeton University Press, 1994.

Kramer, Lawrence. *Music and Poetry: The Nineteenth Century and After.* Berkeley: University of California Press, 1984.

Kranefeld, Ulrike. *Der nachschaffende Hörer: Rezeptionsästhetische Studien zur Musik Robert Schumanns.* Stuttgart: J. B. Metzler, 2000.

Kreisig, Martin, ed. *Gesammelte Schriften über Musik und Musiker von Robert Schumann.* 5th ed. 2 vols. Leipzig: Breitkopf & Härtel, 1914.

Kristeva, Julia. *Revolution in Poetic Language.* New York: Columbia, 1984.

Kross, Siegfried, ed. *Briefe und Notizen Robert und Clara Schumanns.* 2nd ed. Bonn: Bouvier, 1982.

Link, Jürgen. "Empirisch-transzendentale Objekte in der Romantik und die empirisch-transzendentale Dublette Mensch." In *Schläft ein Lied in allen Dingen? Romantische Dingpoetik*, edited by Christiane Holm and Günter Oesterle, 43–54. Würzburg: Königshausen & Neumann, 2011.

———. "Metamorphosen der romantischen Kulturrevolution." *Kulturrevolution* 12 (1986).

Liszt, Franz. *Gesammelte Schriften.* Edited by La Mara and Lina Ramann. 6 vols. Leipzig: Breitkopf & Härtel, 1880–83.

Litzmann, Berthold, ed. *Clara Schumann: Ein Künstlerleben. Nach Tagebüchern und Briefen.* 6th ed. 3 vols. Leipzig: Breitkopf & Härtel, 1920. Translated by Grace E. Hadow as *Clara Schumann: An Artist's Life.* 2 vols. London, Macmillan & Co.; Leipzig: Breitkopf & Härtel, 1913.

Loos, Helmut, ed. *Robert Schumann: Interpretationen seiner Werke.* 2 vols. Laaber: Laaber-Verlag, 2005.

Lossewa, Olga. *Die Russlandreise Clara und Robert Schumanns.* Mainz: Schott, 2004.

Macdonald, Claudia. *Robert Schumann and the Piano Concerto.* New York: Taylor and Francis, 2005.

Mahlert, Ulrich. *Fortschritt und Kunstlied: Späte Lieder Robert Schumanns im Licht der liedästhetischen Diskussion ab 1848.* Munich: Katzbichler, 1983.

Mann, Thomas. *Buddenbrooks*, translated by H. T. Lowe-Porter. London: Vintage Books, 1999.

———. *Gesammelte Werke.* 12 vols. Edited by Hans Bürgin et al. Berlin: S. Fischer, 1960–74.

———. *Große kommentierte Frankfurter Ausgabe: Werke — Briefe — Tagebücher.* Edited by Eckard Heftrich et al. Frankfurt: S. Fischer, 2002–.

McCorkle, Margit L. *Schumann-Werkverzeichnis.* Munich: G. Henle Verlag, 2003.

Mendelssohn, Felix. *Briefe aus den Jahren 1830 bis 1847.* Edited by Paul and Carl Mendelssohn Bartholdy. Leipzig: Hermann Mendelssohn, 1870.

Moscheles, Ignaz. *Aus Moscheles' Leben. Nach Briefen und Tagebüchern*. Edited by His Wife. 2 vols. Leipzig: Duncker & Humblot, 1872–73.

Münch, Stephan. "'Fantasiestücke in Kreislers Manier': Robert Schumanns 'Kreisleriana' op. 16 und die Musikanschauung E. T. A. Hoffmanns." *Die Musikforschung* 45 (1992): 255–75.

Nauhaus, Gerd. "Der Rose Pilgerfahrt op. 112: Schumanns Abschied vom Oratorium." In *Schumann in Düsseldorf: Werke — Texte — Interpretationen*, edited by Bernhard R. Appel, 179–99. Mainz: Schott, 1993.

———. "Robert Schumann: Jünglingswallfahrten," in *Zwischen Poesie und Musik: Robert Schumann — früh und spät*, edited by Ingrid Bodsch and Gerd Nauhaus, 41–50. Bonn: Stroemfeld, 2006.

Nauhaus, Gerd, and Ingrid Bodsch, eds. *Clara Schumann: Blumenbuch für Robert*. Frankfurt: Stroemfeld, 2006.

Nauhaus, Gerd, and Ulrich Tadday, eds. *Prosa und Poesie: Robert Schumanns Schulaufsätze*. Sinzig: Studio, 2010.

Neuenfels, Hans. *Wie viel Musik braucht der Mensch?* Munich: Bertelsmann, 2009.

Nietzsche, Friedrich. *Sämtliche Briefe: Kritische Studienausgabe*. 8 vols. Edited by Giorgio Colli and Mazzino Montinari. Munich: Deutscher Taschenbuch Verlag, 1986.

———. *Sämtliche Werke: Kritische Gesamtausgabe*. 15 vols. Edited by Giorgio Colli and Mazzino Montinari. Munich: Deutscher Taschenbuch Verlag, 1988.

Ostwald, Peter. *Schumann: The Inner Voices of a Musical Genius*. Boston: Northeastern University Press, 1985.

Ozawa, Kazuko. "Merkwürdige Zeiten: Bemerkungen zu Schumanns Neugier." In *Robert Schumann und die Öffentlichkeit: Hans Joachim Köhler zum 70. Geburtstag*, edited by Helmut Loos. Leipzig: Schröder, 2007.

Perrey, Beate. *Schumann's "Dichterliebe" and Early Romantic Poetics: Fragmentation of Desire*. Cambridge: Cambridge University Press, 2002.

Pfitzner, Hans. *Die Neue Ästhetik der musikalischen Impotenz: Ein Verwesungssymptom?* Munich: Süddeutsche Monatshefte, 1920.

Platinga, Leon B. *Schumann as Critic*. New Haven, CT: Yale University Press, 1967.

Pousseur, Henri. "Schumann ist der Dichter: Fünfundzwanzig Momente einer Lektüre der Dichterliebe." In *Sonderband Robert Schumann II*, edited by Heinz-Klaus Metzger and Rainer Riehn, 3–128. Munich: text + kritik, 1982.

Preiß, Friederike. *Der Prozeß: Clara und Robert Schumanns Kontroverse mit Friedrich Wieck*. Frankfurt: Peter Lang, 2004.

Rang, Florens Christian. *Historische Psychologie des Karnevals*. Edited by Lorenz Jäger. Berlin: Brinkmann & Bose, 1983.

Reich, Nancy B. "Clara Schumann and Johannes Brahms." In *Brahms and His World*. Rev. ed., edited by Walter Frisch and Kevin C. Karnes, 57–71. Princeton, NJ: Princeton University Press, 2009.

Reiman, Erika. *Schumann's Piano Cycles and the Novels of Jean Paul*. Rochester, NY: University of Rochester Press, 2004.

[Rellstab, Ludwig]. "Ueberblick der Erzeugnisse." *Iris im Gebiete der Tonkunst* 4 (1833): 110–12.

Riemann, Hugo. *Geschichte der Musik seit Beethoven*. Berlin: Spemann, 1901.

Roesner, Linda Correll. "The Chamber Music." In *The Cambridge Companion to Schumann*, edited by Beate Perrey, 123–47. Cambridge, Cambridge University Press, 2007.

Rosen, Charles. *The Romantic Generation*. Cambridge, MA: Harvard University Press, 1995.

Roth, Philip. *Exit Ghost*. London: Vintage Books, 2008.

Samuels, Robert. "Narratives of Masculinity and Femininity: Two Schumann Song Cycles." In *Phrase and Subject: Studies in Literature and Music*, edited by Delia da Sousa Correa, 135–45. Oxford: Legenda, 2006.

Saponov, Mikhail. "Schumann im Kreml." In *Robert Schumann und die Öffentlichkeit: Hans Joachim Köhler zum 70. Geburtstag*, edited by Helmut Loos. Leipzig: Schröder, 2007.

Schlegel, Friedrich. *Lucinde and the Fragments*, translated by Peter Firchow. Eugene, OR: Wipf & Stock, 1971.

Schleuning, Peter. "'Ein einziger Liebesschrei' — 'an die ferne Geliebte.' Der erste Satz von Schumanns Klavierfantasie op. 17." In *Musik, Deutung, Bedeutung: Festschrift für Harry Goldschmidt zum 75. Geburtstag*, edited by Hanns-Werner Heister and Hartmut Lück, 80–85. Dortmund: Edition V im Pläne-Verlag, 1986.

Schnebel, Dieter. "Rückungen — Ver-rückungen. Psychoanalytische Betrachtungen zu Schumanns Leben und Werk." In *Sonderband Robert Schumann I*, edited by Heinz-Klaus Metzger and Rainer Riehn, 4–89. Munich: text + kritik, 1981.

Schumann, Clara, ed. *Jugendbriefe von Robert Schumann: Nach den Originalen mitgetheilt*. Leipzig: Breitkopf & Härtel, 1885.

Schumann, Clara, and Robert Schumann. *Briefwechsel: Kritische Gesamtausgabe*. 3 vols. Edited by Eva Weissweiler. Frankfurt: Stroemfeld, 1984–2001. Translated by Hildegard Fritsch and Ronald L. Crawford as *The Complete Correspondence of Clara and Robert Schumann*. 3 vols. New York: Peter Lang, 1994–2002.

Schumann, Eugenie. *Robert Schumann: Ein Lebensbild meines Vaters*. Leipzig: Koehler & Amelang, 1931.

Schumann, Robert. *Briefe. Neue Folge*. 2nd ed. Edited by F. Gustav Jansen. Leipzig: Breitkopf & Härtel, 1904.

———. *Briefedition*. 45 vols. Edited by Thomas Synofzik et al. Cologne: Dohr, 2008–.

———. *Erinnerungen an Felix Mendelssohn Bartholdy*. Edited by Georg Eismann. Zwickau: Predella-Verlag, 1948.

———. *Neue Ausgabe sämtlicher Werke*. Edited by Akio Mayeda et al. Mainz: Schott, 1991–.

———. *Tagebücher*. 4 vols. Edited by Georg Eismann and Gerd Nauhaus. Basel and Frankfurt: Stroemfeld and Roter Stern, 1971–82.

Seibold, Wolfgang. *Robert und Clara Schumann in ihren Beziehungen zu Franz Liszt*. 2 vols. Frankfurt: Peter Lang, 2005.

Shaw, Bernard. *Shaw's Music: The Complete Musical Criticism of Bernard Shaw.* 3 vols. Edited by Dan H. Laurence. London: The Bodley Head, 1989.

Struck, Michael. *Die umstrittenen späten Instrumentalwerke Schumanns.* Hamburg: Wagner, 1984.

———. "Kunstwerk-Anspruch und Popularitätsstreben: Ursachen ohne Wirkung? Bemerkungen zum *Glück von Edenhall* op. 143 und zur *Fest-Ouvertüre* op. 123." In *Schumann in Düsseldorf: Werke — Texte — Interpretationen,* edited by Bernhard R. Appel, 265–313. Mainz: Schott, 1993.

Synofzik, Thomas. "Ein Rückert-Kanon als Keimzelle zu Schumanns Klavierkonzert op. 54." *Die Musikforschung* 58 (2005): 28–32.

Tadday, Ulrich. *Das schöne Unendliche: Ästhetik, Kritik, Geschichte der romantischen Musikanschauung.* Stuttgart: J. B. Metzler, 1999.

———. ed. *Schumann Handbuch.* Stuttgart: Bärenreiter, 2006.

Tchaikovsky, Pyotr Ilyich. *Erinnerungen und Musikkritiken.* Edited by Richard Petzoldt and Lothar Fahlbusch. Leipzig: Reclam, 1974.

Todd, R. Larry. "On Quotation in Schumann's Music." In *Schumann and His World,* edited by R. Larry Todd, 80–112. Princeton, NJ: Princeton University Press, 1994.

Tovey, Donald Francis. *Essays in Musical Analysis: Chamber Music.* London: Oxford University Press, 1944.

Tunbridge, Laura. "Schumann as Manfred." *Musical Quarterly* 87 (2004): 546–69.

———. *Schumann's Late Style.* Cambridge: Cambridge University Press, 2007.

Wagner, Cosima. *Die Tagebücher.* 2 vols. Edited by Martin Gregor-Dellin and Dietrich Mack. Munich: Piper, 1976–77. Translated by Geoffrey Skelton as *Cosima Wagner's Diaries.* 2 vols. London: Collins, 1978–80.

Wagner, Richard. *Gesammelte Schriften und Dichtungen.* 4th ed. 10 vols. Leipzig: C. F. W. Siegel, 1907.

———. *Mein Leben.* Edited by Martin Gregor-Dellin. Munich: List, 1976. Translated by Andrew Gray as *My Life.* Edited by Mary Whittall. Cambridge: Cambridge University Press, 1983.

Wasielewski, Wilhelm Joseph von. *Aus siebzig Jahren: Lebenserinnerungen.* Stuttgart: Deutsche Verlagsanstalt, 1897.

———. *Robert Schumann: Eine Biographie.* 4th ed. Leipzig: Breitkopf & Härtel, 1906.

———. *Schumanniana.* Leipzig: Breitkopf & Härtel, 1883.

Weiner, Marc A. "Reading the Ideal." *New German Critique* 69 (1996): 53–83.

Weissweiler, Eva. *Clara Schumann: Eine Biographie.* Hamburg: Hoffmann und Campe, 1990.

Wenke, Corinna. "Aspekte zu Robert Schumanns Entwicklung in seiner Kinder- und Jugendzeit in Zwickau." PhD diss., University of Leipzig, 1987.

Wittgenstein, Ludwig. *Werkausgabe.* 8 vols. Frankfurt: Suhrkamp, 1984–88.

Index of Names

Index of Schumann's Works